Understanding Polit Science Statistics

In politics, you begin by asking theoretically interesting questions. Sometimes statistics can help answer those questions. When it comes to applied statistics, students shouldn't just learn a vast array of formula—they need to learn the basic concepts of statistics as solutions to particular problems. Peter Galderisi demonstrates that statistics are a summary of how to answer the problem: learn the math but only after learning the concepts and methodological considerations that give it context.

With this as a starting point, *Understanding Political Science Statistics* asks students to consider how to address a research problem conceptually before being led to the appropriate formula. Throughout, Galderisi looks at problems through a lens of "observations and expectations," which can be applied to myriad statistical techniques, both descriptive and inferential. This approach links the answers researchers get from their individual data analysis to the research designs and questions from which these analyses are derived.

By emphasizing the underlying logic of statistical analysis for greater understanding and drawing on applications and examples from political science (including law), the book illustrates how students can apply statistical concepts and techniques in their own research, in future coursework, and simply as an informed consumer of numbers in public discourse.

The following features help students master the material:

- Legal and Methodological sidebars highlight key concepts and provide applied examples on law, politics, and methodology;
- End-of-chapter exercises allow students to test their mastery of the basic concepts and techniques along the way;
- A Sample Solutions Guide provides worked-out answers for odd-numbered exercises, with all answers available in the Instructor's Manual;
- Key Terms are helpfully called out in both Marginal Definitions and a Glossary;
- A Companion Website (**www.routledge.com/cw/galderisi**) with further resources for both students and instructors;
- A diverse array of data sets include subsets of the ANES and Eurobarometer surveys; CCES; US Congressional district data; and a cross-national dataset with political, economic, and demographic variables; and
- Companion guides to SPSS and Stata walk students through the procedures for analysis and provide exercises that go hand-in-hand with online data sets.

Peter Galderisi has taught political science methods and statistics for more than three decades, and is currently a lecturer and local internship director in the Political Science Department at the University of California, San Diego. Previously, Galderisi was a Professor or Visiting Professor at Utah State, UCLA, UC Santa Cruz, and Cal State Fullerton. He specializes in U.S. political parties, campaigns and elections, American political development, interest groups, and election law.

Understanding Political Science Statistics

Observations and Expectations in Political Analysis

Peter Galderisi

Routledge
Taylor & Francis Group

NEW YORK AND LONDON

First published 2015
by Routledge
711 Third Avenue, New York, NY 10017

and by Routledge
2 Park Square, Milton Park, Abingdon, Oxon, OX14 4RN

Routledge is an imprint of the Taylor & Francis Group, an informa business

Library of Congress Cataloging-in-Publication Data

Galderisi, Peter.
   Understanding political science statistics : observations and expectations in political analysis / Peter Galderisi.
       pages cm
   1. Political statistics.   2. Political science—Statistical methods.
   3. Political science—Methodology.   I. Galderisi, Peter F.   II. Title.
JA71.7.G35 2015
320.01'5195—dc23
2014030207

ISBN: 9780415890052 (pbk)
ISBN: 9780203830031 (ebk)

Typeset in Adobe Garamond Pro
by Apex CoVantage, LLC

This volume is dedicated to my friend and colleague of over three decades, William L. Furlong. About eight years ago, as I was leaving another academic institution, Bill took my wife, Holly, aside and said that "Peter needs to finish this text. It will be good for his soul." Its completion, I believe, has been good for both of our souls.

Contents

Tables, Figures, and Sidebars

▌TABLES

FIGURES

METHODOLOGICAL AND LEGAL SIDEBARS

Preface

OF OBSERVATIONS AND EXPECTATIONS

This textbook has been decades in the making, informed by 30 years of teaching undergraduate political science statistics. It started off as a series of supplemental notes for my course, Introduction to Quantitative Research Methods, at UCLA (1990s). I had not found any statistics text geared to an entry-level class of primarily innumerate students that did not water down the math so much as to be useless to those who wished to develop the foundation for more advanced study. Students (many from fields other than political science) constantly asked (no, pleaded) for extra notes. Eventually, after many trials at distributing notes, I decided that a full text that presented the material as one would lecture would be most helpful. In almost two decades, this text has gone through multiple iterations and changes. Its original title was *Statistics as if Understanding Mattered*, a handle deemed too "cheeky" by a reviewer for my first publisher. During the long and arduous transition to my new publisher, I developed a better understanding of the interconnecting themes of methodology and statistics. As a result, this text consistently discusses and takes its name from the concept of "observations and expectations." Most students of statistics are aware of this concept, but only in the context of one statistic—chi-square. In reality the comparison of observations and expectations can apply to a myriad of statistical techniques, both descriptive and inferential. More importantly, this concept of observations and expectations links the answers we derive from our individual, real-world tests of data to the research designs and questions from which these tests are derived. Given, for example, our *expectation* that, based on history and logic, partisans are more likely to vote than non-partisans can be examined through an exploration of whether that expectation is confirmed when we *observe* the results of our statistical analysis in any given election year or type. It is this consistent theme of observations and expectations that ties together methodology and statistical analysis and, I believe, makes this book different from others in the field.

This text is rich with features that help guide students through the material, from chapter-opening learning objectives that frame topics to end-of-chapter exercises that allow students to test their mastery of concepts and techniques along the way. A Sample Solutions Guide provides worked-out answers for odd-numbered exercises, with all the solutions provided in the online instructor's material, allowing students to check their work and not only see if they have the right answer but also understand how to arrive at it and what that answer means for political analysis. Political science examples throughout and integration with a diverse array of data sets make the text truly applicable to the field and statistics in the real world. Legal and methodological sidebars show students applied examples of law, politics, and methodology; other sidebars highlight key concepts in statistics. More than 150 figures and tables help clarify concepts and make the text visually engaging. Student learning and studying is enhanced by bolded key terms, marginal definitions, and a glossary, which provide multiple ways to find terms and concepts. Additionally, a free companion website (www.routledge.com/cw/galderisi) includes further resources for both students and instructors.

Along with this text, I and Ellen C. Seljan (Lewis & Clark College) have produced corresponding volumes that walk students through the use of statistical programs that help to match the expectations of our research designs with observations of real-world data: *Understanding Political Science Statistics Using SPSS* and *Understanding Political Science Statistics Using Stata*. A future volume discussing the use of R is planned, but only after enough library entries have been created to lower the curve needed to learn how to use a program during a small part of a brief quarter- or semester-long political analysis class. The data sets offered with these companion volumes include subsets of the 2008 and 2012 American National Election Studies as well as a Eurobarometer survey. We are fortunate to have been given permission to incorporate the 2012 CCES (Cooperative Congressional Election Study) data study into another file with enough cases to allow any instructor to lead her or his students through the parsing and dissecting of relationships while controlling for a myriad of factors. Along with these individual cased sets of surveys, two detailed U.S. congressional district files (2008 alone and an integrated 2008–2012 to allow for analyzing the effects of redistricting) have been developed and are also included. Finally, a multinational data set composed of political, economic, and demographic variables from multiple sources has been added. More data sets and examples will be added to this volume's website as time and copyright laws allow. I welcome the adopters of this text to offer suggestions about other sets that could be included. Although, for purposes of easy demonstration, artificial examples will often be employed, the majority of examples from this text will use data gleaned from these data sets as well as other real-world examples.

The text follows the assumption that any student can learn the basic concepts of statistics if those statistics are introduced as solutions to particular problems, and not formulas with a life of their own. In this text, students are introduced to a problem and asked to consider, conceptually, how one would address that problem, and then are led through to the appropriate statistical formula. Students are required to learn the math, but only after they understand the concepts. Statistical formulas are offered as generic, mathematical summary tools for concepts with fairly clear meaning. Students are walked through the formula in plain language to increase their understanding of both the procedure and the interpretation of results. The real-world importance of the differing interpretations of different statistics can then be highlighted. Another basic assumption is that most of the statistics covered in an introductory political analysis course are connected through a small number of basic statistical concepts. These concepts, in my estimation, are better understood when, at the beginning of a course, the mathematical complexity of the statistic is comparatively limited. Thus, for example, much more time is spent in the first few chapters discussing basic statistics such as frequency distributions, modes, medians, and means, as well as some simple measures of variation than in many other analysis texts. *Standardization* is one of the most important, if not the most important, concept in statistical theory. Introducing this concept while discussing how to compare frequency distributions (Chapter 2) takes away much of the complexity that many students struggle with when the concept is not introduced until a discussion of standard scores. The importance of understanding the effects of outliers is easier to understand when discussing the difference between medians and means (Chapter 3) than when applied to regression analysis. In addition, an understanding of basic, nominal statistics, too often ignored by my profession, provides the conceptual cornerstone for statistical analyses that assume more precisely measured data.

Another reason for the extra time spent on basic statistics is that more mathematically complex statistics are based on both the math and logic of mathematically simpler ones. Regression, after all, is calculated with means and variances. Its measure of goodness of fit (*R*-squared) is based on comparison of the calculated best-fitting line with the variance from the mean. Even this notion of proportional reduction of error or variance can be introduced when discussing a basic and easily understandable measure of association with nominal data, lambda (Chapter 9). Measures like lambda naturally follow the logic of the concept of *goodness of fit*, introduced as early as the discussion of the variation ratio (Chapter 4). Although logistic regression is not covered in this text, an understanding of error reduction (e.g., lambda) and cross product or odds ratios (derived from the concept of paired comparisons introduced in the discussion of the Index of Qualitative Variation in Chapter 4) is essential in understanding the derivation and interpretation of binary logistic estimates.

The last, and perhaps most important, basic assumption driving the underlying theme and development of this text is that statistics are summary measures that are only useful (other than mental exercises) when tied into basic but important methodological considerations. Statistics help us to answer questions that have been formulated after a thorough consideration of concept development, hypothesis formation, and theoretical importance. They help us to answer questions that are naturally derived from these formulations. The "what" and "why" that we try to answer to confirm our methodologically derived questions are answered in the real world with statistical summaries of individual tests that are derived from those questions. This volume is not meant to substitute for a more thoroughly written and example-laden research design volume, but it is written with the understanding that statistics without research design and methodology is just mathematics, not analysis.

I would like to thank two decades of students at four universities who have, both willingly and unwillingly, forced me to think continuously about how to best explain statistics to those with a wide array of logical and mathematical skill sets. This volume is a far cry from what I originally produced as class notes at UCLA decades ago, and I thank my students for holding me to the task of finding better ways, without dumbing down the presentation, of teaching political analysis. I am especially indebted to those students, too numerous to name, who, often on their own initiative, took the time to help me understand when that presentation was not clear enough and to those who, over the years, offered suggestions that helped me edit the work as it transitioned from class notes to locally published copyrighted manuscript to this final text. I would be remiss not to acknowledge the dozens of graduate students who worked with countless variations of this manuscript as they assisted me in my classes over the past 20 years. Special thanks go to Vladimir Kogan, Patrick Rogers and, most recently, Zachary C. Steinert-Threlkeld who, with their intensive knowledge of the R programming language, set up many of the graphs found in this text. I can never thank my wife, best friend, and partner, Holly, enough for her love and support over the two decades during which this manuscript slowly progressed. I am forever grateful to Seidy Cruz and her staff at Cognella Press who, for almost 8 years, gave this manuscript a copyright home as I used it in my Political Analysis course at UC San Diego. I am especially indebted to Michael Kerns and his team at Routledge Press (most prominently the ever-patient and surviving—I wore out several—development editor Alison Daltroy) who, some 5 years ago, took on this orphaned project and allowed me to concentrate on the analysis of politics rather than my original publisher's insistence on a statistics text that attempted to cover every subject in the social sciences and beyond. Statistical analysis is not just some "one size fits all" set of rote procedures meant to process and interpret any set of numbers. It is not just a listing of steps that one must complete to get the "right" mathematical answer. Rather, it is a tool to help understand real-world outcomes and the types of events that cause them. I have been a political scientist for well over three decades, and it is politics that I best understand, interpret, and can relate through these procedures. It is my hope that I help the students who read this text to do the same. Let us begin.

Peter Galderisi
Cardiff by the Sea, California

CONTENTS

Political Science, the Scientific Method, and Statistical Analysis

An Overview

Learning Objectives:

◼ To understand that political science can be studied scientifically
◼ To understand the language of science
◼ To understand what a hypothesis is and how it should be structured
◼ To understand the components necessary to make a causal argument

Political Science is the study of actors and agencies within a legal, institutional setting. As with any science, the observations derived from measuring and analyzing actual data must follow from the creation of questions of interest that are derived from a proper and logically reasoned generalized statement of the relationship between or among *types* of political events. In order to understand, for example, the reasons why Barack Obama did better in most areas in 2008 than John Kerry did in 2004, we need to investigate the reasons why individuals choose to vote the way that they do in more than just those two elections. Comparing differences between those two years may help to confirm or disconfirm our general explanation of why candidates win and by what margin. But so can comparing any other two elections. And they should also, by finding irregularities or anomalies, help us to understand the circumstances under which our statistical findings do not match our causal expectations.

Statistics can help us to summarize our findings for any given two years, or any other combination of events, but, as mentioned in the Preface, they can do so only as tests that are naturally derived and implied from theoretically sound methodological formulations. Without proper and generalizable measurements and designs, they are of interest, they are suggestive, but they are not fully scientifically consequential. They are an important but not the only essential component of scientific inquiry.[1]

Part of the nature of scientific inquiry is the sharing of knowledge. One's study is not to be read in a vacuum, but in the context of other work investigating similar, and sometimes quite different, political, economic, social, and psychological relationships. Knowledge cannot be shared if we are all speaking our own language. Part of the difficulty of sharing in the "social," sometimes pejoratively categorized as the "soft" sciences, is that, unlike many of the more traditional or "harder" sciences, we often use terms for which there is no or little common definitional agreement. What do we mean by "democracy," "political authority," and, even more narrowly, "voter intention" (as the 2000 recounts in Florida and 2008 in Minnesota demonstrated)? Does the discipline share the same common understanding of these terms as say, "wind velocity," "distance," or "white cell count"? As science is partly defined as this "sharing of common knowledge," a lack of a common vocabulary hampers the growth of our discipline.

This text, with its greater, if not exclusive, interest in statistical analysis will not try to single-handedly resolve all of these definitional conflicts (other than to advise one to state as clearly and precisely as possible what one means). It will, however, offer a brief accounting of the definition of basic terms that are the core of scientific inquiry.[2]

THE LANGUAGE OF SCIENCE

Following is a simple vocabulary for terms of scientific research that will be used throughout this text. Later, we will discuss how these terms interact with each other.

Units of Analysis, Case, or Fact

units of analysis, case, or fact Entities from which measurements are taken.

The **units of analysis, case, or fact** are the entities, drawn from a known or theoretical population, from which we take or may later be able to take measurements. Some examples follow:

a. Peter Galderisi
b. My dog, Treana
c. The chair I'm now sitting on as I write this text
d. The United States
e. The European Union
f. Congressman Darrell Issa (my current representative)

For example, in an exit survey of voters, each surveyed individual would be a "unit of analysis." The "units" of analysis would be survey respondents. In a comparative study of election laws in different countries, the unit of analysis would be each country. The **number of cases** for each study is usually abbreviated as *n* or *N*. For example, if we were to list ballot forms in the different states, *N* would equal 50 (51 if Washington, D.C., is included for analysis). If we were to study roll call votes in the U.S. Congress, *N* would equal 435 for the House and 100 for the Senate. The number of cases in an exit poll would equal the actual number surveyed.

Properties, Concepts, and Variables

Properties exist in nature whether we know them or not, **concepts** are our guesses about those properties, and **variables** are our observable or potentially observable measurements of those concepts. The important factor about properties is that, unlike units of analysis, they are *generalizations* or *abstractions*—characteristics, behaviors, attitudes—that can be used to discuss and describe many different units of analysis. Any unit of analysis can be described using categories of a host of properties. For example, in describing Peter Galderisi, we can use gender (category male), ethnicity (category Italian-American), marital status (happily married), height (69 inches in stocking feet), age (62 years, probably 63 when this is finally published), weight (don't ask), hair color (brown with a dusting of gray), partisan preference, ideology, vote choice, views about gay rights, and so forth. Notice that these properties can not only be used to "define" me, but also other units of analysis. Those units don't even have to share the same biological type. All of the unit of analysis examples listed previously can be described by their age. "Partisan preference" can be used to describe both myself and Congressman Issa (although my dog does seem to react differently given which political pundit is on TV).

What is both important and difficult is to ascertain which properties are most important in our analyses of political behavior. Gender and ethnicity (or at least the values associated with them) are probably important determinants of partisan preference. Height is probably not (although it may act as a surrogate for gender or ethnic differences). Although we tend to eliminate

number of cases The total units of analysis from which measurements are taken.

properties/concepts The generalizations we believe are important to measure from our cases.

variable The actual, real-world measurement of properties/concepts.

certain properties as politically irrelevant in a given analysis, we may find out later that they are very relevant (keep this in mind when we discuss the importance of *randomization* later on).

Students often confuse variables (which must vary) with the categories of those variables (which don't). "How one voted for president" would be a common variable in an exit poll. The "Republican percentage of the presidential vote" would be a variable measured from each state (or voting precinct). Each possible response or measurement is referred to as a *category* of the relevant variable. For each voter, the category would correspond to the vote choice (Republican, Democratic, Green, etc.). For each state, a category would be listed as the percentage (46%, 54%, etc.) that voted Republican in each state.

Laws and Hypotheses

Laws exist in nature, and **hypotheses** are our guesses about laws.[3] These are our *generalized* guesses or expectations about how properties relate to each other. Stating that "men are more likely to support Republican candidates than are women" is a statement about our expectations about the interaction between gender and partisan preference. Hypotheses (more on this later) are never just about two facts (we don't just compare one man and one woman—although that might act as a limited *test* of that hypothesis)— they are generalizations about the relationship between and among properties that can be tested in many ways. Stating that "I am more likely to vote Republican than my wife" is an expected outcome that naturally follows from our hypothesis. It is a "**factual statement**," that is, one that can be proved true or false on limited investigation, not a hypothesis itself (it's not a generalization). We'll discuss "how to create a good" hypothesis in the next section.

laws/hypotheses The actual and perceived relationships between or among properties/concepts.

factual statement Test of a hypothesis that is proved true or false on limited investigation.

TABLE 1.1 Listing and Comparison of Terms

In Nature	Our Guesses about Them	Our Measurements of Them
Property	Concept	Variable
Law	Hypothesis	Test Implication/ Factual Statement

In this text, I will take the liberty to use "properties" and "concepts" interchangeably. "Variable" will be used when we discuss their actual measurement in the real world.

Theories

Theories are a broader generalized knowledge that help to explain *why* properties are related to the way we hypothesize. Let's take a simple example. Do any of us have to see someone cut a limb from a tree to be able to predict that it will fall to the ground? Well, no, for two reasons:

1. Experience—you have seen this occur so often that you are fairly certain about its predictive force (common sense). A myriad of *observations* have always met your *expectations*.
2. Theoretical link—it can not only be predicted *but also explained* by the theory of gravity, stated simply as:

   - Objects of mass greater than zero are attracted to each other.
   - The attraction favors the object of greater mass.
   - A limb has less mass than the earth.
   - Therefore: if I cut a tree limb, it will "fall" to the ground unless held up by some other means.

Notice the importance of theory here. It not only predicts *that* but explains *why* the tree limb *should* fall. Like a hypothesis, it has generalizable utility. It can predict and explain the falling of any severed tree limb, the unfortunate collapse of a building whose structure is compromised, and the falling of a duck when shot (thereby removing its innate ability to keep itself airborne). However, the theory of gravity helps explain so much more. It helps to explain why the moon revolves around the earth as we revolve around the sun. It helps to explain tidal patterns. Many scientists believe that gravitational pulls might help to explain the timing of certain types of earthquakes. To really move out there, some believe that planetary gravitational forces can help to explain mood swings. Remember that the term "lunatic" is derived from the Latin name for the moon. The "explanation," factually absurd, is that the moon exerts greater force when it is "full." The "fullness" of the moon, of course, has nothing to do with mass, but earthly shadows.

Granted, few if any full-blown theories exist in political science, although "rational choice" theory probably comes close. However, we should, at least, come up with some sort of "**theory sketch**" to help explain *why* our hypotheses-based expectations are borne out by specific data-based observations, not just that they do. What is it about the social status, differential childhood socialization, or different needs and expectations from government that "causes" women to gravitate more to the Democratic Party than do men?

Theories or theory sketches allow us not only to explain what we expect to see, but also to relate our research to that of others, even outside of our narrow field of study. A thorough understanding of a theory that we use to

theories/theory sketches
A broad explanation of why we expect to observe what our hypotheses predict.

help explain a generalized outcome might also, given proper conditions, reverse what we would expect. Take for example the commonly held hypothesis that "older citizens are more likely to vote than younger ones." Those who have most recently benefited from changes in the franchise, those from 18 to 20 years of age, vote at a dismally poor level—only 37.4% claim to have exercised their franchise in the 2012 presidential election. Turnout increases linearly as one gets older, with those 65 and over voting at almost twice the rate of their younger cohort (72.0%). Only with advancing years does turnout start to decline, most likely due to the infirmities that inevitably come with age. Only 3.1% of those under 24 claim illness or disability as a reason for not voting. That figure climbs to 42.0% for those 65 and older.[4]

Two theories can be offered for this age bias in voting. The **life-cycle theory** basically states that one becomes more likely to vote as one gets older because one's interest in what government does and does not do becomes more salient. Taxes and mortgage deductions become more relevant, as do educational policy, business regulation, medical policies, and social security benefits. Additionally, age brings a form of education gained through experience if not formal training. Although not a perfect relationship, as one gets older, one is also less likely to move, thus decreasing the time and effort necessary to re-register (most other countries have national voter IDs) and learn about the local political terrain. This life-cycle explanation helps to explain the decline in voting turnout in the late 1960s. Two events coincided to increase the proportion of potential young voters during this period. The first was the coming of age of the baby-boom generation (i.e., those born in exceptionally high numbers following the return of troops after World War II and the Korean conflict). The second was the previously mentioned enfranchisement of 18- to 20-year-olds. In essence, a large cohort of young citizens, those least inclined to participate, flooded the political marketplace, much like the enfranchisement of women had done in the 1920s. Unfortunately, unlike the history of women's suffrage, these newly enfranchised citizens did not vote as they got older in the proportions that the life-cycle theory would predict. If they had, voting turnout would have increased in the 1970s, 1980s, and 1990s, rather than continuing to decline.

The second explanation, the **generational theory**, helps to explain this seeming anomaly. Older citizens are not more likely to vote because they are older. They were also highly likely to vote when they were young, with life-cycle tendencies only increasing their turnout marginally. Perhaps partisan politics seemed more salient, with differences over New Deal policies offering clear choices to voters coming of age. More importantly, however, older citizens are more likely to vote because they have and, most importantly, have *always had* a higher sense of civic duty. These are citizens who came of age during the Great Depression and World War II, when a sense of civic community, born of surviving two long-term dramatic events, was much more prevalent than has been the case since. Additionally, this adherence to

life-cycle theory Explaining political behavior based on differences in circumstances that occur as one ages.

generational theory Explaining political behavior based on differences in what was occurring when an individual entered political awareness.

democratic perspectives was passed down to the next generation (baby boomers), even if at a somewhat diminished level. By the time that the grandchildren of the "Greatest Generation" were born, this democratic transmission was all but lost.

Note that these theoretical assessments open up an entire range of possible additions or new areas of study. Each of the assumptions of the theory can be separately tested ("are older citizens more likely to have a sense of civic duty?"). They may help to explain discrepancies in our findings ("are younger citizens as likely to vote as older ones if, for whatever reason, they share the same sense of civic obligation?"). They may also "travel" differently in time and space. If the generational theory is relevant, then we would expect our hypothesis to predict an opposite relationship if we make the same age comparisons in the 1940s when the effects of depression and war should have been more immediately salient for younger generations. In newly emerging democracies, younger generations, raised during the fight or transition to democratic norms, should be more tied into a democratic civic culture and, therefore, more likely to vote than their parents. The same theoretical generalizations can therefore lead to different expectations that follow from well-formed hypotheses that can be studied by testing those expectations in the real world.

THE STRUCTURE OF HYPOTHESES

As mentioned, our hypotheses are our best-informed guesses or expectations about the relationship between two or more properties or concepts, measured as variables that can be tested with real-world data. They should automatically lead to testing for their confirmation (what I will call direct confirmation) but also logically follow from a theoretical backdrop (indirect confirmation). Both direct and indirect confirmation are essential for a hypothesis to be useful.

Several texts do a very good job of delineating all of the components of good hypothesis formation and, later, testing.[5] Let me offer a way to summarize the numerous variations many others make by combining them into two general categories.

Falsifiability

Hypotheses are generalizations that, although we would like to think will always be proved true, must also be written and structured in such a way that evidence *could be* found that would disconfirm them. Science, after all, is not just about the sharing of knowledge; it is also about the ability to challenge that knowledge in order to gain greater understanding. The following are several factors that affect potential **falsifiability**.

falsifiability The possibility that what we observe will not confirm what our hypotheses predict.

1. Lack of clarity—if we don't have an agreed on meaning of our properties, then at least describe exactly what you mean. For example:

The higher the overall level of education, the more likely a country will be democratic.

Problem: "Democratic" is what we call a cluster concept. It has several components. Which one does the author mean (ability to vote, voter turnout, freedom of speech and press, economic democracy, or some combination)? If we don't know, then we don't know what observed evidence might contradict it. What if we found a country with high overall levels of formal education, but little tolerance for a free press? Well, the author could always claim that he/she meant "ability to vote," not "freedom of the press." Be as specific as possible without necessarily detailing exactly how it would be measured (that will come later).

One improvement:

The higher the overall education level within a country, the greater the level of voting turnout in a country.

2. Lack of direction—do the two properties increase together, change direction, or have no directional consistency at all (statistically, the null hypothesis). Terms like "are related," "is a function of," and "is associated with" might make some intuitive, common sense, but they don't tell us what observed evidence could contradict the statement. The expectation is not clear. Thus, we don't know for sure what observations might contradict it. For example:

Education and democracy are related.

Problem: What if, after better defining "democracy," we compare two countries and find that the "more highly educated" one is *less* democratic? That doesn't negate the original statement—maybe that was the author's expectation. The definitional improvements listed previously can work here also. The two properties listed ("overall education level" and "level of voting turnout") are hypothesized to increase together.

3. No explicit comparison—only one side of one property is posited. Remember, comparison is the fundamental key to research. For example:

Stating that "*voting turnout among individuals with low education levels is low*" sounds intuitively correct but doesn't negate the possibility that, upon observation in any given instance, turnout might be even lower among "highly educated" people. A better comparative expectation might be stated as:

Voting turnout among individuals with low education levels is lower than among those with higher education levels.

As we will see in a later chapter, the failure to understand this distinction may have led many to misread the meaning of the gender gap in politics (i.e., that "men are more likely to vote Republican than are women").

4. **Value (normative) judgments**. In science, we constantly leave ourselves open to contradictory information. In religion, we don't. There is nothing wrong with that (I consider myself to be a very religious person)—the two are just different. One is based on fact and is subject to falsification. The other is based on faith and, unless we are non-denominational theologians, we don't try to find evidence contradictory to our beliefs. For example:

The death penalty is bad (or good).

If we mean that even the state should not have the ability to terminate a life because it is morally wrong (or, adversely, "an eye for an eye . . ."), then what is there to study? These are religiously held beliefs. However, is there anything that can be analyzed scientifically? Certainly. Define "bad" or "good" as something measurable, concrete, and as devoid of moral or value judgments as possible (e.g., does it deter other would-be criminals?). Then, as an example:

States with a death penalty will have lower capital crime rates than states without that penalty.
Or
When a state abolishes the death penalty, capital crime rates increase.

Not Immediately Verifiable

Students seem to have the most trouble with this. If a statement can be "proved" true or false on limited investigation (**verifiability**), then we don't have a hypothesis—just a **test implication**[6] or observation of a potential hypothesis. Test implications are factual statements (true or false on limited investigation) that help to confirm or disconfirm our more generalized hypotheses and expectations. They are not, however, hypotheses themselves. They do let us know whether what we expect from our hypothesis is actually observed in the real world. For example:

Senator Dianne Feinstein (D-CA) is more powerful than Senator Barbara Boxer (D-CA).
Problem 1: What do we mean by "more powerful?" Better at arm wrestling? Let's define "power" as "the ability to have one's proposed legislation passed by the entire Congress."
Now: *Senator Dianne Feinstein has a greater proportion of her proposed legislation passed than does Senator Barbara Boxer.*

However, there is still a problem: This is true or false on limited investigation. It is therefore a factual statement—not a hypothesis. Look up some congressional records, and your job is done (at least when both retire). Here's

value (normative) judgment A moral or religious sense that a certain occurrence or action is "good" or "bad" that is based on religious or philosophical principles not subject to testing.

verifiability The ability of a factual statement or test implication to be proved true or false on limited investigation.

test implication An observable test of a hypothesis that is implied by that hypothesis.

the test—is there any hint of cause? That hint comes from specifying two properties/measurable variables. The **independent property** is the posited causal agent. The **dependent property** is the expected outcome. We have the outcome: "the ability to have one's proposed legislation passed by the entire Congress." What is the possible cause, or independent property—"degree of Boxerness"?

Individual senators share certain characteristics, but not all. The question is, what might be different (on a separately measured property) between these two, or any two, representatives that might explain *why* one is more "powerful" than the other? On what property might they vary in such a way as to both predict and help explain the outcome?

One possibility:

> *The more seniority a member of Congress has, the higher the proportion of his/her proposed legislation that passes.*

We now not only have two properties listed, but the statement is generalizable beyond an immediate comparison of just these two senators. The independent property (i.e., the one that we hypothesize or expect is the causal agent) is "level of seniority." The dependent property or outcome is "proportion of legislation passed."

THE BEAUTY OF HYPOTHESES FOR RESEARCH

Once we specify a properly worded hypothesis, we now have a lead into how our research should develop. Too often, I've had students come and state that their "topics" cannot possibly lend themselves to 12- or 20-page papers. Once the topic (e.g., "I'm fascinated by the *fact* that the congressperson from my neighboring district seems more 'powerful' than my own representative") is turned into a hypothesis (e.g., "The more seniority a member of Congress has, the higher the proportion of his/her proposed legislation that passes"), different avenues of research and "filling" those 20 pages become obvious.

Increasing the Number and Types of Tests

Because the hypothesis is a generalized statement of expectations, we can find several ways to test (observe) what is logically expected or implied from that hypothesis:

1. We can compare one or many pairs of congresspersons at a given time (comparative analysis).
2. We can rank order all congresspersons on both properties at a given time and compare those rankings (traditional "quantitative" analysis).

independent property That property that we hypothesize has a causative effect on another.

dependent property That property that we hypothesize was caused by another.

3. We can follow the success/power of the same congressperson over time (case study).

If the original hypothesis is correct, then our expectation should lead to the following observations. These are all tests, which can be proved true or false, that are directly implied from our generalized expectation or hypothesis:

1. A congressperson with more seniority will be observed to be "more powerful" than the congressperson of lesser seniority to whom he/she is compared.
2. As we move from congresspeople with the lowest to highest seniority, we should observe a movement from the least to most "powerful."
3. As any individual congressperson increases, over time, his/her seniority, we should observe an increase in his/her "power."

Broadening Our Frame of Reference or Context

We can also test this with state legislatures or legislative bodies in other countries. I have often told my undergraduate students, when they are trying to find a research topic, to take a hypothesis that has been well tested at one level and see if it can be generalized to another. This is an important component of any research area. Does the expectation travel? Do we observe this expected relationship between seniority and "power" in other countries? Does it make a difference in a specified direction whether the country's legislature operates, as does the U.S. Congress, under a winner-take-all (WTA), proportional, or mixed regime? Do we observe our expected differences in state legislatures (and what happens when a state institutes term limits)? A test on a narrow subject might not be of much interest to someone in another field. However, the more generalizable the hypothesis, the more others can learn from another's study and perhaps use a similar analysis in their own research.

Uncovering Theoretical Relevance

Because a hypothesis must also admit to "indirect" confirmation, we should spend some time researching the underlying theoretical reasons for why we think our two properties are related as hypothesized. This should cause us to do a thorough "literature search" on seniority or the legislative process or personal relationships among congresspersons, and so forth.

Even after going through all of the processes discussed previously, and even if we can run every comparative, quantitative, and case study imaginable, we are never finished. Although we may have enough confirmation (both direct and indirect) to feel comfortable that our cause-effect expectation is correct, we can never fully prove it. Why? Unless we drastically change our (and other nations') institutional arrangements, legislators will exist in the future. There will always be more tests where our observations might contradict our hypothetical expectation. Once we have a true hypothesis, we have much to write about, now and in the future. A factual statement, one that is true or false on limited investigation, can be discussed on a note card.

▌THE LOGIC OF CAUSATION—A REVIEW

Science is more than just about cataloguing information and making predictions. Science deals with explaining and examining why properties are related in the ways our hypotheses specify. We are not satisfied in finding out that two properties as measured *are* related, but *why* a change in the independent or causal property *should* cause a change in the dependent property or outcome.

In order to demonstrate causality (at least with a certain degree of certainty), we need to fulfill the following conditions.

Test

Test the hypothesis in the real world. This is what we call a *direct confirmation* of our hypothesis. Do our observations match our expectations (based on our hypothetical statement)?

Example: If we are stating that voter turnout is higher in systems that employ a proportional representation rule than they are in systems that employ (like the United States) a WTA, single-member districting provision, then we need to actually measure whether the hypothesis is borne out or observed in the real world. Note that the statement is a hypothesis—even if it is completely true at this point in time we may find past or future examples when the outcomes do not come out as predicted.

Theory or Theory Sketch

Provide a logical reason for the causal direction of the hypothesis. This is called theory or *indirect confirmation*. Why *should* we expect turnout to be lower in WTA than proportional systems? Several reasons can be offered, the most important being that unless you live in a district, state, or other WTA electoral unit where elections tend to be perennially close, you won't feel that your single vote has an impact. A senator from a deep red state can win re-election in a two-party race with 60% or 80% of the vote. The margin of victory is not important (at least in deciding a winner). On the other hand, in a proportional representation (PR) system, a legislature is divvied out to parties roughly in direct proportion to the vote they receive. Whether a party nationally gets 60% or 70% of the vote means a difference of 10% of the legislative seats.[7]

Why do we need theory? Well, for a number of reasons. The first is to eliminate what we call accidental, **historical generalizations**. For years, the outcome of the baseball World Series victories (which league wins) seemed to fairly consistently predict presidential election victories (which party wins). Although they seemed to be in sync for a large portion of history, one would be hard pressed to find an explanation for *why* they *should be* related.[8]

The other reason is to help rule out alternate explanations. We'll go through a fuller rendition of this when we cover design and associational statistics. For now, we need to ask whether there may be other reasons why turnout is higher in PR systems that have nothing to do with PR and may be the true cause of turnout differences. Can we ever eliminate every alternate explanation—of course not, as we are not divine. Our job, however, is to eliminate the most obvious ones. Go back to our example. Perhaps citizens in a nation choose proportional representation because they are more committed to the democratic premise that every vote should count. That commitment might be the cause of both the choice of electoral system and high turnout (what we'll refer to later as a **spurious relationship**). Perhaps systems operating under PR have higher overall educations, and it is that level of education that positively drives voter turnout, *independent* of the type of electoral aggregation employed.

One problem students often face is in finding a theory or theory sketch that already exists and that can be used for a full understanding of their hypothetical links. The same is true with finding pre-existing studies that might have already offered some direct confirmation of that hypothesis. Often, we must generalize beyond what we think our original hypothesis is meant to study. Many years ago, I had one student who noticed something unusual as she was studying the gender gap in U.S. electoral politics ("men are more likely to support Republican causes and candidates than are women"). Indirectly, she discovered that, at least for that survey and year, the partisan gap was even stronger between married (more Republican) than unmarried individuals. Little had yet to be written about this marriage gap. On the other hand, she decided that, like much of the rational choice voting literature indicated, voting decisions can be analyzed much the same (with the limitation that a choice is made regardless of whether one votes) as economic ones. Although the relationship between marriage, having children, and political choices was not yet supported by a massive political science literature, much was written about marital and child status and economic decisions. Married individuals were more reserved and conservative in their economic choices. They were also more socially conservative. Particularly after the 1970s, that would make them more likely to lean Republican than their single counterparts.

historical generalization Our hypothesized independent and dependent properties are only related accidentally and are not causally linked.

spurious relationship Our hypothesized independent and dependent properties are actually both dependent on a third property.

Similarly, another student was studying, across time, the hypothesis that those who anticipated a close election were more likely to vote than those who anticipated a one-sided result. Anthony Downs's classic economic model of democracy and its progeny had already dealt with this issue.[9] However, following a collective class hunch, my student also noticed that among those who anticipated a one-sided election, those who supported the anticipated winning candidate were more likely to vote than those who were more closely aligned with the anticipated loser. Where could one find research that might offer the theoretical backdrop to explain why that relationship should exist? The decision was made to treat elections much like a sporting event. After all, rabid supporters of a team will watch the game until the end for the personal satisfaction of seeing the opposition (often hated) crushed. Those supporting the losers tend to head for the parking lot. Lo and behold, journals associated with sports psychology and the like did address such behavior, and a literature and potential theoretical confirmation were found.

Triangulization

We will find that no form of measurement is perfect, nor is any design in which we check our guessed causal relationship. We are safer if we measure our properties in more than one way (as each will have a different potential source of bias). We are also safer if we create different designs. This varied measurement and testing is called **triangulization**. For example, if the general hypothesis about voting systems and turnout is true, then we could "design" our analysis two ways:

a. At any point in time, compare all countries with PR against all countries with WTA. We would hope to observe turnout higher in all of the former or, at least, for turnout to be higher "on average" (see Chapter 3).
b. See if a country changed from one type of system to another. Italy, for example, moved from PR to WTA and back. We would expect to find turnout dropping then rebounding.

Alternate Explanations

Alternate explanations[10] can come from two sources. First, is there something potentially problematic with how we measure our evidence? Second, is there something potentially problematic with how we set up the design in which we collect our measurements and check for correct causal sequences? All of these problems are potential (i.e., just because they might be of concern does not mean that they are). We might only have a partial print and therefore can't legally define a match. However, that doesn't mean that the partial did not come from the suspect. This is an outline of potential measurement and design problems that will each be more thoroughly addressed along with statistics in subsequent chapters.

triangulization Measuring our concepts and testing our hypotheses in as many different ways as possible.

alternate explanations Reasons other than that which are hypothesized for why our properties/variables are related as hypothesized.

"Potential" Measurement Problems

Three potential problems with measurement follow.

- **Reliability of measurement**—are we measuring anything with consistency? (random error)
- **Internal validity of measurement**—are we measuring what we think we are measuring? (systematic error)
- **External validity of measurement**—can we generalize out our evidence to a broader "target" population/time/circumstance? (generalization error)

"Potential" Design Problems

Just as with measurement, internal validity and external validity can also apply to designs (i.e., how we test our hypotheses in the real world). Just as with measurements, it is virtually impossible to create a test situation (design) totally free of internal and external validity problems. Before I elaborate, let's clarify our terms. IV stands for our hypothesized and measured independent variable; DV is the hypothesized outcome or dependent variable (named "dependent" because we are hypothesizing that it is caused or conditioned by another variable). The distinction is much the same as we made for measurement problems:

- **Internal validity of design**—is the change in the IV the cause of the change in the DV, or is it *something else*?
- **External validity of design**—change in the IV causes change in the DV, but perhaps only given certain other conditions, only for a certain subpopulation, only during a particular time period—*how generalizable* are our results?

If "X" refers to the hypothesized causal (independent) variable, then an "internally invalid" conclusion would occur if some variable other than "X" caused the outcome (e.g., another type of historical event). An "externally invalid" conclusion would occur if "X" *did* cause the outcome, but only because of some other condition or circumstance. It is only, therefore, a partial or conditional cause. "External validity" refers to how far we can generalize our results, both in terms of target populations (all voters), all times (historical elections as well as present ones), and research conditions (that may increase the intrusion of alternate explanations).

You will quickly discover that, even under the best experimental conditions of measurement and design, no measurement or design is devoid of potential problems, either internal or external. The best we can hope for is to do the best we can do, control for the most obvious alternate explanations, be careful and as precise as possible in our measurements, and measure and test in as many ways as possible. Each test, as with each type of measurement, will have a potential internal or external validity problem. We can't control for all of

reliability of measurement Measurements are consistent and meaningful.

internal validity of measurement We are actually measuring what we think we are measuring.

external validity of measurement Our measurements are generalizable to our targeted populations and circumstances.

internal validity of design Our hypothesized independent variable is actually the cause of our outcome or dependent variable.

external validity of design Our hypothesized independent variable is actually the cause of our outcome or dependent variable for all targeted populations and circumstances.

them but, if each test has a different type of validity problem yet our observations always match our hypothesized expectations, then we are much more confident in our conclusion (although never fully sure). Again, this is called "triangulization" or, in some texts, "triangulation." Think about the evidentiary burden again as one would in law. If we were to wait until the hypothesis has been confirmed beyond a reasonable doubt (the standard in a criminal law case), we may never feel satisfied with our research. On the other hand, if we can demonstrate that the preponderance of evidence confirms our expectations, and that the most obvious alternate explanations have been addressed (the standard in a civil trial), we should have enough to present our findings.

Sidebar 1.1: Causation—*Law & Order* Edition

Some of you reading this text are considering law school (in some departments you are in the majority) and are wondering why you need to know any of this (OK, maybe you all are). You actually go through this sequence every time you watch an episode of *Law & Order*, *CSI*, *NCIS*, or other legal drama.[1] Here are the legal analogies (you may use your favorite TV show sound or music as background):

Test = evidence. We can better demonstrate that the suspect was the killer if his/her fingerprints are found on the murder weapon.

Theory = motive. We can make a better case if we can explain *why* the suspect would be likely to kill the victim. Was the spouse having an affair? Did the suspect just take out a huge insurance policy on the victim?

Alternate explanations. Any good prosecutor will try to make sure that the defense counsel does not try to sow doubt about how the evidence was collected or whether it is sufficient. One needs to be ready to address these alternate possibilities. Might the weapon be one that was a commonly used household item such as a kitchen knife? Was the suspect the primary cook of the house? Was the evidence tainted by a police officer or prosecutor with a hidden agenda or vendetta against the suspect?

Triangulate—get as much evidence, collected as differently as possible. You have a safer bet if you find fingerprints tested by one lab technician and DNA (under the fingernails of the victim that matches the suspect) tested by another. Having a record that a large insurance settlement was set away in an offshore bank account doesn't hurt either.

These issues of measurement and design will be covered more fully in subsequent chapters as we delve into the concepts and mathematics of statistics. Let us begin.

[1] Actually, statistics and law are constantly intertwined. For example, how do we gauge the accuracy of a DNA sample as matching that of a suspect? How can a defense attorney argue that a jury might not be reflective of the community? More commonly, how do we show that new ballot forms might increase or decrease discarded ballots? We use statistics, especially those involving probabilities.

KEY TERMS

alternate explanations (14)

dependent property (10)

external validity of design (15)

external validity of measurement (15)

factual statement (04)

falsifiability (07)

generational theory (06)

historical generalization (13)

independent property (10)

internal validity of design (15)

internal validity of measurement (15)

laws/hypotheses (04)

life-cycle theory (06)

number of cases (03)

properties/concepts (03)

reliability of measurement (15)

spurious relationship (13)

test implication (09)

theories/theory sketches (05)

triangulization (14)

units of analysis, case, or fact (02)

value (normative) judgment (09)

variable (03)

verifiability (09)

QUESTIONS AND EXERCISES

1. In the following statement, what is the independent property?
   Catholics are less likely to support abortion rights than non-Catholics.
   a. Members of the Catholic faith
   b. Support for abortion rights
   c. Religious denomination/affiliation/faith
   d. The Catholic faith

2. What is *not* a requirement for a statement to be considered a hypothesis?
   a. Clear specification of direction of relationship
   b. Falsifiability
   c. Not normative or value based
   d. Must be completely verifiable

3. Which of the following is a property/variable (not a fact or category)?
   What are the other choices examples of?
   a. Education level
   b. A highly educated person
   c. Educated people
   d. Twelve years of education

4. When discussing measurement, internal validity refers to:
   a. Whether taking the survey validates one's internal sense of tranquility
   b. Only whether a measure is consistent

    c. Whether a measure is generalizable to a larger target population

    d. Whether a variable measures what it's supposed to measure

5. Which of the following is the best-phrased hypothesis? What problems exist with the others?

    a. The economy is related to crime.

    b. Educated individuals are tolerant.

    c. Younger Americans were more likely to vote for Obama than older people.

    d. Those who see a difference between political alternatives are more likely to vote than those who don't.

6. Rephrase the other statements in Question 5 so that they better match the requirements of a hypothesis.

7. The presumed relationship between variables X and Y is said to be "spurious." This means that

    a. Both X and Y are dependent on some third variable. They have no direct impact on each other.

    b. The causal relationship between X and Y is reversed (Y is really the independent variable).

    c. Another variable influences changes in Y but *not* X. No causal link exists between the two.

    d. The two variables are just connected by historical coincidence.

8. Turn each of the following statements into researchable hypotheses. You need to:

    ▪ Explain, in detail, why each statement does not meet the requirements of a researchable hypothesis,

    ▪ Rephrase each statement so that it is a researchable hypothesis, and

    ▪ List the independent and dependent properties/variables for each of your revised statements.

      (1) *The Democratic Party lost the U.S. House in 2010.*

      (2) *Turnout tends to be high in traditional democracies.*

      (3) *The economy and immigration regulation are related.*

9. Hypotheses do not need theoretical, indirect confirmation (T/F) to be confirmed.

10. For the following hypotheses, specify the independent and dependent properties.

    Republicans are more supportive of the military than are Democrats.

    College graduates earn more than do high school graduates.

    Democratic countries are less likely to engage in military conflict than are non-Democratic countries.

11. Going back to our opening example, develop a hypothesis that would help explain why Barack Obama did better in 2008 than his predecessor, John Kerry did in 2004. Remember, the hypothesis should also predict and explain diff erences between any other two candidates/years. A full discussion of this appears on the web page for this volume.

NOTES

1   See Exercise 11 in this chapter.

2   The definitions here are those found in the traditional philosophy of science literature. See, for example, Carl G. Hempel's *Philosophy of Natural Science* (Prentice-Hall, 1966). Even within political science, however, these definitions are not always as rigidly applied as in this text.

3   In traditional sciences, the terms "laws" and "hypotheses" are often interchangeable, especially when the hypothesis has been tested often enough and in enough different ways to provide scientists with an established sense of certainty. I prefer to keep the distinction.

4   All census estimates taken from an analysis of the 2012 U.S. Census. Source: U.S. Census Bureau, *Current Population Survey* (U.S. Census Bureau, November 2012).

5   See Maryann Barakso, Daniel Sabet, and Brian Schaffner, *Understanding Political Science Research: The Challenge of Inference* (Routledge, 2013), the companion volume in this series, for a full discussion of the components of research methodology and the study of politics.

6   Many authors use *hypothesis* and *test implication* interchangeably. This author prefers the distinction based in the philosophy of science literature, while admitting that the distinction is sometimes clouded.

7   Of course, the theory behind our hypothesis should also predict that turnout would be high in perennially closely contested electoral districts.

8   See Martin Kelly, "Predicting the Presidential Election with Baseball," About. com, 2004, http://americanhistory.about.com/od/elections/a/baseballpres.htm

9   Anthony Downs, *An Economic Theory of Democracy* (Harper, 1957).

10   A more generalized research methods text will cover this in much greater detail as will we in later chapters (6 and 10) dealing with hypothesis testing and controls.

CHAPTER 2

CONTENTS

How Do We Measure and Observe?

Learning Objectives:

■ To understand the benefits and limits of statistics
■ To learn about problems with how concepts are measured
■ To understand differences in the level or precision of measurements
■ To interpret data summarized in a frequency distribution
■ To understand the critical importance of standardization
■ To interpret the different types of graphs that can be used to present visualizations of your data distributions
■ To realize that how we present and categorize our data can lead to different interpretations

In every election, candidates differ over who is at fault or should gain glory for current economic conditions and offer alternatives as to how to "grow" the economy in future years. They all seem to make a decent argument for their claim, sometimes even citing different economic decline or growth statistics. Are these just political slogans without substance? Perhaps. Are they legitimate accusations against the misuse of statistics by the opposition? Perhaps. In every election year, candidates rely on different sets of data, based on different conceptual assumptions and baselines of comparisons and analyzed using different statistical procedures. They often talk past each other, and most of the American public has to depend on its own sense of each candidate's veracity and understanding to assess the merits of candidates' claims. The political world will always be, well, political, colored by partisan and ideological lenses. However, as students of politics, we have an obligation to try to make independent, objective assessments of the relative worth of each candidate's proposals. In order to do so, we must have not only a basic understanding of statistical procedure, but also a firm grasp of what data are being statistically analyzed and how those data differ from other similar measures. We also need to understand how those data and statistics help to answer the questions that we propose.

As introduced in the last chapter, one begins research by asking theoretically important questions. Sometimes, *and only sometimes*, statistics can help us to answer those questions. Statistics are merely a summary tool. They help us with our research, but they are not the driving force behind it. They are as good as the data we collect and the research we design—no better. The basic premise of this text follows sound methodological guidelines: statistics can sometimes help us to answer certain questions; therefore, we need to understand exactly which question each statistic answers. Remember, statistics can never substitute for the English (or any other) language—they only complement it by serving as summary tools. Before these tools can be employed, theoretically useful questions about the relationships between and among well-defined and measurable properties must first be asked.

STATISTICAL MEASUREMENT—AN INTRODUCTION

With that introductory premise in mind, let us present two simple, but often overlooked facts about statistical measurement. Each will be developed further as we progress through the chapters.

First, as we summarize information, we lose information. Before we analyze data statistically, we need to make a decision about how much information we can afford to lose or need to lose to simplify our analysis. For example, a simple summary measure of the relationship between education and voting turnout would tell us that a strong and positive mathematical relationship exists between years of schooling and the expectation that one will vote. Most college-educated individuals will vote in any given presidential election, but not all. Any summary measure that causes us to predict that any particular college-educated person will vote will sometimes be incorrect, even if it usually allows for a correct prediction. That summary also masks the individual reasons why each college-educated person does vote (it might be something other than education). We may need to include more "pieces" of information in our analysis such as race, partisanship, and age; however, at a certain point, we need to reach a tentative conclusion. As soon as we do, we are probably leaving out some important distinction among certain individuals that also explains differences in voting turnout. Research is a continuous, not finite process.

Second, politicians, journalists, and the general public love the expression, "Lies, damn lies and statistics." Statistics, however, don't lie. They have no life and, therefore, no conscience. They have no capacity to lie. Individuals (often the politicians and journalists who decry their use), however, do lie—or at least choose information and statistics that place their point of view in the most favorable light (sometimes unintentionally). Statistics just summarize information—good or bad. If the information acquired doesn't accurately measure a certain property or relationship, or if there exists no commonly agreed on measure of that property, then no statistical summary of that measure will give us an accurate or satisfactory assessment of any proposed relationship. Even if the data collected do adequately measure the property at hand, different statistics might give us different impressions about those data. We will see in Chapter 9, for example, that given a certain distribution of party affiliation and voting by members of a legislature, we can choose one statistic that implies that the legislature is totally partisan, another that implies that it is somewhat partisan, and another that implies that the voting tendencies of legislative members are not related to partisanship at all—and even that seeming complexity does not take into account the different meaning of "partisanship" itself. Is it difference just for the sake of opposition, or is it backed by truly felt philosophical differences? Each statistic makes different assumptions about the data and the meaning of a relationship between two variables (in this example, partisanship and the vote). A statistic doesn't lie, but one can easily understand how two analysts can give two totally different assessments of the partisan divisiveness of a legislature using the same data but different statistics. A candidate can run for re-election claiming that she was able to bring together both Democrats and Republicans in a common effort. Her partisan opponent can claim that the partisan divisions within Congress are as bad as ever. The statistics their flacks will present will not lie. However, they may be based on a different set of congressional roll call votes, or they might be summarized using different statistical techniques.

The same can be said of the different tax and budget proposals offered by candidates in any country. Each is often dependent on a different projection of future budget surpluses and deficits. Are these projections always based on a careful, multidimensional analysis that takes into account the impact of the respective proposals, or are they just assuming that the surplus or deficit can be measured as a continuation of a current trend? Each may also be politically motivated by a different assessment of the validity of the public's desire to pay down the national debt or to preserve the integrity of entitlement funds like pension allotments or Social Security. When survey respondents overwhelming state they prefer certain options, are they expressing their true feelings (on which their vote might be based), or are they giving what they thought was a politically correct response? After all, in most U.S. national surveys, these are the same respondents who claim to have voted and to have voted for the winner in proportions that are often well above what actually occurred in the election. The statistics that summarize these survey results don't lie. They just reflect the potential internal invalidity of the responses.

Our task as scholars is to understand the limitations of the data we use. We can then embark on the task of understanding what each statistic measures, what data and relationship assumptions it makes, and how it precisely calculates that measurement. If we do so, then we can make our own, independent decision about the validity or worth of the assessment. We sometimes have a tendency to accept others' statistical findings as gospel or reject them as trivial when, in fact, we make no attempt to try to understand what the politician, pundit, or researcher tried to accomplish. Ignorance may be bliss, but it is not academically virtuous.

Many methodological factors—the reliability of our measurements and the internal and the external validity of measurements—must be considered when collecting data and analyzing relationships found within them (a broader discussion of external validity will be addressed in Chapter 6). Let us turn to a short list of some potential *measurement* problems. Again, a more elaborate discussion of each, and how these problems can be minimized, can be found in the accompanying or other research design texts.

Reliability of Measurement

Are we measuring with consistency? If we measured the variable twice, would we obtain the same results?

Cause: 1. Erratic, unexpected events that are not consistent or measurable
2. Incomplete information/instructions on which to base a measurement

Example: What if we measured someone's height with a tape measure that had a tendency to bend? The exact measurement would change from attempt to attempt. The biggest reliability threats occur when, in deciding how to measure, we come up with an inexact measuring device or instrument. Take, for example, a survey. If we asked people whether they approve of a certain bill, referenced by the House or Senate number only (e.g., House Bill #2087), but didn't give them the option of stating, "I don't know," we'll probably get an unreliable measure. The respondent might say "yes" once and the next day say "no." He/she would be making up an answer each time unless the respondent has a certain response bias (e.g., always saying "no" when unfamiliar with the question). That would be consistent and reliable but wouldn't tell us much about attitudes (other than detesting anything done by Congress).

This problem frequently occurs when researchers hire others (or entice their graduate assistants) to help with "content analysis" (i.e., the extraction of meaning and emphasis in, e.g., newspaper articles as a way of measuring the "partisan or ideological bias" of the paper or correspondent). When the instructions are not clear and open to interpretation, content analyzers might just guess meaning or intention. Given another pass through, they might code the articles differently.[1] Probably the most obvious example of reliability issues comes with the re-counts that have increasingly become part of U.S. elections and folklore. How does one measure "voter intention," a guideline used in many state re-counting laws, when no clear instructions are provided? Note, this is not the same as bias inherent with vote re-counters consciously or not consciously estimating intent in a way that produces the most votes for their party. Those re-counts would be consistent if redone. They might, however, be consistently biased in the same direction as they will always coincide with the partisan interests of the counter. It is that partisan interest, rather than actual intention, that may be measured. This is an example of a potential internal validity problem.

Internal Validity of Measurement

Are we measuring what we think we are measuring, or are we measuring something else? Even if reliable (the measurement is always the same), might the measurement not match the property we think we are measuring?

Example: Let's use surveys again. If I try to limit reliability problems, I might want to be more specific on the wording of the question. What if I state: "Do you approve or disapprove of the House Speaker's proposed bill #2087?" We might really be measuring how individuals feel about the House Speaker, not the bill itself.

Example: In a survey, ask people their age. Many will reliably (consistently) understate it. Even more obvious—in most post-election surveys, more people say they voted than is possible. You are asking whether or not they voted. They are responding to, "What is the politically correct answer?" A better example comes in the form of what we call the "**Bradley effect**." Tom Bradley was a long-term, Democratic, black mayor of Los Angeles who ran for governor of California in 1982. The exit polls indicated he would win, but he didn't. The general view about why the polls were off was because many white citizens, especially Democrats, did not want to acknowledge a racial bias. In fact, the polls were not all that wrong. Bradley only lost after the absentee ballots (at that time mostly Republican) were counted. There was still an external validity problem—but it was that exit polls do not always validly measure all votes (same day, early, and absentee voters are excluded). Barack Obama, for example, in both of his presidential elections did much better proportionately among those who voted early than those who voted on Election Day.[2]

Bradley effect The tendency for individuals to give responses that they feel are more politically or socially correct or reflect better on their own perceived moral values.

Internal invalidity is always problematic but may not be as dysfunctional as one might guess. What if, in a host of studies, we discover that surveys overestimate the vote for minority candidates, especially among Democrats? In a new survey conducted right before an election in a heavily Democratic district with a black Democrat running against a white Republican, the results indicate overwhelming support for the Republican candidate. If we are fairly certain of the potential problems inherent with the "Bradley effect," then, although we might not be able to estimate the Republican's winning percentage with any kind of accuracy, we would feel fairly certain that, given how the survey would be biased against her, she will most likely win.

Example: Are surveys the only problem? No. They are certainly replete with potential validity problems, but, as we will see when we discuss designs, they offer benefits not derived from other types of more aggregated measures. For now, let's just use an example. From the 1930s to the 1960s, voter turnout for Democrats was notoriously overstated in Chicago. Sometimes, turnout exceeded the size of the electorate in certain areas (especially districts containing cemeteries). Are politicians likely to "misstate"? I like to call this the "**Chicago effect**." In a sense, it is the "Bradley effect" brought up to institutional proportions. What needs to be stated by governments or other large institutions to stay in the good graces of their constituents and/or maintain funding for their agency? In 2014, we witnessed a very depressing example of this as we discovered that several Veterans Administration hospitals underreported the wait times of their patients, many of whom died waiting for service.[3]

Sidebar 2.1: The Chicago Effect and Crime Statistics

In 2010, an investigation into the collecting and categorizing of crime statistics by the New York City Police Department found that, in an effort to show reduced crime figures, many property crimes were downgraded from grand larcenies (>$1,000) to misdemeanors. There was also an increase in attempts to persuade victims not to file a complaint. To be fair, the accuracy of this report was questioned by several police officials and politicians who used other data to argue that New York had indeed become a safer city.

Source: William K. Rashbaum, "Police Manipulated Crime Data, Retired City Officials Say," *New York Times*, February 7, 2010, http://www.nytimes.com/2010/02/07/nyregion/07crime.html?_r=0.

Reliability versus Internal Invalidity

The best way I have ever found to demonstrate the difference is to think of an archery contest. Someone who is reliable but internally invalid would consistently miss the center, but in the same location (say outside,

Chicago effect The author's term for the intentional or unintentional misreporting of information by governmental or other agencies.

bottom-right). That person is a reliably bad shot. Someone who is unreliable would scatter the arrows all over the target, with no apparent pattern. Someone who is reliable and internally valid would consistently hit the center mark.[4] Note that, as with many research dilemmas, providing enough information to assure reliability might call into question the internal validity of our survey question.

PRECISION IN MEASUREMENT

Part of the problem with collecting data is that we cannot always collect it in as precise a way as we would like, or, more likely, the data are not collected or reported as precisely as we would like by another group of researchers or agency. Much of what we study has already occurred and been measured in the past, without the imposition of the standards we would have preferred. As far as measurement goes, this would not pose as great a problem as it does except for the potential limitations imposed by the precision, or lack thereof, of the data collected. These limitations might be conceptual. For example, if age is collected in categories (young, middle aged, old) rather than precise years, we may not be able to test our generational theory of voting unless that threefold categorical breakdown closely corresponds to our generational ones. Of greater importance in this text is that the level of precision often limits the type of statistic we can choose to measure our properties and test for their interactions.

There are a myriad of statistics from which to choose. We make our choices based on several fundamental criteria. Each can be considered a constraining device, narrowing down our options of choice. The first constraining device is the level of measurement, or mathematical precision with which data are collected. What are the mathematical assumptions we can make? What mathematical rules can apply, and what manipulations can we perform? Statistics are mathematical summary tools. We need to be careful that our manipulations of the data do not go beyond what the data have to offer mathematically.

All collection methods allow our cases or units of analysis (people in surveys, countries in comparative analyses) to be placed into different categories of a particular variable. The general rules for the creation of categories are that the categories are clearly *mutually exclusive* (i.e., distinctly different from each other—we should have no trouble deciding in which category to place any case), *exhaustive* (all possibilities are included—no cases are left out), and fairly *parsimonious* (although we lose information in the process, we generally try to limit the number of categories to those essential for maintaining conceptual diversity, or to guarantee sufficient case sizes for useful analysis, particularly when we are trying to generalize from a small sample). These rules apply to all levels of mathematical precision.

Data can be collected and measured with differing levels of mathematical precision. There are three basic levels: nominal (sometimes called qualitative), ordinal (ordered qualitative), and interval (continuous or quantitative).

Nominal is the least precise; very few mathematical assumptions can be made about the data. Interval is the most precise. These levels are, in the language of computer operating systems, backwards compatible, both in measurement and application. If data can be mathematically assumed to be interval, they also automatically carry ordinal and nominal properties. Ordinal data only carry ordinal and nominal assumptions. Additionally, with intervally measured data, interval, ordinal, and nominal statistical summary tools are possible. Nominal data can only be summarized nominally.[5] Consider that all data are nominal. With some extra mathematical assumptions, they can also be considered ordinal; with some more, interval. A description of each follows.

LEVELS OF MEASUREMENT—MATHEMATICAL ASSUMPTIONS

Nominal Data

All data can be categorized according to the rules of mutual exclusiveness and exhaustiveness. Nominal comes from the Latin root *nomen*, or "name." If data are purely **nominal data**, then all we can say is that the categories are different from each other (different names). The codes or numbers we assign to each category are purely arbitrary and are only necessary to ease data entry (it is easier to enter a "1" than a "Romney"). They just set a place for cases or units of analysis with similar classifications to be listed together. As an example, take a survey item that asked individuals to specify how they voted in the 2000 presidential election (when third-party candidates played a small but significant role in the outcome). For simplicity, let's assume that the respondents mentioned only the following four candidates (many more candidates were on the ballot in each state):

1. Al Gore, Jr.
2. George W. Bush
3. Ralph Nader
4. Pat Buchanan

For this variable, four categorical placements are possible. The number we assign to each category is *purely arbitrary*. The only mathematical requirement here is one of equivalence (=). For this variable, everyone with a code of "1" is considered to be similar (they all voted, or claim to have voted, for Gore). They are different from everyone coded "2" or "3" or "4" (ignore the problem with butterfly ballots or hanging chads). The operative term here is "difference."

nominal data Data that are assumed to be measured only by differences in categorization. All data are, by their very nature, nominal.

We could just as easily assign the numbers "1, 4, 3, 2" to the four listed possibilities or any other numerical (or alphabetic) scheme that provided four different entries. The numbers themselves are *meaningless*. They just create statistical boxes into which we can place voters who voted differently.

As another example, in many standard European surveys (Eurobarometers), respondents are asked which of the following is most important in determining a country's or group of countries power.

1. Its economic power
2. Its political influence
3. Its military strength
4. Its cultural influence
5. Other/don't know

Again, the numerical entries are arbitrary. Any five different numbers would maintain the mathematical property of equivalence.

Ordinal Data

Certain data allow us not only to categorize differently, but also to assign rank orderings to the categories. Data measured at the **ordinal data** level allow us to discuss not only differences between categories, but also the *direction* of that difference. Let us explain by way of example. Take the following variable coding from the American National Election Studies of the variable IDEOLOGY:

1. Strongly Liberal
2. Liberal
3. Moderately Liberal
4. Moderate
5. Moderately Conservative
6. Conservative
7. Strongly Conservative

As with any variable, the data are measured nominally. An individual coded as a "Conservative" (6) is different in ideology from one coded as "Moderately Liberal" (3). Another way of looking at this variable is to treat it as "degree of conservativeness." Not only is "Conservative" different from a "Moderately Liberal," but the former is "more conservative" than the latter. Anytime it makes sense to talk about "more" or "less," "greater" or "lesser," then we have ordinally measured data. The numbers we assign are still rather arbitrary. There is nothing intrinsically meaningful about coding "Conservative" as a "6." The number "6" only has meaning when we trace its coding within a particular study. The only requirement is that the numerical entries

ordinal data Data for which we can discern differences among categories and for which a set rank ordering of categories makes conceptual sense.

we arbitrarily assign to the seven ideological categories be *different* and maintain the proper conceptual *rank ordering*. Coding "Strongly Conservative" as a "75" would maintain the requirement of ranking ("maintaining the ordering through a monotonic transformation" is the official language that we will all now forget). Mathematically, ordinal data maintain the mathematical rule of equivalence (=), but also those associated with rankings, such as transitivity. If a strong liberal (1) is less conservative than a moderate liberal (3), and a moderate liberal is less conservative than a moderate conservative (5), then, by definition, a strong liberal is less conservative than a moderate conservative. The numbers assigned to each should confirm this (1 < 5).[6]

Go back to our presidential vote example. Can we rank order these categories in a consistently meaningful way? Although it may be possible to say that someone who voted for Pat Buchanan (4) in 2000 was more supportive of him than one who voted for George W. Bush (2), does it make sense to say that a Nader voter (3) was more supportive of Buchanan than one who voted for Bush (or Gore)? Can we reclassify the variable as "degree of support for Buchanan," or by reversing the scale, "degree of support for Gore"? A European who believes that "military strength" (3) is the major characteristic that defines a country's power is more likely to believe in that defining characteristic than one who believes it is a country's political influence (2), but also more likely than someone who believes it lies in a country's cultural influence (4). These categories are different, but not different in a *consistent* direction. Other data considered ordinal would be any survey item measured on a standard Likert scale (Strongly Disagree to Strongly Agree) or any common assessment of presidential performance (poor, fair, good, excellent).

Interval Data

Interval data (also called continuous or quantitative) maintain all the mathematical properties of nominal data (=) and ordinal data (< , >). In addition, standard mathematical rules of addition and subtraction apply. With interval data, the numbers assigned are no longer arbitrary; they must have *intrinsic meaning*. Let us say we ask several people their income. The category "$40,000" is not arbitrary but precisely measures one's annual salary. Of course, the individual might be purposely understating his true income, thus producing a potential internal validity problem. As with all nominal data, someone earning "$40,000" earns a *different* income than someone earning "$20,000." As with ordinal data, someone earning "$40,000" earns *more than* someone earning "$20,000" (*different in a specified direction*). However, in addition, we can subtract the two values and say that someone earning "$40,000" earns *exactly "$20,000" more than* someone earning "$20,000" (*different by how much*). "Income" therefore qualifies as intervally measured data. If these two

interval data Data for which we can discern differences among ranked categories and that allow us to answer the question, "different by how much?"

income earners marry, we can add their salaries and list their family income as "$60,000." If we can consider "Income" as having a meaningful zero point ($0 = no income), then these data can also be considered *ratio* since rules of multiplication and division apply. One earning "$40,000" earns *twice as much* as one earning "$20,000" (*different by a certain factor*).

Return to our ideology scale. Does it make sense to say that a "Conservative" (6) is 2 units more, or 1.5 times more conservative than a "Moderate" (4)? Can we marry the two and create a family that is unbelievably conservative ("10")? Can we subtract the two and produce a "Liberal" (2)? It would be even more conceptually ludicrous to add and subtract religions, presidential vote categories, and views about what defines a country's prominence. Other true intervally measured variables would be age, years of schooling, height, weight, percentage of the vote, population counts, number or percentage of a given ethnic group, and temperature. All can also be considered ratio, except for temperature. A "40"-year-old is different in age than a "20"-year-old, is older, is 20 years older, and is twice as old. Seventy degrees is different from 35°, is hotter, is 35° hotter, but is not twice as hot. Zero degrees Fahrenheit is, after all, not the absence of temperature, a fact to which anyone living in states like Minnesota or Maine can attest.

Data collected at a lower level of measurement can often be aggregated to produce a set of data with more precise mathematical properties—a source of confusion for many students. Let's return to our 2000 presidential election example. If individuals are our unit of analysis, then the data are clearly *nominal*. What, however, if we aggregated individual voters into states or congressional districts, adding all those who voted the same way together? The unit of analysis would now be states, and the sum total or percentage of individuals who voted for, say, George W. Bush would be *interval*. Candidate Nader, for example, won slightly more than 10% of the total presidential vote in Alaska. In Ohio, he won approximately 2.5%. His percentage support was different in both states (nominal), higher in Alaska (ordinal), and higher by roughly 7.5 percentage points (interval).

LEVELS OF MEASUREMENT—CONCEPTUAL ASSUMPTIONS

Even if data comply with all the mathematical properties needed to qualify as interval/ratio (the greatest level of precision), we still need to make sure that those data are measuring a property that we conceive of as precisely. Let us take age. Mathematically, as we have shown, the data are interval/ratio. However, what if we are using age as a way of measuring a less precise concept, "maturity"? We might be willing to claim that someone who is 60 is generally more mature than someone who is 30 (an ordinal claim), but are we comfortable with the claim that the first person is 30 units more mature, or twice as mature? "Maturity," for some, is at best an ordinal concept.[7] Think carefully about whether or not you wish to summarize it with interval statistics. The same can be said if we are using income as an indirect measure of "standard of living." Take the following four individuals (A, B, C, D) listed with their incomes:

A earns $10,000
B earns $80,000
C earns $50,000,000
D earns $50,070,000

Mathematically, the difference in earnings between B and A is the same as the difference between D and C ($70,000). Making the interval assumption that the difference in living standards between B and A is the same as the difference between D and C carries the conceptualization a bit too far. B is comfortably middle class; A is a struggling grad student. D and C are both rich. Of course, to match the data more closely to our concept, we can transform them using logarithms or other mathematical tools or perhaps think of them in purely ratio terms (B earns eight times more than A, but D earns only .14% more than C). For the most part, however, we are probably not willing to think of "standard of living" in such precise terms. We should therefore probably not use a statistic that mathematically assumes too much precision in the data.

Mathematical and conceptual assumptions constrain the class of statistic we can use. A third consideration may also constrain the class, but more precisely, it will narrow down our choices within classes. This final constraint in choosing the appropriate statistic has to do with the question that we ask. The more precise the question, the easier the choice. How to choose a certain statistic from interval (or ordinal or nominal), **descriptive** (or **inferential**),[8] **univariate** (or **bivariate** or **multivariate**)[9] **statistics** is the subject of the rest of this and several more advanced texts. Let us for now just offer one conditional statement. Even if data are measured intervally, and conceived of intervally, we may still wish to use an ordinal statistic to mathematically answer our question. For example, if we need to find out if individuals who stay in school longer generally have *higher* salaries, we are asking an ordinal, bivariate question. The fact that "years of schooling" and "income" are interval is inconsequential. If, on the other hand, we need to estimate exactly how much additional income is to be expected for each additional year of schooling, then we are asking an interval question that requires a mathematically interval, bivariate statistic. Don't choose statistics before you know which question you are asking. The more precise the question, the easier choosing the appropriate statistic will be.

descriptive statistics A class of statistics that allow us to measure and analyze what we actually observe.

inferential statistics A class of statistics that allow us to make inferences or estimates about populations based on our samples.

univariate statistics A class of statistics that allow us to measure and analyze only one variable at a time.

bivariate statistics A class of statistics that allow us to measure and analyze the relationship between two variables.

multivariate statistics A class of statistics that allow us to measure and analyze the relationship among three or more variables.

FREQUENCY DISTRIBUTIONS AS MEASUREMENT AND OBSERVATION

Throughout U.S. history, and the history of other democracies, questions have been raised as to the authenticity of the vote. How internally valid are the numbers produced by the respective election officials of each state or country? This issue came to prominence in 2000, when the U.S. presidential election hinged on the counting of irregularly marked or processed ballots in Florida. The answer to the question, "Who won?" (translated as, "Who received the most votes?") was dependent on the standards that were used for counting and, thus, the standardized baseline of comparison among the candidates. Was it the number of ballots clearly cast? Or was it the number of ballots for which a preference could be ascertained (vote intention)? Although highlighted in 2000, this undercounting of votes has reached epidemic proportions in the United States, with the number of discarded ballots estimated from 1 to 6 million per national election year.

Lost in the midst of the 2000 controversy over hanging chads and butterfly ballots was an important point. More individuals who were eligible to vote in Florida stayed home on Election Day than voted for any one of the presidential candidates. In fact, for certain elections in many states, the number of "stay-at-homes" often exceeds the vote count for all of the candidates combined. How then do we measure if, in a given election, a candidate has a mandate to rule? Conceptual assessments of the *mandates* given by the public to their elected officials, and ultimately appraisals of the success of democratic institutions, are dependent on how we count, whom we count, and on which total we base our count.

Previously in this chapter, we stated that a statistic is nothing more than a summary measure. In fact, most of you are probably already familiar with one statistic—a type of summary called a **frequency distribution**. Every day, in every newspaper, certain magazines, and many websites, for example, you come across summaries of responses of survey questions. Whom do you feel won the debate? Which motion picture should win the academy award? Do you feel that the country is moving in the right direction? Should your country join the European Union? Should pornography be restricted on the Internet? These summaries can all be considered statistics, as they provide in a nutshell or quick listing the feelings and attitudes of hundreds, thousands, or, in certain cases, millions of respondents.

The summaries of election results that we awaited in November 2000 were also stated as frequency distributions. We did not, after all, produce a listing of each voter's preference, one by one, until more than 100 million preferences were listed. Instead, we summarized the results—how many voted for George W. Bush? By what margin did he win a particular state? This was not, of course, intended to diminish the significance of each particular voting act.

frequency distribution A presentation of a distribution's cases summarized by their respective categories.

Indeed, in states like Florida, the presidential election was determined by an interpretation of each and every voting act in several counties. However, once again, statistics are summaries, intended to give us a quick impression of the behavior or characteristics of a large number of cases.

Frequency distributions can be listed in several ways, depending on the information that we need to summarize. Let us start off with a simple example. In November 2010, the state of California, along with 36 other states, held an election for governor. Roughly 10 million votes were cast in that race (10,095,485 to be exact).[10] Listing each voter's preference would fill countless volumes. Instead, the election results could be summarized using the following frequency statistics. Let us briefly describe each statistic and then relate it to an interpretation of the "mandate" granted by the California gubernatorial results.

Absolute Frequency

The **absolute frequency** (also called the **tally** or **count**) is simply the actual number of cases observed within each category (in this example, the number of voters who voted for each candidate). Absolute frequencies are useful in evaluating one population or group. For example, in Table 2.1 voting results for the 2010 California gubernatorial election are listed. The Democrat, Jerry Brown, received 5,428,458 (*absolute*) votes. The absolute frequencies tell us who won most elections (whichever candidate had the highest absolute frequency).[11] The Democrats regained the governorship (held previously by Republican Arnold Schwarzenegger) in California because their candidate received more votes than his closest opponent, Republican Meg Whitman, who received 4,127,371 votes.

Absolute frequencies, however, don't allow us to answer factual statements like "which state is the most Republican?" even just in terms of gubernatorial

TABLE 2.1 2010 California Gubernatorial Vote

Party of Candidate	Cat. Code*	Absolute Frequency
Democrat	1	5,428,458
Republican	2	4,127,371
Green	3	129,231
Libertarian	4	150,898
Other/Write-In**	5	259,527
Total Base (*n=*)		10,095,485

*Remember that these are arbitrary as is the order of the parties listed.
**Often, "other" includes all but the top two or three vote getters.

absolute frequency/tally/ count The actual observed number of cases within each category of a frequency distribution.

TABLE 2.2 2010 Utah Gubernatorial Vote

Party of Candidate	Cat. Code*	Absolute Frequency
Democrat	1	188,911
Republican	2	381,531
Green*	3	0
Libertarian	4	11,723
Other/Write-In	5	11,842
Total Base (*n=*)		594,007

*The "Desert Green" Party did not have a candidate on the ballot that year. The entry is left so as to match the table with the California results.

voting. More citizens voted Republican for governor in California than in, for example, Utah (4,127,371 vs. 381,531); however, more also voted Democratic (5,428,458 vs. 188,911), Libertarian (150,898 vs. 11,723), and just about any other party you can think of (Table 2.2). California just has many more people and, therefore, will be likely to have more people who vote a certain way, who think a certain way, who dress a certain way, and so forth.

Relative Frequencies: Percentages and Proportions

Absolute frequencies, therefore, are not very useful in making comparisons between populations with different case sizes. In order to make comparisons, we need to *standardize* the bases. Percentage (often called **relative frequency**) accomplishes this end.[12] With percentages, the total of the categorical entries is always equal to 100%, *regardless of the number of cases* those percentages represent. We need to be careful, however, in deciding which base to use or in understanding which base was used by others in calculating that percentage.

In order to compare relative partisan strength, we need to *standardize* the base. Percentages or relative frequencies allow us to do so. Percentages for each category are simply the relevant absolute frequency divided by the total number of cases or, in this example, voters, multiplied by 100. Utah gubernatorial candidate Herbert received only a fraction of the *absolute* vote of his Republican counterpart in California, Meg Whitman (see Tables 2.3 and 2.4).

However, he received 53.8% of the ballots cast in his state (381,531/594,007 × 100). Whitman received only 40.9% (2,990,822/8,541,476 × 100). In terms of gubernatorial voting, Utah is therefore more Republican. The listed percentages also tell us that in 2010 Utah was less Democratic (31.8% vs. 53.8%), more Libertarian, and so forth.

relative frequency The proportion or percentage of observed cases within each category of a frequency distribution.

TABLE 2.3 2010 California Gubernatorial Vote

Party of Candidate	Cat. Code*	Absolute Frequency	Proportion/Relative Frequency
Democrat	1	5,428,458	53.8%
Republican	2	4,127,371	40.9%
Green	3	129,231	1.3%
Libertarian	4	150,898	1.5%
Other/Write-In**	5	259,527	2.6%
Total Base (*n=*)		10,095,485	100.0%*

*Due to rounding error (the percentages are carried out to only one decimal place), the totals will sometimes equal 99.9% or 100.1%.
**Category 3 (Green) is kept in Figure 2.4 to maintain consistency. This can be considered another form of standardization.

TABLE 2.4 2010 Utah Gubernatorial Vote

Party of Candidate	Cat. Code*	Absolute Frequency	Proportion/Relative Frequency
Democrat	1	188,911	31.8%
Republican	2	381,531	64.2%
Green	3	0	0.0%
Libertarian	4	11,723	2.0%
Other/Write-In	5	11,842	2.0%
Total Base (*n=*)		594,007	100.0%

THE IMPORTANCE OF STANDARDIZATION

This notion of **standardization**, quite simply understood in the context of frequency distributions, is an extremely important concept in statistical theory, perhaps the most important, and we'll devote much time to it in subsequent chapters. Percentages standardize by eliminating the differences in the number of cases. The total of all percentages in a table will always equal 100% (give or take some rounding error), regardless of the number of cases those percentages represent. Therefore, "100%" becomes the *standardized* base. As in our example, percentages allow us to compare election results across states with different populations. They also allow us to compare election results across races in a given year (more people usually vote for president than senator or House member) and elections across years (Democrat Franklin Roosevelt won the 1936 election with more than 60% of the votes cast even though he received only about half the votes of Barack Obama

standardization The application of a common numerical and/or conceptual base to different data so that different measurements can be compared.

in 2012). In 1976, a younger Jerry Brown won a second term as governor with a higher percentage (56.1) but many fewer absolute votes (3,878,812). Other methods will be needed to standardize on other differences. For example, one statistic (regression) will allow us to compare differences on one variable (say education) with differences on another (say income), even though education and income are measured in different units (years and dollars).

One main consideration in the standardization that allows us to measure outcomes in comparative ways is to decide on the appropriate base for comparison. In computing percentages or relative frequencies, we first need to ask the question, "relative to what?" In the previous example, the base on which we calculated our percentages was equal to the number of individuals who voted for governor in their respective states. On that basis, Jerry Brown received a majority of the total votes cast for governor. However, some individuals voted on Election Day, but not for governor (perhaps only voting for senator or one of California's many ballot propositions). The total number of individuals who cast a ballot on Election Day was 10,302,324. The total number of registered voters, many of whom did not vote on Election Day, was 17,205,883. The total number of eligible voters, as estimated by census figures, was 23,551,699.[13] Dividing the absolute frequency for Brown by these different bases (and then multiplying by 100), we find that although the governor-elect received a vote from 53.8% of the total number of individuals who voted for governor, he received a vote from slightly less, 52.7%, of all those who voted on Election Day, from only 31.6% of all registered voters, and from a mere 23.0% of the estimated eligible electorate. Unless we are certain that those who did not vote would have split their support for Brown in roughly the same proportions as those who did (and a general survey of voters and nonvoters can help us to ascertain this), the idea of a mandate for the Democratic governor-elect only holds up if we use as our base the number of people who showed up at the polls. Among the eligible electorate, more than three-fourths voted against or withheld their vote from Brown. In fact, in many recent U.S. elections, the percentage of non-voters usually exceeds the percentage of voters and certainly almost always exceeds the percentage received by the winning candidate. Always be careful to understand the base used in the proportions. Whether Brown conceptually received a mandate depends on which figures you use. He did not receive active majority support from everyone who could have voted, nor from even everyone registered to vote. Lest the Republicans amongst you rejoice too quickly, remember that regardless of the base used, GOP candidate Whitman fared even worse. Partisanship aside, however, this exercise does demonstrate that active support for candidates in the United States is generally limited at best. The candidate with the most votes wins regardless of the turnout, but public acceptance of the victory may be questionable, especially in low-turnout elections like primaries or in countries where eligible voters stay home to protest what they feel will be a rigged election.[14]

Cumulative Frequency

Before we move on to other statistics, let's discuss one more type of frequency calculation. A **cumulative frequency** is the percentage of relevant cases that has a certain level or degree of a variable or less. Consider the following distribution of ideological preference (degree of conservativeness) taken from the 2000 American National Election Studies (ANES) survey of the U.S. eligible electorate.[15]

Table 2.5 lists, as before, both the absolute frequencies and percentages for each category of ideological placement. Because the categories are ordered from the least conservative (Strongly Liberal) to the most conservative (Strongly Conservative), it also allows us to determine what percentage of individuals place themselves at a certain level of conservativeness or less. For example, 36.1% of all respondents categorized themselves as Moderately Liberal or less conservative (or more liberal); 76.8% of those respondents who expressed an ideological preference were Moderately Conservative or less conservative.

Note that cumulative frequencies only make sense with data that are measured at the ordinal or interval level. The phrase "or less" doesn't make sense with data that are only nominally measured. Refer back to our California percentage table. Would it make sense to state that 94.7% of the voters voted "Republican or less othered?" The ordering of the voting categories is

TABLE 2.5 Ideology, United States, 2000 ANES

Ideology (degree of conservativeness)	Cat. Code	Absolute Frequency	Proportion/ Relative Frequency	Cumulative Frequency
Strongly Liberal	1	70	4.4%	4.4%
Liberal	2	156	9.8%	14.2%
Moderately Liberal	3	350	21.9%	36.1%
Moderate	4	110	6.9%	43.0%
Moderately Conservative	5	539	33.8%	76.8%
Conservative	6	231	14.5%	91.2%
Strongly Conservative	7	140	8.8%	100.0%
Total Base		1,596	100.0%	

cumulative frequency A display within a frequency table that indicates the proportion or percentages that are contained within a certain category and categories ranked below it. Data must be measured at least at the ordinal level.

arbitrary. The ordering of ideology is not, as it follows a certain conceptual ranking.[16]

FROM NOMINAL TO INTERVAL DATA

As mentioned before, data collected at a lower level of measurement can often be aggregated to produce a set of data with more precise mathematical properties. In our California gubernatorial example, the data are purely nominal. The variable is the gubernatorial vote or "for which candidate did the individual cast his/her ballot." The case or unit of analysis is the individual voter; the number of cases (*n*) equals 10,095,485 (only gubernatorial voters will be used for this example). The frequency distribution summarizes the categorical choices of those millions of voters. A similar frequency distribution can be created for the other 36 states in which gubernatorial elections were held in 2010. We have already produced one for Utah. If we take, as one possibility, the percentage of the vote received by the Democratic candidate in each state, we can create a new variable, "% Democratic gubernatorial vote," with each state now serving as the case or unit of analysis, and with the number of cases now equaling 37. This variable is mathematically interval. The Democratic candidate received a different percentage of the vote in California and Utah (nominal). He received a higher percentage of the vote (ordinal). The percentage he received was roughly 22% higher (interval). Considering the data as ratio, we can also state that his percentage was roughly 1.7 times higher. In many research studies, both individual and aggregate data are analyzed to substantiate one's claims. Each have their potential limitations, so each are used as a check against the other.

Scaling techniques can also be used to create interval data from nominal data even at the individual level. One, for example, could add the number of all of the Democratic candidates chosen by an individual in any given election and, then, divide by all of the elections in which one voted. We would then produce the number or percentage of times a candidate voted Democratic in any given election year. In many comparative country studies, a scale is produced using individual items measuring different democratic procedures in use in each country—whether free elections take place, the transparency of the electoral process, freedom of speech and the press, and so forth. Adding the number of items on which a country scores (nominally) as democratic produces an interval "level of democracy" scale. Of course, although the numbers are easily added, scholars disagree as to which items conceptually should be included and whether or not they should be weighed equally.

GRAPHS AS VISUALIZATIONS OF OUR OBSERVATIONS

The adage that "one picture is worth a thousand words" applies to statistical summarization as well as crime scene photos. Different graphing methods can be used to visualize the distributions listed in a table (or the relationship between variables discussed in subsequent chapters). We will only present a few here. Use graphs when they help your audience understand what the data are relating. Don't use them if they complicate the presentation.[17]

Bar Chart

For nominal, categorical data, two types of graphical displays are usually appropriate, bar charts or histograms and pie charts. In a **bar chart**, the absolute frequency or percentage of each relevant category is displayed by the height or length of the bar, with each category represented by a separate bar. Generally, the categories are listed, equally spaced, along a horizontal axis, with the vertical axis representing the number or percentage of cases within each category.[18] The bars can be two- or three-dimensional, with the latter often providing a more dramatic display. The absolute frequency or percentage can be included in the chart in order to provide the reader with precise information. Return to our California example. Figure 2.1 graphically represents the distribution of support for each party's candidate (or combination of minor-party candidates). The victor is the person with the highest bar, Democrat Jerry Brown.

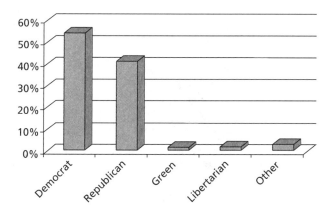

FIGURE 2.1 Bar Chart of the Vote for California Governor, 2010

bar chart A graphical representation of data where each category is separated into bars. The height or length of each bar represents the number or proportion of cases within each category.

Pie Chart

Alternatively, a **pie chart** can be constructed, with each candidate's support represented by a proportional slice of a pie. In Figure 2.2 the slices for the top two candidates are separated from the others. Both types of charts present a strong visual image of the Democratic candidate's victory, the majority (>50%) nature of that victory, and the lack of third-party support. A note of caution: many analysts consider pie charts to lack usefulness because it is often difficult to truly estimate, without percentages attached, the exact magnitude of each "slice." With a small number of slices, however, and especially when one or two are predominant, the visual impact may actually be more compelling than a bar chart.

Consider how different the charts, particularly the pie chart, would appear if the base for percentages and, thus, the size of the individual pie slices factored in all eligible voters. Both Figures 2.2 and 2.3 represent the same election, but the sense of victory or mandate differs greatly.

In order to compare the election results in both states, a combined bar chart, rather than pie chart, would prove extremely useful (see Figure 2.4). Remember to use percentages, and not absolute frequencies, since you wish to visualize *relative* differences of support for each party in each state.

Frequency Polygon and Line Charts

What if we have a large number of categories, and those categories represent data that can be measured intervally? As part of a 2004 Eurobarometer survey (and most surveys), respondents were asked their age. These ages ranged from 18 to 97. For each of those ages, a bar is drawn (as in our example of the

pie chart A graphical representation of data where each category is separated into wedges. The area of each wedge represents the number or proportion of cases within each category.

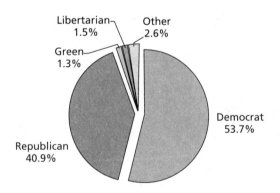

FIGURE 2.2 Pie Chart of the Vote for California Governor, 2010

California vote) whose height represents the number, proportion, or percentage of respondents who specified that exact age (see Figure 2.5). On the horizontal axis, each category is listed in order, with each bar directly adjacent to each other. We represent the distribution with a whole series of bars, one

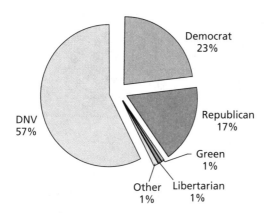

FIGURE 2.3 Pie Chart of the Vote for California Governor, 2010—Non-Voters Included

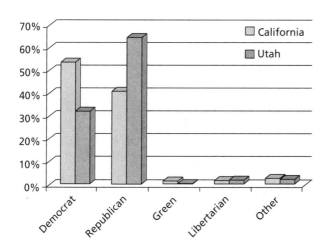

FIGURE 2.4 Bar Chart of the Vote for California and Utah Governors, 2010

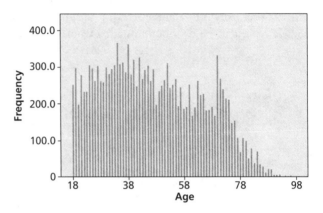

FIGURE 2.5 Bar Chart of Age, Eurobarometer 62

for each of the 81 possible age categories. In simple terms, assume that each voter is the same height. Voters of similar ages stand atop each other. They line up next to voters of proximate ages.

Alternatively, we can hide the bars, and connect their tops by a line (see Figure 2.6). Although the graph is represented by a line, it is, in reality, a smoothed-over bar chart with a large number of categories.

As we will see later, this **frequency polygon** allows us to visualize, and later measure, the proportion or percentage of individuals between any two given ages. That proportion will be measured as the area under the curve between those two age points (much like the proportion of a wedge of a pie chart).[19]

Time Series Charts

The line chart, or frequency polygon, displayed on the previous page represents a distribution of *each category* (18, 19, . . . 98) of one intervally measured variable (age) *at one point in time*. A different type of line chart, commonly called a **time series chart** or graph, represents *one or more categories* of one variable measured at *different points in time*. As such, it can be very useful in showing proportional changes of a variable over time. The horizontal axis displays the years; the vertical axis displays the relevant percentage for the variable in question. Although no data are collected for points between years (which the lines would seem to indicate), the lines do allow the reader to visualize a flow of change over time.

Consider the following listing for the estimated percentage voter turnout in the United States in every presidential election since 1952.[20] Turnout

frequency polygon A graphical representation of data with bars representing each of a large number of categories. A line is then drawn connecting the tops of each bar.

time series chart A graphical representation where data for one or more categories of a variable or variables are plotted for each year and where the yearly data points are connected. The area of each wedge represents the number or proportion of cases within each category.

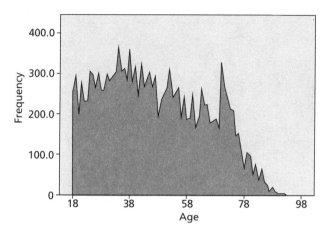

FIGURE 2.6 Frequency Polygon of Age, Eurobarometer 62

figures are calculated with both the voting age and voting eligible figures (see endnote 13). Each point in Figure 2.7 represents one category (percentage voting) for each year (refer back to our discussion in the section "From Nominal to Interval Data"). For example, in 1976, 55.2% of the eligible electorate voted while 44.8% did not. Note that *more* people voted in 2000 than in 1960. The population of the country increased, and the franchise had been extended to residents of the District of Columbia and 18- to 20-year-olds by constitutional amendments ratified in 1961 and 1971, respectively. The *percentage* voting, however, generally decreased over this time (partially as a result of the extension of the franchise to groups less likely to vote than others). The data for each year could be listed, but that form of presentation would not be as dramatic as the graph. Time series charts, like frequency polygons, are really a set of bars with lines connecting the top of each bar, with the bars themselves disguised to make for easier presentation. In our example of voting turnout, only one category is graphed for each year. The line connecting the top of the percentage of nonvoters for each year is left out, as it would be directly and inversely proportional to the line representing the percentage of voters. If more than two categories are possible, as would be the case for party identification, ideology, or presidential vote (third-party candidates included), then one line can be graphed for each category of the variable. Also note that, for clarity of presentation, the bottom of the graph is truncated, with the *y*-axis starting at a point well above the theoretical minimum turnout figure of 0%.

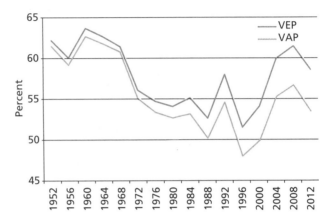

FIGURE 2.7 Presidential Vote Turnout, 1952–2012

Sidebar 2.2: Felony Disenfranchisement and Standardization

Traditionally, this voting age population (VAP) underestimate was caused by the counting of legal immigrants to the United States who, by the twentieth century, had lost their ability to vote in any election. Their inclusion in the denominator of our voting turnout calculations deflated the quotient. In the last quarter century or so, however, an increasingly sizeable proportion of the remaining calculation base is disenfranchised because of a felony conviction. Some states deny the franchise to those currently incarcerated (although in some states these same individuals can run for office). Others delay the franchise until parole and/or probation have been completed. However, in several states, particularly in the South, a felony conviction bars an individual from voting for life—sometimes even when the individual has satisfied the franchise terms in a state from which he moved.

Current estimates range as high as nearly 6 million individuals who could not vote in 2012 due to a felony restriction. That burden falls disproportionately on the black, male population. In Florida, the percentage of that population disenfranchised because of a conviction has now reached 23%.

Although the voting eligible population (VEP) seems a more valid base on which to calculate turnout, many comparative scholars feel that using the VAP provides a more accurate cross-national view as most countries do not restrict the vote in as many ways as does the United States.

Source: http://www.sentencingproject.org/doc/publications/fd_Felony%20Disenfranchisement%20 Primer.pdf.

A word of caution in reviewing graphical representations. Even small changes can seem pronounced if the minimum and maximum chart values are distant from each other, or if the graph is rescaled. One picture might be worth a thousand words, but one can easily change the meaning of those words. The previous chart has been resized to give the appearance of maximum (Figure 2.8) and minimum (Figure 2.9) change and variation over time.

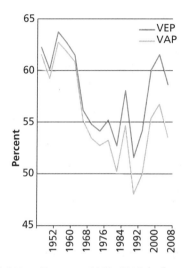

FIGURE 2.8 Presidential Vote Turnout, 1952–2012 (reformatted)

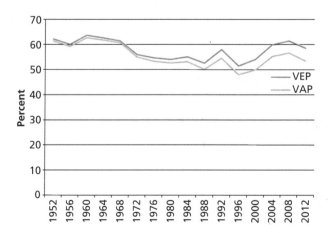

FIGURE 2.9 Presidential Vote Turnout, 1952–2012 (reformatted again)

One More Example

It is often possible to combine some level of time series with aggregations of individual data. In the following example, using data from the Latinobarómetro surveys[21] (2008–2009), data are summarized for each country on the individual survey question representing the percentage of respondents who agreed that "democracy is preferable to any other type of government." The within-country percentages for each country aggregated for 2008 are subtracted from the aggregations produced for 2009. We now have a "within-year" measurement of change for each country (for simplicity, only five countries are listed). The differences can be positive (faith in democracy increased in that country), negative (decreased), or 0 (stayed the same). As the percentage differences can be positive or negative, a standard bar chart would have bars that rise above or fall below the axis (no change). In Figure 2.10 countries are listed alphabetically, although some prefer to list countries in the order of the differences.

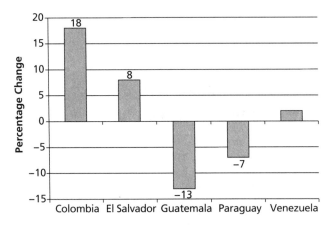

FIGURE 2.10 Change in Views about Democracy, 2008–2009

▌MEASURING PROPERTIES AND THE IMPORTANCE OF CATEGORIZATION

Before moving on to the next chapter, one important methodological point needs to be made. Frequency distributions and the charts that represent them can lead to differing conclusions based on how we originally categorize the data. Presidential job performance ratings, for example, often differ between survey organizations based on the number and type of choices offered respondents. Adding middle-of-the-road choices such as "fair" leads to a much less positive (or negative) appraisal than if only "good" or "not so good" are offered. Similarly, researchers and journalists will often combine categories to further simplify their analyses, especially if they are interested in presenting easily interpretable graphics (a pie sliced three ways is easier to picture, and uses fewer newspaper colors or shades, than one sliced seven ways). How they combine or collapse categories, however, can have significant effects on how data are interpreted.

Notice what happens to the table and our summary understanding of ideological preferences when we collapse categories (Figure 2.11). If we consider categories 1–3 to be liberal (L), 4 to be moderate (M), and 5–7 to be conservative (C, in pie chart A), we come up with a frequency distribution that implies that the electorate is rather polarized with 36.1% identifying themselves as liberal, 57.0% as conservative, and only 6.9% as moderate. If, instead, we consider categories 3–5 to be some level of moderation (chart B), then our liberal/conservative/moderate breakdown becomes 14.2%/62.6%/23.2%, and we would consider the electorate to be very moderate. Remember, statistics don't lie. However, we have to be careful how we choose to categorize the data they summarize. The two pie charts in Figure 2.11 visually demonstrate very different outcomes based on similar responses. Consider that a time series of ideology would also appear differently depending on how we categorized that variable.

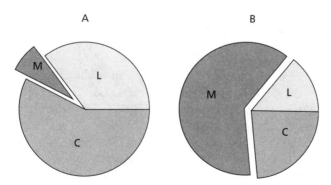

FIGURE 2.11 Pie Charts of Ideology by Exclusion/Inclusion of Moderate Ideologues

Let's turn to another example, one which will be brought up in a subsequent chapter. The ethnic or racial diversity of a culture, for example, can be viewed differently depending on how different ethnic and racial categories are combined. Whether or not an individual who is both racially black and ethnically Hispanic is categorized as "black" or "Hispanic" can change our perception of a group's or geographic area's ethnic composition. It can also dramatically affect how the courts evaluate redistricting plans that are sensitive to racial and ethnic considerations.

KEY TERMS

absolute frequency/tally/count (33)	interval data (29)
bar chart (39)	multivariate statistics (31)
bivariate statistics (31)	nominal data (27)
Bradley effect (24)	ordinal data (28)
Chicago effect (25)	pie chart (40)
cumulative frequency (37)	relative frequency (34)
descriptive statistics (31)	standardization (35)
frequency distribution (32)	time series chart (42)
frequency polygon (42)	univariate statistics (31)
inferential statistics (31)	

QUESTIONS AND EXERCISES

NOTE: Several more examples and exercises can be found in both the SPSS and Stata manuals that accompany this text. Sections 3.1 (RECODE), 3.2 (COMPUTE), 3.3 (IF), and 3.4 (SELECT IF) demonstrate how to re-categorize, select, and create scales of data. A video on re-categorizing data with SPSS is also available on this text's website. Section 4.1 demonstrates how to create your own frequency distributions and graphs. Another video presents examples on how to export your SPSS output into MS Excel in order to produce more vivid graphs.

1. Which one of the following is true?
    a. A measure can be internally valid but unreliable.
    b. A measure can be reliable but internally invalid.

2. The term "Bradley effect" generally refers to:
   a. Survey responses that are mere guesses
   b. Survey responses that may be internally invalid because individuals choose to give politically correct responses
   c. The problem with re-counting ballots
   d. None of the above

3. A government agency overreports its success rate in order to maintain or increase its funding. According to the author, this is an example of a
   _____.

4. Which of the following is most true?
   a. Nominal data always carry ordinal properties.
   b. Ordinal data carry interval properties.
   c. Ordinal data carry nominal properties.

5. Which of the following can be considered (mathematically) interval data?
   a. Country of origin for a group of immigrants (Nigeria, Colombia, Italy, Japan, etc.)
   b. Total percentage of Nigerian immigrants
   c. A four-point scale of support for a tax increase (Not supportive, Somewhat supportive, Supportive, Very supportive) asked of survey respondents
   d. Total PAC contributions received by each congressional candidate

6. Several questions were asked from sampled respondents in the 2012 ANES survey (a subset of these data can be found in the SPSS and Stata manuals that accompany this text). Which of the following are purely nominal (no other assumptions made), purely ordinal, and purely interval?
   a. Marital status (married, divorced, widowed, single, partnered)
   b. Hispanic or Latino heritage (yes, no)
   c. Age (in actual number of years)
   d. Education (none, grade school only, high school, some college, bachelor's degree, master's or equivalent, more than master's)
   e. Does religion provide guidance? (some, quite a bit, a great deal)
   f. View about death penalty (approve strongly, approve not strongly, disapprove not strongly, disapprove strongly, don't know)
   g. Religious denomination (eight categories including mainline Protestant, Roman Catholic, Jewish, Other, Not Religious)
   h. Candidate affect: Does the Democratic candidate make you happy? (yes, no)
   i. A scale that measures the number of times the respondent checked off a positive affect for the Democratic candidate.
   j. A feeling thermometer rating President Obama on a scale from 0° (most negative) to 100° (most positive) with 50° indicating neutrality. All values between 0 and 100 are allowed.

7. In a district file of members of Congress (two are provided in the SPSS and Stata manuals that accompany this text), which of the following are interval?
   a. Member's seniority in years
   b. Percentage received by the Democratic candidate
   c. Total amount of PAC contributions given to each candidate
   d. Presidential support score: the proportion of times a member supported the president on a vote for which the president expressed a preference
   e. The party whose candidate won the district (Democrat, Republican, Independent)
   f. Percentage of a district's population whose citizens are 65 or older
8. Conduct an anonymous survey of your classmates. Query them on at least ten variables. Make sure that at least two are purely nominal, two purely ordinal, and one interval.
9. The following table lists the absolute frequencies of party identification from the 2000 ANES survey. Compute and interpret the proportions and cumulative frequencies (assume independents to be categorically between Democrats and Republicans). Re-compute your figures after collapsing the seven categories into three. First, treat "Independent Leaning Democrat" and "Independent Leaning Republican" as Independents (categories 0–1, 2–4, and 5–6 combined). Next, treat each group as partisans (categories 0–2 and 4–6 combined, with category 3—true independents—standing alone). How do the different methods of combining categories affect your interpretation of the partisanship of the U.S. electorate? For reasons unknown to the author, "Strong Democrats" have always been listed

TABLE 2.6 Party Identification, 2000 ANES

Party ID (degree Republican)	Cat. Code	Absolute Frequency
Strong Democrat	0	345
Weak Democrat	1	274
Independent Leaning Democrat	2	275
Independent	3	221
Independent Leaning Republican	4	231
Weak Republican	5	209
Strong Republican	6	221

(until 2012) as category "0" in the ANES codebooks. Remember, however, that as the data are only ordinal, and not interval, the numbers are arbitrary as long as they maintain a proper rank order.

10. Cumulative frequencies make sense for which of the following types of data?
    a. Nominal
    b. Ordinal
    c. Interval

11. Produce a frequency table with all relevant percentages for the following set of class grades: 8 A's, 24 B's, 12 C's, 4 D's, 7 F's. Interpret all figures. For example, what proportion of students received a B or better? Produce a bar or pie chart for this distribution.

12. Produce a frequency distribution for each of the variables in your class survey. If more than seven categories exist, collapse the distribution into no more than three categories. Justify your scheme for combining categories.

NOTES

1 John Geer admits that, when judging the negativity of political ads, he himself coded the ads differently 15% of the time. See John G. Geer, *In Defense of Negativity: Attack Ads in Presidential Campaigns* (University of Chicago Press, 2006).

2 See Michael P. McDonald, "The Return of the Voter: Voter Turnout in the 2008 Presidential Election," *Forum* 6, no. 4 (2008): Article 4, http://www.bepress.com/forum/vol6/iss4/art4.

3 See Michael Shear and David Oppel, Jr., "V.A. Chief Resigns in Face of Furor on Delayed Care," *New York Times*, May 30, 2012, http://www.nytimes.com/2014/05/31/us/politics/eric-shinseki-resigns-as-veterans-affairs-head.html?_r=0.

4 This analogy is found in W. Phillips Shively, *The Craft of Political Research*, 4th ed. (Prentice Hall, 1998).

5 When only two categories exist—what we call a dichotomy—we can actually employ ordinal and even interval statistics. More on this later.

6 In dealing with ranked data, expect to see the notations "<" and ">" (less than and greater than). Since this scale of ideology is ordinal, we can actually reverse the ranking and treat the variable as "degree of liberalness." A lower number denotes "more liberal," a higher number "less liberal."

7 This is really a subjective assessment on my part. I would like to thank one reviewer for informing me that some developmental psychologists are comfortable with an interval assessment of "maturity" based on age.

8 "Inferential" is a class of statistics that allow us to make estimates about populations from which samples are taken. They will be taken up in subsequent chapters.

9 "Univariate" is a measurement of one variable; "bivariate," a measure of the mathematical relationship between two; and "multivariate," a measure of the relationships among three or more.

10　The year 2010 was a midterm election. During the presidential election years of 2004 and 2008, voting turnout in California was much higher.

11　Most U.S. elections require a mere plurality to achieve victory. The candidate with the most votes wins, even if all other candidates received more votes. In some cases, a certain threshold must be reached for the highest vote winner to be declared the winner. Many Southern states, for example, particularly in primaries, require the victorious candidate to win a majority, that is 50% + 1, or more than all other candidates combined. If no candidate breaks this mark, a runoff is held between the two candidates who garnered the most votes. Louisiana uses this method to narrow down the general election field to two candidates, as does, in a somewhat different manner, California. In both, the top two candidates may be, and often are, of the same party. Several countries also require a second vote (Two-Tiered System) if no presidential candidate receives 50% + 1 on the first ballot.

12　We could also use proportions. Percentages are merely a proportion (out of 1) multiplied by 100 (to sum to 100%).

13　All California voting figures come from the California secretary of state's office. In Utah, the lieutenant governor's office maintains these figures.

14　The "eligible" electorate itself is subject to some interpretation. We often are presented with different voting turnout figures because different bases are used in calculating turnout proportions. Some use the voting age population (VAP) while others use the voting eligible population (VEP = VAP – noncitizens – non-voting felons). McDonald and Popkin (2001) argue that a reliance on the former might have led to an overestimation of turnout decline between 1970 and 2000. McDonald and Popkin (2001), "The Myth of the Vanishing Voter," *APSR* 95 (2001): 963–974.

In some reference works, Brown's vote will be listed as 56.8% of the *two-party* vote (only Republican and Democratic votes included). In certain respects, this is another, conceptual form of standardization. Some states make it easier for third parties to gain access to the ballot, and third-party access was much easier in the nineteenth century, prior to the adoption of the Australian (secret) ballot. Whether or not we include third-party votes in our base is a subject of much theoretical debate.

15　For simplification, I've included only those who expressed an ideological preference. Many others refused to answer or stated that they could not place themselves on this type of left-right continuum.

16　One could argue that a "Moderate" might not be categorically in the middle of the liberal-conservative distribution, but might be an individual who doesn't think in terms of a left-right continuum. Since an option is left for respondents to opt out of such categorizations, however, it is safe to assume that most moderates can be placed in this fashion.

17　Edward Tufte, former political scientist turned graphing expert, warns that, on occasion, too complicated a graph or figure might be better expressed in a few words. For a thorough and interesting rundown on using graphs to visualize large quantities of data, see Edward R. Tufte, *The Visual Display of Information*, 2nd ed. (Graphics Press, 2001).

18　This is not sacred. Depending on your circumstances, you may want to reverse the axes. Many newspapers and websites report poll results this way.

19　These figures were produced using the SPSS statistical software package: IBM Corp., IBM SPSS Statistics for Windows, Version 22.0 (IBM Corp., 2013).

20 My thanks to Dr. Michael P. McDonald for providing estimates of both the voting age (VAP) and voting eligible (VEP) population (see endnote 14). Summaries of his data can be found at http://elections.gmu.edu/voter_turnout.htm.

21 These years are chosen as they reflect a year in which a major recession hit most countries (the United States included). The analysis sought to measure in which countries faith in democracy diminished as a result of bad economic times and the resilience of democratic sentiment in spite of it. Source: The Latinobarometre Poll: "A Slow Maturing of Democracy, *Economist*, Dec. 12, 2009, pp. 55–56.

Central Tendency as Summary Observation

Learning Objectives:

▦ To understand the meaning of central tendency
▦ To understand the differences among measures of central tendency
▦ To understand measures of central tendency as games of chance
▦ To understand the problems inherent with using the term "average"
▦ To know when to use a weighted mean

Frequency distributions impart a great deal of information about data. As summary devices, however, they start to become less useful as we increase the number of categories (as would be the case with most interval, continuous data) or when we need to summarize the distributions for a large number of different populations. Just imagine listing the frequency distributions for all candidates in each of the 37 states that held gubernatorial contests in 2010. Because of our need to present our findings in a readily available fashion, we need to develop other measures that do even more to summarize our data (remember, however, that the more we summarize, the more information we lose). With frequency distributions, several numbers (absolute frequencies, relative frequencies, etc.) have to be listed and discussed. We now turn to statistics that summarize a distribution of data with only one number. These summaries help us to create measures that are directly applicable to the tests we derive from our hypotheses.

For univariate (one variable) summaries, statistics can be broken into two classes. The first determines one number that defines the **central tendency**

central tendency A summary measure that describes the central or most prevalent category of a distribution.

of the distribution. These numbers are often referred to as averages, although, as we will see, this term can apply to several different measures. The second derives one number that measures the *dispersion* or *variation* of the entire distribution, often relative to that measure of central tendency. This second class is sometimes used as a measure of how useful the associated measure of central tendency is in summarizing the distribution. This notion of goodness of fit is, along with standardization, a major, consistent focus of statistical theory and explanation. Measures of central tendency and measures of variation can be both descriptive (what do the data tell us about the cases from which they were measured?) and inferential (what do they allow us to infer about a larger population from which the cases were sampled?) in nature. For now, we will deal only with descriptive measures.

MEASURES OF CENTRAL TENDENCY

Statistics are available for summarizing the central tendency of a distribution for each level of measurement already discussed. The mode assumes only nominal properties. The median also assumes ordinality. The mean takes into account the full precision of interval or continuous data. The level of measurement limits our choices. Purely nominal data can only be summarized by the mode (dichotomies are an exception). Ordinal data can be summarized by the mode or median, depending on the question asked. With interval/continuous data, of course, all the listed measures are mathematically appropriate. The choice of statistic will then be determined by what question we need to answer about the distribution.

Mode

The **mode** is that category or categories (if there are ties) that contain(s) the largest absolute frequency or highest proportion/percentage of cases. It is the category appearing with the greatest frequency.

Review the 2010 California gubernatorial vote tables (Tables 2.1 and 2.3) The mode, or modal category, is "1," standing for Democrat. More people voted for the Democratic candidate, Jerry Brown, than for any other candidate. Mr. Brown won more votes (absolute frequency) and a higher percentage (relative frequency) than did anyone else. He had the largest slice of the pie; his bar is the tallest. In our original seven-point table of ideology (Table 2.5), the category with the highest number of respondents is "Moderately Conservative" (5). Category 5 is thus the modal category, even though it only comprises 33.8% of the survey distribution. If we include all eligible voters in the distribution, the modal category for recent U.S. elections will almost always be "did not vote." With non-voters excluded, the mode is usually the

mode The category within a distribution that has the most cases.

winner of an election. "Usually" because in certain Southern states, particularly in primaries, candidates need to win by a majority in order to be declared the winner. A runoff election would be required between the top two contenders if a majority is not secured by any candidate on the first ballot. In the 2014 Mississippi Republican primary, eventual Senate winner Thad Cochran did not win his party's nomination until a primary runoff was held, as he obtained only 49% in the first round of balloting. His opponent, Tea Party favorite Chris McDaniel beat him (49.4%) but did not secure the necessary majority victory. In the runoff between these two candidates, Senator Cochran won by a bare majority, most likely due to the crossover support of Democrats fearful of a McDaniel victory. Democratic incumbent Wyche Fowler (49%) was the modal (plurality) but not majority winner of the 1994 Georgia Senate race. In the two-candidate runoff, however, the Republican Paul Coverdell secured the modal (now majority) victory. French legislative elections follow a similar rule. Candidates do not win the first ballot unless by majority. On the second ballot, however, all candidates who receive more than 12.5% make it to the second round. The winner of that election may be either plurality or majority. Similar systems exist in other countries.

Sidebar 3.1: Election Law in the United States

Other than a relatively small but important number of constitutional provisions and amendments, federal law, and a larger number of court cases, almost all standards that govern the time and manner in which elections take place in this country are determined by state law. For example, states differ not only as to the winning threshold in either primaries or general elections (plurality or majority), but also as to the qualifications and application procedures for being a candidate in these elections, as well as who can vote in them (see the sidebar on felony disenfranchisement, Sidebar 2.2, in Chapter 2). This is especially true in primaries, where some states allow only registered or announced voters of each party to vote in their respective party primaries (closed), some allow independents to vote in a party primary (semi-open), and others allow primaries to be open to all voters (open)—and this is a simplified categorization.

Most countries do not allow such local autonomy. Although this makes for a great deal of difficulty in teaching about U.S. electoral politics, it also allows for a great deal of analysis as, in any given year, 50 cases are available to study comparatively.

Many texts and articles have been written about the variety of laws that affect our electoral process, including voting rights, primary types, campaign finance regulations, and how votes get counted. For one excellent overview, see Matthew J. Streb, *Law and Election Politics: the Rules of the Game*, 2nd ed. (Routledge, 2013). For a full, if dated, overview of the laws that govern and the results of primaries and primary types, see Peter Galderisi et al. (eds.), *Congressional Primaries and the Politics of Representation* (Rowman & Littlefield, 2001).

UNDERSTANDING STATISTICS AS GAMES OF CHANCE

Statistics, even descriptive ones, can often be understood as we would games of chance. This concept will take on great importance later on as we discuss inferential statistics, but let us introduce it now while we are dealing with statistical manipulations that are simpler and more intuitive.

Let us say that we are sitting in a restaurant trying to pass the time with a companion. An individual walks into the establishment who claims to have voted in the 2010 California gubernatorial election. Your companion challenges you to guess how that person voted. You can guess any single candidate. The rules of the game are fairly simple and stipulate that if you guess correctly, you gain $1; if you guess incorrectly, you lose $1. Your choices can only come from the five categories listed in our table (you can't guess a collection such as "she didn't vote for the Democrat, Brown"). You are allowed to see the listed distribution. Which is the safest guess? The answer is the mode, category 1, Democrat, Brown. That would be your best overall *expectation*, but you may be wrong with any single *observation*. The probability of being correct here is better than guessing any other single category. You would have a 53.8% chance (our relative frequency or percentage), or .538 probability, of guessing correctly. Stated differently, if every eligible voter was paraded before you and you could only make the same guess for each, you would lose the least amount of money, and gain the most, by guessing category 1. Of course, given our seven-point ideological scale (the modal category contained fewer than 50% of all respondents), you would lose more than you would gain. However, any other guess would prove even more costly. The same would be true for the presidential races from 1992 to 2000. The Democratic candidates always won the popular vote, but each time with less than 50%. Returning to our restaurant example, you might try to use other information such as the voter's age or gender or race to come up with a better guess, but these are the subject of measures of association (bivariate and multivariate).

All data can be summarized using the mode. However, as the number of categories increases, the mode produces a less useful summary. The mode is obviously less useful as a summary measure in our seven-point ideology scale than in either of the three-point scales (although note that the modal category is different in those two different three-point scales). Much of the information reported in the U.S. census, unless collapsed into fewer categories, is even less usefully summarized by the mode. If we include all categories of ancestry, for example, over 1,000 categories would be listed. According to the 2010 U.S. Census estimates, more people might be 19 than any other single age, but only a very small percentage would be 19. Many other age categories, from 1 to over 100, will have frequencies close to that number. If the data are purely nominal (as with ancestry), then we might collapse categories according to general geographic location (European, Asian, etc.), keeping in mind the concern that the more we summarize information with the creation of fewer categories, the more information we lose. If those with Italian ancestors from different regions of Italy might be fairly distinct in terms of physical and cultural attributes, those with European roots (including Italian) would of necessity be more distinct still.[1] On the other hand, if the data are measured ordinally or intervally (as with age), other measures can be used to summarize a distribution's central tendency without necessarily collapsing categories.

Median

The **median** is that category below which 50% of all cases in the distribution fall (i.e., half of the cases would be at that categorical point or less). Refer to your table on ideology (Table 2.5). Take the 1,596 individuals from that survey and place them side by side. The most conservative 140 students would be on the extreme right of the line (no pun intended). The most liberal 70 would be on the extreme left. All others would be placed in the line according to their degree of conservativeness. Where you place individuals with similar rankings (say the 350 moderate liberals) is arbitrary, as long as they are all to the right of the 156 liberals, and to the left of the 110 moderates. Starting from the left, count off the respondents until you have counted half. With a sample of 1,596, the halfway point is reached after the 798th respondent, with 798 respondents still to go. That point is reached between the 798th and 799th respondents, both of whom are within the group of "moderate conservatives." Half of the respondents will be moderately conservative or less conservative. Half will be moderately conservative or more conservative.

Remember our discussion of cumulative frequencies. Go down that column until you reach 50%. That would not occur until category 5. Remember that the median is not necessarily the middle category (in this example, category 4), but it can coincidentally be so. What if we had 200 more moderates, or 200 fewer moderate conservatives? The 798th and 799th respondents would be within category 4. Also note that the median doesn't need to be an actual existing value (unlike the mode). For example, consider the following list (not frequency distribution) of incomes earned by ten individuals (measured in thousands of dollars).

20 20 30 40 50 *90 90 100 320 360*

The median would separate the first five individuals (incomes of 20, 20, 30, 40, 50) from the last five (90, 90, 100, 320, 360). The median could be any number between 50 and 90. By convention, we usually specify the exact midpoint, in this instance 70. Half of the individuals in this list earned less

median The category that represents the midpoint of a distribution at or below which half of all cases lie. Data must be measured at least at the ordinal level.

than $70,000, and half earned more. If we only had the first nine in the distribution, the median would be that category corresponding to the fifth person ($50,000), with four earning less and four earning more.

Listed as a very basic formula, when the number of cases is odd, the case with the median would be as follows. Remember all cases must first be rank ordered (N = total number of cases).

$$(N + 1)/2 \tag{3.1}$$

When there is an even number of cases, the median would be that category that falls between the following two cases:

$$N/2 \text{ and } (N/2) + 1 \tag{3.2}$$

Notice that medians must assume rankings. Purely nominal data cannot be summarized in this way. We cannot rank religion or presidential vote. Refer back to the Utah gubernatorial table (Table 2.4). We cannot state that 50% voted Republican or less "othered." Terms like "less than" or "more than" have no meaning with purely nominal data. Remember that the ordering of the categories (do we place Democratic or Republican voters first?) is purely arbitrary. Also note that in distributions re-categorized into fewer categories, the median might be the same, even though the original distributions are fairly distinct. Let's take 2000 Census figures for both Florida and Utah (Table 3.1). To simplify our analysis, we limit our categories to four (some rounding error is visible):

The median category for age in both our Florida and Utah examples is the second category, "Young Adult." Fifty percent of all residents in either state are "young adults" or younger. Note, however, that we would have to virtually exhaust all of the individuals in the second category in Florida before the 50% cutoff is achieved. We almost reach it with the first category in Utah. In reality, when the age distribution is not collapsed into four categories, but maintains its full, original, interval listing, the medians for each state are

TABLE 3.1 Age Groupings, Florida and Utah (2010)

Age Group	Cat. Code	Florida	Utah
Youngest (0–24)	1	31.1	46.4
Young Adult (25–44)	2	28.5	28.0
Older Adult (45–64)	3	18.0	17.0
Oldest (65 and above)	4	17.6	8.5

quite different. The median age in Florida was 38.7 years, in Utah it was only 27.1 years. In Florida, 50% of the residents were 38.7 or younger. In Utah, 50% of the residents were only 27.1 or younger. Because both "27.1" and "38.7" are within the range of our second category, however, the medians in the four-point tables are the same.

Later we will discuss in detail the concept of percentiles. For now, let us just state that the median can be considered to be that category that corresponds to the *50th percentile*. In gambling terms, the median allows us to equalize our odds of success. If one of the ten individuals whose incomes are listed walked into the restaurant, we would have an equal chance of being correct if we guessed that person to be above or below the median value. Medians, as with any statistic based on percentiles, allow us to make comparisons in a *relative* way. Medians separate the bottom half of a distribution from the top half. They don't tell us anything about the intrinsic importance of the individual values within those halves. For example, if we were to determine that only those individuals in the top half of their high school classes should be admitted to college, we would not necessarily know much about the quality of that top 50% and how that might differ from school to school. Judgments about absolute qualities (students who can maintain a 3.0 GPA) must take into account more precise information. This is the characteristic of continuous or interval statistics.

Mean

Let us define the measurement intuitively by way of an example. Go back to our list of ten individuals' incomes. There are two modes (two individuals earned $20,000 and two earned $90,000). Half earned less than $70,000 (the median). Another way of summarizing the central tendency of this distribution is to consider how much everyone would have earned *if everyone earned the same amount* (i.e., if you could take from the rich and give to the poor until contributions were equalized). How would you compute this value? If you are redistributing wealth, you would need to take the sum total of all incomes and then divide them equally among all members of the distribution. In this example, you would add the ten incomes and then divide by the total number of cases in the distribution (10):

The total of all incomes would be as follows:

$20(000) + 20 + 30 + 40 + 50 + 90 + 90 + 100 + 320 + 360(000) = $1,120,000

Evenly distributed ten ways:

$1,120,000/10 = $112,000

The **arithmetic mean** of that distribution is $112,000. Notice first that in order to add values, the data have to be measured intervally. Ideology and party vote cannot be added. Notice also that the mean, like the median, does not need to be an actual value earned by any particular individual. No individual person earned $112,000. As a game of chance? The rules become more complex. The rules for the modal and median game penalized you each time you were wrong, that is, each time you placed someone in the wrong category (penalized for the wrong category) or half (penalized for the wrong direction). Here you would be penalized not if you guessed the wrong income but by *how much* your guess was off. If you were told that you would be given the difference between your guess and the actual income of the unsuspecting income earner if your guess were too high, but that you would lose the difference if your guess were too low, you would break even by always guessing the mean for each of these ten individuals. Go through the computations to prove this. In doing so, you will learn something about an essential element of interval measures of dispersion, the *deviation score*. Hold that thought for now.

Notice that for our ten individuals, the mean is higher than the median. The median separated our distribution of people in half, five above and five below. In this example, however, the mean separated our individuals much differently. Eight had incomes less than $112,000. Only two had incomes above $112,000. The difference is rather simple to explain. Medians treat data only as ordinal. All we are stating is that half earned incomes above $70,000. How much above, or below, makes no difference. If our wealthiest person earned $3,000,000, the median would remain the same (but the mean would be higher still—compute the mean to demonstrate this to yourself). With someone earning $3 million, we would have much more money to redistribute. In our gambling scenario, we would have to move our guess upward in order to reach the break-even point. If our top two individuals earned $120,000 each, the median would still not be altered (but the mean would be lower). The median only takes into account whether a case has a higher or lower value. "How much" higher or lower is inconsequential. "How much" implies that our data, and our questions, assume interval properties. The mean takes that into consideration and uses the data in the most precise way. The median does not. The median separates cases (in this example, individuals) into the lower and upper halves. The mean separates total value (in this example, income) into lower and upper halves. Collectively, our ten individuals earned $1,200,000. Half of that total is $600,000. If we added the incomes from that of the poorest to the wealthiest, we would not reach that total until after the eighth person.

Arithmetic means can be computed for any interval/continuous distribution of data.[2] Although it seems intuitively if not politically plausible to redistribute wealth, consider the mean of other variables to be that value of that variable that everyone would have if everyone had the same value. Heights, weights, years of education, age, any aggregated data such as proportions, and so forth,

arithmetic mean The category that all cases would have if the total value of a variable for all cases were evenly distributed among them.

can be summarized this way even if we cannot actually (and unfortunately for me with age and weight) ever hope to redistribute these values.

Let us examine the difference between medians and means graphically. Take our ten income recipients. If we are to compute the median, we would only need to place each individual side by side in order of their income. The order of individuals with similar incomes is arbitrary. Let us imagine that they are standing, evenly spaced, on a board. We also need to assume that each weighs the same.

20 20 30 40 50 90 90 100 320 360

—————————————————————————

▲

$70,000

In order to balance the bar, we would need to place our fulcrum, or balancing wedge, midway between the fifth and sixth persons, at a point corresponding to $70,000. Let us now replace the individuals on a balancing board, again in order of their income, but now spacing them according to their differences in income, as if the board were a ruler with income indicators rather than inches:

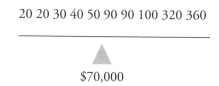

The fulcrum needs to be moved over to the right (in a positive direction) because the two wealthiest persons are far off on the positive side of the board. If we placed the fulcrum at the median of $70,000, the board would tip over to the right. The fulcrum, and thus the mean, must be adjusted to the right in order to accommodate these positive outliers. When a distribution is stretched to the positive, or graphically right direction, we state that the distribution is positively skewed (see Figure 3.1). In a positively skewed distribution, the mean will be greater than the median in most circumstances. If the outliers are on the low, or left, end of the distribution, we state that the distribution is negatively skewed (see Figure 3.2). In a negatively skewed distribution, the mean is usually lower than the median. For example, take the following income distribution, again expressed in thousands of dollars:

20 20 200 220 240 260 280 300 300 340

The median equals $250,000 (half above and half below). The mean equals $218,000. The distribution is negatively skewed or stretched by the two individuals earning far below the others (perhaps two part-time clerks in a law office).

Generally, the greater the difference between the mean and median, the greater the skewness. If the distribution is a **symmetrical distribution**, with both the number of cases and their spacing even on both sides of the fulcrum (i.e., the distribution above the mean is a mirror image of the distribution below the mean), then the mean and median will be equal (see Figures 3.3 and 3.4). For example, take the following income distribution:

40 40 60 70 80 90 100 110 130 130

Both the median and mean equal $85,000. No skew exists. The distribution is perfectly symmetrical.[3]

Median < Mean

FIGURE 3.1 A Positively Skewed Distribution

Mean < Median

FIGURE 3.2 A Negatively Skewed Distribution

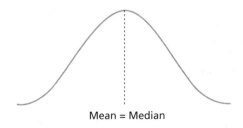

Mean = Median

FIGURE 3.3 A Symmetrical, Unimodal Distribution

symmetrical distribution
A distribution of a variable where the side to the left of the median is a mirror image of the side to the right.

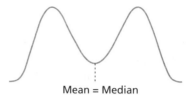

Mean = Median

FIGURE 3.4 A Symmetrical Bimodal Distribution

As these examples demonstrate, medians are insensitive to extreme values or **skewness**, but means are not. Any statistic that uses the mean as part of its calculation (e.g., linear regression) will also be sensitive to extreme values. Differences in skewness are not politically inconsequential. Consider two tax proposals that would be written specifically for our original ten income earners. One proposal is to increase taxes on the wealthier half of individuals. Five of our earners would be adversely affected. The other proposal would increase taxes on those earning above the mean. Only two would be so affected. The second would obviously be more popular, at least in terms of potential votes (of course wealthier people are more likely to vote and generally carry more political influence). We do ourselves no service when we talk about raising taxes for those who earn above the "average." Do we mean $70,000 or $112,000 (or one of the modes)? Remember that income in the United States, and elsewhere, is positively skewed. The bulk of the population has incomes spanning across a fairly small range. As we move to the wealthier income brackets, we find fewer and fewer individuals and families making more and more money, falling further and further away to the right of the bulk of citizens, or on the positive end of the income distribution. The mean income is therefore higher than the median.

For example, according to the 2000 decennial Census estimates, the median family income was $48,950, but the mean was $62,636.[4] Half the families in the United States earned incomes equal to or above $48,950, and half earned that income or less. The mean income of $62,636 is exceeded only by about one-third or so of the population. Remember, as an extreme example, one Bill Gates (to the right of the mean) earns as much as thousands of lower-income wage earners (to the left of the mean).

Similar differences existed in 1976. In the 1976 presidential election campaign, Jimmy Carter, the Democratic candidate and eventual victor, offered his general views on tax reform. He suggested that the tax code be revised so that those who earned more than the "average" would pay more in taxes and those who earned less than the "average" would pay less. The Republican candidate, President Gerald Ford, quickly countered that Carter's plan would raise the taxes of 50% of all taxpayers, including many middle-class

skewness The degree to which a distribution (think frequency polygon) is pulled or stretched. A stretch to the right or highest values of the distribution indicates a **positive skew**, and to the left, **a negative skew**.

families. Governor Carter countered that his proposal would raise the taxes of roughly only the wealthiest 30% to 40%, and actually lower taxes for many in the middle class. Who was lying? Actually neither. Each was using a different measure of "average." Their lack of specificity created a political controversy that did not really exist.

When Jimmy Carter suggested raising taxes on those earning above the average, he was referring to the mean. About one-third of the population had taxable incomes above that level. Since the term "average" can refer to different measures of central tendency, President Ford's staff interpreted his comments to refer to the median wage earner, suggesting that Governor Carter wanted to raise the taxes of 50% of the population. Since those earning between the median and mean incomes are more likely to vote than those earning below the median, the political significance of the difference was greater still. The moral of the story is to be specific.

Sidebar 3.2: Medians versus Means in Liability Cases

In order to award reparations for injury or wrongful death for someone without an established employment history, forensic economists have to estimate earnings losses throughout one's expected lifetime. Whether one calculates those estimates using medians or means for the appropriate demographic group (age, education level) in which the plaintiff belongs can have a significant impact on the award granted. One study finds the difference can range from 9.74% to 59.48%. The differences only increase as inflationary adjustments are made for each additional year. Needless to say, the difference between medians and means can be quite important in determining monetary judgments in these and other such cases.

Source: Lawrence M. Spizman, "Developing Statistical Based Earnings Estimates: Median versus Mean Earnings," *Journal of Legal Economics* 19, no. 2 (2013): 77–82.

FORMULAS AS SHORTHAND DEVICES

Now for the part that initially intimidates many students in statistics classes. Statistics usually appear as, and we normally associate them with, bizarre formulas. These formulas are just shorthand devices that generically apply our conceptual understanding to any variable for any number of cases (thus, *standardizing* the math). They allow us to easily program computers to interpret any type of data set. They can be easily interpreted if broken down into their component parts. Let's start with the mean as its calculation is fairly straightforward. The basic format of this calculation will be consistently reapplied as we look at interval measures of dispersion (Chapter 4).

We have already determined that the mean is computed by adding all the individual values of a variable and then dividing by the total number of cases. Let us introduce mathematical shorthand. We normally designate a generic variable by the use of an uppercase letter. The standard convention is to use the letters X or Y.[5] Individual cases (in our income example people) are designated generically by the lowercase i, where i can take any number from the first to the last person in the distribution (in our example 1 to 10). The individual value for any case is generically listed as a lowercase letter (x) followed by a subscripted i.[6] The total number of cases in any distribution (whether the 10 here or several hundred in a survey) is designated as N. The mean is designated by our uppercase X with a line or bar across the top. Think of this as a "leveling" designation. The mean is the equalized value.

For our distribution of ten incomes, the mean is defined as follows:

$$\overline{X} = (x_1 + x_2 + x_3 + x_4 + x_5 + x_6 + x_7 + x_8 + x_9 + x_{10})/N$$

where $x_1 = \$20,000$, $x_9 = \$320,000$, etc.
$N = 10$

This same generic formula can be used to compute the mean of any other intervally measured variable, such as height or weight from any *ten* individuals. It can also be the shorthand for a calculation of the mean of voting turnout across ten election years. However, what if there were only five cases, or 5,000? Would we have to come up with a different shorthand for each (and run out of paper for the second)? One more shorthand designation is needed, that of summation notation. The uppercase Greek letter Σ (sigma) tells us to perform an operation (listed to the right of it) for every designated case (designated by inserting the first case below it and the last above), and then sum or add each of the individual results of that operation.

The arithmetic mean is therefore defined mathematically and generically as follows:

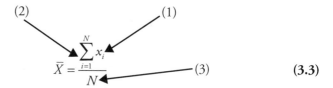

$$\overline{X} = \frac{\sum_{i=1}^{N} x_i}{N} \qquad (3.3)$$

where N refers to the number of cases
x_i is the value for each case (1 to N)

Essentially, (1) take the value of each and every case (all of the x_i's), from the first (x_1) to the last (x_n), (2) add them (Σ), and then (3) divide by the total number of cases (N). That's how we calculated the mean income. It's that simple. Don't let the formula intimidate you.

Formula for the Mean Derived from a Frequency Distribution

On occasion, we might not have direct access to the full listing of data for a sizeable distribution of cases. For example, take Table 3.2, which shows the frequency distribution of the number of times that an individual visited his or her favorite political website in a particular month.

TABLE 3.2 Frequency Distribution of Political Website Visits

Number of Visits	Absolute Frequency	Relative Frequency Proportion
1	2	2.1%
2	44	46.8%
3	38	40.4%
4	5	5.3%
6	3	3.2%
10	2	2.1%

We can first convert this distribution into a list, with one entry for each of the 94 web patrons:

$$(0,0,1,1,1,1,1,1 \ldots 4 \ldots 10,10)$$

We would then add the number of visits for each patron, and then divide by the total number (94). That seems, however, a bit tedious. We can instead do some simple math. Adding 1 + 1 is the same as multiplying 2 (the number of patrons who visited only once) times 1 (the number of times that those two visited). Instead of adding the number 2 44 times (2 + 2 + 2 . . . + 2), we can just multiply 44 (the number of patrons) by 2 (the number of visits). Continue for each category. The calculation then becomes:

$$\frac{[(2 \times 1) + (44 \times 2) + (38 \times 3) + (5 \times 4) + (3 \times 6) + (2 \times 10)]}{94}$$

The 94 patrons collectively visited their favorite site 262 times in the given month. If the patrons did not vary in their number of visits, each would have made 262/94 = 2.79 visits. The number 2.79 is therefore the mean. Generically, for any variable, with any number of cases, the mean can be computed as follows:

$$\bar{X} = \frac{\sum_{k=1}^{K} f_k * x_k}{N} \tag{3.4}$$

where x_k is the value assigned to each category (1, 2, 3, 4, 6, and 10 in our example)

f_k is the frequency count for each category (2, 44, 38, 5, 3, and 2 in our example)

K is the total number of categories (six in our example). Later we'll understand why K rather than C is used.

In simple words, we would first multiply the number of cases within each category (f_k) by the value of each category (x_k). We would do so starting from the first ($k = 1$) category to the last ($k = K$) category. This would be the same as adding each value for each case individually. We would then add all of these products (Σ) and divide by the number of cases in our distribution (N).

We can also use proportions, or relative frequencies, to compute our mean. Since the proportion is the number of cases within each category (x_k) divided by the total number of cases (N), the formula can be rewritten as follows:

$$\bar{X} = \sum_{k=1}^{K} p_k {}^* x_k \tag{3.5}$$

where p_k is the proportion or relative frequency for each category

x_k is the value of each category

Since the relative frequencies introduce rounding error, however, the first two formulas are preferable if the relevant information exists.

One final potential adjustment needs to be discussed, and we'll do so by way of a recent example. In the 2012 presidential election, the Democratic candidate and winner, Barack Obama, won 51.06% of the popular vote (see the appendix to this chapter). If we calculate the percentage of the vote that he won in each of the 50 states and the District of Columbia (whose residents can vote for president but not Congress), and then take the mean of those 51 percentages, we come up with a value of 49.03%, very close to Romney's 49.00%. Why the difference? If each state had the same population, then the mean of the individual state values should equal 51.06%. However, states have different populations and voter turnouts. More than 13 million people cast their votes for president in California (where Obama won by a wide margin), and roughly one-quarter million did the same in Wyoming (where Romney won comfortably). In taking the mean of each state's vote percentage, we treat California and Wyoming the same, although the contributions of the total, national vote for Obama (or Romney) from each state are substantially different. Aside from the effects on the winner-take-all nature of the Electoral College vote,[7] this fact also explains why the mean of the individual state values is less than the actual, nationwide vote Obama received. In order for the two figures to coincide, we must calculate what is called a **weighted mean** (i.e., add each state's value in proportion to its total impact on the vote). To do so, we would multiply the candidate percentage in each state by the number of presidential voters in each state, add them all, and then divide by the total number of individuals who cast their ballot for

weighted mean The arithmetic mean adjusted for the number or proportion of cases within each unit of analysis, used when a full listing of individual values is not obtainable.

unimodal symmetrical distribution A distribution in which both sides of the distribution are mirror images of each other and where the mode is the median category.

bimodal symmetrical distribution A distribution in which both sides of the distribution are mirror images of each but two modes; one on each side of the distribution exist equally distant from the median.

president (which equaled 129,085,403 by the final certified count listed by the Federal Election Commission). The full listing is available at the end of this chapter for those who wish to check the figures.

A NOTE ON MEDIANS AND MEANS

As a review, take the last two distributions presented in Figures 3.3 and 3.4. The first distribution is a **unimodal symmetrical distribution**. The mean, the median, and the mode are the same. The second distribution represents a **bimodal symmetrical distribution**. In the first, incomes are clustered around the middle, with a tail of poverty and wealth. This represents a classic middle-class society. In the second, incomes are polarized; there exist very poor and very wealthy individuals with a limited middle class. It is important to note that the means and medians might be the same for both. However, unlike the first distribution, the incomes represented in the second distribution are clustered around the two extremes. Obviously, just knowing the median and mean does not give us any sense of the differences between the first and second distributions. For that, we need to discuss our second class of statistics— measures of variation or dispersion—in the next chapter.

APPENDIX

2012 PRESIDENTIAL VOTE

TABLE 3.3 2012 Presidential Vote

State	Obama	%	Romney	%
Alabama	795,696	38.36%	1,255,925	60.55%
Alaska	122,640	40.81%	164,676	54.80%
Arizona	1,025,232	44.59%	1,233,654	53.65%
Arkansas	394,409	36.88%	647,744	60.57%
California	7,854,285	60.24%	4,839,958	37.12%
Colorado	1,323,102	51.49%	1,185,243	46.13%
Connecticut	905,083	58.06%	634,892	40.73%
Delaware	242,584	58.61%	165,484	39.98%
District of Columbia	267,070	90.91%	21,381	7.28%
Florida	4,237,756	50.01%	4,163,447	49.13%

Georgia	1,773,827	45.48%	2,078,688	53.30%
Hawaii	306,658	70.55%	121,015	27.84%
Idaho	212,787	32.62%	420,911	64.53%
Illinois	3,019,512	57.60%	2,135,216	40.73%
Indiana	1,152,887	43.93%	1,420,543	54.13%
Iowa	822,544	51.99%	730,617	46.18%
Kansas	440,726	37.99%	692,634	59.71%
Kentucky	679,370	37.80%	1,087,190	60.49%
Louisiana	809,141	40.58%	1,152,262	57.78%
Maine	401,306	56.27%	292,276	40.98%
Maryland	1,677,844	61.97%	971,869	35.90%
Massachusetts	1,921,290	60.65%	1,188,314	37.51%
Michigan	2,564,569	54.21%	2,115,256	44.71%
Minnesota	1,546,167	52.65%	1,320,225	44.96%
Mississippi	562,949	43.79%	710,746	55.29%
Missouri	1,223,796	44.38%	1,482,440	53.76%
Montana	201,839	41.70%	267,928	55.35%
Nebraska	302,081	38.03%	475,064	59.80%
Nevada	531,373	52.36%	463,567	45.68%
New Hampshire	369,561	51.98%	329,918	46.40%
New Jersey*	2,125,101	58.38%	1,477,568	40.59%
New Mexico	415,335	52.99%	335,788	42.84%
New York*	4,485,741	63.35%	2,490,431	35.20%
North Carolina	2,178,391	48.35%	2,270,395	50.39%
North Dakota	124,827	38.69%	188,163	58.32%
Ohio*	2,827,710	50.67%	2,661,433	47.69%
Oklahoma	443,547	33.23%	891,325	66.77%
Oregon	970,488	54.24%	754,175	42.15%
Pennsylvania	2,990,274	51.97%	2,680,434	46.59%
Rhode Island	279,677	62.70%	157,204	35.24%
South Carolina	865,941	44.09%	1,071,645	54.56%
South Dakota	145,039	39.87%	210,610	57.89%
Tennessee	960,709	39.08%	1,462,330	59.48%
Texas	3,308,124	41.38%	4,569,843	57.17%
Utah	251,813	24.75%	740,600	72.79%
Vermont	199,239	66.57%	92,698	30.97%
Virginia	1,971,820	51.16%	1,822,522	47.28%
Washington	1,755,396	56.16%	1,290,670	41.29%
West Virginia	238,269	35.54%	417,655	62.30%
Wisconsin	1,620,985	52.83%	1,407,966	45.89%
Wyoming*	69,286	27.82%	170,962	68.64%
U.S. Total	65,907,213	51.06%	60,933,500	47.20%

*Four states adjusted their totals after the official count was released.
Source: Federal Election Commission (FEC), Official 2012 Presidential General Election Results: http://www.fec.gov/pubrec/fe2012/2012presgeresults.pdf.

KEY TERMS

arithmetic mean (61)

bimodal symmetrical distribution (68)

central tendency (54)

median (58)

mode (55)

negative skew (64)

positive skew (64)

skewness (64)

symmetrical distribution (63)

unimodal symmetrical distribution (68)

weighted mean (68)

QUESTIONS AND EXERCISES

NOTE: Several more examples and exercises can be found in both the SPSS and Stata manuals that accompany this text. Modes, medians, and means can be calculated as part of a frequency distribution (Section 4.1). Means can also be calculated with the MEANS procedure (Section 4.2).

1. The median can be used to summarize which of the following types of data?
   a. Nominal
   b. Ordinal
   c. Interval
   d. All of the above
2. If a distribution's mean is higher than the median, that distribution is most likely:
   a. Positively skewed
   b. Negatively skewed
   c. Symmetrical
3. If a distribution of data is symmetrical, the median will always equal the mean (T/F).
4. A number of lawyers in a firm make contributions to a candidate. The candidate reports that the mean contribution of the lawyers is $1,500, but the median is $150. Are the candidate's records incorrect, or can such a difference be possible? If so, how?
5. A state advertises that it pays back 60% of all money gambled on its education lottery. However, about 99% of those who purchase lottery tickets win nothing. Explain this seeming paradox.
6. We collect data on the percentage of the vote received by the Republican gubernatorial candidate in each of a state's congressional districts. The number of districts is odd. We calculate the median of that vote as equal to 54.5%. Fully interpret that median value.

7. A listing is given specifying the percentage of the eligible voting age population that voted in each country for representatives to the European Parliament. The mean for that listing is lower than the median. Describe the distribution.

8. Compute and interpret the mode and median for the grade list presented in the exercises for Chapter 2 (Exercise 11).

9. Consider the following two distributions of total PAC contributions given to five members of Congress:
   Distribution 1: $20,000, $40,000, $60,000, $80,000, $100,000
   Distribution 2: $20,000, $40,000, $60,000, $80,000, $1,000,000
   Compute the mode(s), median, and mean for each. Verbally interpret each figure, and compare the two distributions.

10. Compute and interpret the mode and median for the distribution of party affiliation presented in the exercises for Chapter 2 (Exercise 9). Repeat the exercise for each of the combined frequency distributions.

11. The following table lists the Democratic vote percentages for House elections in ten state districts before and after the Supreme Court forced states to reapportion districts to guarantee equal populations in each. Compute the mode, median, and mean for each list (all ten districts). Interpret and compare the figures for each list (1964 vs. 1966). Note: this is a list, not a frequency distribution—the unit of analysis is a congressional district, the number of cases = 10.

TABLE 3.4 Democratic Percentage of the Vote, 1964 versus 1966

	1964	1966
D1	56	62
D2	65	62
D3	57	58
D4	72	67
D5	71	64
D6	67	62
D7	35	41
D8	45	48
D9	62	68
D10	48	49

12. Following is a list of median ages estimated from the yearly census samples over a span of 100 years. What can we say about the age of the U.S. population over this time, as well as the difference between males and females?

TABLE 3.5 Median Ages by Gender, 1900–2000

	1900	1910	1920	1930	1940	1950	1960	1970	1980	1990	2000
All	22.9	24.1	25.3	26.5	29	30.2	29.5	28.1	30	32.9	35.3
Males	23.3	24.6	25.8	26.7	29.1	29.9	28.7	26.8	28.8	31.7	34
Females	22.4	23.5	24.7	26.2	29	30.5	30.3	29.3	31.2	34.1	36.5

13. Following is a list of 21 African nations for which information is available on voter turnout (percentage of the voting age population) for president between 2005 and 2008. Compute and interpret the median and mean percentage turnout.

TABLE 3.6 Presidential Voter Turnout, 21 African Countries, 2005–2008

Country	Year	% Turnout VAP
Burkina Faso	2005	36.4
Cape Verde	2006	78.59
Central African Republic	2005	45.14
Chad	2006	71.4
Comoros	2006	52.14
Djibouti	2005	67.82
Egypt	2005	16.41
Gabon	2005	51.47
Gambia	2006	50.66
Guinea-Bissau	2005	66.84
Kenya	2007	54.49
Liberia	2005	59.01
Madagascar	2006	50.85
Mali	2007	48.18
Mauritania	2007	53.55
São Tomé and Príncipe	2006	69.76
Senegal	2007	55.11
Seychelles	2006	97.08
Sierra Leone	2007	62.02
Zambia	2008	34.18
Zimbabwe	2008	47.27

Source: IDEA (Institute for Democracy and Electoral Assistance), http://www.idea.int/vt/viewdata.cfm.

14. For each of the variables in your class survey, compute (where appropriate) and interpret the mode, median, and mean for each variable.

15. (Three separate assignments possible). Table 3.7 shows the 2012 election results for 16 counties in Central-Southern California. It includes the percentage of the vote received by the Democratic presidential candidate (incumbent Barack Obama), by the Democratic Senate candidate (incumbent Dianne Feinstein), and for Prop 34 (yes = abolish the death penalty), as well as the partisan leaning of the county:

TABLE 3.7 Vote Percentages, 16 California Counties, 2012

County	Party Leanings*	% Vote for Obama	% Vote for Feinstein	% Vote for Prop 34
Monterey	D	67.1	69.6	53.2
San Benito	D	59.2	61.1	42.3
Fresno	D	49.9**	51.1	35.5
Kings	R	41.3	42.6	30.1
Tulare	R	41.3	42.9	31.5
Inyo	R	42.6	42.6	32.8
San Luis Obispo	R	48.8**	50.8	43.1
Kern	R	40.4	42.3	31.2
Santa Barbara	D	57.6	59.6	49.0
Ventura	D	52.3	54.4	43.2
Los Angeles	D	69.7	71.5	54.5
San Bernardino	D	52.5	54.0	38.8
Orange	R	45.6	47.5	39.1
Riverside	R	49.7	51.9	37.9
San Diego	D	52.6	54.4	45.5
Imperial	D	65.2	67.2	43.9

*Defined by their most proximate registration figures (Source: California Secretary of State, Voter Registration Statistics by County: http://www.sos.ca.gov/elections/sov/2012-general/02-voter-reg-stats-by-county.pdf; President: http://www.sos.ca.gov/elections/sov/2012-general/10-president.pdf; United States Senator: http://www.sos.ca.gov/elections/sov/2012-general/11-us-senator.pdf; State Ballot Measures: http://www.sos.ca.gov/elections/sov/2012-general/15-ballot-measures.pdf).

**In several counties where President Obama received less than 50% of the vote, he still beat Governor Romney. Third parties picked up a small percentage of the vote in many. For example, in Fresno County, the president received 49.9%, Governor Romney received 48.1%, with the remaining 2% going to six other minor party or independent candidates. California's "top two" primary system limits general election placement to the top two Senate primary candidates—no third parties in this case.

a. Compute the median and mean for *one* variable for ALL 16 counties. Describe and interpret *fully* what each figure tells you *in words*. (For example, don't just calculate the median; describe what it tells you about this group of counties.)

b. By comparing the median and mean, comment on the expected skew (+/–/none?) of your distribution.

c. Now, do the same (a and b) for only the Democratic and, separately, only the Republican-leaning counties. Be complete in your calculation and answers.

d. Give as detailed a written summary as you can comparing your results for all 16 counties, the 7 Republican and 9 Democratic ones.

e. Why isn't the mean of the percentages of all 16 counties equal to the actual total percentage of the vote for your variable in those 16 counties? Try to offer two reasons. The major one is discussed in the text. The other will take some more thought.

16. Using the data in Question 15, answer the following questions:

a. Compute the median and mean for *both* the county vote for Obama and the county vote for Feinstein for ALL 16 counties. Describe and interpret *fully* what each figure tells you *in words*.

b. By comparing the median and mean of each variable, comment on the skew (+/–/none?) of your distributions.

c. Compare the results between the percent vote for Obama and the percent vote for Feinstein. What might this tell you about the difference and/or similarities between presidential and senatorial voting?

NOTES

1   For the two records that I have of my grandfather's arrivals to the United States, his nationality was listed as "Italian" in the first, but "Italian-Southern" in the second. That distinction, based on a presumption of education and occupational class distinctions between Italian regions was not just part of changing U.S. immigration quota law, but has also defined Italian culture and politics for centuries. See David Abulafia, *The Two Italies* (Cambridge University Press, 2010).

2   In other disciplines, geometric and harmonic means are often computed with slightly different calculations. From this point on, we will use the generic term "mean" to refer only to the "arithmetic mean."

3   It is possible for the mean and median to be the same in a non-symmetric distribution. I would like to thank an anonymous reviewer for bringing up this point with the following example, with mean and median equal to 20: 11, 11, 13, 15, 25, 25, 25, 35.

4   Congressional action now prevents the full Census from including full income data. Analysts must now use one or a series of smaller ACS (American Community Survey) Census collections or follow-up supplements.

5   Some texts use "*Y*." Most use "*X*." The designation is arbitrary. In this text, I'll use the more customary "*X*."

6   Some texts keep the uppercase designation here.

7   George W. Bush lost the popular vote nationwide in 2000, but he won the popular vote in more states than did his Democratic competitor, Al Gore, Jr. More importantly, he won more small states.

CHAPTER 4

Dispersion/ Variation/Goodness of Fit as Summary Observation

Learning Objectives:

▮ To understand the measures of dispersion/variation and goodness of fit
▮ To understand those measures' relationships to measures of central tendency
▮ To learn about error measures and deviation scores
▮ To introduce yourself to the concept of paired comparisons
▮ To once again understand the critical importance of standardization

Measures of central tendency give us a single number that we can use to make the best guess (under different Vegas house rules) about any individual within a distribution, no matter how varied or diverse. The measures don't, however, indicate the usefulness of that guess and may often give us the wrong impression about any given distribution. The modal category of state age distributions originally listed in Table 3.1 is "1," "youngest (0–24)," but most residents of Utah and especially Florida are not correctly specified by that category. Review the California gubernatorial frequency distribution. Our best guess would be to guess the mode, that is, to claim that since more people voted for Jerry Brown (category 1), we would be more likely to be correct in guessing that category for any eligible voter than any other category. However, we would still be wrong a large proportion of the time, a majority if all registered voters are included in our base. Additionally, the mode only tells us the value of the most popular category. It tells us nothing about how the cases are spread throughout the other categories. Was the California race close, or were the remaining votes spread among several different candidates? In the first instance, we would be helped with some statistic that would indicate how well the mode fits the distribution (termed "**goodness of fit measure**"). In the second, we would want to calculate some measure of spread, dispersion, or variation. I will spend more time in this text than in most discussing nominal measures of variation. I do so not only because of my own sense that such measures have been underutilized as is the entire field of qualitative analysis, but also because they allow us to introduce and discuss certain concepts (standardization, observed versus expected outcomes, and paired comparisons), early on in our development, that are instrumental in understanding more complicated measures later on.

Much attention has been paid in recent years to the question of racial, ethnic, ideological, and cultural diversity. What if our hypothesis were to start with "the more ethnically diverse a country is . . ."? How would we measure that property of "diversity"? Even more debate has centered on the role of government in fostering that diversity. Beyond politics, however, diversity can be viewed in both a positive and negative light. All but the most prejudiced amongst us would argue that cultural diversity adds to a nation's character, providing all with an opportunity to experience a wide and interesting array of food, music, literature, and folklore. Great diversity, or perhaps better expressed, disparity in incomes, however, would not be viewed favorably by many, particularly those in the bottom end of the income distribution. Mathematically, the level of diversity can be understood in terms of measures of dispersion or variation. Those measures themselves imply no direct negative or positive connotations. It is up to the researcher or reader to make those judgments. The statistical measures we will cover only provide the numerical foundation for those judgments and the social and political debates that follow.

▍ MEASURES OF DIVERSITY FOR NOMINAL DATA

goodness of fit measure
A statistical procedure that measures how well a measure of central tendency summarizes a distribution.

One way of discussing the usefulness, or goodness of fit, of nominal data is to calculate how much information is lost in using the mode as a summary measure. The modal category in our age example correctly places 31.1% of our Florida residents and 46.4% of our Utah residents. For Florida, 68.9% would be placed incorrectly by this modal guessing procedure (i.e., 68.9% of the data would be "lost" with our summary), and 53.6% in Utah. The probabilities of *incorrectly* guessing a person's age category by guessing the mode are .689 (in Florida) and .536 in Utah, respectively. When we calculate the probability of an incorrect guess or placement using the mode, we define a statistic called the **variation ratio** (*VR*), calculated as described subsequently.

Variation Ratio

$$VR = 1 - p_{mk} \qquad (4.1)$$

where p_{mk} is the proportion of cases within the modal category

Quite simply, the *VR* is the proportion of all cases *not* contained within the modal category. For example, if we guessed that a particular individual in Florida was to be found within the "youngest" category, the probability of our guessing incorrectly would be equal to the *VR*, .689.

A proportion, as discussed in Chapter 2, is simply the number of cases within a particular category divided by the total number of relevant cases. We can therefore alternately write the equation as follows:

$$VR = 1 - \frac{f_{mk}}{N} \qquad (4.2)$$

where f_{mk} is the *number* of cases (absolute frequency) within the modal category

Note that our probability of incorrectly guessing the vote choice in our California gubernatorial example increases as we include all those who voted on Election Day ($N = 10{,}302{,}324$, $VR = .473$). The mode becomes less useful (fits the data worse) and actually changes as we include all those who were registered or eligible to vote but didn't.[1]

A simple mathematical transformation ($1 = N/N$) allows us to rewrite the equation as follows:

$$VR = \frac{N}{N} - \frac{f_{mk}}{N} \qquad (4.3)$$

or

$$VR = \frac{N - f_{mk}}{N} \qquad (4.4)$$

The *VR* is, after all, the proportion of non-modal cases. The number of non-modal cases is equal to ($N - f_{mk}$). The formulas are all the same, so use whichever is easiest, or possible (perhaps you are only given voting percentages, not raw counts, thus limiting you to only the first equation). The last formula, however, presents us with a useful introduction to two fundamental

variation ratio A goodness of fit measure that indicates the proportion of cases that vary from or are not within the modal category.

concepts in statistical theory—error terms or deviation scores and the difference between what we *observe* and what we *expect*. Let's discuss this further.

The formula $N - f_{mk}$ can be interpreted as an error term that is the number of times we would be incorrect in applying a certain guess, in this instance the mode. In guessing the mode, we are expecting that any of the N individuals that might randomly enter the California restaurant would have voted for Brown (at least that's our best *expectation*). If every individual did enter the restaurant, however, we would observe that only f_{mk} actually fit in that category. The difference between our *expectation* (all N cases are the same) and *observation* equals the number of times we would err in guessing the mode for each individual. It is the number of times we would deviate from the correct answer. Since that number is a function of the total number of cases (the more people we have, the greater the likelihood that one will be misplaced), we need to *standardize* that error term. We obviously have a greater absolute chance of miscategorizing an individual among a voting population of 10 million than only 10. As with a frequency distribution, we therefore standardize this error term by the total number of cases (N). The VR is therefore the total number of miscategorized cases standardized by the total number of cases possible from our distribution. If we represent the number of times we would *expect* each person to be categorized by the mode if the mode perfectly fit the data (N) as f_e (expected frequency), and the number of times each person actually is categorized by the mode (f_{mk}) as f_o (observed frequency), the formula can also be listed as follows:

$$VR = \frac{f_e - f_o}{f_e} \qquad (4.5)$$

Most students of statistics will be familiar with a variation of this standardized formula as it applies to an inferential measure called chi-square (covered in Chapters 8 and 9). The concept of observations and expectations, however, can also be used in our discussion of other descriptive statistical measures, such as the one to which we will soon turn. First, one more point needs to be made about the VR.

Most, but not all statistics are standardized to allow the calculated values to range from 0 to an absolute value of 1 (directional statistics can produce a negative calculation down to –1). The VR will be 0 when 100% of the cases fall within one category ($p_{mk} = 1$). For elections, this would be the case with a non-contested election if non-voters are excluded. You would guess that everyone voted for the winner, and you would always be correct (1 – 1 = 0). A "0" therefore stands for no variation from the mode. The mode "perfectly fits" the data. You would always *observe* what you *expect*. In 2010, for example, 12 members of the U.S. Congress ran totally unopposed, thus receiving 100% of the vote. That number increases if we discount minor vote incursions by third parties. As late as 1998, more than 10% of House seats were won by 100%. Before the 1960s, when the South was a virtually one-party (Democratic) regime, that number was much higher. When one party predominates, competition is more likely to occur within that party's primary.

What is the highest value that the *VR* can reach? That is partially a function of the number of categories, but it approaches yet never reaches 1. For the *VR* to be 1, p_{mk}, our most popular category, would have to equal 0, and we would have no distribution at all. Just consider that as the value approaches "0," the goodness of fit of the guessing procedure (the mode) is quite high, and the mode is a useful summary measure; when the value calculated is close to 1, there is much greater variation from that modal guess, and the goodness of the modal fit is quite poor. This would generally be the situation when we have a very large number of categories. For example, if we list U.S. residents by their age, more might be 19 years old than any other single age, but only slightly more than 1% (.01) would be 19. The *VR* would therefore be close to 1.

The *VR* measures goodness of fit (i.e., *variation from the mode*). Let us now turn to a statistic that measures dispersion or spread. If the data are dichotomous (i.e., only two categories are possible), then we can measure the evenness of the distribution by subtracting the two relative frequencies. In a two-candidate election, for example, a tie would produce a difference of 0%, indicating an even split. As the value gets closer to 100% (or a proportion of 1), the vote is more one sided. Note that the *VR* for a tie would be .5; a one-sided race would have a value close or equal to 0. Most variables, however, consist of more than two categories. A more complex measure of dispersion therefore needs to be found that can assess the differences among categories.

Index of Qualitative Variation

Let's start with a simple example. As part of the standard Eurobarometer survey set, individuals are asked to place themselves on a ten-point ideology scale ranging from 1 (Left) to 10 (Right). For simplicity (but always worrying about how categorization can affect outcomes), we produce three categories for Table 4.1: Left, Center, and Right. In a pre-test of the measure, 240 respondents are chosen from three different towns in one of the sampled countries.

For each distribution, the mode is category 1, Left-leaning. The *VR* is .25 for the first two distributions (25% are not Left-leaning), but .625 for the third. The *VR* therefore differentiates the last from the first two distributions. The mode (Left) is at its worst as a summary measure for the ideology of the selected members of the third town. It is equally and more useful in summarizing the ideology in the first two towns. Notice, however, that the degree of spread across the categories differs in the first two distributions, even though they share the same *VR*. There is a much greater spread or diversity of cases in the first than the second. How can we measure this variation *across all categories* (not just variation *from the mode*)?

We first need to introduce a new concept here that you will run into again in any discussion of ordinal measures of association, that of *paired comparisons*. So let's take some extra time introducing and understanding it now. There are 240 residents in each example. If we continually pull 2 different individuals from any group (a unique pair), how many unique pairings of residents will we produce? Let us start with a basic example. With 3 residents, we will produce three unique pairings (Figure 4.1):

TABLE 4.1 Ideological Divisions in Three European Towns

Ideology	Cat. Code	Absolute Frequency Town 1	Absolute Frequency Town 2	Absolute Frequency Town 3
Left	1	180	180	90
Center	2	30	59	80
Right	3	30	1	70

FIGURE 4.1 Paired Comparisons with Three Residents

With 4 residents, we will produce six unique pairings:

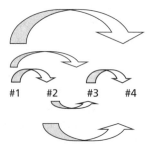

FIGURE 4.2 Paired Comparisons with Four Residents

Generically, the total number of unique pairings will always be equal to:

$$\frac{N(N-1)}{2} \qquad\qquad (4.6)$$

where N equals the number of cases

> For a distribution of 3 cases, the total number of unique pairings equals $3(2)/2 = 3$.
> For a distribution of 4 cases, the total number of unique pairings equals $4(3)/2 = 6$.
> For a distribution of 30 cases, the total number of unique pairings equals $30(29)/2 = 435$.
> For a distribution of 240 cases, the total number of unique pairings equals $240(239)/2 = 28,680$.

In the first instance, we can pull 2 different residents from our group three possible ways. In the last, there exist 28,680 possible unique pairs of residents.

The numbers we just calculated indicate how many ways we can pull out 2 different residents, *without regard to their ideology*. Each pair can share the *same* ideological preference (2 Left, 2 Center, or 2 Right) or a *different* ideological preference (1 Left, 1 Center; 1 Left, 1 Right; or 1 Center, 1 Right). Conceptually, the variation or diversity of any group can be thought of as a function of the number of times we can randomly draw two cases with *different* categories of a variable. If we always pulled out 2 residents with the same ideological preference, we wouldn't consider that town to be very ideologically diverse (of course, assuming the 240 residents chosen represent the town). If we always pulled out 2 residents with different ideologies, we would consider the group to be highly diverse.

In example #1, how often can we possibly pull out 2 residents (from the possible 28,680 combinations) with different ideological preferences? Well, every time we pull out a Left-leaner and a centrist, the two will be different. Each of the 180 Left-leaners can be matched with each of the 30 centrists. This will occur 180 × 30, or 5,400, total possible times. Left-leaner with Right-leaner matchups will also be different, again 180 × 30, or 5,400, total possible times. A centrist can be matched with a Right-leaner 30 × 30, or 900, total possible times. The sum total of unique pairings of town residents with *different* or *diverse* ideological preference will therefore equal 11,700. The other 16,980 pairings will be of residents who share the same ideology. That 11,700 is (11,700/28,680), 40.79% of the total number of possible pairings, or a fractional equivalent of .4079. If we pull out every one of the 28,680 unique pairings or combinations of residents, we will pull out a differently matched (diverse ideological preference) pair 40.79% of the time. Stated differently, if we randomly pulled two residents out of town #1, the probability of drawing two with different ideological preferences would be .4079. We have just computed the **index of diversity**, calculated by dividing the number of differently paired matchups (11,700) by the total possible number of unique matchups (different or the same, 28,680).

The problem with the index of diversity is that its value varies as a function of the number of categories. The only time that this index can be close to 1 (i.e., you will be correct in guessing that any two residents are ideologically different close to 100% of the time) is when the number of categories (K) is close to the number of cases (N). The index can only be equal to 1 when $K = N$; otherwise residents with similar ideological preferences will have to be drawn. Consider the following simple example. We have a small group of six residents. We only have three ideological choices (L, C, R). By definition, some residents have to share the ideology. For example:

Resident	Ideology
1	L
2	C
3	R
4	R
5	L
6	C

With six cases, we have 15 possible unique pairings ($6 \times 5/2$). The first resident has a different ideology than the second, different than the third, different than the fourth, and different than the sixth (4 different or diverse pairings). The second resident is different from the third, from the fourth, and from the fifth (3 different or diverse pairings). Note that we don't compare the second and first resident again since that has already been done. We only want unique pairings. The third resident is different from the fifth and sixth (2 different or diverse pairings). The fourth resident is also different from the fifth and sixth (2 different or diverse pairings). Last, the fifth and sixth resident differ (1 different or diverse pair). Twelve of the 15 possible unique pairings are between residents with different ideological preferences. Three pairings are of residents with the same preference (1 and 5 are both Left-leaning, 2 and 6 are both centrists, and 3 and 4 are both Right-leaning). The index of diversity is therefore equal to 12/15 = .8. We will draw two residents with different ideological preferences 80% of the time. With three ideological categories and six residents, however, this distribution is *as diverse as it can possibly be*. The residents are evenly distributed among the three ideological categories, with two in each.

To solve this problem (which only worsens as the number of cases continues to exceed the number of categories), we need to *standardize* our statistic one more way. One way of doing this is to divide the number of

index of diversity A variation or dispersion measure calculated as the total proportion of times that two unique cases that categorically differ on any variable can be drawn from any distribution.

different pairs *observed* by the total number of different pairs that we could ever possibly *expect* given the number of categories in our distribution. Consider the following: as we increase the disparity between the categories, we will decrease the number of different matchups. By the same logic, we would increase the number of differently matched pairs (ideologically diverse) as we more evenly divide the residents among the three categories. For example, if all 240 residents were Left-leaning, we would be able to randomly pull out 2 residents with different ethnic backgrounds 0 times. If the breakdown were 238, 1, and 1, we would draw 2 residents with different ideologies 477 times ([238 × 1] + [238 × 1] + [1 × 1]). Our current example (180, 30, and 30) produced 11,700 pairs of ideologically diverse residents. If the 240 were *evenly distributed* among the three categories (80 in each), we would produce the *maximum number of differently paired (ideologically diverse) matchups possible*, 19,200 ([80 × 80] + [80 × 80] + [80 × 80]). If we divide the *observed* number of different or ideologically diverse pairings (11,700) by the maximum possible number (given the number of categories) of different or ideologically diverse pairings (19,200), we come up with a rounded figure of .6093.

Congratulations, you have just calculated the **index of qualitative variation** (or IQV), a *standardized* version of the index of diversity. We use term "qualitative" to denote categorical differences. "Quantitative" would denote the ability to treat the categories mathematically (such as age or income). Let's review the calculation. The observed paired differences were computed by multiplying the actually *observed* frequency (f_o) in each category by the frequency in each other category and then adding the products. The maximum possible paired differences were similarly computed, but this time assuming that the cases were even distributed among the categories (i.e., 80 in each). That would be the number of residents we would *expect* (f_e) in each category if the residents were evenly distributed among the three ethnic categories. The calculation breaks down as follows:

observed differences = (180 × 30) + (180 × 30) + (30 × 30) = 11,700

maximum possible differences *expected* if cases were evenly distributed = (80 × 80) + (80 × 80) + (80 × 80) = 19,200

IQV = observed different pairings/maximum possible different pairings = 11,700/19,200 = .6093

Translation: the distribution of cases among the three ideological categories is 60.93% of the best (most diverse) distribution possible.

I suggest listing the observed and expected frequencies in tabular form (see Table 4.2) to make sure that you understand the logic (this will also come in handy when we look later at the chi-square calculation).

index of qualitative variation A variation or dispersion measure that standardizes the index of diversity by dividing by the maximum qualitative variation possible.

TABLE 4.2 Observed and Expected Frequencies

Ideology	Cat. Code	Observed Frequency (f_o)	Expected Frequency (f_e)
Left	1	180	80
Center	2	30	80
Right	3	30	80

Now for the (not so) hard part. One can compute the IQV intuitively as we have done previously. Remember, however, that statistics can be defined by generic formula, not just one limited to 240 cases and three categories. Let's make the conversion from specific (our example) to generic (any distribution). For the numerator, we compute the total number of different pairings that we actually *observe* in the distribution. As in our example, we do so by multiplying the number of *observed* cases in each category by the number of observed cases in every other *different* category. We do this for every possible pair of different categories. We then add those products together. Multiplying the observed cases in one category (generically noted as category I), by those in another (category J) can be generically listed as:

$$f_{oI} \times f_{oJ} \qquad (4.7)$$

where $I \neq J$ (i.e., the categories are different)

The sum of these can be listed as follows:

$$\sum f_{oI} \times f_{oJ} \qquad (4.8)$$

The denominator is the same, except that we substitute for each frequency the number that would exist, or that we would *expect*, if the cases were evenly distributed. We designate the expected frequencies as f_{eI} and f_{eJ}.

Generically, this calculation can be represented as the following:

$$IQV = \frac{\sum f_{oI} \times f_{oJ}}{\sum f_{eI} \times f_{eJ}} \qquad (4.9)$$

where $f_{oI}f_{oJ}$ equals the product of each unique pair of frequencies *observed* in each category (I, J)

$f_{eI}f_{eJ}$ equals the product of each unique pair of frequencies *expected* in each category if the cases were evenly distributed

We can, and perhaps should, end here, but we can re-specify the formula one more way. Remember that the expected frequency of each category is found by dividing the total number of cases by the number of categories. In our example, this would be 240/3 = 80. Generically, we can list this as follows:

$$\frac{N}{K}$$

where N equals the number of cases

K equals the number of categories

We then multiply this number by itself (the number of cases in each category is the same), which is the same as squaring that number. Each product is therefore generically defined as follows:

$$\left[\frac{N}{K}\right]^2$$

We then add the products, but how many products will we have? In our example we had three, not because we have three categories (that is just a coincidental outcome of our example), but because there are three ways in which individuals with different ideological preferences can be matched (category 1 with category 2, category 1 with category 3, and category 2 with category 3). As with the computation of case pairings, the number of times that we will need to multiply the frequency in one category by the frequency in another is generically equal to $K(K-1)/2$, where K equals the number of categories. With only 2 categories, we would perform the multiplication only once. If, for example, we were to test for the degree of gender diversity in a class, the only possible different pairing would be between a male and female student. With 4 categories, we would have six different ways to pull different pairs. With 20 categories, the number of different types of pairs equals $20 \times 19/2 = 190$, and we then discover the benefits of computers and generic formula.

Generically, therefore, the IQV is defined as follows:

$$IQV = \frac{\sum f_{oI} \times f_{oJ}}{\frac{K(K-1)}{2} \times \left[\frac{N}{K}\right]^2} \qquad \textbf{(4.10)}$$

where N equals the total number of cases in the distribution

K equals the number of categories

f_{oI}, f_{oJ} equals the product of each unique pair of categorical frequencies (I, J)

I, J refer to different categories $(I \neq J)$

Translation: for the numerator, multiply each category's actual *observed* frequency by the frequency of a different category, until you exhaust all possibilities. Then sum (Σ) each of these products. This gives you the number of times you *can actually draw or observe a pair from different categories*. For the denominator, divide the total number of cases (N) by the number of categories (K) to produce the number of cases that each category would have *if each category had the same number of cases* (even distribution). You would then, as in the numerator, multiply the frequency of each category by the frequency of each other category. Since the frequencies are the same (N/K), this is the same as squaring the frequency. How often would you perform this calculation? Again, as often as there are different categories to multiply, $K(K-1)/2$ times. The denominator produces the maximum number of different pairings possible or *expected* given the number of categories in the distribution.

The IQV reaches its minimum value of 0 when the numerator is 0 (i.e., when all the cases fall into one category, such as everyone is a centrist). The IQV reaches its maximum value of 1 when the numerator equals the denominator. This can only happen when the actual distribution matches the best possible distribution (i.e., when the cases are actually observed to be evenly divided among the categories). Consider values between the two to represent the degree of variation among the categories. In our example, we calculated an IQV of .6093 (i.e., 60.93% as evenly distributed as possible).

Sidebar 4.1: Does Ending Affirmative Action Reduce Diversity?

In 1996, California voters passed Prop 209, a measure that would ban affirmative action in college admissions for schools within the University of California and California State University systems. Other states passed similar initiatives or legislation, while other affirmative action programs were successfully challenged in the courts.

Many felt that the passage of Proposition 209 would deprive California universities of the benefits of a diverse ethnic and racial student body, and that it would undermine the state's mandate to serve its broad-based constituency. Some worried that it would actually decrease admission rates for white, non-Hispanic students as the number of students of Asian heritage would increase.

Were any of these expectations actually observed in the changing demographics of college admissions? The answer depends on how one reads the data. Indeed, the proportion of graduating white, non-Hispanic students, the largest single group if not any longer a majority, who entered the California system declined (and the *VR* consequently increased marginally from, by my calculations, .579 to .583). However, the proportion of white, non-Hispanics among California's high school graduates declined by an even greater amount, with corresponding *VR*s of .535 to .553.[1] Similarly, the IQV for the pre- and post-209 era changed only marginally upward, indicating a slightly greater diversity in the entering college pool.

Does this mean that Prop 209 and similar state changes had no effects? As one multistate analyst described it, although the total levels of entry may have seemed to change little, the quality of the universities attended did: "affirmative action bans can cause a large fall in underrepresented minority enrollment at certain universities and an increase at others. Estimating the effects only on the mean university may mask these distributional effects."[2] We will return to the hidden effects of other variables in Chapter 10.

[1] Data derived from figures in Peter Arcidiacono et al., "The Effects of Proposition 209 on College Enrollment and Graduation Rates in California," December 2011, http://public.econ.duke.edu/~psarcidi/prop209.pdf.
[2] Peter Laroy Hinrichs, "The Effects of Affirmative Action Bans on College Enrollment, Educational Attainment, and the Demographic Composition of Universities," *Review of Economics and Statistics* 94, no. 3 (2012): 712–722 (719).

Refer back to our California gubernatorial distribution. Computing an IQV here can be rather trying, especially if you do not have a calculator that allows for power notation (try multiplying the number of Democratic voters by the number of Republican voters). An alternate proportion-based formula for the IQV can be computed, however, with a slight possibility of rounding error introduced. Substitute the proportion of cases for the number of cases in each category (e.g., .538 for California Democrats). For the total number of cases (*N*), substitute 1 (the total of all proportions must equal 1).[2] The rest is the same. One of the chapter exercises will ask you to compute the IQV for both California and Utah. Which is more partisanly diverse?[3]

MEASURES OF DIVERSITY FOR ORDINAL AND INTERVAL DATA

The *VR* measures the proportion of times we would be wrong if we guessed the modal category of a distribution for all cases within that distribution. The IQV measures the degree of variation among categories. As we move to interval data, we can derive measures of dispersion that take into account not *whether or not* we have guessed the right category or differences, but by *how much we are off*. Let's look at the following three distributions of incomes for police officers in three different cities, all unimodal and symmetrical with the same modes, medians and means:

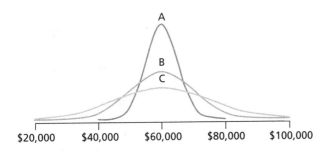

FIGURE 4.3 Three Symmetrical Income Distributions

Reporting the modal, median, or mean value for each distribution ($60,000) would imply that the distribution of income is similar in each city. A *VR* would provide some differentiation between the distributions, but since very few officers share the exact modal value (there are many categories), the *VR* would be rather high for each. The distributions, however, are rather different. In distribution A, most officers earn somewhere around the mean income, with a low tail in both the negative (lower income) and positive (higher income) direction. In this city, very little distinction is made among most officers, but a few seem to be relatively disadvantaged or advantaged compared to their peers. Perhaps salary adjustments are fairly uniform with a limited ability to reward or punish only a handful of outstanding individuals. Perhaps salaries are low during a short training period, settle toward the mean during one's service, and rise only for those who achieve supervisory status. In city B, salaries tend to be more evenly distributed along the pay scale. Perhaps the reward system is much more forcefully applied and varied, or promotions are steady throughout one's career, with a small percentage added for each year of service. City C seems to have a similar method of salary distribution than B. Most salaries are concentrated around the mean, but there seems to be less variation at the extremes. The reward/punishment or seniority system seems less severe.

The Range and Interquartile Range

One way to discuss the differences in the degree of dispersion is to compute the range. The **range** is the difference between the highest value in the distribution and the lowest. For income, the range would tell us what the maximum difference or income disparity would be between any two individuals picked at random from the distribution (remember that the IQV only takes into account whether two cases are different, *not by how much*). The range allows us to differentiate between the distributions in cities A and C ($40,000 vs. $80,000), but not between cities B and C (both $80,000). One solution is to calculate a "middle range," say the maximum difference in salaries for individuals within the middle 50% of the cases. In order to calculate these figures, we would figure out the salary below which 75% of the cases fell (the 75th percentile) and the salary below which 25% of the cases fell (the 25th percentile), and we would subtract the latter from the former. This **interquartile range** (IQR) calculates the range of dispersion for the middle of a distribution. Without looking at precise figures, we can visualize that the middle 50% of the cases in distribution B would spread over a more narrow range than the middle 50% in distribution C.

Remember that for the range and IQR to be computed, we need to be able to measure data at the ordinal or interval level. Purely nominal data cannot be ranked; therefore, like the median, percentiles cannot be ascertained. The range and IQR can be calculated for ordinal data, but the interpretation is not very precise. Calculating differences generally implies that the categorical numbers have intrinsic meaning. At best, we can say that the middle 50% of cases span across a certain number of ordinal categories (e.g., moderately liberal to moderately conservative). The range, IQR, and similar measures of spread or diversion are most appropriate, however, for data measured at the interval or ratio level, where the numbers, and their differences, have intrinsic meaning.

range The maximum categorical difference possible between any two cases in a distribution.

interquartile range The maximum categorical difference possible between any two cases in a distribution's middle 50%.

As an example, let us return to our example of ten incomes in Chapter 3. The mean for that distribution was $112,000. These incomes have a range (maximum disparity) of $340,000 ($360,000–$20,000). If we guessed that the difference between any two randomly picked individuals was no greater than $340,000, we would never be wrong. To compute the IQR, we need to figure out that salary associated with the 75th percentile. This value would be that of the eighth case ($100,000). Two and a half cases would be at that level or higher, and seven and a half would be at that level or less. The 25th percentile would correspond to the value associated with the third case ($30,000). The IQR would therefore be calculated as $100,000–$30,000. The range, or maximum disparity, of the middle 50% is therefore $70,000. The middle 50% of income recipients vary by no more than $70,000.

```
I<-------    $340,000    -------->I
20 20 30 40 50 90 90 100 320 360
     I<--- $70,000 --->I
```

Measures like the IQR eliminate the impact of extreme values. Note that, like the median, the IQR would not change if the highest income was $3,600,000. The range would, however, be much higher ($3,580,000) because the disparity between the lowest and highest incomes would be much greater. The IQR would not, however, differentiate between our original listing of ten incomes and one with much less variation around the mean, such as:

```
20 20 30 100 100 100 100 100 320 360
```

We don't necessarily want to discount the importance of extreme values. Inequalities of wealth are, after all, important components of a society's economic and social character. Can we use the full richness of our data to measure the precise level of diversity or dispersion of incomes? Yes. If the data are interval, we can derive an even more precise measure of dispersion.

Each of our individuals has an income that can vary from the mean. The precise amount of that variation for each case can be measured by subtracting the mean from that individual's income. Our first individual would vary from the mean by –$92,000 (i.e., he earns $92,000 less than the mean income for the entire group). The last person would vary by +$248,000 (i.e., she earns $248,000 more than the mean income for the entire group).

Deviation Scores

For each of the ten cases, we can calculate the difference between the actual value and the mean value. This difference is called the individual **deviation score** and is calculated as follows:

$$d_i = x_i - \overline{X} \qquad (4.11)$$

deviation score The difference between an individual case's value and the mean of all values within a distribution.

where $\overline{X}$ is the mean of the distribution and
x_i is the value for each individual case

The deviation score can be interpreted as the disparity between an individual's value (in this instance, income) and the mean value for all of those in the distribution. Returning to our discussion of observations and expectations, it can also be considered an *error term* between what an individual's actually *observed* income is and the income we would *expect* or guess if that income equaled the mean.

Table 4.3 lists the actual value for each of the ten cases (x_i), as well as the associated deviation score (d_i). For the first case, the individual's actual value falls $92,000 short of the mean. If you guessed the mean for his/her income, you would overestimate by $92,000. For the tenth case, you would underestimate by $248,000. Remember that the mean is that value that each case would get if the total value of income (not the cases) were evenly distributed. The tenth individual would have to relinquish $248,000 to the redistribution pool. The first person would receive a subsidy of $92,000.

We now have a listing of ten deviation scores. We now need to summarize that listing. Remember that when we had ten actual incomes (x_i), we computed the mean as a summary measure of the distribution. It would therefore make sense to summarize the distribution of ten deviation scores by calculating their mean:

$$\overline{d_i} = \frac{\sum_{i=1}^{N}(x_i - \overline{X})}{N}$$

(4.12)

TABLE 4.3 Deviation Scores of Income

Case	x_i	d_i $(x_i - \overline{X})$
$i = 1$	$20,000	−$92,000
$i = 2$	$20,000	−$92,000
$i = 3$	$30,000	−$82,000
$i = 4$	$40,000	−$72,000
$i = 5$	$50,000	−$62,000
$i = 6$	$90,000	−$22,000
$i = 7$	$90,000	−$22,000
$i = 8$	$100,000	−$12,000
$i = 9$	$320,000	+$208,000
$i = 10$	$360,000	+$248,000
Mean	$112,000	

We have a problem. Unfortunately, the mean of the deviation score for this distribution, and for *every* distribution, is equal to 0. Why? Remember, the mean is that value that balances the case values (i.e., the point of redistribution). Guessing the mean for each case would force us to totally overestimate by as much as we totally underestimate. The amount that would be taken from the top two income earners ($456,000) would be redistributed to the other eight individuals (check this calculation).

A statistic that always equals 0 is obviously not very useful. We need to find some way to prevent the negative deviation scores from cancelling out the positive deviation scores. Recall your basic math training. One way to get rid of the negativity problem is to take the absolute value of a score (treat it as a positive value), and the other is to square the number.

Table 4.4 redisplays the absolute deviation scores and the squared deviation scores listed. Two new mean-based measures can now be calculated. One calculates the mean of the absolute deviations, and the other the mean of the squared deviations. The first, called the *absolute deviation*, or, as I like to call it, *mean absolute deviation*, is calculated as follows.

TABLE 4.4 Absolute and Squared Deviation Scores of Income

Case	x_i	d_i $(x_i - \bar{X})$	$\mid d_i \mid$ $\mid (x_i - \bar{X}) \mid$	d_i^2 $(x_i - \bar{X})^2$ E10
$i = 1$	$20,000	−$92,000	$92,000	$$.8464
$i = 2$	$20,000	−$92,000	$92,000	$$.8464
$i = 3$	$30,000	−$82,000	$82,000	$$.6724
$i = 4$	$40,000	−$72,000	$72,000	$$.5184
$i = 5$	$50,000	−$62,000	$62,000	$$.3844
$i = 6$	$90,000	−$22,000	$22,000	$$.0484
$i = 7$	$90,000	−$22,000	$22,000	$$.0484
$i = 8$	$100,000	−$12,000	$12,000	$$.0144
$i = 9$	$320,000	+$208,000	$208,000	$$4.3264
$i = 10$	$360,000	+$248,000	$248,000	$$6.1504
Mean	$112,000	$0	$91,200	$$1.3856

Mean Absolute Deviation

$$\overline{|d_i|} = \frac{\sum_{i=1}^{N} |(x_i - \bar{X})|}{N}$$

(4.13)

First take the absolute value of each of the deviation scores $(x_i - \overline{X})$, and then compute the mean of those absolute values. For our distribution, the **MAD (absolute or mean absolute deviation)** equals $91,200. On mean average, each individual's income varies from the mean by $91,200. If we *expected* everyone's income to be equal to the mean (i.e., the same), the actual *observed* incomes would be off, on mean average, by $91,200. Note that with the MAD, direction is not taken into account. We are just computing generic differences. We don't concern ourselves with whether or not we are overestimating or underestimating, just that we would be *mis*estimating by a certain amount. If we were to be penalized for guessing the mean for each individual, we can expect to be penalized, on mean average, $91,200. The MAD treats deviation scores like driving distances—the odometer on a car would increase by the same amount for each mile that we drive in *any* direction. The mean mileage for ten drivers would not consider direction.

If we were only concerned about describing distributions, the MAD would be a sufficient, easily interpretable measure of variation or dispersion. Because of our need also to make inferences about populations based on samples (discussion starts in Chapter 6), however, variation measures based on the squared deviations become more useful. We now turn to the calculation of a statistic called the **variance**. Note, however, that the basic formula (the mean) stays the same. What we add for each case is what changes. You will see that the variance is an essential part of the last statistical procedures covered in this text, regression analysis.

Variance (Mean Squared Deviation)

$$d_i^2 = \frac{\sum_{i=1}^{N}\left(x_i - \overline{X}\right)^2}{N} \tag{4.14}$$

To compute the variance, we square each of the deviation scores $(x_i - \overline{X})$, and then take the mean of those squared deviations (add them and divide by the number of cases). Notice what happens to our measure. In the first place we wind up with an incredibly large set of numbers: $(-92,000)^2$ equals 8,464,000,000. When we square dollars ($), we come up with squared dollars ($$). So the numbers are large and the units are confusing (squared inches make sense, but not any other squared unit of measurement). The sum (Σ) of all the squared deviations is equal to $$138,560,000,000. Dividing by 10 (N) produces a variance for our distribution equal to $$13,856,000,000 (i.e., 13 billion, 856 million squared dollars). In order to bring both the unit of measurement and magnitude of the value back to standard terms (thousands of dollars), we take the square root of the variance. This produces the most commonly used measure of dispersion for continuous data, the **standard deviation**.

MAD (absolute or mean absolute deviation) The mean of the absolute values of deviation scores.

variance The mean of the squared values of deviation scores.

standard deviation The square root of the variance.

Standard Deviation

$$\sqrt{d_i^2 = \frac{\sum_{i=1}^{N}\left(x_i - \overline{X}\right)^2}{N}} \qquad (4.15)$$

First, compute the variance (the mean of the squared deviations or error terms), and then take its square root. Remember, the final calculation is to compute the square root. Make sure that you don't first take the square roots of each individual squared deviation score before you add them. The standard deviation of our distribution equals $117,711.51. Note that the standard deviation (s_x) is higher than the MAD. That is because the larger deviation scores (computed from the outliers that positively skew our distribution) carry even greater weight when they are squared.[4] There is, for the moment, no simple verbal description of the standard deviation. Consider it to be the same as the MAD, but with an extra penalty assigned for extremely incorrect (outlier) estimations.

We now have completed measures of central tendency and measures of variation or dispersion. We have introduced concepts of standardization, goodness of fit, paired comparisons, and the comparison of observations and expectations. Review all that you have learned. It comprises most of the building-block concepts of statistical theory. You have also learned how to create and interpret generic formulas, including some that seem rather bizarre at first glance (IQV and standard deviation). Other than the concepts of relative placement and association, you are well on your way to understanding statistics.

Sidebar 4.2: The Polarization of Congress

Do you ever get the sense that the U.S. Congress has become polarized recently? One (and only one) way to measure this is to look at the level of dispersion in support for the president. Each year, each member of Congress is rated according to the percentage of times that he/she supported the president on legislation for which his position was known. Assuming that a greater difference denotes a larger divergence between the parties (and further investigation supports this—see Figures 4.4 and 4.5), any increase in the range and MAD of presidential support scores would be indicative of increased polarization. This polarization can be caused by greater ideological differences between the parties (as well as greater consistency within each one with few in the middle), an indication that parties are offering increasingly greater choices. It may also indicate that, in order to make political points, members of the opposition are not willing to grant the president a victory and, perhaps, the president's party is willing to do so.

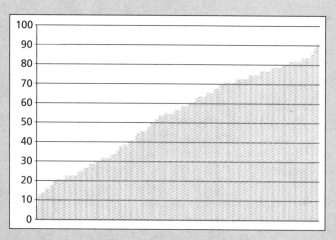

FIGURE 4.4 Presidential Support Scores, 1981

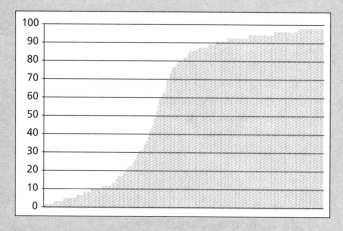

FIGURE 4.5 Presidential Support Scores, 2009

In 1981, the first year of Republican Ronald Reagan's presidency, the range of presidential support scores was 84%; that is, there was an 84% (91% if generally non-policy unanimous votes are excluded) difference between the support percentage of the most supportive Congress member and the least. In 2009, the first year of Democrat Barack Obama's presidency, the range had increased to 96% (98%). Of course, ranges are influenced by outliers, and perhaps a few extreme outliers anchored both ends. In order to keep these outliers in check, the MADs for each year was also calculated. The results were 15.6% (20.0%) in 1981 and 30.2% (36.3%) in 2009.

My thanks to Professor George C. Edwards III for compiling and granting permission to use the data from which these results were derived: http://presdata.tamu.edu/ArchiveData/prezscor. html.

A SUMMARY EXAMPLE WITH AGGREGATED DATA

Table 4.5 lists the 25 European Union countries admitted as of 2005. The figures refer to the percentages of respondents in each country who were satisfied with how democracy worked in the EU, ranked from the country most satisfied to the country least satisfied.[5] The median (52%) and the mean (52.7%) are fairly close, indicating a small positive skew (check the calculations). In half of the nations, 52% or less of the sample was satisfied with democracy in the EU; in half, the satisfaction level was 52% or more. Although the mean for the 25 nations is 52.7%, the percentage satisfaction for the entire European Union (composed of those 25 nations) is only about 49%. Why the difference? Once again, as was the case with states within the United States, the mean of the countries does not take into account the difference in country populations. The fewer than half a million residents (or at least the sample of residents) from Malta carry as much weight in the calculation of the mean as do the roughly 80 million residents of Germany.

Now, compute the range, the IQR, and, using that mean figure, the deviation scores, the mean absolute value of the deviation scores, and then the variance and standard deviation. You should come up with the following. The range of percentage values is 25%; that is, no country's citizens collectively differed by more than 25% from any other country in their positive assessment of democracy in the EU. The IQR would assess the maximum difference between the middle 50% of the distribution of countries. With 25 countries, the IQR would cut out the lower "6.25 countries" and the upper "18.75" countries—leaving us with the middle 12.5 countries, or 50%. We, therefore, after ranking the countries from lowest to highest proportional support, subtract the value of the 7th country (in which the 6.25 case would reside—Finland) from the 19th (Czech Republic). The IQR is equal to 10%; that is, the middle 50% of countries do not vary in their support by more than 10%.[6] The MAD and standard deviations should be 5.67% and 7.24% respectively. Try the calculations yourself.

TABLE 4.5 Percentage of Sampled Individuals in Each Country Satisfied with the Level of Democracy in the European Union

Country	%
Entire EU	49
Luxembourg	66
Belgium	65
Slovenia	65
Ireland	61
Denmark	60
Spain	59
Czech Rep.	58
Cyprus	57
Italy	53
Estonia	53
Malta	53
Hungary	53
Latvia	52
Poland	52
Greece	52
Portugal	49
Slovakia	49
Lithuania	49
Finland	48
Germany	47
Austria	46
France	45
Sweden	42
The Netherlands	42
United Kingdom	41

KEY TERMS

deviation score (91)

goodness of fit measure (78)

index of diversity (84)

index of qualitative variation (85)

interquartile range (90)

MAD (absolute or mean absolute deviation) (94)

range (90)

standard deviation (94)

variance (94)

variation ratio (79)

QUESTIONS AND EXERCISES

NOTE: Several more examples and exercises can be found in both the SPSS and Stata manuals that accompany this text. Ranges, variances, and standard deviations can be calculated as part of a frequency distribution (Section 4.1). Remember to suppress the actual frequency tables if you don't want too much output.

1. Interpret the following *VR*s: .00, 1.00, .43.
2. The modal ethnicity for a certain group of 140 European Union legislators is German. The *VR* is .7. How many Germans are in that group?
3. The MAD is calculated for the number of terms served by each of those 140 legislators. That MAD is 2. Explain what that "2" represents.
4. Compute and interpret the *VR* and IQV for each of our three category listings of party ID presented in Chapter 2, Exercise 9.
5. Exam scores for a class of 200 students produce a standard deviation of 0. What can be said about the exam scores of those 200 students?
6. Compute and interpret the IQV for the second and third ideological distributions in this chapter.
7. Compute the range, MAD, and standard deviations for the two distributions of PAC contributions listed in Exercise 9 in Chapter 3. Notice how the difference between the MAD and the standard deviations changes from one distribution to the other. Why?
8. Compute, interpret, and compare the *VR*s and the IQVs for the California and Utah gubernatorial races in Chapter 2.
9. Following is a listing of the 1996 presidential support scores for each of the 17 Illinois members of the U.S. House of Representatives who won re-election in 1996. The score represents the proportion of times that each Congress member supported the president (Clinton) on a bill on which he had a stated position. The party of the member is listed along with his/her respective score. Compute and interpret the median, mean, range, and MAD for each of the following: all 17 members, all Democrats, and all Republicans. For all statistics calculated, compare the results between Democrats and Republicans. You must show all calculations. Don't just give the results. (Presidential support scores as well as a host of other district data for the U.S. House of Representatives from 2008 to 2012 can be analyzed with data supplied with the SPSS and Stata manuals that accompany this volume.)
10. Turn to the list of African presidential elections in Chapter 3 (Exercise 13). Compute and interpret the range, MAD, and standard deviation.
11. Compute the range, MAD, and standard deviation for the two election lists found in Exercise 11 in Chapter 3.

TABLE 4.6 Presidential Support Scores for 17 Illinois U.S. House Members, 1996*

CD1	Rush	(D)	78%
CD2	Jackson	(D)	85%
CD3	Lipinski	(D)	65%
CD4	Guitierrez	(D)	81%
CD6	Hyde	(R)	39%
CD8	Crane	(R)	34%
CD9	Yates	(D)	72%
CD10	Porter	(R)	42%
CD11	Weller	(R)	41%
CD12	Costello	(D)	66%
CD13	Fawell	(R)	43%
CD14	Hastert	(R)	37%
CD15	Ewing	(R)	34%
CD16	Manzullo	(R)	33%
CD17	Evans	(D)	75%
CD18	LaHood	(R)	39%
CD19	Poshard	(D)	61%

*Two members were not in office long enough in 1996 to have been included.

12. Turn to your class survey. Compute and interpret the *VR* and IQV for one of your purely nominal variables (with at least three categories). Compute and interpret the range, IQR, MAD, and standard deviation of one of your interval variables (if applicable).

13. See Chapter 3, Exercise 15 (Three separate assignments possible).
    a. Compute the range and the MAD for each of the three vote distributions. Describe and interpret *fully* what each figure tells you *in words*. (For example, don't just calculate the MAD; describe what it tells you about this group of counties.)
    b. Now, do the same for only the Democratic and, separately, only the Republican-leaning counties. Be complete in your calculation and answers.

14. Using the data in Question 13, compute the range and MAD for *both* the county vote for Obama and the county vote for Feinstein for *all* 16 counties. Describe and interpret *fully* what each figure tells you *in words*.

NOTES

1   If our base from which to guess is all registered (17,205,883) or eligible voters (23,551,699), then our mode changes to that category representing those who *did not vote* for a candidate. What would be the variation ratio for each?

2   Alternately, one can use percentages (relative frequencies). *N* then becomes 100 as the total of all proportions must equal 100%.

3   Many texts use alternate and easier formulas for proportions that produce the same results. One is the following:

$$\frac{K}{K-1}\left(1 - \sum p_i^2\right) \text{ where } i \text{ refers to each of the different categories}$$

My preference is based on understanding the comparison between *observed* and *expected* frequencies that allow students a more intuitive understanding of the IQV.

4   A simple example will demonstrate this point. The mean of two numbers, 2 and 4, is 3. If we first square those numbers (4, 16), then the mean equals 10. The square root of that mean is 3.16.

5   Source: *Eurobarometer 63: Public Opinion in the European Union* (European Commission, 2005).

6   Many computer programs will artificially parse out the actual differences among the cases when calculating the median and IQR. You may see fractional differences between your hand calculations and what these programs produce. SPSS, for example, produces an IQR of 11%.

CHAPTER 5

Standardized Scores and Normal Distributions

The Concept of *Relative* Observation

Learning Objectives:

▨ To learn the importance of standardizing measures
▨ To understand the concept of a normal distribution
▨ To learn to interpret individual Z-scores
▨ To begin to understand the idea of confidence intervals
▨ To understand what confidence intervals can and can't tell us

As we have seen, standard deviations are not yet easily interpretable, except as a variation of the mean absolute deviation (MAD) with an extra penalty assessed for the greatest deviations from the mean. If we were only concerned about description, the MAD would probably be the only measure of dispersion necessary. If we are concerned about making inferences about populations from randomly drawn samples, however, the standard deviation becomes necessary. Standard deviations are fairly consistent from sample to sample drawn from any given population, provided the sample sizes are relatively large.

We'll get back to the use of sample standard deviations later. For now, let us address their use in the computation of something new, standard or (I prefer) standardized scores. We have already introduced the concept of standardization. Standardization allows for comparisons between and among different distributions. Relative frequencies, for example, standardize absolute frequencies by dividing them by the total number of cases in their distribution. All relative distributions add to the same number, 100%, regardless of the size (N) of the distribution. The index of qualitative variation ranges between 0 and 1 regardless of the number of categories (K) or cases (N) in the distribution. Let us now move to the computation of standardized scores.

HOW WELL OFF ARE WE?

Consider the following problem. A major part of the political dialogue in any election is the question of whether or not one believes he/she is better off than in the past or will be better off in the future. Ronald Reagan's parting line in the 1980 presidential debate, "Are you better off now than you were four years ago?" has become, in varying forms, part of the vernacular of challengers in campaigns. For each of us, the notion of "better off" is premised not only on the basis of where we are financially at any given time, but where we *expected* to be. For decades after the Second World War, for example, families prided themselves on leaving their children better off than they had been. We had developed the expectation (now badly bruised) that each generation would be better off than the ones preceding it. A noble idea, but how do we measure "better off"? Allow me to use a personal example. When I was 55 (2006), my combined family income was approximately $100,000. When my father was 55 (1973), his last year of full-time employment, his family income was approximately $10,000. Who was better off? Economists can provide us with a precise comparison based on an assessment of how much purchasing power each income has in its respective time period. Using the standard consumer price index (CPI) inflation scale, we *observe* that the purchasing power of $100,000 in 2006 was equivalent to the purchasing power of approximately $22,000 in 1973.[1] Looking at this from my father's perspective, he would have had to have made more than $45,000 to equal my purchasing power. By either calculation, I'm much better off financially. Or am I?

One's assessment of financial worth or living standard is often premised on more than just absolute purchasing power or a simple observation of what one can buy. That assessment often also includes an evaluation of how well off one is compared to or *relative to* one's peers. Poor people sometimes feel fairly well off if they live in a poor area, as long as they are relatively better off than most of their neighbors. By the same token, a teenager in Beverly Hills, Malibu, or Marin County, California, may feel relatively deprived even if his standard of living is objectively rather high. We oftentimes make judgments based on our *relative* position in society, not just an absolute measure of wealth. Expectations of what constitutes a decent standard of living change (smartphones, laptops, or tablets) over time and influence the political battle over what we expect families, societies, and governments to provide.

What if, in 2006, my wife and I earned less than most of the people with whom we regularly associated, or more than just a small percentage, and my father and mother earned more than most of their equivalent peer group? My parents might have felt relatively better off, even if they had less expensive and fewer if any cars (none) and TVs (1) and a less elegant home (a three-room apartment to be exact) than their son at the same time in his life. Their judgment was based not on what they could purchase in *absolute* terms, but what they could purchase in *comparison to others* with whom they associated. In hindsight, we might *observe* fewer material goods in my father's household, but those goods, after serving in the military for five years during World War II, might have more than exceeded his *expectations*.

How do we precisely compare *relative* worth (i.e., relative to others in their area)? First, as in our calculation of relative frequencies, we need to establish the peer base against which to compare, or standardize, each salary. Is it one's colleagues or neighbors, or the residents of an entire city? For sake of argument, let's make the base the large, metropolitan neighborhood in which each lived. Next we need to determine the proportion of households in each neighborhood whose income they each exceeded. The assessment of wealth then becomes not better off by *how much*, but rather better off than *how many*, or, since the size of the neighborhoods may differ, better off than "*what proportion*." Both father and son can be ranked by their incomes, as we did to calculate the median, against others in their neighborhood to determine their income percentile (i.e., the percentage of households whose income they exceeded). My parents might have been better off than roughly

Sidebar 5.1: Standardization in Surveys

Certain data-gathering organizations perform a routine standardization of particular measures in order to allow for relative comparisons across countries and time. In listing income categories for respondents in each of the countries in the regular Eurobarometer survey, for example, incomes are standardized into quintiles (five equally populated 20% of the population categories) to standardize relative income within countries and across time. In a poorer country, one can earn the same salary, measured in euros, than a colleague in a wealthier one. What each can buy may be relatively equal. However, the individual in the poorer country would be relatively better off as that person would be able to buy more than a higher percentage of others in her country, thus placing her in a higher quintile (see Exercise 6 at the end of this chapter).

90% of their neighborhood's households. In 2006 in California, my family might have been better off than roughly only 68% of ours. In relative terms, therefore, my parents were better off.

You are probably most familiar with the notion of relative standardization when you look at scores from some national testing programs such as the SAT, GRE, MCAT, or LSAT. Your absolute score is only important as it places you in a certain position relative to others who took the exam. Standardized scores can be converted into percentiles. An LSAT score of 160 is meaningless except that it may place you in the top 20% of exam takers. It is this relative position that is of interest to law schools, not your actual score, although the two should be positively and closely related.[2] Some state university systems allow entry to the top 9% or 10% of graduates of each high school. The absolute educational talent of those students is not as important as the fact that they have scored better than 90% of their local peers.

We can always figure out an individual's percentile on any measure by ranking all individuals from lowest to highest and counting off until we reach the appropriate cutoff. We have already employed this technique in the calculation of the median, the point that defines the 50th percentile. Rank ordering a large number of cases within a distribution can be tedious, although computers can help. If the distribution is of a known shape, however, calculus can be employed to measure the points that define each percentile cutoff. One commonly analyzed distribution is what is called the **normal distribution**, a particular family of bell-shaped symmetrical curves, which match or approximate distributions of cases for many different types of variables such as age, height, and weight. The following discussion will assume that the family incomes of our two neighborhoods were normally distributed. Although this may not be the case, the logic that follows would work with any type of distribution in which we rank order cases from the lowest to the highest value. The formula and calculations would be different, but the logic would remain the same. We need to start with one, so we'll start with the normal distribution. Later, we'll see why this particular unique distribution is so important.

We first need to know if each family earned more or less than the mean for its neighborhood and by how much. We've already calculated this figure. It's the deviation score discussed in Chapter 4:

$$d_i = x_i - \overline{X} \tag{5.1}$$

If the mean household income in my parents' neighborhood was \$8,000, then their deviation score would be +\$2,000 (i.e., they earned \$2,000 more than the mean income in their neighborhood that year). What if I lived in a fairly upper-middle-class neighborhood with a mean income of \$80,000? My family deviation score is +\$20,000 (i.e., we earned \$20,000 more than the mean income in our neighborhood). So were we relatively better off?

normal distribution A family of symmetrical distributions whose mathematical equation is determined by its mean and standard deviation.

That depends. One's relative standing is not only a function of how much one is above or below the mean, but also how diverse their neighborhood's income is. The distribution of incomes in my father's neighborhood might not have varied much. An income of $10,000 might have been at the very top of that neighborhood's income distribution. The distribution of incomes in our California neighborhood might vary by a much wider amount, placing an income of $100,000 relatively closer to the mean salary than the 100th percentile.

STANDARDIZATION AVND Z-SCORES

Because the spread of each distribution might vary, we need to *standardize* the respective deviation scores by some measure of that dispersion or distribution. As we discussed in Chapter 4, the standard deviation is the most commonly used measure of dispersion for interval data. The standardized deviation score is then calculated as the deviation score divided by the standard deviation for the given distribution. If the data are normally distributed, with a mean of 0 and a standard deviation of 1, this standard score, or, as I prefer, standardized score, is called a **Z-score** and is represented by the following equation:

$$Z_i = \frac{x_i - \overline{X}}{s_x} \qquad (5.2)$$

where x_i is the observed value for any individual case (i)
$\overline{X}$ is the mean of all the values in the distribution that contains x_i
s_x is the standard deviation of all of the individual values in that distribution

The Z-score standardizes any particular value, in our example income, in relation to the distribution of which it is a part. That distribution is defined by both its mean ($\overline{X}$) and its standard deviation (s_x). Let us say that we find from census figures that the standard deviation of incomes for my neighborhood was $20,000, and $1,000 for my parents' neighborhood. Let's calculate the Z-score for each of us, father and son, respectively:

$$Z_{father} = \frac{\$10,000 - \$8,000}{\$1,000} = 2$$

$$Z_{son} = \frac{\$100,000 - \$80,000}{\$20,000} = 1 \qquad (5.3)$$

Z-score A measure of deviation from the mean standardized by the standard deviation of a distribution when the mean is 0 and the standard deviation is 1.

Z-scores convert absolute deviations (how many dollars above or below the mean is our income?) to standardized ones (how many standard deviations above or below the mean is our income?). My parents earned 2 standard deviations above the mean of their neighborhood. We earned only 1 standard deviation above the mean of ours. We were therefore *relatively* worse off (i.e., relatively worse off for our local comparison group) than my parents were at the same point in their lives, even if our purchasing power was greater.

Before we move on to a more precise interpretation of these values, one important point needs to be made. Notice that when we computed *Z*-scores the unit of measurement ($) drops out. This allows us to make *standardized* relative judgments about incomes across time (1973 dollars vs. 2006 dollars) and across cultures (dollars vs. euros or pesos). Again remember that these are comparisons of *relative* worth, not absolute purchasing power. To figure out the latter, we would need to turn to inflation charts and currency converters. As we will see when we discuss regression (Chapter 11), standardized scores also allow us to make comparisons between distributions measuring entirely different properties (e.g., education [measured in years] and income [measured in dollars]). *Z*-scores have no differential unit of measurement. The units are measured as standard deviations and are therefore *universally* comparable.

A normal distribution, which we are assuming our neighborhood incomes follow, has a well-defined shape and allows us to pinpoint the exact percentile of any particular value. That percentile defines the proportion of all cases in the distribution below that value. A normal distribution is presented in Figure 5.1, along with the percentile cutoffs for each value associated with a whole *Z*-score. Other types of distributions could be similarly plotted, along with their corresponding cutoffs.

Since the distribution is symmetrical about the mean, the mean and the median are the same. As it is unimodal, the mode also equals the median and mean. Fifty percent of the distribution must therefore lie at or below the mean, and 50% at or above. An individual value equal to the mean would have a *Z*-score of 0 since that value would not deviate at all from the mean. In 2006, an income of $80,000 would be associated with a *Z*-score of 0, corresponding to the 50th percentile. Half of the neighborhood families earned $80,000 or less, and half $80,000 or more. In a normal distribution, 34.13% of all cases lie between the mean and a *Z*-score of +1, and, since the distribution is symmetrical, 34.13% lie between the mean and a *Z*-score of –1. An additional 13.60% of the normal distribution lies between a *Z*-score of +1 and +2, or –1 and –2. Adding these figures, 47.73% of all the cases in a normal distribution lie between the mean (*Z* = 0) and a *Z*-score of +2, and 47.73% between the mean and a *Z*-score of –2. In a normal distribution, 95.46% of all the cases lie between a *Z*-score of –2 and +2, and 68.26% between –1 and +1. An additional 2.13% of all cases lie between a *Z*-score of +2 and +3, or –2 and –3; 49.86% of all the cases lie between the mean and a value associated with a *Z*-score of +3 or –3; and 99.72% of all the cases lie between these two values.

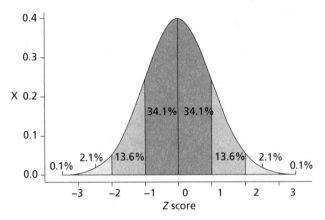

FIGURE 5.1 The Normal Distribution (Z)

Let us return to our example. My family Z-score of +1 placed us at the 84.13% cutoff or percentile of the income distribution of our neighborhood (50% + 34.13%). In 2006, we earned more than 84.13% of the families in our area and less than the remaining 15.87% (Figure 5.2).

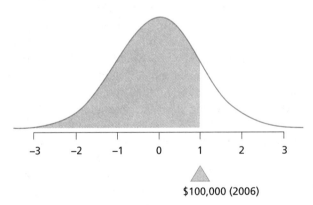

$100,000 (2006)

FIGURE 5.2 $Z = 1$

My parents' income computed to a *Z*-score of +2 (see Figure 5.3), thereby placing them at the 97.73 percentile (50% + 47.73%). Rounding off, we can say that they ranked in the upper 2.5% of their distribution (actually 2.17%). My parents were therefore relatively better off because they earned more than an additional 13.6% of all the individuals in their comparison group than we did. Note that these percentiles refer to *proportion of cases*, not to *how much more* each made. They were relatively better off because they earned more than a higher proportion of individuals in their neighborhood. If our views about our living standards were based exclusively on our relative worth, then our expectations of government policy and our evaluations of the promises made by candidates would most likely have been different.

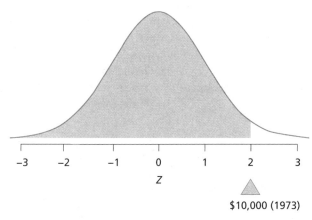

FIGURE 5.3 $Z = 2$

A Policy Example

What if, at both points in time, the local government decided to apply a surtax to those families whose incomes placed them in the top 10% of income earners (let's assume that the relevant comparison group for father and son was all citizens within that local government's jurisdiction)? Although my father had a much lower absolute standard of living, he would have been hit by that tax as his relative status placed him in the top 10% of his comparison group. Living a much more comfortable life, but within a wealthier community, I would be free of that extra assessment.

As it is, most government programs that deal with taxes and benefits are not set by percentiles, but usually by actual dollar amounts. Surtaxes usually apply across the board to everyone who pays taxes. To help pay for the Vietnam War, a 10% surtax was added to each individual's already existing tax liability (therefore exacting a greater percentage from high-income earners who were originally taxed at a higher marginal rates). Recently, surtaxes on those who made more than a certain specified income (not percentile) have been suggested as a way to pay for the revamping of our nation's health care system. Low-income benefits programs operate in much the same way, with cutoffs for eligibility based not on one's percentile ranking but on a certain dollar income figure based on the poverty rate. The financial problems with these programs occur as the costs can swing even more widely than one based on percentiles. During a recession, for example, the percentage of individuals who fall below the pre-established cutoff rises dramatically, thereby increasing the cost of the program. The alternative is to only provide benefits to those below a certain percentile threshold—perhaps more fiscally sound but morally questionable. Of course, one can achieve similar results by increasing the absolute income cutoff or changing how income is measured, thus allowing a smaller percentage of families to qualify. In 2011, for example, Michigan added a family's bank assets over $5,000 and vehicles valued over $15,000 to the base from which food stamp eligibility was determined. The state argued that it could no longer handle the growing number of recipients who, by past income determinations, increased by more than 40% from 2008 to 2011.[3]

Furthering Our Understanding of Z-Scores

Z-scores are not always whole integers. A 2006 salary of $87,000 would correspond to a *Z*-score of +.35 (.35 standard deviations above the mean). Table 5.1 lists the proportions of cases that fall between the mean ($Z = 0$) and any given positive *or* negative *Z*-score. Look down the leftmost column to find a given *Z*-score carried out to only one decimal place. Stop at the line beginning with the *Z*-score of .3. Next move along that line until you reach the column headed by .05. This carries the score to a second decimal place. At the intersection of that line (.3) and column (.05), you will find a proportion associated with a *Z*-score of .35, .1368. In a normal distribution, 13.68% of the area, or cases, is found between the mean ($Z = 0$) and a value associated with a *Z*-score of plus or minus .35. Since 50% of all cases must lie below the mean (the distribution is symmetrical), then a family earning $87,000 earned more than 63.68% (50% + 13.68%) of all individuals in that neighborhood and less than 36.32% (100% – 63.68%) (see Figure 5.4).

   Z-scores can also be negative (values are below the mean). In 2006, a family with an income of $50,000 would have a corresponding *Z*-score of –1.5 (1.5 standard deviations below the mean); 43.32% of the area under the curve (i.e., 43.32% of all the cases in a normal distribution) would lie between the mean and a *Z* of –1.5 (see Figure 5.5). A family earning $50,000 therefore made more than only 6.68% of the families in their neighborhood

TABLE 5.1 Areas under the Normal Curve

Proportion of Cases between a Z-Score of 0 and a Z-Score of ± Z

Z	.00	.01	.02	.03	.04	.05	.06	.07	.08	.09
.0	.0000	.0040	.0080	.0120	.0160	.0199	.0239	.0279	.0319	.0359
.1	.0398	.0438	.0478	.0517	.0557	.0596	.0636	.0675	.0714	.0753
.2	.0793	.0832	.0871	.0910	.0948	.0987	.1026	.1064	.1103	.1141
.3	.1179	.1217	.1255	.1293	.1331	*.1368*	.1406	.1443	.1480	.1517
.4	.1554	.1591	.1628	.1664	.1700	.1736	.1772	.1808	.1844	.1879
.5	.1915	.1950	.1985	.2019	.2054	.2088	.2123	.2157	.2190	.2224
.6	.2257	.2291	.2324	.2357	.2389	.2422	.2454	.2486	.2517	.2549
.7	.2580	.2611	.2642	.2673	.2704	.2734	.2764	.2794	.2823	.2852
.8	.2881	.2910	.2939	.2967	.2995	.3023	.3051	.3078	.3106	.3133
.9	.3159	.3186	.3212	.3238	.3264	.3289	.3315	.3340	.3365	.3389
1.0	.3413	.3438	.3461	.3485	.3508	.3531	.3554	.3577	.3599	.3621
1.1	.3643	.3665	.3686	.3708	.3729	.3749	.3770	.3790	.3810	.3830
1.2	.3849	.3869	.3888	.3907	.3925	.3944	.3962	.3980	.3997	.4015
1.3	.4032	.4049	.4066	.4082	.4099	.4115	.4131	.4147	.4162	.4177
1.4	.4192	.4207	.4222	.4236	.4251	.4265	.4279	.4292	.4306	.4319
1.5	*.4332*	.4345	.4357	.4370	.4382	.4394	.4406	.4418	.4429	.4441
1.6	.4452	.4463	.4474	.4484	.4495	.4505	.4515	.4525	.4535	.4545
1.7	.4554	.4564	.4573	.4582	.4591	.4599	.4608	.4616	.4625	.4633
1.8	.4641	.4649	.4656	.4664	.4671	.4678	.4686	.4693	.4699	.4706
1.9	.4713	.4719	.4726	.4732	.4738	.4744	*.4750*	.4756	.4761	.4767
2.0	.4772	.4778	.4783	.4788	.4793	.4798	.4803	.4808	.4812	.4817
2.1	.4821	.4826	.4830	.4834	.4838	.4842	.4846	.4850	.4854	.4857
2.2	.4861	.4864	.4868	.4871	.4875	.4878	.4881	.4884	.4887	.4890
2.3	.4893	.4896	.4898	.4901	.4904	.4906	.4909	.4911	.4913	.4916
2.4	.4918	.4920	.4922	.4925	.4927	.4929	.4931	.4932	.4934	.4936
2.5	.4938	.4940	.4941	.4943	.4945	.4946	.4948	.4949	.4951	.4952
2.6	.4953	.4955	.4956	.4957	.4959	.4960	.4961	.4962	.4963	.4964
2.7	.4965	.4966	.4967	.4968	.4969	.4970	.4971	.4972	.4973	.4974
2.8	.4974	.4975	.4976	.4977	.4977	.4978	.4979	.4979	.4980	.4981
2.9	.4981	.4982	.4982	.4983	.4984	.4984	.4985	.4985	.4986	.4986
3.0	.4987	.4987	.4987	.4988	.4988	.4989	.4989	.4989	.4990	.4990

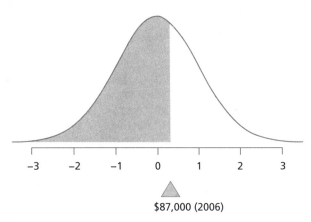

FIGURE 5.4 $Z = .35$

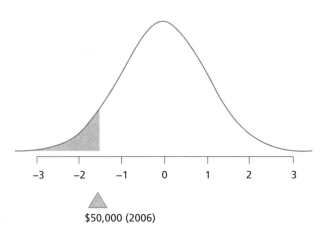

FIGURE 5.5 $Z = -1.5$

and less than 93.32% (that 43.32% plus the 50% above the mean). Make sure that you understand how to use the chart by finding the percentile rankings corresponding to a Z-score of +1.12 (86.86), –.75 (22.66), and 1.96 (97.50). I suggest that you always draw out a normal curve and place a mark close to where the Z-score would be. This prevents you from confusing positive (always above the mean and higher than the 50th percentile) and negative (always below the mean and below the 50th percentile) scores.

Relative Placement:
Why a Student Should Never Ask That Grades Be Curved

The *Z*-score formula can be quite useful in determining relative placement. As an example, let us say that you scored 90 points on an exam (out of 100). Should you receive an "A" in this class? Well, if the professor has made an *objective* judgment that 90 out of 100 constitutes "A" performance, then the answer is yes. If the professor, on the other hand, makes *relative* judgments, then your grade is dependent on how well you have done *relative to others* who have taken the test. If the mean exam score is 85, with a standard deviation of 5 points, then your corresponding *Z*-score is +1, placing you in the top 15.87% of the class. If your professor will only give "A's" to the top 10%, then you won't receive an "A," no matter how well you may have otherwise, objectively, done. What is the minimal score needed to receive an "A"? In order to answer this question, we need to find the *Z*-score that corresponds to the top 10%, that is, the 90% cutoff. Remembering that the chart lists proportions on each side of a symmetrical normal curve, we need to look at the body of the chart to find a proportion close to .4000 (50% + 40% = 90%). A *Z*-score of 1.28 is pretty close (see Figure 5.6).

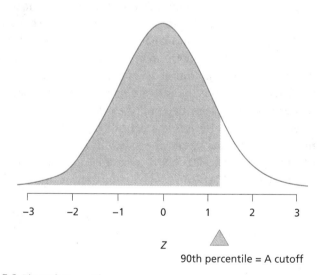

90th percentile = A cutoff

FIGURE 5.6 The 90th Percentile

CHAPTER 5 STANDARDIZED SCORES/NORMAL DISTRIBUTIONS

Now, enter that Z-score into the Z-score equation, and solve for the actual score (x_{90} will be used to designate the score corresponding to the 90th percentile) that corresponds to that cutoff:

$$1.28 = (x_{90} - 85 \text{ pts})/5 \text{ pts}$$
$$6.40 \text{ pts} = x_{90} - 85 \text{ pts}$$
$$x_{90} = 91.4 \text{ pts}$$

You would have to earn at least 91.4 points, or 92 if a fraction is not possible, to place you above the 90% cutoff and receive an "A." Close, but, as they say, no cigar. Students often ask their professors to "curve" their grades, assuming that everyone gets bumped up. A curve just means granting grades based on relative placement. If the grades are normally distributed (i.e., fit in the normal "curve"), and the professor only grants A's to the top 10%, then only a score of 92 or better will do. This is true regardless of the difficulty level of the exam or the mean average intelligence of the class. If you are in a class of geniuses with easy exams, watch what you ask for.

Sidebar 5.2: Forced Ranking and Job Discrimination

For years, companies have used a ranking method to promote, give out bonuses to, or fire employees. One controversial case involved Ford Motor Company's attempt to rate its managers on an A, B, C scale, with the top 10% rated an A and the bottom 10% rated a C. Two consecutive "C" ratings could lead to a manager's dismissal—even if that manager met or exceeded all of the expectations of his job. It was not absolute but relative performance that mattered. The AARP and other organizations argued that this was a less than subtle way of releasing older and more expensive employees, especially in light of the fact that the ranking method seemed somewhat arbitrarily biased against older workers. Ford eventually settled out of court for $10.5 million. For a full discussion of forced ranking systems and their effects, see Meredith Myres, "Grades Are No Longer Just for Students: Forced Ranking, Discrimination, and the Quest to Attain a More Competent Workforce," *Seton Hall Law Review* 33 (2003): 681–709. The case in question is *Siegel v. Ford Motor Co.*, No. 01–102583-CL (Mich. Circ. Ct. Wayne Co. Jan. 23, 2001).

Continuing the example, this professor wishes to grant an A+ to any student who scores in the top 2.5% of this class and an F to those in the bottom 2.5%. What are the corresponding actual exam scores?

Let's first find the score below which a student would receive an F grade; 97.5% of all scores would be above that cutoff. Fifty percent would be above the mean (85, $Z = 0$), and the remaining 47.5% would be between that score and the mean. Look at the Z-score table. Find the figure .4750. The corresponding Z-score is 1.96; 47.5% of all cases lie between a Z-score of 0 (the

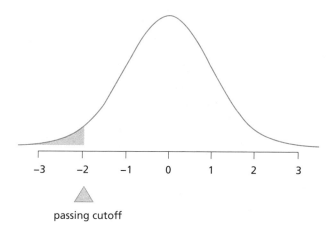

passing cutoff

FIGURE 5.7 The 2.5th Percentile

mean) and a Z-score of 1.96 (upper end), and 47.5% of all cases lie between the mean and a Z-score of -1.96. The 2.5% cutoff is therefore associated with a Z-score of -1.96 (see Figure 5.7).

Now solve for the unknown (i.e., the exact score associated with that cutoff):

$$-1.96 = (x_{2.5} - 85 \text{ pts})/5 \text{ pts}$$
$$-9.80 \text{ pts} = x_{2.5} - 85 \text{ pts}$$
$$x_{2.5} = 75.2 \text{ pts}$$

Rounding off, anyone who scores 75 points or less fails the exam. Note that a score of 75 would normally be associated with a "C" grade. However, we are looking at *relative* placement. This might be a smart class, or this might be an easy exam. It doesn't matter. What matters is that a grade below 75 points places you in the bottom 2.5% of the class. Thus, you fail.

An A+ will be given to anyone who scored in the upper 2.5% (see Figure 5.8). That score is associated with a Z of $+1.96$ (50% below the mean, 47.50% above).

The calculation is as follows:

$$+1.96 = (x_{97.5} - 85 \text{ pts})/5 \text{ pts}$$
$$+9.80 \text{ pts} = x_{97.5} - 85 \text{ pts}$$
$$x_{97.5} = 94.8 \text{ pts}$$

Rounding off, anyone who scores 95 points or better receives an A+.

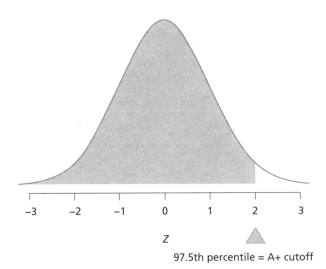

97.5th percentile = A+ cutoff

FIGURE 5.8 The 97.5th Percentile

Let's review this one other way. The middle 95% of all exam takers would have scores between these two cutoffs (47.5% below the mean, 47.5% above). The corresponding actual values are 75.2 and 94.8. The corresponding Z-scores are −1.96 and +1.96. In a normal distribution, 95% of the cases would always lie between these two Z-scores. The range of that middle 95% in *this* example is 94.8 − 75.2, or 19.6 points (3.92 standard deviations). In a fashion similar to one interpretation of the range, if you randomly chose two individuals within the middle 95% of all exam takers, they would differ by no more than 19.6 points.

Remember the interquartile range? That corresponds to the middle 50%. What are the corresponding Z-scores? Refer once more to the Z-score table. To find the relevant scores that border the middle 50%, we need to find a Z-score (− and +) that corresponds to a table value of .2500 (25% below the mean, 25% above). That value is somewhere between .67 and .68, so let's call it .675. The middle 50% of all cases in a normal distribution will always lie between Z-scores of −.675 and +.675. The middle 50% will span across 1.35 standard deviations. As a review, compute the actual scores between which 50% of all our exam takers lie (81.625 and 88.375 points).

Let's end this chapter by going back to our original 2006 income example. In my neighborhood, the mean income was $80,000 with a standard deviation of $20,000. Therefore, 97.5% of this neighborhood's households had incomes below $119,200 because:

$$+1.96 = (x_{97.5} - \$80,000)/\$20,000$$
$$\$39,200 = x_{97.5} - \$80,000$$
$$x_{97.5} = \$119,200$$

Similarly, 2.5% of the households had incomes below, and 97.5% will have incomes above $40,800 because:

$$-1.96 = (x_{2.5} - \$80,000)/\$20,000$$
$$-\$39,200 = x_{2.5} - \$80,000$$
$$x_{2.5} = \$40,800$$

Ninety-five percent of all households in this town will have incomes between these two values (Figure 5.9), and we can represent this middle 95% range as follows:[4]

$$\$40,800 < x_i < \$119,200$$

Next, note that if we were to randomly draw a household, the chance or probability of drawing a household with an income between these two values

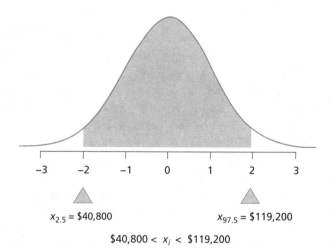

FIGURE 5.9 The Middle 95%

would be .95 or 95%. Is it *possible* to randomly sample a household with an income of less than $40,800 or greater than $119,200? The answer is yes, but the *probability* of such a random draw is less than 5%. Thus, if we were placing bets on the incomes of households randomly drawn from this neighborhood, we could "safely" or "confidently" bet that each household drawn would earn between $40,800 and $119,200—"confidently" because we would chance being wrong *only 5% of the time*. Notice, that 5% refers only to *how often we might be wrong* (commonly called **alpha error**), not by how much. Five percent of the households earn incomes outside of that middle 95% range—2.5% below $40,800 and 2.5% above $119,200. This game of chance is much like the one we introduced in discussing the median. We could guess someone to be above the median, with a 50% chance of guessing correctly. We would be allowing ourselves a 50% confidence range (all on one side of the distribution). Fifty percent of all the cases would have values at or above the median value. In the current example, we are allowing ourselves a 95% confidence range (47.5% on each side of the distribution)—a pretty safe bet, but one that we will discover is common in statistical applications.

alpha error The probability of erroneously rejecting the null hypothesis.

Sidebar 5.3: The Prosecutor's Fallacy

In court trials, probabilities are often offered as a way of providing evidence against a suspect—often incorrectly. Just because only 1% of a given population (incidence rate) carries a certain characteristic also carried by the suspect does not mean that there is only a 1% chance of the suspect being innocent. This "transposition of the conditional" is so commonly used that it has been named "the prosecutor's fallacy." Arguments have been made for a more thorough approach based on Bayes Theorem that would include the use of prior odds of being a suspect along with the incidence rate evidence offered. For three very useful overviews of the misinterpretation of evidence by both prosecutors and defense attorneys in criminal cases, see William C. Thompson and Edward L. Schumann, "Interpretation of Statistical Evidence in Criminal Trials: The Prosecutor's Fallacy and the Defense Attorney's Fallacy," *Law and Human Behavior* 11, no. 3 (Sep. 1987): 167–187; Philip Dawid, "Probability and Statistics in the Law," Proceedings of the Tenth International Workshop on Artificial Intelligence and Statistics, January 6–8, 2005, Barbados, edited by Zoubin Ghahramani, Robert G. Cowell, and Robert G. Cowell. http://www.gatsby.ucl.ac.uk/aistats/fullpapers/123.pdf; and Michael O. Finkelstein, *Basic Concepts of Probability and Statistics in the Law* (Springer-Verlag, 2009). Bayes Theorem, which allows prior information to condition our interpretation of future outcomes, incidentally, has been successfully used by Nate Silver and other analysts to predict electoral outcomes.

A CAUTIONARY TALE

Let us proceed one step further. We are told that a household was randomly drawn from a neighborhood in 2006, but not told which one. That household's income was $40,000. Could we "confidently" guess that this household was not randomly drawn from our neighborhood (with a mean income of $80,000)? Yes. While the possibility exists, it is highly unlikely because the probability of randomly drawing a household from that town with an income below $40,800 is only 2.5% (we halved the 5% figure because we are not even considering individuals who earn less than the mean; when we are only concerned about one side of the curve, we perform such a one-tailed test). Might we be wrong in rejecting them as residents of that neighborhood? Certainly, but the probability of being wrong in that rejection is slim, and therefore we would be willing to take that chance.

Note that even if we are correct in stating that they are probably not residents of that town, this *does not* tell us what neighborhood they might be a resident of (although we may wish to guess that it has a higher mean income and/or a larger standard deviation). Several different neighborhoods might have household incomes that, if we computed their middle 95% range, would include $40,000. Certainly, a town whose mean income was $40,000 is a possibility. So would a town with the same standard deviation ($20,000) but a higher mean of, say, $60,000. Being 1 standard deviation below the mean, this household's income ($Z = -1$) would be greater than 15.87% of all households, certainly within that 95% range. Similarly, that income would be within the middle 95% range of a town with an income standard deviation of $10,000 and a mean income of $30,000 ($Z = 1$). There is no *single* possibility. If you understand this, you already understand a very important concept in the study of inferential statistics discussed in the next chapter. We will always be able to confidently reject some limited possibility (knowing that there is a slight chance of being wrong in rejecting that possibility). However, we can never state *exactly* what the random sampling procedure will produce. At best we can offer a range of outcomes within a certain **confidence interval**. With that knowledge, we will now turn to an introduction to inferential statistics.

KEY TERMS

alpha error (118)

confidence interval (119)

normal distribution (105)

Z-score (106)

confidence interval A range of values that we use to safely predict a random choice.

■ QUESTIONS AND EXERCISES

NOTE: Several more examples and exercises can be found in both the SPSS and Stata manuals that accompany this text. Means and standard deviations can be calculated as part of a frequency distribution (Section 4.1). Remember to suppress the actual frequency tables if you don't want too much output.

1. a. In any symmetrical distribution, what percentile would be associated with the mean value?
   b. What Z-score?
2. In a normal distribution, the mean will always equal the median. (T/F)
3. We compare two scores on a normal distribution. We find that the first score has a Z that is 2.5 times the size of the second score's Z. Is the corresponding percentile of the first Z also 2.5 times the size of the percentile corresponding to the second score's Z?
4. What percentage of cases (or area under the normal curve) lie BELOW a Z-score of .87?
5. If cases are normally distributed, what proportion of cases would lie between a Z-score of –1.0 and a Z-score of +1.73 (carry out to two decimal places)?
6. We wish to compare the relative standard of living for two government officials. One lives in an Italian village with a mean income of 20,500 euros and standard deviation of 4,800 euros. The other lives in a U.S. town, with a mean income of $52,000 and standard deviation of $22,750. Their respective incomes are 19,000 euros and $48,000, respectively. Who is relatively better off (compared to their locale)? Why?
7. The mean taxable family income in a state is $42,000, with a standard deviation of $17,000. That state's legislature plans to issue a special tuition voucher to each family whose taxable income falls in the bottom 15% of the distribution of family incomes. Assuming that taxable incomes are normally distributed (and that the voucher program passes constitutional muster), what is the maximum family taxable income that could be earned before being disqualified from the program? (You can use the closest applicable Z-score.)
8. A survey is conducted in one European Union nation in 2012, asking 600 respondents of voting age their views about newly re-elected U.S. president Barack Obama. One of the items in the survey asks the respondents to rate their feelings toward the U.S. president on a scale from 0 (very cold/negative) to 50 (neutral) to 100 (very positive/warm). The distribution of data is surprisingly normal. The calculated values for these 600 individuals are as follows:

Mean = 70.4 degrees
Standard deviation = 9.6 degrees

a. What percentage of respondents gave President Obama a scale rating above 85 degrees?

b. What percentage gave him a rating below 65 degrees?

c. What would be the lowest and highest ratings that define the middle 95% of the ratings given by these 600 individuals?

9. For Question 8c, is it possible to randomly draw an individual who gave President Obama less than or more than the calculated ratings? What is the probability of doing so?

10. We collect information from the FEC (Federal Election Commission) cataloguing all individual contributions given to a presidential primary candidate's election campaign. The distribution of those contributions is (surprisingly) normally distributed about the mean for that distribution. The mean is $575, with a standard deviation of $250. The candidate's advisers suggest giving out special certificates to those who contributed at least $100 (bronze), $250 (silver), $500 (gold), and $1,000 (platinum diamond). What percentage of contributors would receive each certification level? Again, drawing a normal curve will help you to understand the process here.

NOTES

1   CPI index calculated from http://www.bls.gov/data/inflation_calculator.htm. One would also need to calculate locational differences in the cost of living between the two cities, but we can probably assume that, if anything, New York City's living costs are equal, if not higher.

2   I recently consoled a student who had taken the LSAT (Law School Application Test) twice, received the same absolute score, but wound up with two different percentile placements. Evidently, in the same year, the quality of students taking the exam differed across examining periods.

3   "Michigan Changing Food Stamp Eligibility Rules," AP: http://www.mlive.com/politics/index.ssf/2011/09/michigan_changing_food_stamp_e.html.

4   We are using the middle 95% for our range of confidence. We could also reject any high income above which 95% of the households fell (one-tailed test). Looking at the normal table chart, the corresponding Z-score would be approximately –1.645 (5% above the mean). The 5% of the households would have incomes below $47,100 because:

$$-1.645 = (x_5 - \$80,000)/\$20,000$$
$$-\$32,900 = x_5 - \$80,000$$
$$x_5 = \$47,100$$

We could then safely guess that a randomly drawn household would have an income below $47,100. For illustrative purposes, we chose the middle 95%, however, much like we did in computing the interquartile range (i.e., the middle 50%).

The discussion of one- versus two-tailed tests will be discussed further in the next chapter.

An Intuitive Introduction to Inference and Hypothesis Testing

Learning Objectives:

▨ To understand the meaning and purpose of inferential statistics
▨ To understand the importance of the sampling distribution of means and the central limit theorem
▨ To understand all of the steps needed in hypothesis testing
▨ To understand the concept of statistical hypothesis testing
▨ To realize the limitations inherent in random sampling and their partial solutions
▨ To know when to use one-tailed tests

The notion of standardized Z-scores discussed so far assumes that data are normally distributed. Many exam scores are. In fact, the types of questions asked are often adjusted over time to guarantee such a normal approximation. Unfortunately, very few sets of data other than height or weight are ever normally distributed around their own mean. The distributions of societal incomes certainly are almost always positively skewed. What then is the importance of the normal distribution to these data? As we will see, several important sample statistics are normally distributed about the statistic of the population from which those samples are drawn. The mean is one such statistic; so, as we will discuss in Chapter 8, are dichotomous (two-category) proportions. The normal and other known sampling distributions are essential in the calculation and interpretation of inferential statistics.

INFERENTIAL STATISTICS

Inferential statistics are that subset of statistical theory that allows us to infer, estimate, or guess about population characteristics on the basis of characteristics of samples drawn from that population.

Before we can investigate the mathematical components of inference, we first need to draw on what we learned briefly in Chapters 1 and 2. We first need to be as certain as possible that our measurements are reliable and internally valid in the data that we collect and observe. We then ask whether that data can be generalized, and, if so, to which population, geography, time period, and so forth. Generalizability is both methodological (do I have a representative sample of the population to which I wish to generalize?) and statistical (given what I observe with my data, what is my comfortable or expected range of estimates of the true population value?).

The latter issue is one of mathematical chance or random error and assumes that the sample is representative. The former issue is one of systematic error or *external validity* (i.e., whether a representative sample actually exists). The most famous example of an externally invalid sample came out of the **Literary Digest poll of 1936**. A very large number of individuals were polled and asked how they would vote in the upcoming election. A majority stated they would vote for Alf Landon, Kansas governor and Republican presidential nominee. In reality, Democratic incumbent Franklin Delano Roosevelt was re-elected to a second term in the largest landslide in U.S. history. What went wrong? Assuming that individuals gave internally valid answers (they weren't lying nor would they legitimately change their minds by Election Day), the problem had to do with the nature of the sample. The sample was drawn disproportionately from upper-middle-class and wealthy citizens who were not only more likely to vote Republican than the voting population at large, but also more likely to respond to surveys. If the *Literary Digest* analysts had limited their conclusion to that particular type of respondent, the results would most likely have been close to reality. The trouble was in generalizing those results to a broader, demographically and politically different population. In a similar vein, polls taken by cable news talk show hosts of their viewers might be good measures of what their most ardent viewers think, but can we generalize to the entire adult population, which is probably less conservative/liberal than those viewers? Assessing whether students want a fee hike for athletics by asking students walking out of a campus gym might not validly assess what the entire student body would be willing to pay for.

Literary Digest **poll of 1936**
Poll infamous for making the wrong prediction about the outcome of the 1936 presidential election. The sample was biased toward individuals more likely to be Republicans than the voting population as a whole.

None of this should imply that unrepresentative samples are without use. An externally invalid measure can, if we can figure out the direction of the bias, work to our advantage. If a majority of ideological cable news viewers offer a majority opinion in opposition to what we would expect (e.g., a conservative audience approving of a liberal president's proposal), then we can be fairly confident that the direction of that viewpoint will be carried out to the general public (even if it is hard to exactly estimate it). If athletes are not willing to pay extra for the facilities that they will use, then we would be fairly safe in assuming that the rest of the campus population would be even more hesitant to do so. Even with its external validity problems (disproportionately Republican), we often forget that the *Literary Digest* correctly predicted FDR's 1932 (if not 1936) victory. To a certain extent, low-income citizens were less likely to vote in 1932; the sample, therefore, might have been more representative of the actual voting population in 1932 than in 1936. Perhaps more importantly, enough Republicans were upset with the Hoover administration's lack of action when the Great Depression started that they decided to punish their own party and temporarily vote like Democrats. When the Democratic Congress and FDR moved this country economically left, those Republicans returned home while poorer individuals became more likely to vote. With a survey that disproportionately interviewed Republicans and a subset of Republicans who were more likely to respond to the survey, the potential misrepresentation of the outcome became much more pronounced.[1]

How might we solve this problem? We can ask every voter how they voted, but that's tactically impossible. We can try to have a proper proportion of each category of each property that we think is theoretically relevant. Aside from the inherent difficulty of such a procedure, what if there were a property that we aren't even aware of as an important determinant of some outcome we are trying to predict? Our best bet is, when taking a sample, to make it a **random sample**, or what I prefer to call **equiprobable**. Figure out the target population to which you want to generalize. Then do whatever you can to make sure that everyone in that target population has an *equal chance* of being drawn into the sample. With a large sample size, differences in political philosophy, gender, and other attributes and behaviors will be mathematically sorted out, and the sample will look close to the targeted population, most importantly even for properties we don't even know exist but might have a causal link to the outcomes we observe.

Drawing a random or equiprobable survey also dictates that the chance of drawing any second case is not affected by the first case that is drawn. For example, if we first randomly draw a male into a sample, that doesn't mean we must next draw a female. The selection of each case must be independent of each other, much like the flipping of a coin.[2] Even if we flip ten heads in a row, since the flips are independent of each other, we still have a 50% chance of flipping a head on the 11th try. Similarly it is possible, although

random (equiprobable) sample A random sample assumes that any case within the target population we are analyzing has an *equal chance* of being drawn into the sample as any other case. Also referred to as an equiprobable sample.

highly unlikely, that we could randomly draw a sample that was almost entirely made up of men. Even if the first nine individuals sampled were male, in a purely random selection process, we would not change our sampling technique to guarantee sampling a female on the 10th try.

The mathematical rules that define inference are based on the laws of chance. Given any kind of Las Vegas game, there is a certain *expectation* about what outcome should be produced. The gambling odds are based on these expectations. In the long run, with a large enough sample, or with repeated samples or trials, what is actually *observed* should look much like what is *expected*. However, with a small sample, or a single trial, what is observed might be rather different from what we would expect *in the long run*. Let's take the example of tossing a coin. Don't worry about the math. Think about it intuitively. The probability of flipping a head or tail at any time is .50 (i.e., you would have a 50% chance of flipping either a head or tail). This assumes, as with any random technique, that there is no bias to either the coin (it is equally distributed between its head and tail) or the flipper (one doesn't always start with the head facing up and flipping it so it rotates the same number of times). Those biases would make the flips internally invalid as we are not measuring the true probability of a random flip, but rather the error produced by an off-center coin or strategic flipper. If you were to flip a coin a large number of times, you would *expect* heads to be produced 50% of the time and tails the other 50%. With a small number of flips, say ten, we would not want to bet the farm on an exact 50%/50% split. Just on the basis of mathematical chance, or, stated differently, the luck of the toss, we might come up with 50%/50%, or 60%/40%, or 40%/60%, and so forth. There is even a slight chance that on one trial of ten we may toss ten heads (100%/0%), or ten tails, although that is unlikely. What we *observe* with any one trial is not always what we would theoretically *expect* (50/50). We always have to allow for a range of possibilities.

The Law of Large Numbers

Does that allowance change as we increase our number of flips? With 1 million flips, we would probably be willing to bet that the number of heads would be within a certain range, and that that range would be proportionately less than with 100 or 10 flips. Think about it. How much would you be willing to bet that the proportion of heads with 10 flips would be neither 0 (0%) nor 10 (100%)? Some, but if you are as cautious as I am, probably not your life's salary. Now, with 1 million flips, would you be more willing to bet or willing to bet more money against 0 (0%) or 1 million (100%) heads? Probably so. As the saying goes, there is safety in numbers. In most of my classes, few students will bet that the number of heads will be between 3 and 7. However, I can usually get most to bet that the number of heads will be between 300,000 and 700,000 (at least hypothetically), even though

law of large numbers As we increase our sample size, our estimates of population values draw closer to the true population value.

the proportions are the same (30%–70%). I actually don't flip a coin 1 million times, although a computer can simulate that occurrence. As we increase our number of tosses, or our sample size, we will be more willing to bet on a smaller proportional range of possibilities. We can say that we are confident with a *proportionately* smaller range of possibilities as we increase our number of tosses. We might be wrong as even 1 million heads in a row is theoretically possible, but we sense that the chance of being wrong in rejecting a range of extreme possibilities (0 to 299,999, 700,001 to 1 million heads) is minimal. So we are willing to risk the bet.

Note that we would never bet on any *particular number* of heads, especially when the number of tosses is high. With 1 million flips, we would have to be enormous risk takers to bet that we will flip *exactly* 500,000 heads and 500,000 tails or any other particular split. We will, however, bet on a range of possibilities. Similarly, when we draw samples of individuals from a large pool, say the entire U.S. voting population, we have to make the same allowance for observing in a sample something different from what we expect (i.e., would find in the population from which a sample is drawn). If 52%

Sidebar 6.1: Sampling and the U.S. Census—Political Changes?

In 2000, the U.S. Census Bureau collected short form schedules from more than 100 million households. The information gathered was limited to the number of individuals per household, age, gender, and race/ethnicity (the first and last needed for redistricting purposes). Roughly 18 million households were asked to fill out the long form that gathered other types of demographic and economic information needed for the allocation of federal, state, and local funds. Some considered the long form too intrusive, costly to administer, and without constitutional justification. Others viewed those concerns as a not so subtle way to make it more difficult to administer governmental programs and perhaps, because of the lack of information, eliminate them. Another concern was the way in which unresponsive households might be counted, if at all. Suggestions were offered that included taking a mean average of the number of individuals in adjacent households or conducting a follow-up, face-to-face random survey of those households.

In 1999, the U.S. Supreme Court argued that only a full counting, or enumeration, could be used to determine the population of each state for apportionment purposes (i.e., the number of congressional districts allocated to each state). However, it left unchallenged the use of annual sampling for estimating a series of demographic figures, such as race, age, and income, for the allocation of government resources. See *Department of Commerce et al. v. U.S. House of Representatives et al.* (525 U.S. 316 (1999)). Congress, however, limited the number of demographic features that could be asked of respondents in the 2010 Census long form. For those figures, one must turn to the annual American Community Survey that, because of its smaller sample size and limited counting of communities with small populations, is not as accurate as was the long form.

of the people in the adult population are female, we may draw a small sample with the same percentage, but we have to allow for some variation just because of the luck of the draw. Inferential statistics basically tell us how much variation we must accept solely based on mathematical chance (i.e., the luck of the random draw). They cannot directly measure the impact of internal bias (the wrong question is asked) or external bias (we purposely/accidentally oversample men by only interviewing in bars). Let's carry out the argument by extending the logic of income distributions and mean incomes presented in Chapter 5. We will turn fully to proportions in Chapter 8.

THE SAMPLING DISTRIBUTION OF MEANS AND THE CENTRAL LIMIT THEOREM

Let us begin by taking a random sample of 100 or more households from my California neighborhood (2006). For that sample, we can compute a mean value for income, designated as $\overline{X}_1$. It may be equal to the mean for all of the households, but it may be somewhat higher or lower, just because of the random luck of the draw. For example, you may have randomly chosen a few extra extremely wealthy households, the equivalent of proportionately more heads than tails, thereby producing a mean for the sample higher than the mean for the entire neighborhood. Say we take a second independent random sample of equal size and calculate its mean ($\overline{X}_2$), we take a third and calculate its mean ($\overline{X}_3$), and so on for a large number of samples. After you calculate each mean, plot it on a graph just as you did for individual values. Place each mean on the line according to its value, designating it as $\overline{X}$. Continue to do so for each sample mean. If you draw a sample with a mean income equal to one drawn previously, stack it atop (give equal heights to each plotted mean value). If we look at all of our sample means together, we have a distribution of sample means, known as the **sampling distribution of means**.

$$\overline{X} \quad \overline{X} \quad \overline{\dfrac{\overline{X}}{X}} \quad \overline{X}\,\overline{X} \quad \overline{X}\,\overline{X}$$

$80,000 = mean of all households in town

If we draw a very large number of independent samples, compute their means, and plot them, our sampling distribution of means will be approximately normally distributed around the mean income for every household in the neighborhood. This phenomenon is referred to as the **central limit theorem**. Since the distribution is normal, the mean (this may seem tricky, so read through it carefully) of all of the sample means will be equal to the mean of

sampling distribution of means The distribution of means drawn from an infinite or very large set of random samples from a population that results in a normal distribution around the true population mean.

central limit theorem The distribution of sample means and dichotomous proportions will be normally distributed around the population mean, regardless of the shape of the original, individual data distribution.

the individual incomes for the entire neighborhood (i.e., *the mean of the sampling distribution is the same as the population mean of the variable*).

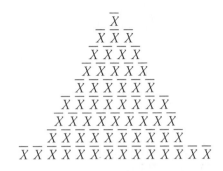

$80,000 = mean of all individual households
$80,000 = mean of all sample means

What is extremely important is that the means of an infinite or very large number of samples of size greater than 100 randomly drawn from a population will be roughly normally distributed around the population mean, *regardless of the shape of the original distribution of individual values* (x_i). Even if our original distribution of household incomes is positively skewed, or negatively skewed, or bimodal, or so forth, the distribution of means computed from a large number of samples ($N > 100$) will *always be approximately normal*.

Before we move on, let's discuss some new terminology. To avoid confusion, we need to find a way to differentiate between the values associated with an entire population (e.g., all of the neighborhood's households) and the values associated with any given sample drawn from that population (e.g., 100 of those households). By convention, statisticians use letters from the Greek alphabet to denote population statistics or parameters and letters from the Roman alphabet to denote sample statistics. The mean of any sample will thus be denoted as we have before as $\overline{X}$. The mean of an entire population from which that sample was drawn is denoted as μ_x, the lower case "mu." Similarly, the standard deviation of a sample of cases will be denoted as s_x, and the standard deviation of the population as σ_x, the lowercase "sigma."

Remember that the mean of all of the sample means ($\overline{X}_1, \overline{X}_2, \overline{X}_3, \ldots$) is equal to the mean of all of the individual values in the entire population (μ_x):

$$\mu_x = \mu_{\overline{X}} \tag{6.1}$$

where μ_x is the mean of all of the individual values (x) in a population
$\mu_{\overline{X}}$ is the mean of all of the means ($\overline{X}$) of samples randomly drawn from that population

Sidebar 6.2: The Central Limit Theorem in Real Time

As a way to visualize the central limit theorem, Figure 6.1 was produced. We started with the 54,535-case 2012 CCES (Cooperative Congressional Election Study) data set as our "population." Next, 1,000 rounds of 1,000 samples of $N = 1,000$ were randomly drawn from that population, with the means of each sample plotted. For simplicity, the means were clustered into 30 equally divided bins or categories. Note that even with sample size of only 1,000 the distribution of sample means very nearly fits the pattern of a normal curve. The mean of all of these samples is 52.23, not very different from the true mean of the population.

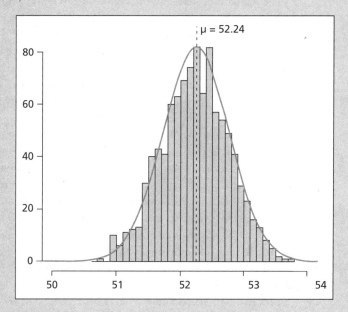

FIGURE 6.1 1,000 samples of $N = 1,000$

The standard deviation of the means ($\overline{X}$'s) of the samples drawn from a population will, however, be smaller than the standard deviation of the individual values (x's) of that population and is a function of the sample size (i.e., the larger the number of cases within the samples, the more closely proximate will the sample means be to the population mean). Think of it in terms of the influence of extreme values. One extremely high income will tend to pull the mean out to the right of the distribution since the distribution will be positively skewed. If the sample size is relatively small, one high value will exert an extremely strong pull as one large income needs to be redistributed among a small number of other cases. However, if the sample size is large, that one income will not have so strong a pull since it will be balanced by many other cases. As another example, think of sampling men in Brooklyn, New York, and computing their heights or weights. New Brooklyn Nets center Kevin Garnett has an equiprobable chance of being drawn into a sample. If the sample is small, say 10, the inclusion of his height (almost 7 feet) will make that sample's mean quite different from the true mean of the entire population, and different from the means of samples in which he is not included. If the sample is quite large, say 2,000, whether Garnett is drawn into the sample makes little difference on that sample's mean computation.

The standard deviation of the sample means is also a function of the standard deviation of the original, individual values. As an extreme example, if everyone had the same income, then the individual values would all be equal to each other and, therefore, would not deviate at all from the population mean. Any sample would have the same mean as any other sample. They would not deviate from each other. The greater the dispersion or deviation among the individual incomes, however, the greater the possible difference between the means of two randomly drawn samples as well as between the mean of a sample and the mean of the entire population. One sample may have randomly drawn a few extremely wealthy individuals, and another a few extremely poor ones.

Sample means within a sampling distribution of means can be thought of exactly the same way as individual values distributed normally about a population mean. Actual sample mean values can be standardized using the Z-score formula, with a few changes in representation. Remember that in the standard *individualized* Z-score formula, our normal curve represented the distribution of individual values (say income) as they deviated from the central point of the distribution, its mean. Those deviation scores were then standardized by dividing by the standard deviation of the *individual* values. The individualized Z-score formula was represented by:

$$Z_i = \frac{x_i - \overline{X}}{s_x} \tag{6.2}$$

where x_i stands for the individual value on a given variable X

$\overline{X}$ stands for the mean of the distribution of a given variable X

s_x stands for the standard deviation of the individual values of a given variable X

Similarly, the theoretical distribution of sample means around the population mean would also be represented by a normal curve. The Z-score formula for sample means distributed around the population mean would be represented by:

$$Z_{\overline{X}} = \frac{\overline{X} - \mu_x}{\sigma_{\overline{X}}} \tag{6.3}$$

where $\overline{X}$ stands for the individual sample mean

μ_x stands for the mean of the distribution of individual values for the entire population

$\sigma_{\bar{x}}$ stands for the *standard deviation of the sample means*, commonly called the **standard error of the mean**

The standard error of the mean, as mentioned, is a function of both the standard deviation of the entire population and the sample size and is computed as follows:

$$\sigma_{\overline{X}} = \frac{\sigma_x}{\sqrt{N}} \tag{6.4}$$

where σ_x stands for the standard deviation of the individual values for the entire population

N stands for the size of the sample (number of cases) randomly drawn from that population

Let us return to our California example (2006). Suppose we draw a large number of random samples of households from the entire neighborhood. The mean of the samples would be equal to the population mean more often than any other single mean (it would be the modal category), but we could also draw samples with means less than or greater than the population mean according to the probabilities associated with the normal curve. If we draw independent random samples of 400 cases ($N = 400$), then the standard error of the mean would be equal to $1,000 because:

$$\sigma_{\overline{X}} = \frac{\$20,000}{\sqrt{400}} = \$1000 \tag{6.5}$$

In other words, the standard deviation of the means of a very large number of samples of size 400 randomly drawn from that population would be $1,000, much smaller than the $20,000 standard deviation of the individual household incomes. As the distribution of sample means is normal, 95% of all possible random independent samples would have means that lie between a corresponding Z-score of -1.96 and $+1.96$. Using our standard Z-score formula for sample means drawn from a population, we see that 95% of the samples of 400 (N) that could be drawn from a population with a mean income of $80,000 ($\mu_x$), and a standard deviation of $20,000, would have means between $78,040 and $81,960 because:

$-1.96 = (\overline{X}_{2.5} - \$80,000)/\$1,000$ $+1.96 = (\overline{X}_{97.5} - \$80,000)/\$1,000$

$\overline{X}_{2.5} = -1.96\,(\$1,000) + \$80,000$ $\overline{X}_{97.5} = +1.96\,(\$1,000) + \$80,000$

$\overline{X}_{2.5} = -\$1,960 + \$80,000$ $\overline{X}_{97.5} = +\$1,960 + \$80,000$

$\overline{X}_{2.5} = \$78,040$ $\overline{X}_{97.5} = \$81,960$

$$\mathbf{\$78,040 < \overline{X} < \$81,960}$$

Translation: 95% of all the possible samples (of size 400) that can be randomly drawn from this population of households will have a *mean sample*

standard error of the mean
The standard deviation of sample means in a sampling distribution of means based on dividing the standard deviation of the individual cases by the square root of the sample size.

income between $78,040 and $81,960. In drawing a sample of 400, therefore, we can expect to be off by as much as $1,960 (give or take) when we calculate a sample mean just by the luck of the random draw of 400. This $1,960 is called the *margin of error* expected with a sample of 400 (and the given standard deviation). We will be off by as much as $1,960 less or more than the true population mean (of $80,000) *95% of the time.* This range is commonly called the 95% "confidence interval" of possible sample means. It is *possible* to randomly draw a sample of this size and come up with a sample mean income less than $78,040 or greater than $81,960, but the *probability* of doing so is less than 5%.

If we randomly drew 400 households from this neighborhood, we would guess the mean income for that sample to be somewhere between those two figures, and we would have a .95 probability of being correct. If we made that guess for all of the samples, we would be correct 95% of the time. Not bad odds by Las Vegas standards. However, always remember that even 95% certainty is not total. On any given random draw, we could produce a sample with a mean income outside of this range, say $83,000 or $77,000 but we rather confidently reject those possibilities as highly, if not totally, unlikely.

An Example: The Gender Gap in Wages

Much has been made over the last several decades about income disparities between men and women. Currently, women as a whole make about 77 cents for every dollar made by men, roughly 82 cents when limited to full-time or salaried workers.[3] Although the gap has narrowed since the 1960s, and is greatly reduced among younger cohorts of men and women, the gender wage gap actually increases as one moves up the economic ladder. Our California neighborhood, with its $80,000 mean household salary, is ranked above all households within the nation with a mean of roughly $71,000 and median of roughly $51,000 (positively skewed).[4] For the sake of argument, let us stipulate that we only have information about the mean and standard deviations of income for the entire metropolitan neighborhood. So now let us say that we are given a listing of households in which men are the sole or main income earner (henceforth labeled "male households"). We are not, however, given a listing of all such households' incomes. We wish to know if male-headed households earn more, on mean average, than households in this neighborhood generally. We have enough time and money to interview only 400 such households. We randomly draw a sample of 400 of these households from among this population, ask their income, and compute a mean household income of $83,000 for male-contributing households, which is higher, on (mean) average, than the population of all households as a whole. Could we have randomly drawn *any* 400 households from the entire population and come up with that high a mean by chance alone (i.e., without specifying any particular demographic subset)? The answer is probably not;

that is, the possibility of randomly drawing a sample of 400 households with a mean income greater than $81,960 is fairly remote (less than 2.5%; mean incomes higher than $81,960 fall beyond the top end of the 95% range specified). Another way of expressing this is to say that the mean of our male sample is "significantly different" from the mean of the population of all households. Thus, we reject the possibility (commonly called the null hypothesis, H_0) that this sample could have been randomly drawn from a population with a mean income of $80,000. Male households in this neighborhood, in all likelihood, have incomes with a higher mean average than the general population. Might we be wrong in this guess? Certainly, but it is highly unlikely.[5]

If, on the other hand, our sample produced a mean income within the specified range of acceptance or confidence interval (e.g., $81,000), we would not be able to reject the null hypothesis, that is, the probability that the mean income of *all* male households equaled the mean income of all households ($80,000). The sample mean of $81,000 is not "significantly" different enough to reject that probability. The $1,000 difference between what we *observed* ($\overline{X}$) in the sample and what we would have *expected* from the original population (μ_x) is small enough to be attributed to the random luck of the draw (i.e., it is within an acceptable level of sampling or random error). Note that not being able to confidently reject the null hypothesis that the true mean of the entire male population is $80,000 *does not* tell us what the true population mean for those households actually is. It does not, for example, give us proof that the mean for this subgroup is exactly $80,000. At best, we can only say that the sample mean ($80,000) is *not statistically inconsistent* with such a possibility.

Similarly, as we cautioned at the end of the previous chapter, confidently rejecting a possibility is not the same as knowing which possibility to accept. We feel safe in stating that a sample with a mean income of $83,000 was probably not randomly drawn from a population with a mean income of $80,000, but *we have no way of exactly knowing* what the mean for the entire population of contributing households may be. Of course, knowing what the population mean probably isn't may not give us as much information as we need. We may wish to derive a range of possible population means; that is, given a certain sample mean, within what range of values could we "safely" or "confidently" say that the mean of the population from which that sample was randomly drawn would lie?

Let us return to our example. The sample of 400 male households produced a mean income of $83,000. We don't know the mean income for the population from which that sample was randomly drawn (i.e., all male households), although we are rather confident that it is not $80,000. If we don't know the mean for that population (μ_x), then, quite obviously, we can't know the population standard deviation (s_x), a necessary element in computing the standard error of the mean ($\sigma_{\overline{X}}$). Do not fear. Because standard deviations are fairly consistent across samples (the reason we use them rather than mean

Sidebar 6.3: The Gender Gap in Wages

Several laws and actions, starting with the 1963 Equal Pay Act, Title VII of the 1964 Civil Rights Act, the 2009 Lilly Ledbetter Fair Pay Act, several state and local acts, and, most recently, President Obama's 2014 Executive Order to enforce provisions of the yet-to-be-passed Paycheck Fairness Act, attempt to enforce a narrowing of the gap in wages between the genders.[1] Some critics of these laws state, with justification, that wage differences are based upon a host of factors including self-made choices, particularly the time that women have spent on the job (disrupted by raising children). Others argue that, even when controlling for all of these differences, a gender wage gap of about 9 percentage points still exists, indicating true discrimination in the workforce.[2] See sidebar, Chapter 10, on Simpson's Paradox for a more thorough discussion of these possibilities.

[1] See U.S. Equal Employment Opportunity Commission, http://www.eeoc.gov/laws/types/equalcompensation.cfm, for a review of all wage discrimination laws.
[2] See Francine D. Blau and Lawrence M. Kahn, "The Gender Gap: Have Women Gone as Far as They Can," *Academy of Management Perspectives* 21 (2007): 7–23. Not surprisingly, this article has been used to justify both sides of the wage gap argument.

absolute deviations), we can usually use the standard deviation of our sample (s_x) as an estimate of the standard deviation of the population from which that sample was randomly drawn. Thus, our formula for deriving the standard error of the mean would be as follows:

$$\sigma_{\overline{X}} = \frac{\sigma_x}{\sqrt{N}} \approx \frac{s_x}{\sqrt{N}} \tag{6.6}$$

where s_x stands for the standard deviation of the random sample (computed using a denominator of $N-1$)[6]

N is the size of the sample (number of cases)

Our task now is to estimate what the mean income of all male households might be. It can be $83,000, but it may be slightly lower or higher than that. Remember, any samples may be off by some margin of random sampling error. We need to determine the range of means of populations this sample may have been randomly drawn from. Stated differently, from what populations could this sample of 400 have *probably* been randomly drawn? Let's begin with a visual presentation. Look at Figure 6.2. The normal distribution to the left represents the distribution of means of random samples around a certain population mean (μ_L). Our sample with a mean of $83,000 could have been randomly drawn from a population with a mean income of μ_L, lying just at the top of that distribution's 95% range, corresponding to a Z-score of +1.96. Our sample would lie on the bottom of the 95% range of the distribution to the right, with a mean represented by μ_H, corresponding to a Z-score

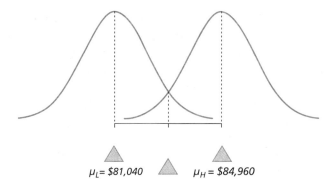

$\mu_L = \$81,040$ $\mu_H = \$84,960$

FIGURE 6.2 Two-Curve Population Estimate

of –1.96. Our sample mean *would also fall within the 95% range of distributions anchored by means between μ_L and μ_H*. Stated differently, a sample with a mean of \$83,000 could have been randomly drawn from populations with means anywhere between those two figures (including \$83,000).

The sample of 400 contributing households produced a sample mean of \$83,000. If the standard deviation of incomes of that sample was \$20,000 (as it is coincidentally for the entire population—they need not be the same), then our estimate of the standard error of the mean ($\sigma_{\bar{x}}$) would be, as before, \$1,000. We now need to compute two formulas to solve for two hypothetical population means (μ_L and μ_H). This would give us the lowest (μ_L) and the highest (μ_H) means of populations from which this sample could have probably been randomly drawn:

$$+1.96 = (\$83,000 - \mu_L)/\$1,000 \qquad -1.96 = (\$83,000 - \mu_H)/\$1,000$$
$$+\$1,960 = \$83,000 - \mu_L \qquad -\$1,960 = \$83,000 - \mu_H$$
$$-\mu_L = \$1,960 - \$83,000 \qquad -\mu_H = -\$1,960 - \$83,000$$
$$-\mu_L = -\$81,040 \qquad -\mu_H = -\$84,960$$
$$\mu_L = \$81,040 \qquad \mu_H = \$84,960$$
$$\$81,040 < \mu_x < \$84,960$$

What we do in computing this "reverse confidence interval" around our sample mean is to specify the lowest and highest theoretical means of a population from which our sample could have been randomly drawn. The mean of \$83,000 would be the highest probable mean for a sample randomly drawn from a population with a true mean of \$81,040; it would be the lowest probable mean of a sample randomly drawn from a population with a true mean of \$84,960. We would not want to reject the possibility that this sample could have been drawn randomly from any population with a mean between these two values (e.g., $82,000 or $84,000), because the sample mean of $83,000 would be within the 95% confidence intervals of the sampling distribution of means of any such population. The differences between $83,000 and those two figures are small enough to attribute to the random luck of the draw. The true mean income of all contributing households might not be either $82,000 or $84,000, but a sample mean of $83,000 is *not statistically inconsistent* with either of those possibilities, or any possibility in between. Might this sample have been drawn from a population with a mean income outside of that range? Certainly, but the possibility is slim.

HYPOTHESIS TESTING

We have just conceptually gone through an example of statistical hypothesis testing. Hypothesis testing is used to see if our real-world observations confirm our hypothesized expectations. In this instance, we were trying to determine if male households earned more, on mean average, than the population of all households. That is the hypothesis that we are trying to confirm (denoted as H_1). In almost all texts, the term "hypothesis testing" refers only to Step 5, and that is what we will concentrate on in this chapter. As research is more than just about numbers, however, we should really be looking at all of the following. Steps 6 and 7 will be covered in later chapters.

- STEP 1: Are our measurements reliable and internally valid? Are our respondents making up numbers, or are they listing higher/lower amounts than they actually earned (an example of the Bradley effect mentioned in Chapter 2). If we are confident enough of the reliability and internal validity of our measurement, then we turn to . . .
- STEP 2: Does our hypothesis make theoretical sense? Do we have an adequate reason to expect the hypothesized relationship to exist? If so, we then turn to . . .
- STEP 3: Is our sample a random, equiprobable representation of all targeted (male) households (i.e., is our sampling method externally valid)? If we are confident enough that it is, then we turn to . . .
- STEP 4: Does our observation match our hypothesized expectation (H_1)? Yes, as in this instance, the mean income level of male households is greater than that of the household population as a whole. We now turn to . . .
- STEP 5: *Is the observed difference small enough to attribute to the random luck of the draw or significant enough to confidently reject that as a possibility? If the latter, then we can confidently (but never absolutely) reject the null hypothesis (H_0) that the incomes of all of the male households and all households generally are the same ($80,000).*
- STEP 6: Along with Steps 1 and 2, are there other reasons why our two variables are related. Are there any alternate explanations? If so, then . . .
- STEP 7: Can we generalize our hypothesis to other populations, times, experimental conditions?

There are actually two ways to statistically test this hypothesis (Step 5). The first, as we saw, is to figure out, using a 95% confidence interval test, the estimated range of the means of populations from which this sample was randomly drawn. The income of $83,000 is outside of that range. The other is to determine the Z-score of a household with an observed income of $83,000 compared to a hypothesized population mean of $80,000. If it is outside of the margin of error used, then we can confidently reject the null hypothesis that this set of households was randomly sampled from that hypothesized population.

$$Z_{\overline{X}} = \frac{\overline{X} - \mu_x}{\sigma_{\overline{X}}} \qquad (6.7)$$

$$Z_{\overline{X}} = \frac{\$83,000 - \$80,000}{\$1,000} = 3$$

A Z-score of 3 is certainly beyond our margin of error (corresponding to a Z of 1.96). We can therefore confidently, but not absolutely, reject the possibility that this male household sample could have been randomly drawn from a population of all male households with a mean income of $80,000 ($H_0$). In all likelihood, male households, on mean average, make more than all households in this neighborhood (H_1).

Two important decisions need to be made regarding any inferential statistic. First, what confidence interval are we comfortable with; that is, proportionately *how often* do we wish to chance being wrong in rejecting values outside of that interval or range (the "null hypothesis" when dealing with single means)? This is a function of our gambling sensitivities and what the profession views as acceptable for mathematical "significance." Ninety-five percent is not a sacred confidence interval, but one that is generally used in the profession. Second, within that confidence interval, by *how much* can we afford to be off? What margin of error between our sample observation and true population value can we accept? This is a function of the sample size, which, as you recall, is used in computing the standard error of the mean ($\sigma_{\overline{X}}$). Look at the formula. Does doubling the sample size reduce our margin of error by half? No. I'll leave it to the reader to figure this out in one of the exercises at the end of this chapter.

CONSIDERATIONS IN SAMPLING

Under most circumstances, it is only the size of the sample, not the size of the population that is important in calculating standard errors and margins of error. When the population is relatively small, however, the margin of error is reduced. As long as the sample size is 5% or less of the population, we need not worry about this adjustment. Most national, state, or even local surveys would usually be sampling far less than 5% of their relevant populations.

The sample size, in and of itself, however, is not as important as how that sample was produced. As mentioned previously, all of our calculations are based on a random, or equiprobable, sample. Each individual in the target population must have an equal chance of being included in the sample. Although modern media and polling agencies are much more careful than the *Literary Digest* had been, a rush to make the first prediction often leads to similar results in kind if not magnitude. In the 2000 presidential election in Florida, the prediction that Al Gore would win that state was partially based on a sample that did not include those western counties where the polls closed later than the rest of the state. These are counties that tend to be more Republican than the state as a whole. Of course, if we look at voter intentions rather than the tabulation of ballots, Al Gore did receive more votes than the certified winner, George W. Bush. Some Floridians seem to have voted for Pat Buchanan even though they thought they voted for Gore. In either case, the margin was so slim, however, that no prediction should probably have been made. The eventual declaration of "too close to call" was perhaps the most responsible.

Totally random samples are usually impossible to produce. The problem is more one of logistics and costs than anything else. Let us say that we want to draw a sample of 2,000 voting-age individuals throughout the country, and we want to interview each of those individuals face-to-face (a procedure that increases both our response rate and the number of questions that we can ask). Even if we could easily acquire a full national listing of every eligible voter, the cost to send an interviewer out to each possible sampling area would be prohibitive. A purely random sample might choose one person in the far reaches of northern Alaska, one in the mountains of Utah, and one in the vast expanses of South or North Dakota. The possibility even exists that the 2,000 respondents will be so geographically distributed that we would have to send out 2,000 interviewers to collect the needed responses in a short period of time.

In order to limit the costs of interviewing, many survey organizations vary their sampling method to approximate but not replicate a pure random sample. The American National Election Studies (ANES) surveys that produce most of the data political scientists use to analyze presidential and congressional elections employ such a strategy—that of a multistage random area sample. Think of it as a series of random samples. A standard procedure would be to first randomly sample congressional districts or some other, U.S. Census–defined, primary sampling units. Next, from each of those units initially sampled, a random sample of geographic subunits, perhaps voting precincts, would be drawn. We would continue this procedure of randomly sampling smaller units until we reached a sample of households. Last, one individual from each household would be randomly selected. Because this is a series of random samples, the margins of error will be a bit higher than those produced by a purely one-shot random sample. The organizations that produce such samples will normally give these adjusted figures. For example, a typical ANES survey would list a maximum margin of error of 6% for a sample size (N) of 500. For a pure random sample, the maximum margin of error would be less than 4.5%. Keep in mind that, unless they can be reprogrammed, standard statistical packages assume total randomness, and thus lower margins of error.

Also note that intentionally or not, samples might be quite different in characteristics than the population, even by more than what the random luck of the draw could produce. The Eurobarometer and World Values Survey series are two that intentionally adjust their samples.[7] In order to produce a statistically meaningful (i.e., fairly low margin of error and representative demographic diversity) sample in each country included, it is necessary for the sample size in each country to be fairly large. The Eurobarometer researchers set the figure at about 1,000, and the World Values Survey sets the figure at roughly 1,500. Not all countries, however, have equal populations. As long as each country is analyzed separately, then no problem exists. However, if all the cases from all the countries are combined, then some countries might be overrepresented given their small size. The 1,500 respondents from Estonia will carry as much weight in the survey as the 1,500 from Russia, even though the Russian population is about 100 times greater. There are two ways to compensate for this over- and underrepresentation. One, to increase the size of the sample in the larger countries commensurate with their larger populations, would be prohibitively expensive. To proportionately match the 1,500 Estonians, more than 150,000 Russians would have to be surveyed. The other is to apply a weight to each respondent to reduce or increase his/her contribution to the results by the proportion by which they are over- or underrepresented. Each Russian's response might be duplicated ten times. Alternatively, each Estonian's could be worth .1. Similar weights need to be applied to samples that purposely oversample certain demographic groups (e.g., African-Americans in a U.S. nationwide survey) or those that unintentionally undersample individuals who work during the day.

Even with careful sampling, responses might not measure what they are intended to measure, producing a source of internal invalidity. Question wording might affect how people answer. Even timing is important. For example, polls conducted several days before an election might accurately portray the intentions of the voters on the day the question was asked. In many recent elections (the 2012 South Carolina primary comes to mind), however, many voters had not made up their minds until a few days before or the day of the election. If that last-minute vote swing is one-sided, the final results can be quite different from the earlier predictions. The now famous, but incorrect headline announcing the 1948 victory of Republican Thomas Dewey over incumbent President Harry Truman was based on a poll that had been conducted more than one week before the election. Many Democrats decided to either turn out to vote for their candidate the week of the election or, as is usually the case, switched their vote intentions away from third-party candidates as the Election Day neared.

Even with careful sampling, question wording, and timing, we need to remember that the margins of error calculated *are not absolute*. Although a sample proportion might be off by as much as or no more than a certain amount 95% of the time, it will be off by more than that amount 5% of the time. In other words, even the most careful of surveyors will be wrong in the range of possibilities they report 1 out of 20 times. In a one-sided race or issue preference, the general prediction will still be correct. However, what about in a close race? One should always remember, but not be paralyzed by, the fact that in 100 flips of a coin, 100 heads can turn up.

T-TESTS AND STATISTICAL HYPOTHESIS TESTING

One last point before we move on. When the population standard deviation is unknown, we should really be looking not at the normal distribution associated with Z-scores, but at a series of distributions known as "t." The *t*-test (or Student's *t*) is a series of curves that look like the normal curve, unimodal and symmetrical, but flatten out and widen as our sample size decreases. A differently shaped distribution exists for each *degree of freedom* (*df*) of our distribution (see Figure 6.3). For "t," the degrees of freedom are equal to $N - 1$. Given a set mean, each value of the distribution can be changed except for the last one, thus $N - 1$ degrees of freedom.[8] For large samples (100 or greater), the *t*-distribution approximates the normal curve, and thus Z-scores can be used as approximations. With sample sizes less than 100, calculations based on *t*-scores would have to be used, even when the population standard deviation is known. The logic, however, is exactly the same. The 95% confidence intervals would just be bounded by *t*-scores with absolute values greater than 1.96. A table of the *t*-score intervals follows (see Table 6.1). Fortunately, most computer programs like SPSS and Stata use *t*-scores for absolute precision.

t-test Also known as the Student's t is a series of symmetrical distributions based on sample size ($N - 1$) that approaches the normal (Z) curve as the sample size increases.

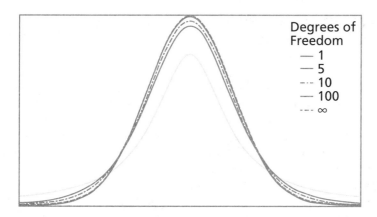

FIGURE 6.3 *t*-Test Values

TABLE 6.1 *t*-Test Values

α (Alpha) One-Tailed	.05	.025	.01	.005
α (Alpha) Two-Tailed	.1	.05	.02	.01
df				
1	6.314	12.707	31.819	63.655
2	2.920	4.303	6.965	9.925
3	2.353	3.182	4.541	5.841
4	2.132	2.776	3.747	4.604
5	2.015	2.571	3.365	4.032
6	1.943	2.447	3.143	3.707
7	1.895	2.365	2.998	3.500
8	1.860	2.306	2.897	3.355
9	1.833	2.262	2.821	3.250
10	1.812	2.228	2.764	3.169
11	1.796	2.201	2.718	3.106
12	1.782	2.179	2.681	3.055
13	1.771	2.160	2.650	3.012
14	1.761	2.145	2.625	2.977
15	1.753	2.131	2.603	2.947
16	1.746	2.120	2.584	2.921
17	1.740	2.110	2.567	2.898
18	1.734	2.101	2.552	2.878
19	1.729	2.093	2.540	2.861
20	1.725	2.086	2.528	2.845
30	1.697	2.042	2.457	2.750
100	1.660	1.984	2.364	2.626
Infinity	**1.645**	**1.960**	2.326	2.576

STATISTICAL HYPOTHESIS TESTING AND ONE-TAILED TESTS

If, as we did in our male household example, posit a certain direction to our hypothesis, then a **one-tailed significance test** can and should be used. The 5% cutoff would not come evenly from both sides of the normal or t-distribution, but only the top, positive end. We are not even considering the alternative that the sample mean may be lower than the mean of the population. Fifty percent of the rejected area is therefore below the mean, and 45% is above. We therefore need to find a figure on the Z-score table close to 45% or .4500. That would lie about equally between 1.64 and 1.65 (see Figure 6.4). We can therefore reject our null hypothesis even if the calculated Z-score is less than +1.96 but above 1.645 (see the last value listed in the first column of Table 6.1). Ours ($Z = 3$) certainly qualifies.

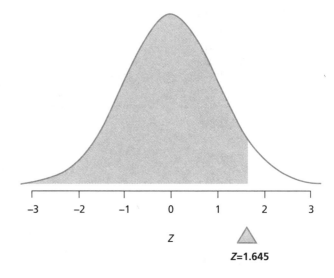

one-tailed significance test A test to gauge the significance of the difference between our sample observation and expected population value when a direction is posited.

FIGURE 6.4 One-Tailed Test, $Z = 1.645$

KEY TERMS

central limit theorem (127)   random (equiprobable) sample (124)

law of large numbers (125)   sampling distribution of means (127)

Literary Digest poll of 1936 (123)   standard error of the mean (131)

one-tailed significance test (142)   *t*-test (140)

QUESTIONS AND EXERCISES

NOTE: Several more examples and exercises can be found in both the SPSS and Stata manuals that accompany this text. *t*-tests for the comparison of a sample and population mean can be found in Section 4.3.

1. If we draw a very large number of random samples ($N > 100$) from a given population, and compute the mean age of each sample, the distribution of those sample means will be approximately normal:

    a. Only if the distribution of individual ages is normal
    b. Only if the mean of individual ages equals the median
    c. Regardless of the shape of the original distribution of individual ages
    d. Only if the standard deviation of age is 0

2. The standard deviation of all of those sample means is a function of both the standard deviation of the individual ages in the population and _____.

3. We compute the mean age of all *individuals* in the population as 47 years. We draw a large number of random samples of individuals from that population ($N > 100$) and compute the mean age for each sample. The mean of all of those mean sample ages would be _____ years.

4. Describe, in words, what is meant by the standard error of the mean.

5. The central limit theorem only applies to the distribution of sample means (T/F).

6. With a randomly drawn sample of 800, a sample mean weight of 170 lbs., and a sample standard deviation of 20 lbs., what would be our estimate of the range of possible mean weights of the population from which this sample was drawn? With a sample size of 400? With a sample size of 200? In each instance, can we confidently reject the possibility that the true population mean weight is 168 lbs.? Can we reject that possibility without any chance of being wrong?

7. A government program in a European country is set up to distribute subsidized business loans in towns with a mean independent, single-owned business income below 30,000 euros. Samples of 600 such businesses are

taken from each town. If a town's mean business income, based on its sample, is calculated as 30,500 euros, with a sample standard deviation of 7,000 euros, should it be disqualified from the program? Why or why not? Base your answer on 95% confidence intervals.

8. Return to our presidential primary candidates contributions in Chapter 5, Exercise 10. Let us assume that this is a random sample of contributions from donors with the same mean ($575) and standard deviation ($250). If the sample size (this group) was 625, and using 95% confidence intervals (and the Z table), what would we be able to confidently claim is our range of estimates for the true mean contribution level of the population from which this sample was randomly drawn? Can the true mean value be outside of this range? Why or why not?

   What if the sample size was twice that (i.e., 1,250)? Answer the same questions.

9. In the 2012 presidential election, much was made of the Republican candidate's religion. W. Mitt Romney is a practicing member of the Church of Jesus Christ of Latter-Day Saints (also known as Mormons). In the 2012 ANES survey (included in the SPSS and Stata guides for this text), individuals were able to rate parties, candidates, and groups on a 0–100 feeling thermometer scale. Measuring their feelings toward Mormons, we calculate a sample mean of 50.48°, a sample standard deviation of 21.902°, with a sample size of 5,385. Using the two-curve method of estimation and a 95% confidence interval, what is range of estimates of the mean from which this sample was drawn (assume random sampling)?

10. Given the results in Exercise 9, can we confidently reject the possibility that, in the population from which this sample was drawn, the actual mean thermometer rating of Mormons is less than 50°? Use either the two-curve estimates or the Z-score calculation demonstrated in equation 6.7.

11. Can we state with any confidence what the population mean exactly is?

12. Can we state with absolute certainty that the population mean feeling thermometer isn't lower than 50°?

NOTES

1 See Peverill Squire, "Why the 1936 Literary Digest Poll Failed," *Public Opinion Quarterly* 52 (1988): 125–133 for a full discussion of why the 1936 poll was so far off in its prediction.

2 This independence also assumes what we call "sampling with replacement." After one individual is sampled, they must then be placed back in the population and could possibly be sampled again. Of course, with a fairly large population (e.g., all households within the United States) the chance of sampling the same household twice is fairly remote. Most sampling organizations therefore don't worry about replacement.

3   Several sources report these *median* differences. See, for example, the U.S. Bureau of Labor Statistics website: http://www.bls.gov/opub/ted/2013/ted_20131203.htm.

4   Carmen DeNavas-Walt, Bernadette D. Proctor, and Jessica C. Smith, "Income, Poverty, and Health Insurance Coverage in the U.S.: 2012." *U.S. Census Bureau Current Population Reports*, September 2013, Table A-1: http://www.census.gov/prod/2013pubs/p60-245.pdf.

5   That 2.5% indicates that 97.5% of the samples that could be randomly drawn from that population, with a mean household income of $80,000, would have sample means of $81,960 or less.

6   Dividing by $N - 1$ produces what is called an unbiased estimate. In essence, since we are estimating the population standard deviation from a sample, we want to be conservative and overestimate its magnitude. By dividing by a smaller number, we increase the size of the standard deviation. Of course, with large sample sizes, whether we divide by N or $N - 1$ is fairly inconsequential.

7   Both the Eurobarometer and World Values Surveys series, as well as the ANES surveys used throughout this text are available through the Inter-university Consortium for Political and Social Research (ICPSR). The author is fully responsible for any errors made in discussing or analyzing these surveys.

8   Let's take four numbers with a mean of 6. Once we set the first three of those numbers (say 2, 4, 6), the fourth is set (it must be 12 for the mean to equal 6). We are, thus, only free to alter the first three cases or numbers.

Hypothesis Testing and the Concept of Association

Observations and Expectations about the Difference between Means[1]

Learning Objectives:

▉ To continue our discussion of hypothesis testing
▉ To understand how to apply the central limit theorem and normal curves to the analysis of differences between means
▉ To understand and learn how to calculate the standard error of mean differences
▉ To understand the difference between groups that are sampled independently and those in which the sampling in the second group is dependent on the first

Thus far, we have acquainted ourselves only with descriptive and inferential measures of univariate statistics. The mathematical logic behind our next set of presentations on bivariate statistics follows the concepts already discussed. Before moving to an analysis of the association between two variables, however, some further terms need to be reintroduced.[2]

We generally are concerned with analyzing bivariate (and eventually multivariate) statistics because we are trying to determine some causal linkage between two (or more variables). Let's review some of the terms used in Chapter 1.

Perhaps we are trying to determine whether one's gender affects one's income in some expected way (with women earning less than men), or if race determines one's chance of being selected for grand jury service (with minorities having a lower chance of selection than white Anglo-Americans), or if the type of voting system influences turnout (with proportional representation systems typically having higher turnout than single member districting systems). In the strictly bivariate case, we are trying to determine if differences in one variable (the causal agent or antecedent condition) affect the value of another (the outcome or consequence). The measured outcome, as you recall, is referred to as the *dependent variable* because its value is dependent on some causal or antecedent variable. The antecedent variable is called the *independent variable*. In our first example, the independent variable is gender (i.e., whether or not one is male or female); the dependent variable is income. In the second, the independent variable is minority (race or ethnicity) status, and the dependent variable is whether or not one is selected for jury service. In the third, the independent variable is the type of electoral system, and the dependent variable is turnout percentage. We would generally posit a guess about the relationship between these two variables. This guess, as we discussed in Chapter 1, is called a *hypothesis*. One such general hypothesis for our first example could be as follows:

Males have a higher income than females.

A hypothesis, as the one stated, must be a general one. It cannot be so specific as to be proved true or false with limited evidence. For example, stating that turnout in a particular country that uses proportional representation in one year is higher than in another country using a single member districting system is not a fully general hypothesis because it can be proved true or false on limited investigation. That statement is what we call a factual or *test implication* of the broader, more general hypothesis. Its truth or falseness, together with evidence about other countries or other times, helps us to understand the usefulness of the general hypothesis. The general statement itself cannot ever be proved conclusively because even if we can investigate every country at every point of time in the past and present, the possibility that we might find an example in the future that does not confirm our hypothesis is still possible. Statistics are helpful in determining the usefulness of a hypothesis by telling us whether the implications of that hypothesis are, for only the data we have at hand, true or false.

Return to our hypothesis. For any particular time or place, bivariate statistics can both describe the observed differences between males and females and make inferences about the population from which a sample of males and females did or did not come. Please note, however, that statistics are only summaries of *mathematical association*. Mathematical association is only one element in a causal argument (e.g., are gender differences in income caused by intentional discrimination against women?). Summarizing the steps listed in the last chapter, one must also be able to determine whether the two variables are theoretically linked (should one have a causal effect on the other, or is the link just a mere coincidence?).[3] One must eliminate alternate explanations. Statistics, as mathematical summaries, can only offer us a baseline mathematical standard of analysis. Knowing that men make more than women in any profession does not necessarily demonstrate actual discrimination, even in just that one profession at any given point in time, but it gives us one indication that discrimination *may* be taking place. It can tell us whether or not the evidence *is mathematically consistent* with a discriminatory effect.

COMPARISON OF TWO MEANS

For our gender and income analysis, many measures of association between two variables can be computed, depending on the exact wording of our hypothesis or test implication. We may have income categorized only as "low," "medium," or "high." Our hypothesis would then be nominal ("Males are more likely to earn high incomes than are females"). Since income is an intervally measured variable, and as the formulas are still fresh in our minds from the last several chapters, let's begin our analysis by using the mean as a summary of the income distributions of males and females. We could then compare the means, rewording our hypothesis (H_1) as follows:

Males have a higher mean income than do females.

Our analysis then becomes a comparison of *the difference between two means.* Say that we take a random sample of males and a random sample of females in a given profession and find their mean salaries to be $32,800 and $32,000, respectively. Can we make at least a mathematical claim that salary discrimination is based on gender?

Let us go through the first five steps of hypothesis testing brought up in the last chapter. We'll assume that the first three steps (reliability and validity of measures, theoretical relevance, and random sampling) have been satisfied. We then move to the following:

STEP 4: Does our observation match our hypothesized expectation (H_1)?

$$H_1: \mu_M - \mu_F > 0 \tag{7.1}$$

Yes: As expected, males make $800 more than females in our samples, since:

$$\overline{X}_M - \overline{X}_F = \$32,800 - \$32,000 = \$800 \tag{7.2}$$

We have one piece of evidence for our claim. The difference we observe is in the hypothesized direction. Our observation matches our expectation of discrimination, however slight.

We now finish our test by turning to the following step:

STEP 5: Is the observed difference small enough to attribute to the random luck of the draw or significant enough to confidently reject that as a possibility? If the latter, then we can confidently (but never absolutely) reject the null hypothesis (H_0) that the incomes of males in this profession is exactly the same on mean average as the incomes of females.

$$H_0: \mu_M - \mu_F = 0 \qquad\qquad (7.3)$$

Stated differently, could we have come up with a slightly higher paid sample of males and a slightly lower sample of females just by the luck of the random draw, even if no difference between the means actually exists in that entire population ($\mu_M - \mu_F = 0$)? Could we have produced an $800 difference in the same way that we could flip 100 coins one time and come up with 52 tails, but produce 52 heads with another flip of those 100 coins? Or is an $800 difference more like two sets of flips producing 92 tails and 92 heads—possible but highly unlikely?

We therefore need to find some way to determine whether the *observed* difference of $800 between our two samples is significantly large enough to reject the possibility that no difference exists in the populations from which the samples were randomly drawn, a posited hypothetical or *expected* difference of $0. Sound familiar? It should. The problem breaks down to a standard *t*- or *Z*-score formulation.[4] As with univariate means and dichotomous proportions, the central limit theorem applies. If we were to draw random samples from any given population for two groups of individuals (say males and females), compute the difference between the sample means, repeat the procedure a very large number of times, and plot the sample mean differences, the distribution of those sample mean differences would be normally distributed around the difference between the means of the two groups in the entire population (Figure 7.1). The theoretical distribution of the difference between sample means around the population mean would be represented by:

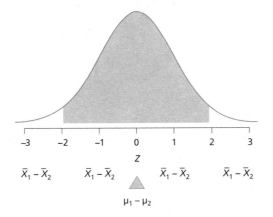

FIGURE 7.1 The Middle 95%, Mean Differences

The Z-score formula for sample mean differences distributed around the population mean ($Z = 0$) difference would be represented by:

$$Z_{\overline{X}_1 - \overline{X}_2} = \frac{(\overline{X}_1 - \overline{X}_2) - (\mu_1 - \mu_2)}{\sigma_{(\overline{X}_1 - \overline{X}_2)}} \qquad (7.4)$$

where $\overline{X}_1 - \overline{X}_2$ stands for the difference between the means of the *samples*

$\mu_1 - \mu_2$ stands for the true difference between the means in the population

$\sigma_{(\overline{X}_1 - \overline{X}_2)}$ stands for the standard deviation of the sample mean differences, commonly called the **standard error of the mean differences**

With large enough sample sizes, if we drew a very large number of independent samples, and subtracted the difference between them, 95% of the time that difference would be between values associated with a Z of -1.96 and $+1.96$. We need to expect that much variation just from the luck of the random draws.

Now let's turn to the calculation of the standard error of the mean differences. Because we have two sampled groups, the standard error is a combined function of the standard deviations and sample size for each group. It is computed as follows:[5]

$$\sigma_{(\overline{X}_1 - \overline{X}_2)} = \sqrt{\frac{\sigma_1^2}{N_1} + \frac{\sigma_2^2}{N_2}} \qquad (7.5)$$

where σ stands for the standard deviation of the individual values of the entire population for each group, 1 and 2

N stands for the size of the sample (number of cases) randomly drawn from that population for each group, 1 and 2

standard error of the mean differences The standard deviation of the differences between two samples randomly drawn from a population.

As with the univariate case, the standard deviations of the respective samples can be substituted for the standard deviation of the populations), giving us the following recalculated formula:

$$\sigma_{(\bar{X}_1-\bar{X}_2)} \approx \sqrt{\frac{s_1^2}{N_1} + \frac{s_2^2}{N_2}} \qquad (7.6)$$

Let us go back to our example. If the mean income of a random sample of 300 males is \$32,800, with a standard deviation of \$4,000, and the mean income of a sample of 200 females is \$32,000, with a standard deviation of \$3,000, then the standard error of the mean differences would be equal to:

$$\sigma_{(\bar{X}_1-\bar{X}_2)} \approx \sqrt{\frac{\$4000^2}{300} + \frac{\$3000^2}{200}} = \qquad (7.7)$$

$$\sqrt{\frac{\$\$16000000}{300} + \frac{\$\$9000000}{200}} = \sqrt{\$\$98333.33} = \$313.58$$

Now, turning to our Z-score formula:

$$Z_{\bar{X}_M-\bar{X}_F} = \frac{(\$32800 - \$32000) - (\$0)}{\$313.58} = \frac{\$800}{\$313.58} = 2.55 \qquad (7.8)$$

Note that the hypothesized difference between the population means is set at "\$0." We can actually set it at any value, but we choose "\$0" because we are trying to determine if we can confidently reject "no difference in incomes in the entire population" as a possibility (our usual null hypothesis, H_0). We therefore want to compare our observed difference of \$800 against a hypothesized or expected difference of \$0. A difference of \$0 *mathematically* indicates no discriminatory results based on gender.[6]

If we randomly draw a large number of samples of the given sizes from a population, 95% of the time we can expect to calculate a Z-score between −1.96 and +1.96. If the Z-score we actually do calculate is *within* 1.96 standard deviations from the true difference (in our case, \$0), we can't confidently reject the possibility that, in the population from which these samples were drawn, no difference exists between the mean incomes of males and females. No direct mathematical evidence of discrimination would exist. Our calculated Z-score of 2.55 is higher. We can therefore confidently reject the null hypothesis that no difference exists between the mean incomes of males and females in the entire profession's population. Males in all likelihood make more on mean average than do females. Might we be wrong in this rejection? Of course, sometimes samples are randomly drawn that vary by more than our set margin of error. Even taking that fact into account, does our calculation conclusively prove discrimination? No, but the evidence is at least mathematically consistent with that claim.[7]

The evidence might actually be stronger. We compared our calculation to a Z-score of +1.96. However, if we were not even considering the possibility that men might make less than women ($\mu_M < \mu_F$), then we might want to use a one-tailed test of significance. (See the discussion of one-tailed tests in Chapter 6.) If the true population means were equal, then 50% of the time we would randomly draw samples where females made the same or less than males on mean average. Forty-five percent of the time, males, on mean average, would make more. The critical cutoff value would then be 1.645; that is, 95% of the time, by random chance, the sample differences would produce Z-scores ≤ 1.645. Using a directional, or one-tailed test (Figure 7.2), we can reject the null hypothesis with even greater confidence.

One more point needs to be made before we move on to another example. We used $0 as our hypothesized difference of mean incomes. We were testing to determine whether we could reject the possibility that gender had no effect on mean incomes in this profession's population (a concept we will later discuss as statistical independence). The Z-score (or t-score) formula, however, need not assume equality as our hypothesis of rejection, although the formula is often presented in other texts as if this were the only possibility (thus leaving off the second half of the numerator). What if the government, limited in its ability or desire to follow up on discrimination claims, wished to set a cutoff for claims that it would pursue? As an example, it chooses to follow up only

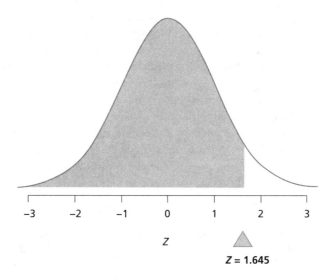

FIGURE 7.2 One-Tailed Test, $Z = 1.645$, Mean Differences

when it can feel confident that the true mean income difference ($\mu_M - \mu_F$) is greater than $500. It will reject claims if it can't confidently reject the possibility that the true population differences are less than or equal to $500. Would the government take action in our case? The logic of the analysis is the same as before, but the theoretical distribution of sample mean differences would be symmetrically distributed around a new null hypothesis:

$$H_0: \mu_M - \mu_F = \$500 \qquad (7.9)$$

Sidebar 7.1: Employment Discrimination

The issue of the limitations of carrying out government regulations is no small matter. The EEOC (Equal Employment Opportunity Commission) has consistently fallen behind in its processing of wage discrimination claims that now include claims based not only on race, national origin, and gender, but also age (after the Age Discrimination in Employment Act of 1965), disability (the Americans with Disabilities Act of 1990), sexual orientation (under an interpretation of the Civil Rights Act of 1964 and recent presidential executive order), and genetic typing information (the Genetic Information Non-discrimination Act of 2008). Part of this is intentional, as a more conservative Congress would prefer less regulation. Budget stalemates that force the sequestering (across-the-board cuts) of funding also adversely impact all governmental activities. Part, however, is purely an instance of the dramatic increase in claims, including workplace discrimination other than wage based, that no level funding could adequately satisfy. An EEOC division director testified to Congress that, although the EEOC is entrusted with examining every case of employment discrimination, by 1995 its director had decided to target resources on the strength of the discrimination evidence and increased its requests that such claims be dealt with by mediation rather than the traditional EEOC charging process.

Source: U.S. Congress, Senate, Committee on Labor and Human Resources, *Burgeoning Workload Calls for New Approaches* (U.S. General Accounting Office, 1995).

Is the observed $500 difference significantly different enough from $500 (not $0) to confidently reject the possibility that the true difference between the mean incomes of males and females was $500 (or less)? The denominator of our equation, the standard error, would remain as before. The numerator will change because the expected or hypothesized population difference changed:

$$Z_{\overline{X}_M - \overline{X}_F} = \frac{(\$32800 - \$32000) - (\$500)}{\$313.58} = \frac{\$300}{\$313.58} = 0.97 \qquad (7.10)$$

Even using a one-tailed test, which would make it easier to reject the new null hypothesis, the *Z*-score that we calculated is lower than the rejection cutoff (1.645). We therefore cannot confidently reject the possibility that the income differences in the population were $500 (or less).

What mean income difference would we have to find in order for the government to take action? Well, that's partially a function of the standard deviations and sizes of any two samples that we drew, as that would produce our standard error estimate. Let's assume that the standard deviation and sample sizes were the same as before. Let's also use a one-tailed test. Our job is to determine the lowest sample mean difference that would qualify for governmental action, that is, a difference that would equate to a Z-score just above the 1.645 critical value.

$$1.645 = \frac{(\overline{X}_M - \overline{X}_F) - (\$500)}{\$313.58}$$

$$\$515.84 = (\overline{X}_M - \overline{X}_F) - \$500 \tag{7.11}$$

$$\overline{X}_M - \overline{X}_F = \$1,015.84$$

The government would follow up only if the mean income difference between males and females in the samples was greater than $1,015.84. Only then would it feel confident that the true population difference was at least $500.

The Marriage Gap and Feelings toward Parties

Let us look at another example. As discussed in Chapter 1, although we tend to concentrate on the gender gap in politics (women are more likely to associate with, have positive feelings toward, and vote for candidates of the Democratic Party than men), there is a growing body of research discussing the even greater importance of a **marriage gap**, with those currently in or who had been in traditional marriages (married or widowed) being more likely to side with the Republicans than those in non-traditional arrangements (single, divorced, partnered).[8]

In 2012, more than 5,000 respondents were interviewed by the American National Election Studies organization (ANES).[9] One survey item asked about their marital status, and two others about their feelings toward each of the two major parties, ranked on a scale of 0 (coldest/least favorable) to 50 (neutral) to 100 (warmest/most favorable). In the following analysis, for each respondent, feeling thermometer ratings for the Democratic Party were subtracted from feeling thermometer ratings for the Republican Party. A positive thermometer difference indicates more warmth or favorability assigned to the Republicans, a 0 indicates equal feelings (not just 0 for each), and a negative difference indicates favorability toward the Democrats.[10] In order to test for the following hypothesis:

marriage gap A recent U.S. electoral division where married couples, especially those with children, are more likely to vote Republican than non-married individuals, especially single females with children.

$$H_{1:} \; \mu_T - \mu_{NT} > 0° \tag{7.12}$$

TABLE 7.1 Differential Thermometer Ratings by Marital Status

	Traditional Status	Non-Traditional Status
Sample Mean	.7623°	−18.5487°
Sample Standard Deviation	47.56289°	48.73523°
N	3,487	2,417

the means and standard deviations of the differences were calculated separately for those in "traditional" (T) marital arrangements and those in "non-traditional" (NT) ones.

Again, let's assume that Steps 1 (measurements are reliable and internally valid) and 3 of our hypothesis testing have been satisfied (although the ANES is not a purely random sample).[11] Let's move on to the following step.

STEP 2: Is there a theoretical reason to believe that marital status and party leanings should be related as hypothesized? Many scholars have addressed this. Reasons include the fact that married individuals are more culturally conservative and more likely to attend church services, both positively related to Republican affiliation. Married individuals also tend to have higher incomes.[12] Having satisfied Steps 1–3, we now turn to Step 4.

STEP 4: Does our observation match our hypothesized expectation (H_1)?

$$H_{1:} \ \mu_T - \mu_{NT} > 0° \qquad (7.13)$$

Yes, as expected, the mean difference of party feelings leans more Republican (slightly positive) for traditionalists than for non-traditionalists (negative) for a combined mean difference of 19.311°. Of course, this difference indicates that marital status is not the only predictor and causal agent of partisan leanings. If it were, the difference would be 200°.[13] Having at least somewhat confirmed our hypothesis descriptively (what we observed), we now need to test it inferentially. Could that difference of 19.311° be an artifact of the mathematical peculiarities of random sampling, or is it significant enough to reject the possibility that, in the population from which these samples were drawn, a difference greater than 0° exists? In other words, is that difference large enough to confidently reject the null hypothesis of equality of means between the two samples?

$$H_{1:} \ \mu_T - \mu_{NT} = 0° \qquad (7.14)$$

Let's carry out our calculations:

$$\sigma_{(\bar{X}_T - \bar{X}_{NT})} \approx \sqrt{\frac{47.56289^2}{3487} + \frac{48.73523^2}{2417}} = \qquad (7.15)$$

$$\sqrt{\frac{2262.228505}{3487} + \frac{2375.122643}{2417}} = \sqrt{1.631435} = 1.27728°$$

Now, turning to our Z-score formula:[14]

$$Z_{\overline{X}_T - \overline{X}_{NT}} = \frac{(0.7623° - (-18.5487)) - (0°)}{1.27728°} = \frac{19.311°}{1.27728°} = 15.1189 \quad (7.16)$$

Clearly, this Z-score is so much larger than the 1.645 one-tailed confidence cutoff for a 95% confidence interval that we can be very confident that those whose marital status is traditional have higher mean difference ratings (+Republican) than those whose status is non-traditional. In actuality, the significance level works out to less than 0.4888 E–51 (the p-value calculated by SPSS or Stata). If the population difference in the population from which these samples were drawn was truly 0, the chance of randomly sampling two groups with a mean difference this high would be infinitesimal. Translation: a marriage gap in all likelihood does truly exist—at least mathematically.

Once again, we should always realize what these findings tell us and what they do not.

- Being able to confidently reject the null hypothesis is not the same as being absolutely certain. With a 95% confidence interval, we still have a 5% probability (called alpha error) of erroneously rejecting the null hypothesis because our calculated Z- or t-value is beyond the cutoff values for that interval.
- Not being able to confidently reject the null hypothesis is not the same as accepting it (i.e., that the true population difference is exactly the same as that specified in the null hypothesis, usually 0). A population difference of 0 is only one of many values consistent with any sample difference that fell within our 95% confidence range, even a difference of 0.

One more qualification must be made. When ascertaining the causal relationship between two variables, two more steps (6 and 7 in Chapter 6) must be satisfied. Is there something internally or externally invalid about how we designed our test other than a problem with measurement? For example, if wealthier individuals are more likely to get married and wealthier individuals are more likely to favor Republicans over Democrats, might we not really have a *spurious relationship* (Chapter 1) where wealth is the real causative agent of marital status and party leanings? Can these results from one test be generalized to other election years? Might the relationship be stronger/weaker for subsets of the population sampled (say different races). This last step requires an understanding of controls and multivariate statistics, subjects to which we will return in Chapters 10 and 12.

SPECIAL COMMENT ON SIGNIFICANCE TESTS

For the most part, I adhere to a traditionalist view of the use of significance tests: only when a random sample of a population is used (or, if not random, where we can estimate irregularities) are significance tests relevant. After all, inferential statistics just deal with how much we need to attribute to the random luck of the draw to feel safe or confident with our estimates. Without random or equiprobable draws, the mathematics of significance levels and tests are somewhat misplaced.

Many in the discipline (often called "frequentists"), however, including the editorial boards of most peer-reviewed journals, believe that significance tests can play a wider role. Everything in life, one could argue, is random. Thus, one can use significance tests, for example, to determine whether the behavior of Republican and Democratic members of Congress are "significantly different" from each other on any single vote or cumulatively throughout a session. As a traditionalist, I might want to argue that one chosen Congress is similar or is representative of a certain *type* of Congress—but that is a research design parameter, not a mathematical one.

In order to satisfy the different methodological views of anyone using this text, let me offer a compromise with two qualifiers: If the difference/association we observe in the real, if not random, world is no better than we would get by random chance alone, then we may want to dismiss the relationship as not important enough to study.

Caveat 1: Never confuse statistical significance with conceptual—especially if sample sizes are extremely large (miniscule differences/associations can be statistically significant; i.e., different from 0). How far would we want to study a relationship based upon a 0.1% proportional difference?

Caveat 2: With small N, little will ever be "statistically significant." Green and Gerber have argued that studies with large N are more likely to be published because they are more likely to come up with "statistically significant" results. But if, for example, members of the U.S. Supreme Court are consistently more likely to defer to the president and Congress on foreign policy issues than domestic ones, might that not be a conceptually significant finding, even if the case size in any one or series of years prevents us from achieving a statistically (mathematically) significant result? Similarly, countries with proportional representation systems might, in every series of elections, have a mean turnout higher than countries with single member districting rules. Unless we increase our "sample size" to all countries for all election years (treated as separate data points) over an extended period of time, our small case size (N) might prevent us from achieving a statistically significant difference. But, if in any decade, the difference that we observe is what we would expect, isn't that result conceptually significant?[15]

APPENDIX

COMPARISON OF TWO VARIABLES, SAME OR MATCHED GROUPS

In the previous examples, we were comparing two different groups against each other, usually referred to as an "**independent samples test**." What if, instead, we were investigating one group and assessing how the individuals within that group differed on two separate issues, or across time on the same issue, or when the sampling of two groups are not independent of each other (e.g., we compare males and females within married couples)? We would then need to employ a paired or **dependent samples test**. The numerator stays the same, as we are still comparing the observed difference of means against a hypothetical population difference (usually 0). The denominator, however, changes substantially, as it must consider the mean differences for each individual in the one group sample in order to calculate the standard error of the paired differences (D). The calculation of that standard error is:

$$\sigma_{\overline{D}} = \frac{\sqrt{\sum_{i=1}^{n}(D_i - \overline{D})^2 / (N-1)}}{\sqrt{N}} \tag{7.17}$$

where D_i equals the difference in scores for each case in the sample
$\overline{D}$ equals the mean of those differences
N equals the number of cases in the sample

The Z-score calculation is therefore:

$$Z_{\overline{X}_1 - \overline{X}_2} = \frac{(\overline{X}_1 - \overline{X}_2) - (\mu_1 - \mu_2)}{\sigma_{\overline{D}}} \tag{7.18}$$

In general, the same differences in sample means for a paired test will yield a higher Z-score than for an independent samples test as the standard error of the differences ($\sigma_{\overline{D}}$) will usually result in a lower value than the standard error of independent means ($\overline{X}_1 - \overline{X}_2$).

Statistical analysis packages, such as SPSS and Stata will run different tests depending on whether you have selected paired or independent samples. They will also adjust for small sample sizes and whether or not the variances between the samples are the same or different.

---

independent samples test
A test of significance for which the cases within each comparison group are drawn independently of each other.

KEY TERMS

dependent samples test (159)

independent samples test (158)

marriage gap (154)

standard error of the mean differences (150)

QUESTIONS AND EXERCISES

NOTE: Several more examples and exercises can be found in both the SPSS and Stata manuals that accompany this text. *t*-tests for the comparison between two means (independent and dependent tests) can be found in Section 4.3.

1. For an entire population, the mean of one variable is calculated for two groups within that population. The difference between those two means is calculated and represented as $\mu_1 - \mu_2$. We draw a large number of large samples of two categories of a variable and compute the difference between the means calculated for each category. The mean of those sample differences will be equal to _____ .

2. We draw a large random sample from a population and measure the campaign contributions that respondents give to a political candidate. We calculate the mean contribution and standard deviations of contributions for those who oppose ObamaCare in that sample and, separately, for those who support it. Using 95% confidence intervals, we find that we *can't* confidently reject the possibility that the difference of the mean contribution level (between opponents and supporters) in the population is 0. Which of the following statements best describes what we found?
   a. The population difference has to be 0.
   b. The population difference might be 0, but that is only one of several possibilities.
   c. The population difference has to be higher than 0.
   d. The population difference has to be lower than 0.

3. Same scenario: We draw a large random sample from a population and measure the campaign contributions given to a certain candidate by each respondent. We calculate the mean contribution and standard deviations of contributions for ObamaCare opponents in that sample and, separately, for supporters. Using 95% confidence intervals, we find that we can confidently reject the possibility that the difference of the means in the population is 0.

   True or False: It is therefore impossible for the population difference to be 0.

---

dependent samples test
A test of significance for which the sampling of each case in the second group is contingent or dependent on the draw on the first.

---

4. Although it is not a necessity, when comparing differences between means we usually set the expected population difference $(\mu_1 - \mu_2)$ to _____ .

5. For several decades, the ANES group has conducted extensive surveys of the voting age population for each biannual election cycle. One of the survey items asks respondents to place a candidate, other political figure, organization, or group on a scale ranging from 0 to 100. On this "feeling thermometer," a "0" represents the least positive, or cold placement; 100 represents the most positive, or hot placement; and 50 represents neutrality (take him or leave him). Following are the relevant means, standard deviations, and sample sizes for males and females for feeling thermometers for Republican Party candidate and eventual winner George W. Bush (pre-election). Using this information, address the following statement:

In 2000, men were more supportive of George Bush than were women.

Note that this is not a hypotheses, but an empirical, factual statement, proved true or false upon limited investigation (the data presented). Hypotheses are more general in their structure and would apply to more than one piece of factual evidence. A possible hypothesis would be that "men are more supportive of Republican candidates than are women," a specification of a political gender gap that might define a whole series of elections across time.

	Feeling Thermometer Ratings	
	Men	Women
George W. Bush	$\overline{X} = 56.65$	$\overline{X} = 55.74$
	$s = 24.55$	$s = 25.12$
	$N = 781$	$N = 980$

Did a gender gap exist in 2000? Answer the question both descriptively and inferentially. Make sure you can explain the difference.

6. As in Exercise 5, use the following statistics to address this statement:

In 2000, women were more supportive of Democratic candidate Al Gore, Jr., than were men.

Al Gore	$\overline{X} = 53.92$	$\overline{X} = 60.44$
	$s = 25.32$	$s = 25.56$
	$N = 781$	$N = 993*$

* N varies because 13 more women had an opinion about Al Gore than they did about George W. Bush.

7. Compare the results in Exercises 5 and 6. In which is the gender gap more evident?

8. A sample is taken measuring the level of total contributions given by individuals to a Senate candidate and all PACs, SuperPacs, 501(c)s, 527s, and other organizations that contributed to or otherwise supported her campaign (in reality, even before Citizens United, this would be very difficult to trace, so let's assume that this is a survey in which individuals answered truthfully). The following figures are produced:

	Mean	Standard Deviation	N
Conservatives	$580	$225	750
Liberals	$450	$185	600

Answer the following question. Can you confidently state, in the entire population of contributors from which this sample was randomly taken, that conservatives gave more (i.e., >$0), on mean average, to the Senate candidate's campaign than did liberals? Or could the $130 sample difference be explained by the luck of the random sampling draw?

9. A random survey of 200 individuals is taken from two European Union nations. Each respondent is asked to estimate how much of his or her total taxes go to pay for national security. The mean of the sample in country A is €1,100, with a standard deviation of €150. The corresponding mean for the respondents in country B is €1,075 with a standard deviation of €160. Can we confidently state that, in the populations from which these samples were randomly drawn, the estimates are exactly the same?

10. For Exercise 9, would your answer be different if the sample size was 2,000?

▌NOTES

1 This volume will only cover the difference between two means. When more than two means need to be compared, statistics such as ANOVA (analysis of variance) would be used.

2 In actuality, we hinted at this when we compared the income of male households against the entire population in the last chapter. Intuitively, when we did so, we were considering the possibility that the incomes of male households was higher than female households.

3 Sports and politics provide us with a classic example of the coincidental association between two variables. Between 1940 and 1976, a baseball World Series victory by the representative of the National League was followed by a presidential victory by the Democratic candidate 100% of the time (5/5). A World Series victory by the representative of the American League was followed by a Republican presidential election victory 80% of the time, the only exception being 1948, when the Republicans were predicted as easy winners, a prediction made by some newspapers as late as the morning after the election. Few social science variables are as closely mathematically associated. One would be hard pressed, however, to claim that election outcomes in November are caused by baseball victories in October. Before the longer, protracted era of primaries, the old adage that Americans would concentrate on presidential politics only after the series

was over certainly made some sense. However, it explained the priority that Americans placed on sports as opposed to politics, not a causal link between the two. See Martin Kelly, "Predicting the Presidential Election with Baseball: Can the Winner of the World Series Predict the Presidential Election?" (2004). http://americanhistory.about.com/od/elections/a/baseballpres.htm.

4   In actuality, the test is usually classified as a *t*-test. Recall from a previous chapter, however, that if the sample sizes are large enough, the *t*-test values will be close to or equal to the *Z*-score values. The degrees of freedom for a one-variable *t*-test would be $N - 1$. The degrees of freedom for a two-variable *t*-test would be $N_1 + N_2 - 2$ if we assume the standard deviations for each group in the sample to be equal, and somewhat less (a function of both sample sizes and standard deviations) if we don't. Most statistical computer packages, such as SPSS or Stata, will compute the test for the proper case sizes, which define the degrees of freedom for both assumptions. A test for equality of variances will also be performed. If that test produces a significantly high number, related to a significance level of less than .05, then we can reject the possibility that the standard deviations are equal in the population and use the *t*-test score for non-equal deviations. With large samples, the differences between the two calculations will usually be slight.

5   Note that this is the standard error formula if the two samples are *independent* of each other. If the women were chosen because they were married to the sample of men, or if two measures were taken from the same group (say the incomes of men before and after completing a probationary period or the temperature of individuals before and after taking medication), then a different formula would have to be used. Additionally, this formula does not assume that the standard deviation for males and females is equal. Again, many statistical packages will provide the ability to test for differences between samples that are not independent of each other.

6   I use the word "indicates" because, absent other information, it does not prove the lack of discrimination. Perhaps women tend to have more seniority or work longer hours. Making the same income under those conditions would certainly lead us to believe that discrimination might be taking place. Perhaps women make more on mean average than men at the lower end of the profession's job scale, but less at the top, indicating two biases that negate each other. See the sidebar in Chapter 10.

7   We have only confidently rejected one *possible* actual population difference. Can we estimate what the true population differences are? Yes, by following the same analysis as in previous chapters. We would compute the lowest mean difference of a population from which this sample, with a difference of $800, could have been randomly drawn ($Z = +1.96$) and the highest ($Z = -1.96$). Having gone through this exercise numerous times, this author leaves the calculations to the student.

8   Although I am not personally comfortable with this "traditional/non-traditional" characterization, I will use it as it is commonly stated this way in much of the literature.

9   The American National Election Studies (ANES; http://www.electionstudies. org). The ANES 2012 Time Series Study [data set]. Stanford University and the University of Michigan [producers].

10 I prefer this difference assessment to looking at individual thermometer ratings as one would expect an individual to vote for the candidate of the party to which they are more warmly or positively disposed. The fact that one has high/ low ratings for the Democratic Party or candidate does not negate the possibility

that she has equally high/low ratings for the Republicans. We may misestimate the influence of partisan feelings by looking only at one side of the equation. More on this when we get to regression (Chapters 11 and 12).

11 We of course could question whether the traditional/non-traditional dichotomization is an internally valid measure of marital status and certainly would question whether the ANES survey is truly random.

12 For a fairly thorough breakdown of the reasons for the marriage gap and its outcomes written by a student, see Shikole Struber, "The Effect of Marriage on Political Identification," *Student Pulse* 2, no. 1 (2010).

13 If someone's rating of Republicans is 100 and of Democrats is 0, the mean difference would be 100. If the reverse holds, the mean difference would be −100. If all traditionally married individuals had a difference in ratings of 100 and all non-traditionalists had a rating of −100, the mean difference would be 200 degrees.

14 This is the more conservative calculation with equal variances not assumed. With equal variances of the two groups ratings assumed, the figure would be roughly 15.185. The difference is slight as the number of cases in each group is large.

15 For an excellent discussion of this problem, see Alan S. Gerber, Donald P. Green, and David Nickerson, "Testing for Publication Bias in Political Science," *Political Analysis* 9(2001): 385–92.

Inferential Statistics for Proportions

Learning Objectives:

■ To understand that inferential tests of dichotomous proportions follow the logic of tests of means

■ To understand the concept of observed and expected frequencies given categorical, nominal data

■ To be able to use chi-square as an inferential measure of one-variable nominal distributions

■ To understand the concept of degrees of freedom with one-variable nominal distributions

■ To further understand what inferential tests can and cannot tell us

The controversy over the 2000 presidential election outcome in Florida began well before the question of hanging chads and butterfly ballots was raised. On election night, the polls first predicted George Bush the winner, then Al Gore, and finally, they decided the election was too close to call. Part of the problem had to do with calling the election before all of the Florida polls had closed, thus deriving the prediction from a potential geographically biased sample. However, polls can be "wrong" even when the sample is not biased. Even with large samples, polls can merely provide estimates, allowing us to make predictions given a calculated margin of error. Sometimes, again only because of the laws of probability, we can be off by even more than that calculated margin. On rare occasions, we can flip close to 100 heads.

We have just discussed how, by using Z-scores and the normal curve, we can estimate the mean value, or a range of mean values, of a population (μ_x) from the mean ($\overline{X}$) of a sample randomly drawn from that population. The logic behind comparing sample observations and mean expectations by way of the normal curve also applies to proportions, but only when the variable we are measuring is dichotomous (i.e., just two categories; see the appendix in this chapter for a demonstration). Some variables, like gender, are naturally *dichotomous*. You are either male or female. Others are dichotomous by the researcher's decision if only two choices are offered, say, "agree" or "disagree." Of course, all variables, regardless of the number of categories, can be dichotomized after the fact. A four-category agreement question ("strongly agree," "agree," "disagree," "strongly disagree") can be collapsed into two categories. So can multicandidate voting outcomes. Several candidates were on the 2000 presidential election ballot other than George W. Bush and Al Gore. The responses to a question asking presidential vote choice can be collapsed to "Bush" or "Other candidate."[1] Electoral systems can be dichotomized into "proportional" or "not," even though the "not" incorporates several forms of single member districting and mixed aggregation methods.

DICHOTOMOUS PROPORTIONS

When we deal with proportions of dichotomies, just as we did with means, there is a fairly straightforward procedure to determine the margin of error that can be attributed to the luck of the draw. Let us designate the first of two proportions of any **dichotomous variable/dichotomies** in a population as the Greek character π. Note that as only two categories exist, and the sum of both proportions must equal 1, the second proportion must be equal to, and can be designated as, $1 - \pi$. Holding to our convention of using the Roman alphabet for sample statistics, let us designate the proportions calculated from any sample as p and $1 - p$. We only need to concern ourselves with calculating estimates for one of the two proportions—the other directly follows. Now, if we draw a large number of random samples from a population with actual proportions of a dichotomous variable equal to π and $1 - \pi$, and if we plotted those sample proportions for either of the two categories (let's use p), then the sample proportions would be normally distributed around their respective population proportion (π). Once again, the central limit theorem and the Z-score formula would apply, with one of the sample proportions (p) substituting for the sample mean ($\overline{X}$), the population proportion

dichotomous variable/
dichotomies A variable for
which only two categories
exist.

(π) substituting for the population mean (μ_x), and the standard error of the sample proportions (σ_p) substituting for the standard error of the sample means ($\mu_{\bar{X}}$):

$$Z_p = \frac{p - \pi}{\sigma_p}$$ (8.1)

where p stands for the sample proportion

π stands for the population proportion

σ_p stands for the standard deviation of the sample proportions around the population proportion, the standard error of proportions

σ_p is calculated as:

$$\sigma_p = \sqrt{\frac{\pi \times (1 - \pi)}{N}}$$ (8.2)

The formula for the standard error of proportions can be restated as:

$$\sigma_p = \frac{\sqrt{\pi \times (1 - \pi)}}{\sqrt{N}}$$ (8.3)

Note the similarity between the formulas for the standard error of the mean ($\mu_{\bar{X}}$) and the reconfigured standard error of proportions (σ_p). The denominator ($\sqrt{N}$) is the same in both. Remember that the standard error of the mean, as well as the calculated margin of error, was not only a function of the square root of the sample size but also of the variance, and thus the standard deviation, of the individual distribution. For nominal data, the margin of error is also a function of variance or the evenness of the split between the two proportions (π and $1 - \pi$) of a dichotomy. Recall that when we discussed the index of diversity and the index of qualitative variation (Chapter 4), we determined that variation could be measured by computing the number or proportion of times that two individuals who differed on a variable (as opposed to sharing the same attribute) were drawn. In order to do so, we multiplied the number in each category by the number in every other category. The highest number or standardized proportion occurred when there existed an even split between or among the categories (the computation of the denominator of the index of qualitative variation [IQV]). Consequently, the numerator of the standard error of dichotomous proportions will be highest when the split is 50/50, that is, when $\pi \times (1 - \pi) = .5 \times .5 = .25$. Any other combination will produce a smaller product (e.g., $.6 \times .4 = .24$). As the split becomes rather one sided, say 90/10, the value of $\pi \times (1 - \pi)$ becomes rather small (.09). Obviously, there isn't much room above 90% for one proportion to vary in any particular sample.

As with means, a range of possible population proportions can be estimated from the proportions of a given sample using the Z-score formula for proportions. Let us take the following example. A survey is taken from a random sample of 500 citizens in a Latin American country. Along with other items, the respondents are asked if they approve of their government's U.S. foreign policy. Fifty-two percent express approval, and 48% do not. Can the nation's leaders confidently assume that a majority (>50%) of citizens support them? Well, assuming that everyone is responding truthfully, and that the question was not worded in a way that would prompt a positive response, a slim majority of the respondents *observed in the sample* do approve.[2] A sample, however, only provides one estimate of what the actual level of approval is in the population from which the sample was drawn (i.e., what we can *expect* in that entire population). The question that still needs to be answered is whether that sample could have been randomly drawn from a population where support is less than majority, or 50%.

We can approach this from several angles. Let's do the following. Fifty-two percent is just an estimate of the proportion that approve in the population. The actual approval rate in the population could be 52%, but it could be more or less. How much more or less? That depends on which confidence interval we choose. As with the mean, let's use 95%, corresponding to an absolute Z-score of 1.96. Although we are just interested in "how much less," we'll calculate both "less" and "more" in order to provide an estimate of the entire range of probable population proportions.

We proceed as we did with the calculation of probable population means and calculate the lowest (π_L) and highest (π_H) proportion of approval in populations from which this sample could have been randomly drawn. The number .52 lies at the top of the 95% confidence interval of a population with an actual approval rating of π_L and at the bottom of a population with an actual approval rating of π_H (Figure 8.1). We would not want to reject the possibility that this sample could have been randomly drawn from a population with actual approval levels as low or as high as these values, or any value in between (including $\pi = .52$).[3]

In order to determine those minimum and maximum values, we first need to calculate the standard error of proportions. We can, as we did when we substituted the sample standard deviation in computing the standard error of the mean, substitute the sample proportions (p and $1 - p$) for the population proportions (π and $1 - \pi$). Thus, our formula for deriving the standard error of proportions would be:

$$\sigma_p = \sqrt{\frac{\pi \times (1-\pi)}{N}} \approx \sqrt{\frac{p \times (1-p)}{N}} \qquad (8.4)$$

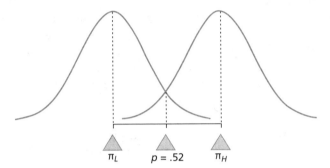

FIGURE 8.1 Two-Curve Population Estimate, Dichotomous Proportions

In our example, this would be:

$$\sigma_p = \sqrt{\frac{.52 \times (.48)}{500}} = \sqrt{\frac{.2496}{500}} = \sqrt{.000499} = .0223 \qquad (8.5)$$

We now need to compute two formulas to solve for two hypothetical population proportions (π_L and π_H). This would give us the lowest and the highest approval proportions of populations from which this sample could have probably been randomly drawn (i.e., would lie at the edge of their 95% confidence intervals):

$$+1.96 = (.52 - \pi_L)/.0223 \qquad -1.96 = (.52 - \pi_H)/.0223$$
$$+.0437 = .52 - \pi_L \qquad -.0437 = .52 - \pi_H$$
$$-\pi_L = .0437 - .52 \qquad -\pi_H = -.0437 - .52$$
$$-\pi_L = -.4763 \qquad -\pi_H = -.5637$$
$$\pi_L = .4763 \qquad \pi_H = .5637$$
$$.4763 < \pi < .5637$$

The .0437 calculated on the second line is the margin of error. That is, given this sample size and this split in approval, we have to allow for the possibility that our sample proportion might be off by as much as 4.37% (more or less) from the true population value just because of the luck of the random draw of respondents. The last line tells us that, if we are using a 95% confidence interval, we would not feel safe in rejecting the possibility that this sample (with a $p = .52$) could have been randomly drawn from a population where 47.63% (52% − 4.37%) approve of their country's foreign policy, where 56.37% (52% + 4.37%) approve, or any rate of approval in between these two figures. To restate our original question, can the country's leaders safely reject the possibility that the true level of support for foreign policy is below 50%? Not quite. Fifty percent is within our calculated margin of error of 4.37%. It is not significantly different enough from .50, or .49, or even .48 to reject these as possibilities. The country's leadership may take a calculated risk. After all, that .4763 is at the bottom end of the probable level of support in the population. Support might be as high as 56.37%. However, also remember, although it is highly unlikely that this sample could have been randomly drawn from a population where the real level of support was even lower than 47.63%, say, 47% or 46%, it is not impossible. Tough call. Of course, this nation's leaders might sense that the issue is not all that important to most citizens, except for the most anti-U.S. citizens. They might therefore decide that, given differing levels of intensity on the issue, they should not proceed for fear of suffering significant political damage.

We could have approached the problem in a more direct way. The nation's leaders have a precise question they need answered. They need to know if .52 is significantly different enough from .50 (or one voter less) to confidently reject that as a possible population value. The null hypothesis is therefore:

H_0: percentage support = 50% or, more accurately, $H_0 \leq 50\%$

and

H_1 percentage support is > 50%

Is that difference of .02 within the estimated margin of error, basing that decision on a 95% confidence interval and a Z-score of 1.96 (or 1.645 in a one-tailed test)? Let's solve for the Z-score and see if it's less or more than 1.96. If it is more, then we can confidently reject the possibility ($\pi_L < 50$) as it is outside of the 95% range of possibilities. If it is less than 1.96, then we can't.

As we are specifying a particular population proportion for comparison (.5), we need not depend on the sample proportions (.52, .48) as estimates of the true population proportions. That .50 is the expected proportion that we are trying to reject as a possibility (our null hypothesis, or H_0). The standard error would therefore be recalculated using .5 × .5 as our variance (the maximum possibility). The standard error would be marginally higher than before, rounded to .0224 (.02236068 carried out). The formula then is listed as:

$$Z_p = \frac{.52 - .50}{.0224} = \frac{.02}{.0224} = .894 \qquad \textbf{(8.6)}$$

The calculated Z-score of .894 (actually .8944272) is substantially less than 1.96 (or 1.645). Thus, we cannot confidently reject the possibility (our null hypothesis) that this sample could have been randomly drawn from a population with an actual level of approval of .50. Fifty-two percent is within the 95% confidence interval of that population.

Now what if the sample size were 5,000? The standard error would then be .0071 (.7071068). Check this to make sure you understand the calculation. The recalculated Z-score would be 2.82 (2.8284271 without rounding error). Although we start with the same sample proportion, we can now confidently reject the possibility that the sample could have been randomly drawn from a population where the true proportional support was .50 or less. With a larger sample size, less of the difference between sample and posited population proportions can be attributed to the random luck of the draw. We can therefore confidently reject a larger range of possibilities (including ≤ .50).

Just as with means, when we are only concerned with one side of the equation, as we are in this analysis, we might want to perform what is called a "one-tailed" test. We only need to know if .52 is significantly *greater* than .50. The difference with a one-tailed, or directional, test is that the Z-score value would be different since we are only concerned with one side of the normal curve. Look at the following normal curve (Figure 8.2). If we randomly draw samples from a population with a proportional support of π, 95% of those samples will have proportional support (p) less than the cutoff designated on the graph.

Refer back to our normal table chart (Table 5.1). Fifty percent of the sampling distribution of dichotomous proportions would lie below a Z-score of 0, or the point corresponding to the true sample proportion (π). Forty-five percent

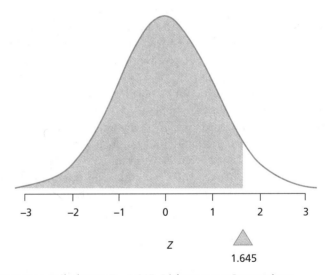

FIGURE 8.2 One-Tailed Test, Z = 1.645, Dichotomous Proportions

would lie between that point and a Z-score somewhere between 1.64 and 1.65, or about 1.645. As we are concerned with only "one tail" of this distribution, the 95% confidence interval would have its upper bound not at 1.96 (the two-tailed version), but 1.645. Is the calculated Z-score still less than this? In our example of a sample of 500, yes. Even with a one-tailed, or directional, test, this nation's leaders could still not safely reject the possibility that the true level of approval was .50.

News agencies and political groups that commission surveys usually list a "maximum margin of error" in reporting their results. This maximum margin is that which, given the sample size, would exist if an even split (50/50) existed between the proportions. Remember from both our discussion of the indices of diversity and qualitative variation and this chapter that the maximum value for the variance (and thus the calculation of the standard error of proportions) exists when the cases are evenly distributed. As they usually report more than one result, with several different splits between categories, they list this maximum rather than a separate calculation for each table. Additionally, since the sample proportions are used as estimates of the true population proportions, this procedure allows for the maximum amount of variance in the population. The actual margin of error will often be less than that which is listed.

CHI-SQUARE (χ^2)

The previous calculations based on the normal curve and Z-scores only work with proportions when the variable is nominally measured with only two possible categories (i.e., dichotomous). For nominal variables with more than two categories, a different inferential test is needed. The **chi-square** (χ^2) procedure is most commonly used. It also deals with comparing the differences between population *expectations* and sample *observations*.

Let's develop the logic of this procedure by way of a *Law & Order* example. Let us say that a task force is formed in a California county to determine whether the composition of capital crimes jury pools (those finally seated on juries) is representative of the demographics of the county as a whole. Throughout the year, 1,000 individuals served as jurors (and, we assume, only served once). Of those 1,000, 44% were of Hispanic origin, 30% were non-Hispanic white, 22% were of some Asian or Pacific Islander origin, and the remaining 4% were non-Hispanic black. The Hispanic community complains that, according to the most recent census figures, their community was underrepresented in jury selection. For the entire population, the relevant percentages of jury-age citizens are 51%, 28%, 18%, and 3%, respectively.[4] Was the recruitment technique biased?

The task force argues that, just as with the flip of a coin, one should expect some difference to occur solely based on the laws of mathematical chance.

chi-square An inferential-only statistic that tests for the possibility that the proportions we observe in a sample could have been randomly drawn from a population with different expected proportions. The chi-square must be used when more than two categories of a variable exist.

They could not hope to contact every citizen in every home, but they did try to come up with a fairly representative sample. They argue that they can't be asked to do better than what could have been produced by a purely random selection process.[5] The problem then gets framed as the following: are the differences between what is *observed* in the sample (the 1,000 jurors) *significantly* different enough from what would have been *expected* from the population to confidently reject the possibility that the recruitment technique was unbiased? Or are the differences so slight that, as with the flip of coins, a purely random procedure could have produced them?

In order to answer this question, we need to compute the chi-square statistic for this sample with the following statistical hypotheses:

H_0: percentage of four ethnic groups equals 51%, 28%, 18%, and 3%, respectively,

and

H_1: percentage support is significantly different from those percentages

Let's do the computations in stages. First, we need to compute the **observed** (absolute) **frequency** for each ethnic category. For example, with a total recruitment jury of 1,000, we observe (f_o) 440 individuals of Hispanic origin (44%). We next calculate the **expected frequency** (i.e., how many Hispanics should we have expected). Given the population breakdown, we would have *expected* an absolute frequency (f_e) of 510 (51%). We therefore find that 70 fewer Hispanic individuals were selected and seated for jury service than would have been expected if the selection process exactly reflected the proportion of Hispanic-Americans in the entire population. The observation deviates from the expectation by –70 ($f_o - f_e$). Compute the observed and expected frequencies for the other three categories, and subtract them to see by how many individuals the observations exceed or fall short of the expectations based on the population figures. It is best to set up a table at this stage (Table 8.1).

Expected values for each category are subtracted from the observed values to produce a *count* of how much deviation there is from our population-based expectation. Think of this as a *categorical*, rather than an individual, deviation

observed frequency The actual number of cases in each category observed in a sample.

expected frequency The number of cases in each category expected from a specified population from which a sample is randomly drawn.

TABLE 8.1 Observed and Expected Number of Jurors

Ethnic/Racial Category	f_o	f_e	$f_o - f_e$
Hispanic	440	510	–70
Non-Hispanic White	300	280	20
Asian/Pacific	220	180	40
Black	40	30	10

score. As with the computation of the individual deviation scores in Chapter 4, summing up these deviations across all categories will cancel each other out (70 fewer Hispanic-Americans must be made up by 70 more from the three other categories). Thus, as in the computation of the variance, we square those deviations (adding them will always produce a value of "0"). Of course, we now have a large number of "squared individuals" (4,900, 400, 1,600, and 100). As with the computation of the standard deviation, we need to bring this number back into alignment with our original values. We could add them and take the square root, but a different method is employed. Additionally, as with the computation of Z-scores, it would be useful to standardize these "squared deviations" to remove the unit of analysis (in this case, individuals).

In order to standardize these squared values, we divide each by the respective expected frequency (f_e) of each category. Think of it this way. With a small number of individuals in any particular category, our sample could not be much different in absolute terms from its population. Having a larger number of individuals, however, produces a much greater range of possibilities for over- or undersampling. Dividing by the expected frequency (our population estimate) re-calculates the squared difference in relative terms (i.e., as a proportion of the number of cases that originally exist). Notice that the oversampling of 10 black Americans produced a higher relative deviation than the 20 non-Hispanic whites. Add these proportional deviation scores to the table.[6] Now take their sum (i.e., add them together).

Again, a generic formula is useful, although not essential, in depicting the needed calculations. The formula for chi-square is as follows:

$$\chi^2 = \sum_{k=1}^{K} \frac{(f_o - f_e)^2}{f_e} \qquad (8.7)$$

where K = number of categories (not cases)
f_o = frequencies actually *observed* for each sample category
f_e = frequencies *expected* from the population for each category

Compute the expected frequency for each category, and subtract it from the observed frequency. Next, square that difference and divide by the expected frequency. Do this for each category, and then add them together.

You may justifiably surmise that a number like 23.26 has no intrinsic meaning. However, neither did a Z-score of 1.96 or any other value until we converted it to area under a normal curve. The logic here is similar, even if the graphs are not normal.

Sometimes, as in the calculation of a sample mean or dichotomous proportion, what we observe in the sample is identical to what we would

TABLE 8.2 Chi-Square Calculation for a Four-Category, One-Variable Distribution

Category	f_o	f_e	$f_o - f_e$	$(f_o - f_e)^2$	$(f_o - f_e)^2/f_e$
Hispanic	440	510	−70	4,900	9.61
Non-Hispanic White	300	280	20	400	1.43
Asian/Pacific	220	180	40	1,600	8.89
Black	40	30	10	100	3.33
					$\Sigma = 23.26 = \chi^2$

observe in, or what we would have expected from, the population. Given this condition, the Z-score will be equal to "0." In our current scenario, if we observed in the sample *exactly* what we expected from the population for each of our four categories, the chi-square value would be equal to "0." There would be no difference between observed and expected frequencies, the square of "0" is "0," "0" divided by any number is "0," and the sum of four "0s" is "0." Of course, it would be highly probable that in any single random sample we would produce a distribution a bit different from that of the population. As we increase the difference between observed (in the sample) and expected (from the population) values, we increase the calculated value of chi-square. However, could we have drawn by random chance enough fewer Hispanic-Americans, enough more black Americans, and so forth, to produce a chi-square value as high as 23.26 (or higher)? The question we need to ask is whether a set of observations producing a chi-square of 23.26 could have been randomly sampled from the given population. Or is it so high that the differences between observed and expected frequencies were probably caused by some bias, intentional or not, in the selection technique? Is 23.26 within a reasonable mathematical margin of error, or is it highly unlikely (like the flip of 100 heads)? In order to determine this, look at the table of critical values of chi-square (Table 8.3). First, figure out which row to peruse by calculating the "degrees of freedom" (*df*). The degrees of freedom for a single frequency distribution are equal to the number of categories (*K*) minus 1. Since we have four ethnic/racial categories, the degrees of freedom are equal to 3.[7] Move over to the column marked ".05" and notice the figure "7.815 (Figure 8.3)." Translation: if we randomly draw a large number of samples from any given population with four categories of any variable (and 3 degrees of freedom), 95% of the time the differences between observed (in the sample) and expected (from the population) frequencies will produce a chi-square between 0 and 7.815 (Figure 8.3). The ".05" represents the area to the right of the **critical value** (i.e., outside of the 95% confidence interval).

critical value The value of a statistic, like chi-square, above which allows us to confidently reject a null hypothesis.

Consider this to be much like the −1.96 and +1.96 Z-score values for the normal curve with two differences. First, because we square the differences,

TABLE 8.3 Critical Values of the Chi-Square Distribution

	Area to the Right of the Critical Value					
	.100	.050	.025	.010	.005	.001
df						
1	2.7055	3.8414	5.0238	6.6349	7.8794	10.828
2	4.6051	5.9914	7.3777	9.2103	10.5966	13.816
3	6.2513	*7.8147*	9.3484	11.3449	12.8381	16.266
4	7.7794	9.4877	11.1433	13.2767	14.8602	18.467
5	9.2363	11.0705	12.8325	15.0863	16.7496	20.515
6	10.6446	12.5916	14.4494	16.8119	18.5476	22.458
7	12.0170	14.0671	16.0128	18.4753	20.2777	24.322
8	13.3616	15.5073	17.5346	20.0902	21.9550	26.125
9	14.6837	16.9190	19.0228	21.6660	23.5893	27.877
10	15.9871	18.3070	20.4831	23.2093	25.1882	29.588
11	17.2750	19.6751	21.9200	24.7250	26.7569	31.264
12	18.5494	21.0261	23.3367	26.2170	28.2995	32.909
13	19.8119	22.3621	24.7356	27.6883	29.8194	34.528
14	21.0642	23.6848	26.1190	29.1413	31.3193	36.123
15	22.3072	24.9958	27.4884	30.5779	32.8013	37.697
16	23.5418	26.2962	28.8454	31.9999	34.2672	39.252
17	24.7690	27.5871	30.1910	33.4087	35.7185	40.790
18	25.9894	28.8693	31.5264	34.8058	37.1564	42.312
19	27.2036	30.1435	32.8523	36.1908	38.5822	43.820
20	28.4120	31.4104	34.1696	37.5662	39.9968	45.315
21	29.6151	32.6705	35.4789	38.9321	41.4010	46.797
22	30.8133	33.9244	36.7807	40.2894	42.7956	48.268
23	32.0069	35.1725	38.0757	41.6384	44.1813	49.728
24	33.1963	36.4151	39.3641	42.9798	45.5585	51.179

chi-square values can only be positive, thus the lowest value is "0." Second, like the set of *t*-distributions discussed at the end of Chapter 6, the shape of the chi-square distribution is different for each degree of freedom, or number of categories (−1). Interestingly enough, as we increase the degrees of freedom (say, 100), the χ^2 distribution becomes less skewed and more normal in its appearance (Figure 8.4).

As we increase the number of categories, we increase the possible ways that a sample can deviate from its population. Therefore, we decrease the likelihood of a computed chi-square close to 0 and increase the probability of a calculated chi-square well above 0. Note that the critical values or cutoff values for any confidence interval increase as we increase the number of categories and, thus, the degrees of freedom. Let us say that we had seven

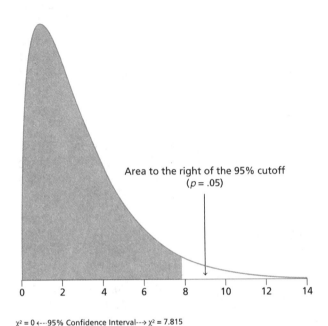

χ² = 0 ←---95% Confidence Interval---→ χ² = 7.815

FIGURE 8.3 Chi-Square Distribution with Three Degrees of Freedom

ethnic/racial categories instead of four. In order to confidently reject the possibility (95% confidence interval) that our sample could have been randomly drawn from a posited population, a chi-square value greater than 12.5916 ($df = 6$) would have to be calculated.

Could a chi-square greater than 7.815 be calculated for a randomly sampled group divided into four distinct categories? Like a high Z-score, it is possible but highly unlikely. "23.26" is so much higher than (significantly different from) "0" (and "7.815") that we can confidently reject the possibility that this sample of jurors was randomly drawn from the adult population.[8] The differences between observed and expected frequencies (and the chi-square produced) are more than we are willing to attribute to a random luck of the draw. The likelihood of bias in the sampling procedure is therefore *statistically* rather high. Hispanic-Americans were either intentionally (prosecuting or defense attorneys were more likely to eliminate them from the pool) or unintentionally (Hispanic-Americans might earn relatively low salaries and can therefore delay or cancel their jury duty) underrecruited. Stated differently,

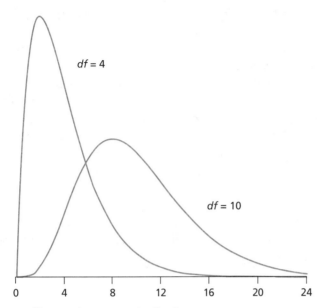

FIGURE 8.4 Different Chi-Square Distributions

the real population from which this group was sampled probably does not mirror the actual total population (but rather a disproportionately non-Hispanic one).[9] Legal controversy still remains over whether one needs to demonstrate intentional bias. Statistics can't answer that question, but they can provide a minimal base of data for its debate—a debate that is often used to question the legitimacy of the pool of individuals who serve on jury duty.

If, on the other hand, the differences between observed and expected frequencies produced a chi-square below our critical value (e.g., 5.6), then we would not be confident in rejecting the possibility that those differences were caused simply by random sampling procedures (much like we couldn't reject the possibility that support for a nation's foreign policy was 50% with a Z-score of less than 1.645). We would have no statistical basis for claiming discrimination. Of course, this does not mean that discrimination does not exist—only that the evidence is consistent with a fair recruiting procedure (as well as several biased ones).

Before we move on to the next chapter, let's discuss this notion of expected frequencies further. Recall that, with the IQV, the expected value was that which would occur if the cases were evenly distributed among all of the

Sidebar 8.1: Discrimination in Jury Selection

Courts will generally not challenge the method of jury selection as long as the discrepancy between the percentage of jurors of a protected group and that group's actual population percentage does not exceed ten percentage points. What that implies, of course, is that any group that constitutes less than 10% of the population can be excluded without question. This also means that black citizens are denied the chance to challenge in 75% of U.S. counties, and Hispanics and Asian-Americans in more than 90%.

Of course, prosecutors, defense counsels, and judges can eliminate a certain number of jurors without a specifically mentioned cause. Former justice Thurgood Marshall complained that, even though the court made challenges based on race easier to pursue, these individuals could "easily assert facially neutral reasons for striking a juror, and trial courts are ill equipped to second-guess those reasons" (*Batson v. Kentucky*, 476 U.S. 79 at 106).

For a full discussion of this issue, particularly the implications of the *Batson* decision, see the report of the Equal Justice Initiative, *Illegal Racial Discrimination in Jury Selection: A Continuing Legacy* (Equal Justice Initiative, 2010), available online at http://www.law.berkeley.edu/files/thcsj/IllegalRacialDiscriminationJurySelection.pdf.

categories. With χ^2, the expected value is based on the proportional breakdown of any given population against which we wish to compare our sample. Could this sample have been randomly drawn from that given population? The cases can be evenly distributed or not. Let us take an example where an even distribution *is* our expectation and the traditional rules of statistical inference apply.

A state gaming commission is concerned that a casino is not using regulation decks, thereby reducing the probability of certain cards appearing. The commission doesn't have time to count and identify every card. Instead, it shuffles all of the casinos decks together and randomly draws 1,000 cards from this master deck. The draw produces 265 Diamonds, 245 Hearts, 260 Clubs, and 230 Spades. Can we confidently claim that the house decks are rigged (i.e., can we confidently reject the possibility that the suits are evenly distributed throughout the decks)?

Once again, we will produce a table comparing observed and expected frequencies for each suit. In a normal deck of cards, the number of each suit should be identical (i.e., the cards are evenly distributed among the four suits). With 1,000 cards, the expected frequency for each suit would be 250.

The calculated χ^2 of 3 is less than the 7.815 critical value cutoff. The commission cannot reject the possibility that, in the population of all cards from which these 1,000 were sampled, the cards were evenly distributed among the four suits. Does that guarantee that the decks are indeed evenly

TABLE 8.4 Chi-Square Calculation of Sampled Cards

Category	f_o	f_e	$f_o - f_e$	$(f_o - f_e)^2$	$(f_o - f_e)^2/f_e$
Diamonds	265	250	15	225	.9
Hearts	245	250	−5	25	.1
Clubs	260	250	10	100	.4
Spades	230	250	−20	400	1.6
					$\sum = 3.0 = \chi^2$

distributed? No, but the evidence does not allow them to reject that as *one* possibility.

What if the commission randomly sampled 10,000 cards with the same proportional results (2,650, 2,450, 2,600, 2,300)? Recalculate the χ^2 value. The value is now 30. The commission now has statistical evidence that the cards are probably rigged. Why the difference? Remember, sample sizes are important when making inferences about any statistic. The larger the sample size, the closer any sample should be to the true population value. The anticipated margins of error should be proportionately less. As with our calculation of the Z-scores for dichotomous proportions, a larger sample size should and does produce a larger chi-square value—even though the observed proportions are the same.

One last question. Is the evidence of bias now absolutely conclusive? No. Just as with means and dichotomous proportions, even extreme differences between sample observations and population expectations are possible, even if highly unlikely. Additionally, the bias might not have been intentional (perhaps a card manufacturing error). This evidence alone would probably not hold up to proof "beyond a shadow of a doubt." However, it would provide at least a piece of the evidence required for a successful prosecution.

Similar to this analysis of observed and expected frequencies of cards, we could use the same logic in trying to determine if a sample of ethnic groups like the one we chose could have been randomly drawn from a population with perfect diversity among those groups. As with our calculation of the denominator of the IQV (Chapter 4), the expectation of the IQV would be an equal number of individuals within each of the four ethnic categories that exist in this community. Of course, one could claim that more ethnic categories would equate with greater diversity. However, given just these four sampled groups, could we reject the possibility that an equal number of each group exists in the population? Carry out the calculations to find out.

The use of the χ^2 statistic as an inferential measure for one variable (univariate) is not commonly found in most statistics texts, although the reason for its omission is not clear to this author. It provides a useful measure of the goodness of fit between a distribution of sample observations and a posited distribution of population observations for data measured at the categorical, or nominal, level. Its interpretation matches nicely with that used for Z-scores.[10] It can be used to judge whether or not a sample could have been drawn from a population with an even distribution among all categories (our expectation for the IQV). Its more common application will be covered as we discuss measures of association between two variables (bivariate), a discussion that we will begin in the next chapter. Other than the concepts of association and control, however, you have now been introduced to the basic elements of statistical theory—description and inference, central tendency, variation, and goodness of fit, as well as the notion of observed and expected values. Each of these will be re-introduced in the coming chapters.

APPENDIX

VISUALIZING DICHOTOMOUS PROPORTIONS AS MEANS

Although we would be hard-pressed to conceptualize dichotomies as interval data (we use ordinal terms like "more male," but can we state "by how much"?), there is, however, a direct mathematical equivalence between the two. Let us say that a statistical program, not knowing the limitation of the data, computed a mean value of gender of 2.6. Males are arbitrarily categorized as "1," and females as "5." Given that mean, and the category values arbitrarily assigned, one and only one combination of proportions of males and females is possible. Why? Let's categorize the proportion of males as "M" and the proportion of females as "F." Because males and females constitute the entire universe of categories for gender (proportion = 1), then the proportion of females can be listed as "$1 - p_M$." In Chapter 3 we stated that the mean can be computed with proportions using the following formula:

$$\overline{X} = \sum_{k=1}^{K} p_k \times x_k$$

Carrying that out with the gender information given:

$$2.6 = (p_M) \times 1 + (1 - p_M) \times 5$$
$$2.6 = p_M + 5 - 5\,p_M$$
$$2.6 = 5 - 4\,p_M$$
$$-2.4 = -4\,p_M$$
$$M = .6$$

The proportion of men equals .60, or 60% of the total. The proportion of women must therefore equal .4, or 40%. Given that mean, and those arbitrarily assigned categories, no other pair of proportions is possible. This exercise might seem silly, but it helps us to understand why dichotomous proportions and means can be analyzed similarly. It also explains why dichotomous variables can be used in regression analysis (dummy variables), a statistical technique that assumes interval properties for its variables. We'll discuss regression analysis in Chapters 11 and 12.

KEY TERMS

chi-square (171)

critical value (174)

dichotomous variable/
dichotomies (165)

expected frequency (172)

observed frequency (172)

QUESTIONS AND EXERCISES

NOTE: Several more examples and exercises can be found in both the SPSS and Stata manuals that accompany this text. Inferential tests for dichotomous proportions and one-variable chi-squares can be found in a set of legacy procedures Section 4.4.

1. A European newspaper reports that the maximum margin of error for its poll sample, using a 95% confidence interval technique, is 4.4%. Seventy-two percent of the sample members state that they support the stricter restrictions on immigration from non-EU countries (28% do not). Using that maximum margin of error, what would be our estimate of the true proportion of supporters of stricter restrictions in the population? Could we confidently reject the possibility that the true, or expected, proportion was 66%? Is that percentage impossible?

2. An exit poll has a margin of error of 5.6%. The observations derived from this poll predict that the incumbent member of Congress will retain her seat with 54% of the two-candidate vote. How safe is the polling agency in calling the race for the incumbent?

3. Return to the figures in Exercise 1. Use the sample proportions as estimates of the true population proportions. The sample size is 500. What can we expect the range of population support to be?

4. A variable has four possible responses. How many degrees of freedom exist for that variable? If we are using a 95% confidence interval test, what would be the critical chi-square value? What does that critical value mean?

5. A variable has eight possible responses. How many degrees of freedom exist for that variable? If we are using a 95% confidence interval test, what would be the critical chi-square value? What does that critical value mean?

6. Why do you think the critical value in Exercise 5 is higher than that in Exercise 4?

7. Return to the three ideological listings in Chapter 4, Table 4.1. The third has 90 individuals on the left of the spectrum, 80 in the center, and 70 on the right. Assume this is a random sample. Could this sample have been drawn from a population where the individuals are evenly distributed (80) among the three categories?

8. Can we specify exactly what the population proportional breakdown is in Exercise 7?

9. Perform the same calculation and analysis as in Exercise 7, but with a population proportional breakdown of 60%, 20%, and 20%.

10. Perform the same calculation and analysis as in Exercise 7, but with a sample ten times larger (2,400) and with the same proportional breakdown in the sample (900, 800, 700). Do our inferential results differ? What does this tell you about the "law of large numbers"?

▌NOTES

1 Of course, as we saw in Chapter 2, how we treat "non-voters" will affect the outcome regardless of which statistic is used.

2 An example of such a biased question would be: "The United States is a trading partner that purchases many of our goods. Although one might not agree with all of our diplomatic relations with the United States, increasing tensions between our countries might lead to economic sanctions against our products. This will most likely lead to a substantial loss of jobs. Do you approve of our nation's U.S. foreign policy?" Notice, this would not be the same as asking: "We have many concerns about U.S. involvement in our region. Do you approve of your nation's foreign policy toward the United States?"

3 We've truncated the discussion here because our discussion of sample means covered this fully. The logic is exactly the same and is based on a series of theoretical sampling distribution of proportions in which .52 would lie within each distribution's 95% confidence interval.

4 Of course, the census is itself an estimate. Many argue that certain ethnic groups are severely underrepresented. It is, however, the best full enumeration we have. For purposes of illustration, let's proceed as if it were complete.

5 Here I am using my compromise version of significance test use.

6 Note the similarity to the variation ratio formula re-calculated as the difference between observations and expectations found in Chapter 4. The order of subtraction differs ($f_e - f_o$ rather than $f_o - f_e$), but squaring the difference removes the disparity (either order would produce the same result). Note, however, that the variation ratio measures the standardized difference from the mode for an entire distribution. For the chi-square, we measure the standardized difference for each category of a distribution based on expected values for each category.

7 If we fix the number of cases of the first three categories and keep the total number of cases constant, then the number of cases in the fourth category is no longer free to vary. Once we know the number of Hispanic, non-Hispanic white, and Asian jurors, then, with a fixed number of individuals of 1,000, we can automatically determine the number of individuals who are black.

8 Most computer programs will actually compute the exact point on the chi-square distribution on which the calculated value falls and specify the area to the right of that point. If that value is less than .05 (as it is in our example), then we can reject the null hypothesis that the sample could have been randomly drawn from the posited population.

9   Unfortunately, unlike means and dichotomous proportions, we cannot even begin to specify a range of actual possible population values from which this group of 1,000 was drawn. With more than two categories, the possibilities are virtually infinite. Of course, using the chi-square formula, we can compare our observed distribution to any hypothesized distribution and determine if the differences are statistically significant or not.

10 This match between interpretations is more than coincidental. Go back to the data from which we calculated our original Z-score (52%/48% split). List the observed and expected frequencies (not proportions). With a sample of 500, the observed frequencies would be 260 and 240, respectively. As we are testing whether this could have been randomly drawn from a population with 50% support, the expected frequencies are 250 and 250. Calculate the chi-square. It should equal .8, which is the square of the Z-score of .8944272. As we shall see later, statistics are often related to each other in more than conceptual ways.

Category	f_o	f_e	$f_o - f_e$	$(f_o - f_e)^2$ *	$(f_o - f_e)^2/f_e$
Approve	260	250	10	100	.4
Disapprove	240	250	−10	100	.4
					$\Sigma = .8 = \chi^2$

In the next chapter, we'll discuss a modification of this formula when only 1 degree of freedom exists, as it does in this example.

CHAPTER 9

Measuring Association for Nominal and Ordinal Data

Learning Objectives:

▧ To learn how to read a bivariate contingency table

▧ To understand the concept of observed and expected frequencies given categorical, nominal data for two variables

▧ To be able to use chi-square as an inferential measure of two-variable nominal distributions

▧ To understand the concept of a proportional reduction of error measure

▧ To learn the differences between alternate definitions of association and no association

▧ To understand why different statistics can produce drastically different results with the same crosstabular data

▧ To realize that many statistics are variations of others

▌ CONTINGENCY TABLES

Thus far, when dealing with categorical, nominal data, we have mainly discussed questions dealing with the distribution of values on one variable (frequency distributions, modes, variation ratios, indexes of qualitative variation, and inferences based on proportions). As we noted in Chapter 7, however, most important issues in the social sciences deal with discussing the relationship or association between and among the values of two or more variables. We will not discuss bivariate (two variable) differences between dichotomous proportions, although the logic and math is similar to those of the difference between means. This chapter will discuss how one measures the differences between proportions with any number of categories. For this we will use a **crosstabulation** or **contingency table**. Just as a frequency distribution provided a pictorial review of the distribution of one variable, a crosstabulation provides similar information about the relationship between two or more variables.

Crosstabulations can provide a wealth of information about the association between variables. Comparing sets of percentages can answer several interesting questions. Each set of contingent percentages, however, answers a different question. We must be careful in how we read those percentages. Let us turn to the following crosstabulation for an example.

In the following table, information is provided from the 1988 American National Election Studies (ANES) survey.[1] Two variables are presented, gender and presidential vote, each with two possible categories (dichotomies). Note that only those respondents who claim to have voted for one of the major party candidates are listed (third-party and non-voters are excluded from this analysis, as they are from most electoral discussions). A claim has been made that there exists a gender gap between men and women over their political attitudes and behaviors. Specifically, women are more likely to think and behave like Democrats than are men. Men, in turn, are more likely to behave like Republicans than are women. The *independent variable*, or property specified is gender; that is, we are hypothesizing that one's gender has a direct effect on one's partisan orientation. Gender is in actuality a surrogate measure for personality and cultural differences. Women, for example, seem to be more likely to be concerned with social welfare issues (an issue cluster beneficial to Democrats) than are men. Remember that by considering all women as a unit, we are losing the distinctiveness among them. Not all women are concerned about social welfare issues. Similarly not all men are not concerned. Multivariate analysis can help us to determine which aspects of gender differences are most important, and which men and women are most likely to behave in a "normal" manner. For now, we'll deal only with a bivariate analysis; but keep in mind that the universe, political or otherwise, is much more complex.

One way to operationalize the outcome of partisan orientation is to determine how people vote for president. Presidential vote, or the partisan direction of that vote, is therefore the *dependent variable*. We provide *one* test implication by analyzing survey results in 1988.

Table 9.1 provides both absolute frequencies (how many), and a series of relative frequencies (what percentage) for the bivariate distribution between

crosstabulation or contingency table A frequency table that represents the distribution of data simultaneously on two or more variables.

TABLE 9.1 The Gender Gap in 1988

PRESIDENTIAL VOTE	Gender		Total
	1 Male	2 Female	
1 Democratic	232	331	563
	43.5%	50.0%	47.1%
2 Republican	301	331	632
	56.5%	50.0%	52.9%
	533	662	$N = 1,195$
Total	44.6%	55.4%	100.0%

our independent (gender) variable and our dependent (1988 presidential vote) variable. Now we need to use this information to confirm or disconfirm the following test implication of our general gender gap hypothesis:

In 1988, women were more likely to support the Democratic presidential candidate, (Michael Dukakis), than were men.

. . . which is a logical test implication of the following general hypothesis:

Women are more likely to vote Democratic than are men.

Notice that we can't answer this question by looking at the absolute frequencies. More females than males voted Republican, but more females also voted Democratic. There just happen to be more females in the survey.[2] Refer back to our discussion of frequency distributions in Chapter 2. When the total case sizes are different, one cannot compare absolute counts. Instead, one must *standardize* to a common base that depends on proportions, or relative frequencies. In order to answer the question, we must first determine what proportion of the 533 men in our sample voted Democratic (232/533 = *43.5%*) and Republican (301/533 = *56.5%*) for president. We then calculate the proportions of the 662 females who voted Democratic (331/662 = *50%*) and Republican (331/662 = *50.0%*).

Women were more likely to vote Democratic than were men. Looking at the column percentages, we can state that, in this sample, females were 6.5 percentage points (50.5–43.5) more likely to vote Democratic than were males. That 6.5% is called the **relevant percentage difference**. Of course both groups gave the Republican candidate, George H. W. Bush, at least half of their support. Certain summary measures of association are sensitive to this, and can indicate very high or very low degrees of association between these variables. We'll return to this example as we cover more statistics of association

relevant percentage difference The difference in the percentages of cases between dependent variable categories for one or more independent variable categories.

in this chapter. First, however, make sure that you understand how to per-centage properly. Our hypothesis asks us to compare the proportion of all 533 males and 662 females who voted Democratic. Thus, we calculated column percentages. Row percentages would tell us what proportion of those who voted Democratic were males (232/563 = 41.2%) and what proportion were females (331/563 = 58.8%). The Republican breakdown would be 47.6% and 52.4%, respectively. These figures, often presented in the press as profiles of partisan supporters, would indicate that Democrats are more dependent on the votes of females than are Republicans, but, while important to cam-paign consultants, would not directly answer the question proposed by our hypothesis.

We have only produced part of the answer to our question. Our sample evidence confirms our guess about the differences between men and women. Women were more likely to support the Democratic presidential candidate (Michael Dukakis) by 6.5 percentage points. Of course, gender is not the only determinant of the vote. If it were, the proportional levels of support for each candidate should be polar opposites or close to it (roughly 100% of women should have voted Democratic, and roughly 0% of men). Whether or not a 6.5% point difference (rather than 100%) is theoretically significant or important is a question that is debated by political commentators and consultants, and the answer to that question is not directly addressed by statistical techniques.

Two-category by two-category tables are fairly unique, so let's hold off on a further analysis to later in this chapter. Let us look at another cross table. The data represented here come from another hypothetical survey of that same Latin American country discussed in Chapter 8. In an effort to bolster support for its U.S. foreign policy, governmental leaders are trying to determine the demographics of support in order to best fashion and target their message. Respondents are asked, among other items, their age and their support for better relations with the United States (support, not support). We'll treat age as the independent variable, one's level of support as the dependent variable (see Table 9.2). For simplicity, we will combine respondents into only three categories based on their age (younger = below 30, middle = 30–50, older = 51 and above).[3] Remember (Chapter 2) that how we combine categories can dramatically affect our understanding of a group's characteristics. It can also affect our interpretation of the relationship between variables.

One might hypothesize that one's age has a direct bearing on one's support for improved U.S. relations:

H_1: *The older one is, the more likely one is to support improved relations with the United States.*

For this sample, our guess is correct. The oldest respondents were 17 percentage points more likely to support improved relations than those in the middle

TABLE 9.2 Age and Foreign Policy Support

| IMPROVED U.S. RELATIONS | Age | | | Total |
	1 Younger	2 Middle	3 Older	
Support	120	110	360	590
	40.0%	55.0%	72.0%	59.0%
Do Not Support	180	90	140	410
	60.0%	45.0%	28.0%	41.0%
Total	300	200	500	$N = 1,000$
	30.0%	20.0%	50.0%	100.0%

age group, 32 percentage points less likely than the youngest. Once again, of course, it seems that other factors also have a bearing on the relationship (income, education, etc.) otherwise we would expect even greater discrimination (e.g., 100% of the oldest respondents favoring improved relations).

THE CHI-SQUARE STATISTIC

We have confirmed our hypothesis by way of this one test, but only descriptively (Step 4 in our process first discussed in Chapter 6).[4] However (Step 5), are those relevant percentage point differences in the sample of 17% and 32% significant enough to be able to confidently claim that differences in support among individuals of different age classifications at some level greater than 0 also exist in the population from which this sample was randomly drawn? Or can those differences be small enough to be attributed to the luck of the random draw (we just accidently drew a few more young respondents who opposed improved relations, etc.)? For nominal, crosstabular data, the null hypothesis that we usually wish to reject is that the proportional support (the dependent variable) for each subcategory of the independent variable (in this example, age) is equal, that is, where the differences in the proportion of support among the youngest, middle, and oldest age categories is 0%. Stated differently, are the proportions that we *observe* significantly different enough from the proportions we would *expect* if our three groups of respondents did not differ in their support in the population at all? Or are the differences small enough to be attributed to random sampling error?

This notion of proportional equivalence is a form of non-association known as **statistical independence**. We say that statistical independence obtains when one's placement on one variable (in this case, age) has absolutely no bearing on one's placement on a second variable. The probability of a young person supporting improved relations is no different from the probabilities for those who are older.

statistical independence
A type of no association between two variables where percentages on the dependent variable are invariant across independent variable categories.

189

A standard, familiar way of addressing this question is by looking at a standard deck of 52 playing cards. Decks of cards have two "variables"—suit (Diamonds, Clubs, Hearts, Spades) and face value (Ace, two, . . . King). There are four jacks in a standard deck. The probability of drawing a jack from an entire deck is therefore 4/52 = 1/13. Now let us pull out only diamonds (13 cards) and shuffle them. The probability of pulling out a jack is still 1/13; that is, the probabilities have not changed even when we have restricted the suit drawn. The same 1/13 probability would exist if we only pulled out clubs or hearts or spades. We therefore say that the suit of a card and the face value of a card are *statistically independent* of each other. Mathematically, statistical significance is said to obtain when the probability of the joint occurrence of two variables is equal to the product of the probabilities of the separate occurrences of two variables. There is a 1/4 probability of randomly drawing a diamond from a deck of cards. There is a 1/13 probability of drawing a jack. The product of these probabilities is 1/52, exactly the probability of randomly drawing a jack of diamonds. Look at our hypothetical survey results. The probability of randomly drawing an older respondent who supports improved U.S. foreign relations (360 of 1,000, or 36.0%) is not the same as the product of randomly drawing out an older respondent (50%) and a supporter (59%), which is equal to 29.5%.

The probability of randomly pulling out someone *in our entire sample* who supports improved relations is equal to 590/1,000 = 59%. We now use the same logic as we did with cards but with different probabilities. If we restrict ourselves to any of the three age categories of respondents, we observe that the probability of randomly pulling out a supporter is different from 59%; it is respectively 40%, 55%, and 72%. If we guessed that any one of the 1,000 sampled individuals support the policy, we would guess wrong a proportionately different number of times depending on the age category of the respondent. Statistical independence is not in evidence here. The question remains, however, whether statistical independence *can* obtain in the population from which the sample was randomly drawn. Is it possible that the level of support in the sampled population from *each* group is *exactly* the same as for all respondents combined (i.e., 59%)? Can the differences between what we observe and what we would expect if the two variables were statistically independent be small enough to be attributed to the random luck of the draw?

As we did with our one-variable chi-square in Chapter 8, we now need to compare our *observed* sample frequencies with what we would have *expected* if statistical independence obtained (i.e., where each group supports improved relations 59% of the time). Once again the formula for χ^2 is:

$$\chi^2 = \sum_{k=1}^{K} \frac{(f_o - f_e)^2}{f_e} \qquad (9.1)$$

where now K = number of cross-classification categories (table cells)

f_o = frequencies actually *observed* for each sample category (cell)

f_e = frequencies *expected* from the population for each cell, in this instance if the two variables are statistically independent

Remember that **chi-square (two variables)** is purely an inferential statistic. A "high" value only tells you that the chance of randomly drawing a sample where the association is not statistically independent ($\chi^2 > 0$) from a population in which statistically independence obtains is less than, say, 5%. Translation: the differences in this sample are so great that we have to assume that a difference (of some unknown size greater than 0) probably also exists in the population from which this sample was randomly drawn. The differences are too great to be attributed to the random luck of the draw alone. We would thus state that some level of nominal association exists in that population (although we don't know exactly at what level). If the calculated chi-square is less than the critical (.05) value, then we could not confidently reject the possibility that there is no difference between the categories in the population from which the sample was randomly drawn. The differences are minor enough to fall within the margin of sampling error.

Also remember that the observed frequency in this chi-square calculation is what the sample actually produces, that is, the actual number *observed* in each cell (cross-category). The *expected* frequency is what we would expect if the two variables are totally independent of each other (like the face value of a card in an unbiased deck of cards is totally independent of its suit). Fifty-nine percent of the total sample supports improved relations. If age (as categorized) and support were statistically independent of each other, then 59% of the youngest age group would have supported improved relations, 59% of those in the middle group, and 59% of those in the oldest. If one's age is independent of one's support for improved relations, then we would *expect* 59% (59/100) of the youngest group to support improved relations (just like Diamonds and Jacks); 59% of 300 equals 177.[5] We sampled 57 fewer young respondents who support improved relations than we would have expected if age and support were statistically independent of each other (again, think of this as a categorical deviation score). The entries for the chi-square statistic are calculated and displayed in Table 9.3. Remember to *standardize* the squared differences by the expected, not observed frequencies (since the expectation is the base against which we wish to compare).

Chi-square gives us an inferential value for the nominal association between two variables. We need to determine if the value computed from the sample is high enough to safely reject the possibility that the given sample could have been randomly drawn from a population where those within different age categories all had the exact same level of support (59%), that is, where statistical independence obtained between those two variables. We can safely reject that

chi-square (two variables) An inferential measure of association that compares the observed frequencies within a contingency table against a certain frequency expectation, usually one that matches statistical independence.

TABLE 9.3 Chi-Square Calculation

Category (Age/Support)	f_o (observed)	f_e (expected)	$f_o - f_e$	$(f_o - f_e)^2$	$(f_o - f_e)^2/f_e$
Youngest/Support	120	177[a]	−57	3,249	18.36
Middle/Support	110	118	−8	64	.54
Oldest/Support	360	295	65	4,225	14.32
Youngest/Not Support	180	123	57	3,249	26.41
Middle/Not Support	90	82	8	64	.78
Oldest/Not Support	140	205	−65	4,225	20.61
					$\Sigma = 81.02 = \chi^2$

[a] Given a cross table, the expected cell frequencies can be calculated by multiplying the appropriate total row frequency (in which the cell resides) by the appropriate column frequency, and then dividing by the total frequency of the table.

$$(Ro \times Co)/To = f_e$$

Where ro is the observed frequency for the entire row, co is the observed frequency for the entire column, and To is the total number of observations for the entire table. The expected frequency within each crosstabular cell is listed as f_e.

So, given our cross table between age and support:

f_e for (Youngest/Support) = (590 × 300)/1,000 = 177

After all, 590 (the column frequency) divided by 1,000 (the total frequency) is the proportion of the entire sample that supported a tax increase. With 300 young respondents, we would expect that 177 of them would have supported improved relations if the two variables were statistically independent. This may seem simple, especially with a total sample size as clean as 1,000, but using this calculation helps to reduce rounding error from that which would be produced if we first calculated a proportion, and then multiplied it by the row frequency.

possibility (as in our one variable example) if the computed chi-square value lies outside of the 95% confidence interval. Remember that the value needed to meet the 5% criterion is dependent not on the number of cases (as in dichotomous proportions), but on the shape of the chi-square distribution, which is contingent on the "degrees of freedom" of the cross-classification table.

The "degrees of freedom" for a cross table are somewhat different than for a univariate distribution and are calculated as the product of the number of categories of one variable (minus 1) times the number of categories of the other variable (minus 1):[6]

$$df = (R - 1) \times (C - 1)$$

where R = number of row categories
C = number of column categories

In our example of a 3 × 2 table, 2 degrees of freedom exist. For a distribution with two degrees of freedom, 95% of the samples that could be randomly drawn from such a population would have, just on the basis of the luck of the draw, chi-square values below 5.9914 (Figure 9.1, Table 9.4). Think of "5.9914" as the maximum tolerable margin of error. Samples with calculated chi-square values greater than 5.9914 could have been randomly drawn from such a population, but the chance of such a random draw is less than 5%. This sample probably was drawn from a population where *some* difference in support exists between different types of respondents. We can't say exactly what it is (it might be less or more than those observed), but the difference is most likely greater than 0%.

A few qualifiers need to be mentioned. First, the chi-square should not be used if the sample size is less than 50.[7] Second, the chi-square should not be used if any expected cell frequency is less than 5. As with most inferential statistics, small values make the inferences very tentative. Also, as the χ^2

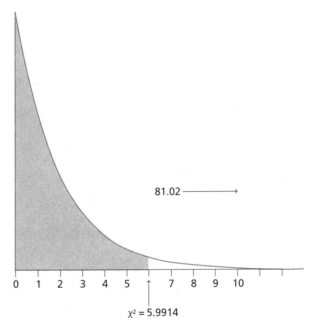

FIGURE 9.1 Chi-Square Example, Degrees of Freedom = 2

TABLE 9.4 Critical Values of the Chi-Square Distribution

| | Area to the Right of the Critical Value | | | | | |
	.100	.050	.025	.010	.005	.001
df						
1	2.7055	3.8414	5.0238	6.6349	7.8794	10.828
2	4.6051	*5.9914*	7.3777	9.2103	10.5966	13.816
3	6.2513	7.8147	9.3484	11.3449	12.8381	16.266
4	7.7794	9.4877	11.1433	13.2767	14.8602	18.467
5	9.2363	11.0705	12.8325	15.0863	16.7496	20.515
6	10.6446	12.5916	14.4494	16.8119	18.5476	22.458
7	12.0170	14.0671	16.0128	18.4753	20.2777	24.322
8	13.3616	15.5073	17.5346	20.0902	21.9550	26.125
9	14.6837	16.9190	19.0228	21.6660	23.5893	27.877
10	15.9871	18.3070	20.4831	23.2093	25.1882	29.588
11	17.2750	19.6751	21.9200	24.7250	26.7569	31.264
12	18.5494	21.0261	23.3367	26.2170	28.2995	32.909
13	19.8119	22.3621	24.7356	27.6883	29.8194	34.528
14	21.0642	23.6848	26.1190	29.1413	31.3193	36.123
15	22.3072	24.9958	27.4884	30.5779	32.8013	37.697
16	23.5418	26.2962	28.8454	31.9999	34.2672	39.252
17	24.7690	27.5871	30.1910	33.4087	35.7185	40.790
18	25.9894	28.8693	31.5264	34.8058	37.1564	42.312
19	27.2036	30.1435	32.8523	36.1908	38.5822	43.820
20	28.4120	31.4104	34.1696	37.5662	39.9968	45.315
21	29.6151	32.6705	35.4789	38.9321	41.4010	46.797
22	30.8133	33.9244	36.7807	40.2894	42.7956	48.268
23	32.0069	35.1725	38.0757	41.6384	44.1813	49.728
24	33.1963	36.4151	39.3641	42.9798	45.5585	51.179

formula is an approximation of the true value, if df equals "1" (2×2 table), a correction for continuity has to be made. This correction occurs in the numerator of the equation as:

$$(|f_o - f_e| - .5)^2 \qquad (9.2)$$

First take the absolute value of the difference and then subtract .5 before squaring the difference. This gives us a more conservative (smaller) χ^2 value, which in turn makes it more difficult to confidently reject the null hypothesis of statistical independence.

Let's return to our original gender gap table. Compute the expected frequencies, i.e., those that would exist if gender and the vote were statistically independent of each other. For example, since 47.1% of all voters in the sample, regardless of gender, voted for the Democratic candidate, we would expect 47.1% of the 553 men and 47.1% of the 662 women to have voted for him. Table 9.5 lists all of the relevant figures, with the correction for continuity added. We used the method of calculation addressed in footnote 1, Table 9.3, to avoid double rounding errors. Although we can't really expect fractional voters, carry out the expected frequency to two decimal places.

With one degree of freedom, 95% of the time, just by the random luck of the draw, we will draw a sample with observed frequencies that will be identical to or different enough from the expected frequencies to create a chi-square value of less than 3.84. Our calculated χ^2 of 4.71 (4.97 without the continuity correction) is greater than that critical value. We can therefore (Step 5) reject the null hypothesis that support for the candidates is

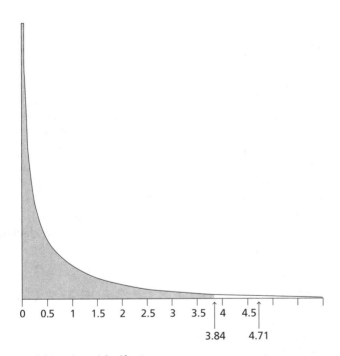

FIGURE 9.2 Chi-Square with $df = 1$

TABLE 9.5 Chi-Square Calculation

Category	f_o	f_e	$f_o - f_e$	$(|f_o - f_e| - .5)^2$	$(|f_o - f_e| - .5)^2 / f_e$
Male/Democrat	232	251.11	−19.11	346.33	1.38
Female/Democrat	331	311.89	19.11	346.33	1.11
Male/Republican	301	281.89	19.11	346.33	1.23
Female/Republican	331	350.11	−19.11	346.33	0.99
					$\Sigma = 4.71 = \chi^2$

proportionately exactly the same between men and women in the population from which this sample was randomly drawn. In all likelihood, women were more supportive of the Democratic candidate, Michael Dukakis than were men in the population, even if not by a majority.

An Important Note

Stating that two variables are most likely not statistically independent must be viewed with care. We must first look at the observed results to see if they are in the right hypothesized direction. Look at either of our previous chi-square examples. We could switch the frequencies between or among categories—say making women more supportive of George H. W. Bush—but the chi-square would not vary. Chi-square, after all, is a nominal measure. Thus, the direction of the association does not matter. Whether women are 6.5 percentage points more or less supportive makes no difference in the calculation of the chi-square statistic (nor any other statistic with which it is associated). As you will notice subsequently, lambda, a purely nominal statistic, must be viewed the same way.

PROPORTIONAL REDUCTION OF ERROR AND LAMBDA

Percentage differences are useful in descriptively summarizing one table. However, what if we have a series of tables, with different numbers of categories (say parties), or measuring different variables (gender, views about health care reform, etc.)? Statisticians rely on several measures of association which, like the mean, mode, or standard deviation, produce a single value for each cross table. Some of these measures are nominal, some ordinal ("The more children one has, the more supportive one is of a property tax increase to support education"). In general, a value of "0" means that no statistical relationship or association between the variables exists, a value of 1 (or −1 if direction is important) means that perfect association exists. We won't have time to cover all of this in detail in this chapter, but different statistics have different interpretations of "no" and "perfect." So be careful which statistics are used. Statistics don't lie, but individuals can choose statistics to make their points more forcefully.

Let us begin our discussion of descriptive nominal measures of association by introducing a new concept and coming back to an old one. Remember our original bar game in our discussion of the mode in Chapter 3 and apply it to our foreign policy support example. If one of these 1,000 Latin American individuals walked into a bar, and all we knew was how the 1,000 felt about improved U.S. relations (referred to as the support marginals), what would we guess the choice for that person to be (see Table 9.6)? We determined that guessing the mode (in this case, "Support") was the safest bet because we would be wrong less often (410) by doing so if we had to guess the preference of all 1,000 individuals. Another way of stating this is to say that our probability of being wrong by guessing the mode, "Support for improved U.S. relations" for any individual is .410. Let's make the game a bit more interesting. What if we were also told that individual's age category, and also given the preference distributions for each "age" group (the entire table). We would still use the mode as our safest guessing rule, but the additional information proves helpful. If the person was within the youngest group, we would bet on his/her being *against* improved relations (the modal category for that group), but be wrong 120 times for that group. If the person was in the middle age category, we would guess a different mode (Support) and be wrong 90 times. If that person were in the oldest, we would guess the same modal category (Support) as for someone in the middle group and be wrong 140 times. Collectively, we would be wrong in guessing the modal category for each group (120 + 90 +140) 350 times. Our probability of being wrong would be reduced to .350.

TABLE 9.6 Age and Foreign Policy Support

IMPROVED U.S. RELATIONS	Age			Total
	1 Youngest	2 Middle	3 Oldest	
Support	120	110	360	590
	40.0%	55.0%	72.0%	59.0%
Do Not Support	180	90	140	410
	60.0%	45.0%	28.0%	41.0%
Total	300	200	500	$N = 1,000$
	30.0%	20.0%	50.0%	100.0%

Did we improve our ability to make a correct guess about support for improved relations knowing information about one's age? Yes, we reduced our probability of error from .410 to .350. Of course, how much we can reduce our probability of error is a function of how high that probability is to begin with (the more we are off the more we can improve). We therefore *standardize* that difference by the original probability. Proportionately, we reduced our probability of error by [(.410 − .350)/.410] .146, or 14.6%. Knowledge of the independent variable (age) reduced our error in predicting ones placement on the dependent variable (support) proportionately by 14.6% over predicting blindly (i.e., without such knowledge).

We have just completed an introduction to a class of statistics known as **PRE (proportional reduction of error) measures**. PRE measures generically tell us by what proportion do we reduce our error in making guesses about the dependent variable by having knowledge about the independent variable. The general formula for PRE measures is the following:

$$PRE = \frac{P(1) - P(2)}{P(1)} \qquad \textbf{(9.3)}$$

where $P(1)$ is the probability (or proportion) of incorrectly guessing placement on the dependent variable blindly (i.e., *without* information about the independent variable)

$P(2)$ is the probability of incorrectly guessing placement on the dependent variable *with* information about the independent variable

We then say that the independent and dependent variables are related or associated if knowledge about the independent variable reduces our probability of error in guessing placement on the dependent variable. "Age" and "Support for Improved U.S. Relations" are associated in our example to the extent that knowledge about age proportionately reduces our probability of error in predicting support by 14.6% over predicting blindly (the mode for everyone). PRE measures can range from 0 (where no reduction is made) to 1 (where knowledge about the independent variable completely eliminates our probability of error).

PRE measures exist for nominal, ordinal, and interval data, and employ different rules for making guesses about the dependent variable. If the data are nominal, and the rule for guessing is the mode (as in our case), then the PRE measure is called **lambda** (λ). Since λ is based on the proportional number of times we make wrong guesses, a raw score formula can be calculated as follows:

$$\lambda = \frac{\dfrac{N(1)}{N} - \dfrac{N(2)}{N}}{\dfrac{N(1)}{N}} \qquad \textbf{(9.4)}$$

PRE (proportional reduction of error) measure Any measure of association that assesses proportionately how much better off we are with information about the independent variable than without.

lambda A nominal measure of association, based on the mode, that assesses how much better off we are with information about the independent variable.

where $N(1)$ equals the number (absolute frequency) of total errors in prediction for the entire table by guessing blindly

$N(2)$ equals the number of total errors in prediction with knowledge about the independent variable

N equals the total number of cases in our crosstabular distribution

Some quick mathematics and our formula for λ becomes, allowing us to use
the number or absolute frequencies of incorrect guesses:

$$\lambda = \frac{N(1) - N(2)}{N(1)} \qquad (9.5)$$

Notice also that $P(1)$ and $P(2)$ are equal to the proportion of cases *not included*
in the respective modal categories. Sound familiar? $P(1)$ is the Variation Ratio
(VR) for the support variable. $P(2)$ is the (weighted) mean average variation ratio
for support for each category of the independent variable, age. Lambda can therefore also be thought of as a PRV (proportional reduction of variation) measure:

$$\lambda = \frac{VR(1) - VR(2)}{VR(1)} \qquad (9.6)$$

where $VR(1)$ is the original variation (from the mode) of the dependent
variable

$VR(2)$ is the variation unexplained (left over) by the independent
variable

We'll return to the similarities between PRE and PRV measures in a subsequent
discussion of regression analysis. For now let's investigate the circumstances under
which lambda will achieve its lowest value (0) and its highest value (1). Lambda
can never be negative. More information can never increase the number or
probability of a wrong guess (some of my students might argue with that).
Lambda will equal 0, indicating no relationship between the two variables, when
the proportional breakdown on the dependent variable (support) within each
category of the independent variable (age) is the same. This is the condition that,
in our discussion of chi-square, we called statistical independence. The variation
ratios of support for those in each age category are equal. Stated differently, our
probability of incorrectly guessing one's support by guessing the mode is the
same regardless of one's age. Refer to our original table, but substituting a set of
observed frequencies that just happen to match our expected ones (Table 9.7).

$$\lambda = \frac{410 - (123 + 82 + 205)}{410} = \frac{410 - 410}{410} = 0 \qquad (9.7)$$

Every statistic has some potential limitations or peculiarities, and lambda,
unfortunately, is no exception. When two variables are statistically independent, lambda will always equal 0. The reverse, however, is not true. A lambda
of 0 does not necessarily indicate statistical independence.

Let's vary the original table just a bit (see Table 9.8). Split the support of those in the youngest age category 151/149. Keep the other breakdowns the same. Re-compute the percentage differences. Re-compute lambda. Compare your results. Notice that although the percentages still indicate a relationship between "age" and "support," lambda (0) indicates that no relationship exists.

$$\lambda = \frac{379 - (149 + 90 + 140)}{379} = \frac{379 - 379}{379} = 0 \tag{9.8}$$

So long as the modal categories remain the same, *regardless of the proportion* within that modal category (which would change the variation ratios), lambda will always equal 0. This is a condition we call **accord**. Statistical independence is only one example, or a subset of accord. The modal category is the same with the same proportions within each independent variable category. Compute lambda for our original gender table. Since women divided evenly between George H. W. Bush and Michael Dukakis, either vote can be considered modal, and lambda will equal 0. Accord also applies here.

TABLE 9.7 Age and Foreign Policy Support—Version 2

IMPROVED U.S. RELATIONS	Age			Total
	1 Youngest	2 Middle	3 Oldest	
Support	177	118	295	590 59.0%
Do Not Support	123	82	205	410 41.0%
Total	300 30.0%	200 20.0%	500 50.0%	N = 1,000 100.0%

TABLE 9.8 Age and Foreign Policy Support—Version 3

IMPROVED U.S. RELATIONS	Age			Total
	1 Youngest	2 Middle	3 Oldest	
Support	151	110	360	621 62.1%
Do Not Support	149	90	140	379 37.9%
Total	300 30.0%	200 20.0%	500 50.0%	N = 1,000 100.0%

accord A type of no association between two variables where percentages on the dependent variable can vary across independent variable categories as long as the modal categories remain invariant.

When will lambda equal 1? When each independent category is perfectly matched with only one dependent category (e.g., if all women voted for Michael Dukakis, and all men voted for George H. W. Bush). Knowing one's gender would reduce our probability of error by 100%. Knowing one's gender would allow us to perfectly predict one's vote (Table 9.9).

TABLE 9.9 Gender and the Vote—Version 2

| | Gender | | |
PRESIDENTIAL VOTE	1 Male	2 Female	Total
1 Republican	533	0	533
	100.0%	0.0%	44.6%
2 Democratic	0	662	662
	0.0%	50.0%	55.4%
	533	662	$N = 1,195$
Total	44.6%	55.4%	100.0%

$$\lambda = \frac{533 - (0 + 0)}{533} = \frac{533 - 0}{533} = 1 \qquad (9.9)$$

DIFFERENT STATISTICS, DIFFERENT ASSUMPTIONS, DIFFERENT CALCULATIONS

Many nominal statistics, if each variable is dichotomous, are derived from ordinal or interval statistics. One such statistic is called **Yule's Q**, a nominal, 2×2 version of an ordinal statistic, gamma. Briefly (we'll cover it in detail later in this chapter), it is based on the cross-products ratio. Let's take the following graphic representation, where the letters (a–d) represent the absolute frequencies within each cross-classification category:

c	d
a	b

Yule's Q is calculated as:[8]

$$\frac{ad - bc}{ad + bc} \qquad (9.10)$$

Yule's Q A measure of nominal association for two dichotomous variables based on the cross products. It is derived from the ordinal measure gamma.

Let's look at the following hypothetical breakdown of a vote in the U.S. House of Representatives in support of adding a provision in a Medicare spending bill (Table 9.10). The Democrats are evenly split, the Republicans are unified in opposition:

Just eyeballing the table would tell us that Democrats were more likely to accept the addition than were their Republican counterparts. They were 50 percentage points more likely to be in support. A considerable relationship between party and this vote seems to be in evidence (and, if we calculated chi-square, the difference would be statistically significant). However, what about the value of Yule's Q?

$$Q = \frac{ad - bc}{ad + bc} \qquad Q = \frac{240 * 95 - 95 * 0}{240 * 95 + 95 * 0} = \frac{22800 - 0}{22800 + 0} = 1 \qquad \textbf{(9.11)}$$

Yule's Q indicates that this was a perfect partisan vote! Let's move on to lambda.

$$\lambda = \frac{N(1) - N(2)}{N(1)} \qquad \lambda = \frac{95 - (0 + 95)}{95} = \frac{0}{95} = 0 \qquad \textbf{(9.12)}$$

Oops. Lambda indicates that this vote had no partisan influence.

The difference lies in the assumptions of each statistic (and the fact that one is derived from an ordinal measure). Let's look at it in this fashion. Someone would use lambda, which reaches 0 under conditions of accord (or weak "no association"), if they only viewed votes where a majority of one party voted in opposition to a majority of the other, as partisan (and these are the only ones used in creating a variety of "party unity" scores). This bill would, well, not fit the bill. Someone would use Yule's Q, on the other hand, if they wished to consider a vote to be partisan if defections only came from one side of the aisle (in this instance, the Democrats).

TABLE 9.10 Party and Medicare Voting

INCREASE SPENDING	Party		Total
	1 Republicans	2 Democrats	
1 Add	0	95	95
	0.0%	50.0%	22.1%
2 Don't Add	240	95	335
	100.0%	50.0%	77.9%
Total	240	190	$N = 430$
	55.8%	44.2%	100.0%

We need to understand that each statistic makes different assumptions about the data, some indicating perfect association and/or no association under different conditions. Some will be sensitive to variations in the marginals (imbalance between and among categories). Some will be symmetrical (i.e., they will not vary if we switch independent and dependent variables). Others will be directional, or asymmetrical. Some, based on notions of accord, will be lower than most others and can be 0 even when other statistics indicate perfect association. Others will be 1 under weak conditions of perfect association (like Q). The moral of the story is to be careful. Choose statistics based on what you conceive a relationship to be and an understanding of each statistic's base assumptions—and be cognizant of the statistics that others choose.

We have already seen that, even with the same cross tabular breakdown, different statistics might lead us to different summary views about the relationship between variables. Often, with two dichotomous (two-category) variables, the differences are partially due to the underlying assumptions about the data. Are they treated as nominal, ordinal or interval (all of which can be mathematically assumed about dichotomies)? In general, however, statistics often differ because they make different assumptions about what is meant by "perfect association" and "no association" as well as how sensitive they are to distributional imbalances between/among categories and whether or not the two variables have the same or different numbers of categories. The following offers a brief description of several nominal (as well as ordinal and sometimes interval) level statistics and how each is affected by the differing conditions just mentioned.[9] An example of each is also presented.

Symmetrical versus Asymmetrical Measures

If a **symmetrical measure** is employed, the same value will be produced regardless of which of the two variables is considered dependent (i.e., the variable we are trying to explain or predict). The calculation and interpretation of an **asymmetrical measure**, however, are contingent on which variable is chosen as the dependent one. If we hypothesize one variable causes another, then we are talking about explaining one variable given another (dependent) and an asymmetrical measure would be generally appropriate (all other criteria being satisfied). Chi-square is a symmetrical measure. We would have the same observed and expected frequencies regardless of whether gender or the presidential vote were treated as dependent (check the proportions here). Since chi-square is generally measured against a baseline of statistical independence, the measure is appropriate even though a causal direction is specified. The probability of drawing an ace is not altered by the suit we first draw; the probability of drawing a diamond is not altered by the face value we first draw.

symmetrical measure
A measure of association that doesn't take into account the direction of an association. Independent and dependent variables are treated equally.

asymmetrical measure
A measure of association that takes into account the direction of an association. Independent and dependent variables must be specified.

Interpretation of the Values of Measures of Association

The value of a measure of association should have some clear, intuitive meaning. We would normally expect the values of a measure of association to lie between 0 and 1, where 0 would refer to the total absence of a relationship given some definition of "no relationship," and 1 would refer to the statistic's definition of "perfect association." What if the statistic changes its value (±) according to the placement of the categories within the variables? After all, these are nominal measures, and their values should be generally invariant given the arbitrary ordering of the categories. Some nominal measures, however, are actually variations of ordinal or interval measures, and thus a "negative" value can be obtained. Absolute values of the measure should, however, be of equal magnitude. The meaning of values between 0 and 1 is dependent on the operational value of the statistic. Statistics will vary according to when they achieve their minimum (0) and their maximum (±1) absolute values. For illustration, we will present analyses of hypothetical roll call results in a state legislature.

No and Perfect Association

Nominal measures of association differ according to their criteria for determining that no association or perfect association exists between two variables.

Statistical Independence

To say that no association obtains between two variables usually, but not always, implies that they are statistically independent. Knowledge of a person's score on one variable, for example, does not help us in predicting his value on another. Mathematically, we can say that the probability of the joint occurrence of both events (placement within a unique pairing of an independent and dependent variable category) equals the product of the probability of their separate occurrences. This is the logic employed in calculating the "expected" cell frequencies for a chi-square test. Given our example, "no relationship" would exist if Republicans and Democrats were *equally* likely to have voted affirmatively. Their proportional support for the bill is identical (80/140 = 40/70).

	R	D
Yea	80	40
Nay	60	30

Accord

It is highly unlikely to ever find a situation where the proportional breakdown within each independent variable category is *exactly* the same. We thus might be willing to say that "no association" existed between two variables if the modal category (of the dependent variable) were the same within each independent variable category. We may not, for example, wish to consider party affiliation as an important explanatory variable in our example if a majority of each party vote the same way. Note that statistical independence is a subset of accord.

Statistics that operate under accord are likely to produce lower values than those operating under statistical independence.

	R	D
Yea	140	50
Nay	0	30

Nominal measures of association differ according to their criteria for classifying an association as "perfect."

Strict Perfect Association

Each value of one variable is uniquely associated with a value of the other. Given knowledge of a category on either variable allows us to perfectly predict the categorical placement on the other. Measures which reach their highest absolute values only under **strict perfect association** must be symmetrical and assume that the table on which the measure is calculated is square (each variable has the same number of categories).

	R	D
Yea	140	0
Nay	0	80

strict perfect association
A type of perfect association between two variables where each category of one variable is uniquely matched with a category of another.

Weak Perfect Association

We may wish an association to be considered "perfect" even if homogeneity exists for only one category of each variable. For example, many congressional bills are so popular that we wouldn't expect much of a vote against (or in favor of) them. We might consider these votes, however, to be strong measures of the inherent differences between the two parties. Under such conditions, we might wish to state that any divergence from the majoritarian position

weak perfect association
A type of perfect association between two variables where variation on the dependent variable occurs only within one category of the dependent variable.

would be an indication of a perfect partisan vote if that divergence emerged purely from within the ranks of only one of the parties. The association between party and the vote would then be as "perfect" as possible given the overwhelming majority given to one position. A measure which would obtain its maximum value under "weak" perfect association does so as long as *one* of the two parties voted as a unit. Statistics that operate under assumptions of weak perfect association are more likely to produce higher values than those operating under strict perfect association. Note that the example given is the same as for accord. Also note that the Democratic breakdown could have been 79 to 1 and weak perfect association would still obtain—even with only one defector.

	R	D
Yea	140	50
Nay	0	30

Implicit Perfect Association

One variable will frequently have more categories than the other and, thus, strict perfect association could never be obtained (and neither could a maximum value be reached under that restriction). Strict perfect association would, for example, be impossible if we had more parties than vote choices. Measures which reach their maximum values under implicit perfect association compensate for the non-squareness of the cross table. Implicit measures need to be asymmetrical: within each category of the independent variable, only one dependent category exists. **Implicit perfect association** adjusts for the discrepancy between differing number of categories. Like the IQV it allows us to measure whether our results are as perfect as would be possible given categorical limitations.

	R	D	Libertarian
Yea	0	80	20
Nay	140	0	0

Sensitivity to Marginal Distributions

implicit perfect association A type of perfect association between two variables where adjustments are made if the number of independent and dependent categories is different.

Several measures will produce a different value, even if the underlying association is the same, if the marginal distributions (the totals for each category) are different. Statistics which are impervious to this problem are said to be insensitive to the skewness of the marginal distributions, that is, invariant to differences in a variable's index of qualitative variation (deja vu). Such a measure would produce the same result for both table A and table B, each representing a different distribution of issue preferences for a sample of 120 legislators:

	A					B		
	R	D	Libertarian			R	D	Libertarian
Yea	140	20	10		Yea	70	60	30
Nay	100	10	20		Nay	50	30	60

Notice that the proportions of support within each partisan category are similar for each table. In table A, however, Republicans comprise a much greater proportion of the legislature than in table B. A measure sensitive to differing marginal distributions (**marginal sensitivity**) would probably give us different, usually lower values for the former, thereby allowing us to "erroneously" claim that the association between party and preferences were different within each of these two samples. Lambda is one such statistic. With one large independent variable category, the number of errors could increase dramatically. Go back to our original age and foreign policy table (Table 9.2). Multiply the number of young supporters and non-supporters by 10. The relevant percentage differences remain the same, but what happens to lambda? When comparing different samples or populations, we would therefore hesitate to use any such measure. Also notice that if we converted or standardized the row entries to percentages, the problem of differing marginal distribution would disappear. Any measure that bases its calculation on proportions or percentages should therefore be insensitive to marginal variation. Percentages, as we mentioned much earlier, allow us to standardize across populations with differing sizes.

All Roads Lead To …[10]

Statistics are often adjustments to or variations of other statistics. As mentioned, Yule's Q is a dichotomous nominal version of an ordinal statistic (gamma). Return to our opening gender and vote table (Table 9.1). As both variables are dichotomies, they can be treated ordinally. A female is more female than a male. A Democratic vote is more Democratic than a Republican one. We can then rephrase our test implication as follows:

H_1: *As one becomes "more female," one becomes "more Democratic" as opposed to more "Republican."*
Or

    As we compare a female to a male, we are more likely to compare a Democrat to a Republican than a Republican to a Democrat.

Our analysis follows the logic of paired comparisons discussed in Chapter 4. This time, however, we are testing not only for the number of unique pairs of different cases, but for pairs of different cases that are also different on

marginal sensitivity A condition that changes values of a statistic as the proportion of cases in each variable's categories change, even if the overall association remains the same.

two variables. There are two possibilities. Pairs that differ in the hypothesized direction (a female will vote more Democratic than a paired male) and pairs that differ in the opposite direction (a female will vote more Republican than a paired male). The former are referred to as **concordant pairs** (i.e., in concordance with our hypothesis), and the latter as **discordant pairs** in *this* example. Generally, concordant pairs are those that differ on two variables in the same direction (greater on one and greater on the other = a positive relationship), discordant in opposite directions (greater on one, but less on the other = a negative relationship). Whether pairs are concordant or discordant will often depend on the arbitrary designation we make in the order of categories (should Republicans be listed first or second?). When we have more than two categories, as with age in Table 9.2, a logical order (youngest to oldest) is easier to discern.

The number of times that we will match a female who voted "more Democratic" than a male (concordant pair) would be 331 (F-D) × 301 (M-R) times. Each one of those 331 voters would be more female and more Democratic than those 301 males. The number of times that we will match a female who voted "less Democratic" than a male (discordant) would be 331 (F-R) × 232 (M-D) times.

The calculation for **gamma** would be:

$$\frac{C-D}{C+D} = \frac{(331 \times 301) - (331 \times 232)}{(331 \times 301) + (331 \times 232)} = \frac{99,631 - 76,792}{99,631 + 76,792}$$

$$= \frac{22,839}{176,423} = .129 \tag{9.13}$$

Translation:

- We come up with two individuals who differ on both variables (gender and the vote) in the direction we hypothesized (concordance) 99,631 times.
- We come up with two individuals who differ on both variables (gender and the vote) in the direction opposite of what we hypothesize (discordance) 76,792 times.
- We therefore have 22,839 more pairs that support our hypothesis than the opposite.
- As we discussed over and over in this text, those numbers are partially a function of how many individuals we have in our group and, therefore, how many concordant and discordant pairs we can generate, so . . .
- We *standardize* by the total number of pairs that differ (both *C* and *D*) on both of our variables.
- We are therefore 12.9% more likely to compare a Democratic female with a Republican male (our hypothesis) than a Republican female with a Democratic male.

concordant pairs All pairs of two unique cases that differ in the same direction on two variables.

discordant pairs All pairs of two unique cases that differ in the opposite directions on two variables.

gamma A measure of ordinal association that assesses the proportional difference between concordant and discordant pairs.

In the language of ordinal statistics, as we increase the level of "femaleness" we increase the level of "Democraticness" 12.9% more often than we decrease that level. Our unique pairings of individuals who differ on both variables are 12.9% more likely to differ in our hypothesized direction than the opposite direction.

Gamma can also be interpreted as a PRE measure by taking the following steps:

■ Without knowing the order of our independent variable (gender), our best guess (expectation) on the order of all pairs that differed on the dependent variable (partisan nature of the vote) would be a 50/50 split. We can either randomly pull a Democratic voter first or a Republican. It is purely arbitrary. Our proportion of error is .50, or 88,211.5 times.

■ We now, as we did with lambda, get to use information about the order of our independent variable, gender. Our hypothesis posits the expectation that as we compare a male to a female we should compare a Republican voter to a Democratic one. We are correct more often than not, but we would still be wrong (discordant pairs) 43.5% of the time or with 76,792 pairings.

■ Using our standard PRE formula, where $P(1)$ is the number or proportion of times we are wrong by blind guessing without knowledge of the order of the independent variable and $P(2)$ is the number or proportion of times we are still wrong with that knowledge:

$$\frac{P(1) - P(2)}{P(1)} = \frac{88,211.5 - 76,792}{88,211.5} = \frac{11,419.5}{88,211.5} = .129 \qquad \textbf{(9.14)}$$

■ Knowledge of the order of the independent variable reduces our error in guessing the order of the dependent variable proportionately by 12.9%.

As a keen observer, you may have noticed that any two individuals in our group of 1,195 could differ on only one variable (same gender, different vote/ different gender, same vote) or on both (same gender, same vote). These are neither concordant nor discordant, but tied cases. We designate these ties as follows:

Tx   tied on the independent variable only (gender)
Ty   tied on the dependent variable only (vote)
Txy   tied on both variables

To determine the number of ties only on the independent variable, multiply the number of female Democrats by the number of female Republicans, the number of male Democrats by the number of male Republicans, and add those two products together. To determine the number of ties only on the dependent variable, multiply the number of Democratic females by the number of Democratic males, the number of Republican females by the number of Republican males, and add those two products together. We are then left only with those unique pairs of individuals who are tied on both. To calculate this number, for each cell within the table, multiple the number of cases in that cell by the number of cases minus 1, then divide by 2.

For our gender and vote table, you should have produced the following:

Tx	179,393
Ty	176,423
Txy	181,176

Adding these "tied" cases to the number of concordant and discordant cases produces a value of 713,415. We can pull out two different individuals from a group of 1,195 713,415 times. Going back to Chapter 4 and the IQV, you will notice that this is the same as:

$$N(N-1)/2 = 1,195(1,194)/2 = 713,415$$

With the exception of a statistic that we will not cover (Spearman's rho), all ordinal measures of association contain the same numerator ($C - D$) but differ as to whether and which ties are included in the denominator. **Somers' D** is an asymmetrical measure in which ties on either the independent or dependent variable are added to the denominator. With a hypothesis, we generally would only use ties on the dependent. In reality, as a PRE measure, this counts ties on the outcome as counting half for us, half against:

$$\text{Somers'} D_y = \frac{C - D}{C + D + T_y} \tag{9.15}$$

As a PRE measure:

$$\text{Somers'} D_y = \frac{\left(C + .5T_y\right) - \left(D + .5T_y\right)}{\left(C + .5T_y\right) + \left(D + .5T_y\right)} \tag{9.16}$$

With more than a two-by-two table, ordinal statistics would follow a similar calculation rationale. For example, return to Table 9.2 (age and foreign policy support). If our hypothesis is, "The older you are, the more likely you are to support improved U.S. relations," then our concordant pairs would be any match between a "younger" person who does not support and an older (middle or older) who does, as well as a "middle" age person who does not support and an older person who does. We'll leave the full calculation to Exercise 13.

Somers' D A measure of ordinal association, based on gamma, with ties on one variable counting as half hypothesis confirming, half disconfirming.

We will cover interval measures of association in Chapter 11. For now, we'll finish up this chapter by quickly demonstrating once again the congruence of different statistics, let's briefly discuss **phi**, a dichotomous version of an interval statistic, Pearson's *r*. Phi has the same numerator as ordinal measures, but a denominator based on the sum of each independent and dependent variable category:

$$\text{Phi } (\Phi) = \frac{ad - bc}{\sqrt{(a+b)*(c+d)*(a+c)*(b+d)}} \qquad (9.17)$$

Phi is also based on the chi-square statistic (without the continuity correction) standardized by the number of cases in the table:

$$\Phi = \sqrt{\frac{\chi^2}{N}} \qquad (9.18)$$

When more than a two-by two table exists, the equivalent statistic to chi-square is **Cramer's *V***, Φ adjusted for the possible difference in the number of row and column categories.

$$\text{Cramer's } V = \sqrt{\frac{\chi^2}{N * m}} \qquad (9.19)$$

. . . where *m* is the smaller of #rows − 1 and #columns − 1.

▌ KEY TERMS

phi A nominal measure of association between two dichotomous variables based on the interval statistic Pearson's *r* as well as chi-square.

Cramer's *V* A nominal measure of association, similar to phi, where more than two categories exist for either or both variables.

█ QUESTIONS AND EXERCISES

NOTE: Several more examples and exercises can be found in both the SPSS and Stata manuals that accompany this text. Crosstabular or contingency table analysis is covered in Section 4.5.

1. Fill in the following to represent an example of statistical independence:

	Southern	Non-Southern
Agree with Tea Party Positions	35%	
Disagree with Tea Party Positions	65%	

2. How many degrees of freedom are in the table in Exercise 1? What adjustment should you make to your chi-square calculation?
3. Fill in the following to represent an example of accord *but not* statistical independence:

	Southern	Non-Southern
Agree with Tea Party Positions	35%	
Disagree with Tea Party Positions	65%	

4. Two variables that meet the requirements of statistical independence also meet the requirements of accord (T/F).
5. In comparing whether Americans or Europeans have differing views about the continuance of the conflict in Afghanistan, we compute a lambda of .297. Interpret that lambda. Can we tell which group is more supportive?
6. The chi-square value for the previous table is above the critical value for the table's degrees of freedom. What can you say about the relationship between the two variables?
7. A cross table is produced with two categories of the independent variable and five of the dependent variable. How many degrees of freedom are there in that table?
8. Using a 95% confidence interval, what is the critical value cutoff for a distribution with that many degrees of freedom?
9. The following is the partisan division of the March 2010 vote in support of the Patient Protection and Affordable Care Act (PPACA), better known as Obama Care (H.R. 3590).

TABLE 9.11 Party and the 2010 Affordable Care Act Vote

| PPAHCA | Party | | Total |
	1 Democrats	2 Republicans	
1 Yea	219	0	219
2 Nay	34	178	215
Total	253	178	$N = 431$
			100.0%

H_1: *Republicans are less likely to support increased nationalization of and spending for health care than are Democrats.*

Test: *In 2010, Republicans were less likely to support the PPACA than were Democrats.*

Test this hypothesis by calculating and interpreting the relevant percentage differences, lambda, Yule's Q, and Somers' D from the data observed in our table. Why are the last three measures different?

10. The following is the partisan distribution for an August 2011 U.S. House vote on increasing the U.S. debt ceiling (H.R. 2480)—a compromise worked out between President Barack Obama and the GOP majority in Congress.

H_1: *Republicans are less likely to support an increase in the debt ceiling than are Democrats.*

Test: *In 2011, Republicans were less likely to support the compromise debt ceiling increase than were Democrats.*

Test this hypothesis by calculating and interpreting the relevant percentage differences, lambda, Yule's Q, and Somers' D from the data observed in our table. Why are the last three measures so different?

TABLE 9.12 Party and the 2011 Debt Ceiling Vote

| INCREASE DEBT CEILING COMPROMISE | Party | | Total |
	1 Democrats	2 Republicans	
1 Yea	95	174	269
2 Nay	95	66	161
Total	190	240	$N = 430$
			100.0%

11. The following table gives the breakdown, by gender, of feelings toward immigration for a random sample of residents of Spain.

TABLE 9.13 Gender and Immigration Support

| | Gender | | |
IMMIGRATION	Male	Female	Total
1 Beneficial	324	334	658
2 Don't Know	59	76	135
3 Not Beneficial	124	116	240
Total	507	526	1,033

Answer the following questions:

a. Using percentage differences in this sample, which gender group was more likely to consider immigration to be beneficial? By what percentage point difference?

Which group was more likely to consider immigration not beneficial?

b. Compute and fully interpret lambda (with views of immigration as the dependent variable). In words, what does that value tell us?

c. Using chi-square, can we confidently claim that men and women differ on immigration in the population from which this sample was randomly drawn? Be precise in your answer.

d. Multiply each cell by 10 and recalculate a, b, and c. What have we learned? Hint: You will notice a major point is made here.

12. The following table represents data from the 2012 ANES (data set available with the SPSS and Stata manuals that accompany this text). The columns represent one's ideological position (Liberal/Moderate/Conservative). The rows represent one's self-proclaimed Party ID (Independents only include true independents, not those who lean toward the Democrats or Republicans—see discussion of difference in Chapter 2).

TABLE 9.14 Party and Ideology

| | IV=Ideology | | | |
	Liberal	Moderate	Conservative	Total
dependent variable = Party ID				
Democrat	219	496	44	759
Independent	4	86	21	111
Republican	9	374	341	724
Total	232	956	406	1,594

Answer the following questions.

a. Using percentage differences in this sample, which ideological group was more likely to consider itself to be Democratic? By what percentage point difference?

Which group was more likely to consider itself Independent? Which group was more likely to consider itself Republican?

b. Compute and fully interpret lambda (with party identification as the dependent variable). In words, what does that value tell us?

c. Using chi-square, can we confidently claim that Liberals, Moderates, and Conservatives are proportionately different (> 0%) in their partisan affiliation in the population from which this sample was randomly drawn? Be precise in your answer.

d. Switch the column entries for lambda and chi-square. Do your results differ?

13. For the data in Table 9.2, calculate gamma and Somers' *D* with "Support for Improved U.S. Relations" as the dependent variable.

NOTES

1. We are using 1988 because of its uniqueness (an even split among women in the sample). The logic and mathematics of the analysis would be the same for a larger table that included more presidential vote categories (Reform, Green, etc.).

2. For the 2008 ANES data set that accompanies this text, a weighting factor has been applied to match the survey distribution of gender to census figures. The 2012 study does this with its normal weighting procedure. Women are still more prevalent in the voting age population.

3. How one breaks down "age" can be done either by a natural, numerical break—say roughly equal thirds—or based on some theoretical construct (e.g., generational experience). Let's assume that some generational derivation was used associated with important events between that nation and the United States.

4. We'll assume that the first three steps—reliability and internal validity of measures, theoretical significance, and external validity (random sampling)—have been satisfied.

5. Actually, any similar proportion would do (50% in each age category, 80%, etc.). Just as with the single-variable chi-square, we can compare our observations against *any* set of expectations. By convention (as with a deck of cards), we use the marginal proportional frequency for the entire group (in this instance 59%/41%) as we normally test against the expectation of statistical independence. We normally do the same when comparing the difference between two means (population difference = 0).

6. Look at Table 9.15. Once we fix the number of cases in two of our categories (0/Support; 1/Support), the number of cases in the other categories are no longer free to vary (they are defined by the difference between the marginal values and the two fixed categorical values).

TABLE 9.15 Visualizing Degrees of Freedom

IMPROVED U.S. RELATIONS	Age			Total
	1 Youngest	2 Middle	3 Oldest	
Support	*120*	*110*	360	590
	40.0%	*55.0%*	72.0%	59.0%
Do Not Support	180	90	140	410
	60.0%	45.0%	28.0%	41.0%
Total	300	200	500	$N = 1,000$
	30.0%	20.0%	50.0%	100.0%

7   Fisher's exact test, produced by programs like SPSS and Stata, would be more appropriate here.

8   Many texts will have "a" and "b" on top. My preference, which fits in with the rest of the discussion here and in subsequent chapters, is to have the "higher" value on the top and to the right. The difference would only be in the sign ± of the calculation.

9   For an early and full discussion of these differences, see Herbert Weisberg, "Models of Statistical Relationship," *APSR* 68 (Dec. 1974): 1638–1655.

10   These statistics are only discussed here descriptively. Inferential tests are associated with each and can be calculated using several statistical packages such as SPSS and Stata.

CHAPTER 10

Research Design and the Use of Control Variables

Learning Objectives:

▓ To be introduced to experimental design
▓ To understand the limitations in producing a true experimental design
▓ To learn the logic of introducing a third variable to control for alternate explanations, theoretical links, and specification and interaction effects

After reading the previous chapters, you might have figured out that life is not as simple as two-variable causal relations. How well a president does in his election in one year will usually predict a Congress member's support for the president in the next—but are they causally related or are they both functions of a third variable, a district's partisan breakdown? Older Europeans are less (or at least were less) likely to support European integration than younger counterparts, but what is the reason? Older U.S. citizens are more likely to vote than younger ones, but is this consistent when broken down by other demographics, like gender or across time?

When we introduce a third (or more) variable into our analysis, we are able to gain insight into this complexity. Statistics alone will not always allow us to determine the way in which a third variable intervenes, especially when the data, as in a survey, are all collected at the same time. That must be joined by our own theoretical and conceptual logic of a causal order between and among variables. However, the standard notion of introducing a third, **control variable** *statistically* uses the same logic.

control variable A third variable that is used to eliminate the mediating effect that may cause us to misread the relationship between two variables specified in our hypothesis.

Control variables allow us to parse out distinctions that our research designs do not directly allow. We cannot, for example, randomly assign individuals into districts or age categories. The notion of "statistical" control is not as valid as a properly designed experiment, but it allows us to approximate what a design, based on reality and often pre-collected data cannot afford us.

We have already discussed potential problems with measurement: reliability, internal validity, and external validity. Internal validity and external validity can also apply to designs (i.e., how we test our hypotheses in the real world). Just as with measurements, it is basically impossible to create a test situation (design) totally free of internal and external validity problems. Before we elaborate, let's once again make the distinction clear. IV stands for hypothesized independent variable; DV is the hypothesized outcome or dependent variable. The distinction is much the same as we made for measurement problems:

■ Internal validity-design—is the change in the IV the cause of the change in the DV or is it *something else*?
■ External validity-design—change in the IV causes change in the DV, but perhaps only given certain other conditions, only for a certain subpopulation, only when another variable also changes—how generalizable are our results?

If "X" refers to the hypothesized causal (independent) variable, then an "internally invalid" conclusion would occur if some variable other than "X" caused the outcome. An "externally invalid" conclusion would occur if "X" *did* cause the outcome, but only because of some other condition, population or circumstance. It is only, therefore, a partial or conditional cause. "External validity" refers to how far we can generalize our results, both in terms of target populations (all states) and research conditions (only looking within a certain time frame).

CLASSIC EXPERIMENTAL DESIGN

classic experimental design The standard against which all research designs are compared. This design assumes random assignment into two groups with the only difference between the groups being differences on the variable hypothesized to be the causal agent.

The best way to determine whether potential validity problems exist is to first look at what a perfect experimental design entails. If anything is missing, then we know that our conclusions might be suspect (i.e., the test might not really confirm our hypothesis). A true or **classic experimental design** can be mapped out as follows:[1]

Test	**R: Y1t**	**X**	**Y2t**
Control	**R: Y1c**	**~X**	**Y2c**

X is the treatment or independent variable. It needs to vary between the test and control (comparison) groups. It can, as in the example, be the presence (X) or absence (~X) of an independent stimulus or treatment, or different levels of that treatment. In medical research, for example, the "treatment" is either a drug (given only to the test group) or different levels of a drug (in either instance, variation exists between the two groups). In policy research it might be whether or not a tax was increased and by how much. You might already be thinking of a problem. Individuals might get better just because they take a pill (a psychological response), regardless of whether or not the compound in it actually causes the benefit (a physiological response). This is why in most medical research a "placebo" is given to the control group—a pill with the same shape, color, and taste as the real drug but without the tested medicinal properties. By doing this, the effects of the medicine, as opposed to just taking the pill, can be isolated. Similarly, many policies travel across state borders. An increase in a sales tax in one state, for example, might influence purchasing behavior both in that state and adjoining ones, making it more difficult to assess the effects of the sales tax increase in the state of origin.

Y is the outcome or dependent variable. In our design we measure it for both groups (t = test, c = control or comparison) and before (time = 1) and after (time = 2) the treatment is administered (or, for policy research as an example, before and after a policy is implemented).

As you all learned when we discussed hypothesis formation, a comparison must be made—thus we need at least two groups to compare. The most difficult, if even possible requirement in our research is to make sure that the two groups are *exactly the same* on every important variable except for the difference on *X*. Remember that, in discussing measurement problems, we decided that any tested group needed to be a random or equiprobable sample of the target population. How can we accomplish this with designs?

One method is by a matching procedure. We try to figure out every possible alternative cause of a difference in outcome. With medical research this might be health, age, gender, race, and so forth. Although this "matching" or "matched pairs" is often employed when the test and control groups are small, it is not preferred. In policy research, we may try to find two or several pairs of communities that are, as best as we can discern, equivalent on all demographic and political variables that we think may influence the outcome of a new policy.

It is very difficult to match on every posited alternate variable (each group must have the same age, health, gender, race, etc., breakdown). More importantly, however, is that we can't know for sure whether we equally parceled out individuals or communities on every variable that might bias our experimental outcome. We are not deities, and therefore can't be sure that other important properties might not exist that are important in determining the usefulness of a treatment (drug/policy) but that we are not even aware exist. What if there is a human property called "zenotone," which influences the usefulness of a drug? This might sound silly, but remember, we didn't even know about DNA and its unique difference among individuals a half century ago. Yet it is critical in understanding both the implications of medical treatments as well as providing excellent data for determining guilt in certain crimes.

How can we possibly equalize out the effects of "zenotone" when we can't measure it because we don't even know it exists? Just as with measurement where we employed random, equiprobable selection, we can do so by **random assignment** of individuals into the treatment and control group. If done properly and with a large enough original sample, each group will have the same proportion, within mathematical margins of error, of individuals with every "zenotone" level. In order to do so, each case in the experiment must have an exactly equal (equiprobable) chance (50/50) of being selected for either the test (drug is given) or control (placebo is given) group. If done perfectly, then a "pre-measurement" or "before measurement," Y1t and Y1c is not even necessary—they should break down within mathematical measurement error the same for each group. We often do the pre-measurement, however, as a way of testing whether or not we were successful in our random assignment process.

Two other conditions, often not mentioned in the Political Science literature should also be met in order for us to have a true experiment:

1. The experiment should be "**double blind**." This means that whether or not a group is being given the treatment (drug) should not be known to those taking the drug or placebo (otherwise different psychological reactions might occur) AND to those measuring outcomes (otherwise it might influence how they perceive those outcomes). Every medical practitioner wants to find a cure, especially if their continued funding depends on it. We often find the same tendency with government agencies. As much as we would like to think otherwise, public officials might want to be able to demonstrate that the programs for which they fought so hard to receive funds had the intended effects if only to make political points or guarantee ongoing funding and subconsciously read data differently before and after funding had increased.[2] When, many years ago, I was working on my dissertation, I wondered if knowing my hypothesis ("the easier it is to enter a primary, the less successful third parties will be in the general election") in any way compromised my interpretation of each state's election law (looking for "ease" in states with limited third-party activity). As a partial check, I had separate graduate colleagues check a handful of coding on both my independent (primary ease) and dependent (third-party activity) variables.

2. No "**cross-contamination**." This means that there can be no "spillover" effects from one group to another. Usually we don't concern ourselves with this because cross contamination will tend to reduce the probability that we

random assignment An experimental condition in which cases have an equal chance of being placed in each test and control group.

double blind An experimental condition in which neither the subjects nor the investigators are aware of the group in which each subject is placed.

cross-contamination/ spillover effect An experimental condition in which investigators cannot limit the influence of a test condition to only the test subjects.

will observe the hypothesized differences. Those on a placebo might get a psychological boost just by seeing their friends get better. If the test group still shows even more improvement than the control, then we can be even more certain that the drug works as intended. On the other hand, what if the "placebo" group gets depressed because they realize that they are not getting better as they notice some of their friends are? This might tend to exaggerate the effects of the drug. Similarly, what if we are trying to determine if increasing a tax on alcohol consumption decreases the purchase of alcohol within a state when we can't prevent individuals from crossing borders to purchase alcohol in a less taxed state? We may very well wind up overestimating consumption in the latter, underestimating it in the former state, thereby leading us to erroneously conclude that taxes are having the desired effect.

At this point, you should all realize the difficulty of conducting a true experiment in Political Science. It's not impossible, but most of what we study has already occurred, with individuals or states or countries deciding on their own whether or not they will be part of a future researcher's test or control group. Even if we are looking at the present or future, we can't force some states, for example, to try a new education or tax program and others not to. They will choose on their own short of any financial inducements from the federal government. Both **laboratory** and **field experiments** have been offered as alternatives but have often been criticized for suffering from potential cross-contamination problems (internal validity) or a lack of generalizability (external validity) outside of a particular town for a particular election at a particular point in time. These potential problems, as we discussed with measurement, however, might actually make it more difficult to uncover our hypothesized findings, and are therefore certainly not without merit. Furthermore, replication of these studies under differing circumstances adds validity to the hypotheses offered.

The best we can hope for is to do the best we can do, control for the most obvious alternate explanations, and measure and test in as many ways as possible triangulation. Each test, as with each type of measurement, will have a potential internal or external validity problem. We can't control for all of them, but, if each test has a different type of validity problem yet the results always come out as anticipated, then we are much more confident in our conclusion (although never fully sure).

Sometimes testing for alternate explanations may be, at first glance, difficult. For example, one might posit that the decline in U.S. voter turnout (most likely underestimated as we saw in Chapter 2) after the mid-1960s might have been due to an increase in the public's distrust in government. Others might claim that it was a function of the entry of "baby boomers" into the population. Younger citizens, at least in contemporary America, are less likely to vote than their older counterparts. Ratifying a constitutional amendment (XXVI) that allowed for still younger citizens to vote would only

laboratory experiments
In the social sciences, experimental studies that occur under controlled settings that attempt to simulate real world settings.

field experiments
Experimental studies conducted in real-world settings.

Sidebar 10.1: Laboratory Experiments and Field Experiments

Laboratory experiments have been utilized in Political Science, especially in the field of rational choice theory. For example, single or iterative games have been played attempting to determine circumstances under which players will behave more or less altruistically or how well they navigate the prisoner's dilemma. Others have studied how outcomes would differ under different voting rules that one could not impose on constituencies in the real world or how individuals react to subtle negativity in political ads. Most recently, studies have been conducted examining brain activity as a way of testing for a partisan or ideological gene. In each of these, the experiments are conducted with relatively small samples in conditions controlled by the investigator. One conducts a "field experiment" by attempting to replicate an experimental design in the real world rather than a laboratory. Examples include the use of vouchers in promoting test taking and test outcomes, the effects of differing types of individual campaign communications on turnout, as well as the imposition of social pressure on turnout and voting choice. What experimenters lose in control, they make up in sample size.

An exceptionally useful rundown of the methodology of these and other examples as well as the overall validity of laboratory and field experiments can be found in Rebecca B. Morton and Kenneth C. Williams, *Experimental Political Science and the Study of Causality: From Nature to the Lab* (Cambridge University Press, 2010). See also Alan S. Gerber and Donald P. Green, *Field Experiments: Design, Analysis and Interpretation* (W. W. Norton, 2012).

exacerbate the decline. However, if an increase in distrust occurred at the same time and pace as the entry of younger potential voters, how can we tell which event was more causative of voter decline? In effect, to use the language of statistics, we would run into a conceptual multicollinearity problem.

The answer to such a dilemma, as with all things scientific, lies with forcing a comparison where only one of the events occurs. We cannot run an experiment, for example, removing distrust from an already established political environment or changing the age demographics of an era. On the other hand, we may be able to find another historical era where one, but not both events took place. If turnout declined during another period of distrust that did not occur when the population was growing proportionately younger, then we have bolstered our hypothesis that "the more distrustful a citizenry, the less likely they are to vote." If turnout did not decline during that era, then we cast doubt on that hypothesis and, perhaps, bolster our base alternative—that "younger citizens are less likely to vote than older citizens." Similarly, we may look for a period in which the population grew proportionately younger but with little evidence of changing levels of trust in government.

Another technique to "force" a comparison would be to separate individuals based on age (surveys are helpful here even if survey responses are often less than internally valid). The expectation that the decline was a result of the disproportionate growth of younger citizens would be bolstered if we indeed discovered that younger citizens were always less likely to vote than their senior counterparts. If our observations consistently followed this pattern, and if the exact level of turnout could be roughly estimated based on the proportion of the citizenry in each age group, then our "youth" hypothesis is better confirmed. If, on the other hand, we find that turnout declined within all age groups during this period, then we would be more likely to posit a period effect (such as growing distrust in government) that had an influence on everyone regardless of age. If we do find that, throughout the period in question, those who distrusted government were indeed less likely to vote than their trusting counterparts, then we have added to the evidence supportive of our "trust" hypothesis. Of course, just as with our original dilemma, we might find that younger citizens were also consistently the most distrustful. The two alternate hypothesized causal agents might be interactive and cumulative.[3]

INTRODUCING A THIRD VARIABLE

Note that just because there might be an alternate explanation does not mean that, in our study, there *is* an alternate explanation. It is easy to find potential fault. Politicians do it all the time. However, as political scientists, we need to find ways to offer confirmation that those alternate explanations are more valid than those originally proposed. As with all other design limitations, we must find ways to control for those other, potentially causative variables. This might be, as in the case of voter turnout decline, to try to find evidence from different time periods. In a matched pair design, we try to find two or two sets of cases that are as similar as possible on all variables we consider potentially significant. Other texts carry out these examples in much greater detail.[4] In this chapter, we will show how we can statistically offer controls to test for the validity of our hypotheses by introducing a third variable into our analysis when we have no control over the conditions under which those data were collected (i.e., we neither have a laboratory nor a field experiment). In particular, we will use a third variable to serve three purposes:

1. Test for an alternate explanation. We already listed five steps needed to help demonstrate causality (Chapter 6). Here we will move on to Step 6, testing for alternate explanations. We will use as our example a very common version—a spurious one.

In a spurious relationship, both our originally hypothesized independent and dependent variables are "caused" by a third variable. The connection between the IV and DV are mathematically coincidental, but X and Y are not causally related. They are, in effect, both caused by that third variable. A spurious relationship is likely to show up when we collect data at the same time, as in surveys, where we have no time sequence to determine causal sequencing. We also notice such relationships when, for example, we try to, at one time, collect information from two or more states or countries that differ on both the independent and dependent variables with both being caused by some underlying third, preexisting cultural or political condition. When I lived in Utah, I was aware of both a high vice tax on alcohol and a fairly low per capita consumption of alcohol. Were high taxes acting as a disincentive to the purchase of alcoholic beverages, or were both an outcome of a religious majority that, for the most part, did not drink and who chose to raise revenue through a source they found detrimental to society?

2. Test for an **explanatory relationship**:

Here, we are correct in stating that a causal link exists between the independent variable (X) and the dependent variable (Y), but we are trying to explain the theoretical link between them (Causal Step 2); that is, *why* should they be related?

explanatory relationship The reason (theoretical link) why our hypothesized variables should be linked as specified.

specification effect The determination that a hypothesized relationship might change when applied to different subgroups within our cases.

interaction effect The determination that a hypothesized relationship might be enhanced or weakened when a third variable changes.

Unlike a spurious relationship, changes in X and Y are not *both* caused by our third variable Z. Instead the relationship between X and Y is mediated by Z. As we will see, Z might account for the entire explanation of the X/Y relationship, or part, leaving a left-over or residual connection between changes in X and changes in Y.

3. Test for a **specification effect** or an **interaction effect**:

Here we are attempting to deepen our understanding of under what conditions the hypothesis can be generalized (Step 7). Is the relationship we observe (Step 4) and successfully test for significance (Step 5) stronger or weaker given other variable differences in population, time period, or other political conditions. Is it at all generalizable beyond our one particular study? In this type of research scenario, we are stating that changes in both X and Y *are related* in the hypothesis as specified, but we are also stating that the relationship might vary based on differences on a third variable (specification) or, in combination with another variable (interaction).

3a. Special case of specification—*Simpson's Paradox*

This unique type of specification states that there is a "lurking" variable that, when controlled for, *reverses* the direction of the original IV to DV relationship.

In each type of test, especially the first two, the logic of the statistical analysis is exactly the same. It is up to us (not the computer) to determine conceptually how our third variable intervenes with the others.

The Logic of Control: Tabular Data

Following is a brief "how to" guide on the introduction on how to test for the conditioning or mediating effects of a third variable when our data are already or can be aggregated into tabular form. The mathematical logic of the analysis is the same whether we are using that third variable to test for alternate explanations including spuriousness, to determine the applicability of an explanation, or to determine whether or not a relationship is enhanced or diminishes as the three variables interact.

1. Start off with the original IV/DV contingency table. See what the percentage point differences and statistical summaries are for the entire sample or population.
2. "Control for" the third variable. Statistics and computer-wise, this means to break down the original table into a series of tables for each category of the control (with nominal controls, I would recode that third variable into no more than three categories). What we are doing is, in essence, attempting to eliminate variation on the third variable from the original table. Each of the "controlled" subsets will have cases that share the same category (no variation) on that third variable.
3. If the original differences and their associated statistics disappear (e.g., relevant percentage differences = 0), then we are more confident that our original relationship is being conditioned or mediated by a third.
4. If the original relationship is maintained, then we should feel more (but never absolutely) confident in our original relationship and less certain that its two variables are mediated in some way by a third. I say "never" because, in science, another alternate explanation might always come up (maybe a fourth variable causing the change in the first three). Tests just confirm, not prove a hypothesis (see falsifiability in Chapter 1).

A Third Variable Used to Test for an Alternate Explanation

The following table is fictitious, set up to demonstrate the circumstances under which one can use a controlled cross table to test for the mathematical effects of a third variable in a neatly presentable manner. Real life is usually more complicated than these three variable interactions. Thus, it would be difficult to find a real life scenario that would come out as neatly. We will start with a test for the existence of a spurious relationship, that is, that differences or changes in a third, exogenous variable might actually be the cause of differences in both our hypothesized independent and dependent variables.

Many students often ask if their college educations are "worth it," with worth measured as one's lifetime income. The assumption is that one's income will be higher with a college education than without.

$$\Delta X \longrightarrow \Delta Y$$

where X is education level (defined as whether or not one has a college
   degree)
   Y is lifetime income

Look at the hypothesized breakdown in Table 10.1. For the sake of simplicity, let us say that education level has been split into two categories— No College Degree/College Degree. Similarly, lifetime income is dichotomized into two categories (e.g., roughly below the median value for all or above).

The table indicates that a relationship, in the posited direction, exists. Those who complete college are 18 percentage points more likely to earn a high lifetime income than those without a college education (63.6%–45.6%). If this table represents a random sample of a larger population, then the chi-square value allows us to confidently reject the possibility that, in that population, the true categorical income difference is 0%. Obviously, the relationship is not perfect. If it were, we would see a 100% point difference. However, the increased chance of earning a higher income may well be seen as worth it to most students. The possibility exists, however, that the

TABLE 10.1 Education by Lifetime Income

| | X = Educational Achievement | | |
Y = Lifetime Income	No College	Completed College	Total
Above Median	205 45.6%	350 63.6%	555 55.5%
Below Median	245 54.4%	200 36.4%	445 44.5%
Total	450	550	$N = 1{,}000$

$\Delta = 18.0$ percentage points, lambda = .09, chi-square = 32.03 ($p < .001$).

relationship between our variables might be spurious. Is there a third variable (*Z*) whose differences might explain both whether or not one finishes college and how high one's lifetime income will be? Perhaps the financial or educational status of one's parents may help to predict and explain both. College-educated parents, by virtue of culture or finances, are better able to advance educational opportunities for their children than non-college educated parents. Additionally, they are more likely to be in occupational or societal positions to afford their children greater future financial opportunities (including taking over the family business).

Graphically, this would be presented as follows:

where *Z* is parents' education level (completed college or not).

A series of possibilities exist when we control for one's parents educational achievement. Let us examine the two most extreme ones.

- Scenario 1: If, after controlling for one's parents' education, the original relationship (Δ = 18.6 percentage points) disappears (Δ = .0 percentage points difference within every category of "parents" education) then we are more confident in claiming that the original relationship, and the difference it produced, is spurious. One's parents' education likely explains differences on *both* our original independent and dependent variable. For each parental group, the relationship between one's own educational achievement and future income are *statistically independent* of each other.
- Scenario 2: If, after controlling for one's parents' education, the original relationship (Δ = 18.6 percentage points) is maintained, then we are more confident that one's own educational achievement *independently* helps determine one's lifetime earnings.

Statistical Technique—Working through the Logic

In order to "control" for a third variable, we need to keep that variable constant so that differences on that third variable cannot intervene in the original relationship between our two variables. For simplicity, we separated out parental education into three categories: no parent completed college, one parent completed college, both parents completed college (see Table 10.2A–C). Within each of these subtables, parental education cannot have a direct or indirect influence on either of our original variables as it *does not* categorically vary.[5]

TABLE 10.2 Scenario 1—*Potentially Spurious*

A. No parent completed college

	X = Educational Achievement		
Y = Lifetime Income	No College	Completed College	Total
Above Median	75	30	105
	30.0%	30.0%	30.0%
Below Median	175	70	245
	70.0%	70.0%	70.0%
Total	250	100	*N* = 350

Δ = 0 percentage points, lambda = 0, chi-square = 0.

B. One parent completed college

	X = Educational Achievement		
Y = Lifetime Income	No College	Completed College	Total
Above Median	90	120	210
	60.0%	60.0%	60.0%
Below Median	60	80	140
	40.0%	40.0%	40.0%
Total	150	200	*N* = 350

Δ = 0 percentage points, lambda = 0, chi-square = 0.

C. Both parents completed college

	X = Educational Achievement		
Y = Lifetime Income	No College	Completed College	Total
Above Median	40	200	240
	80.0%	80.0%	60.0%
Below Median	10	50	60
	20.0%	20.0%	20.0%
Total	50	250	*N* = 300

Δ = 0 percentage points, lambda = 0, chi-square = 0.

Note that, within the first subset (no parent completed college), statistical independence obtains between our original two variables. One's own educational achievement has no statistical bearing on one's lifetime income. The same holds true for the next two subsets.

Within each category of parental education (our *Z* variable), no lifetime income differences exist between one's own educational achievement and

TABLE 10.3 Parents' Education and Child's Lifetime Income

Y = Child's Lifetime Income	Z = Parents' Educational Achievement			
	None	One	Both	Total
Above Median	105	210	240	555
	30.0%	60.0%	80.0%	55.5%
Below Median	245	140	60	445
	70.0%	40.0%	20.0%	45.5%
Total	350	350	300	$N = 1,000$

TABLE 10.4 Parents' and Child's Educational Achievement

X = Child's Educational Achievement	Z = Parents' Educational Achievement			
	None	One	Both	Total
Completed College	100	200	250	550
	28.6%	57.1%	83.3%	55.0%
No College	250	150	50	450
	71.4%	42.9%	16.7%	45.0%
Total	350	350	300	$N = 1,000$

one's lifetime income. Also note the relationship between parental education and both of our original variables, created from the marginals of our three subsets (see Tables 10.3 and 10.4).

Two education parent children are 20 percentage points more likely to earn high lifetime incomes than those with one college-educated parent, 50 percentage points more likely than those where neither parent completed college, regardless of their own academic achievement.

Children with two educated parents are, within rounding error, 26.2 percentage points more likely to have gone to college than one parent offspring, 54.7 percentage points more likely than those where neither parent completed college. The premise behind our spurious control receives some confirmation. Now let's look at another possible scenario, one in which are third variable control has little effect on our outcome (Table 10.5).

Note that, within the first subset (no parent completed college), the original 18.6% point difference is pretty much maintained. Controlling for one's parental achievements seem to have little influence on financial outcomes. The same holds true for the next two subsets.

TABLE 10.5 Original Relationship Maintained (as well as possible given numerical constraints)[1]

A. No parent completed college

Y = Lifetime Income	X = Educational Achievement		
	No College	Completed College	Total
Above Median	114	64	178
	45.6%	64.0%	50.1%
Below Median	136	36	172
	54.4%	36.0%	49.1%
Total	250	100	N = 350

Δ = 18.4 percentage points, lambda = .128, chi-square = 8.95 (p < .01).[2]

[1] Given the total numbers used, one could either make the data perfectly fit the first or the second scenario. Individuals cannot be dissected into parts.

[2] Although each of our chi-square values here is significant, it is possible, when we break out our original table that it may not be, even if the percentage point differences remain the same. Recall that, as the sample size decreases, the likelihood of a significant chi-square decreases as well.

B. One parent completed college

Y = Lifetime Income	X = Educational Achievement		
	No College	Completed College	Total
Above Median	68	127	195
	45.3%	63.5%	55.7%
Below Median	82	73	155
	54.7%	36.5%	44.3%
Total	150	200	N = 350

Δ = 18.2 percentage points, lambda = .09, chi-square = 10.74 (p < .001).

C. Both parents completed college

Y = Lifetime Income	X = Educational Achievement		
	No College	Completed College	Total
Above Median	23	159	182
	46.0%	63.6%	60.7%
Below Median	27	91	118
	54.0%	36.4%	39.3%
Total	50	250	N = 300

Δ = 17.6 percentage points, lambda = .03, chi-square = 4.7 (p < .05).

Sidebar 10.2: Welfare and Crime

Analysts continue to argue over the relationship between welfare and crime. One side argues that households that are dependent on welfare (food stamps and housing assistance) are more likely to produce children who behave in a delinquent fashion and commit crimes than those that are not. Their claim is bolstered by the explanatory argument that fathers are less likely to remain in a home where the financial situation has been made stable enough by government aid. Children of one-parent, particularly female-headed households, lacking paternal guidance, are more likely to join the ranks of juvenile delinquents than others.

The opposition argues that delinquency has little to do with the safety net of welfare. More importantly, both the need for welfare assistance and the potential for criminal activity are both caused by poor economic conditions. Thus, the relationship between welfare and crime is, in this situation, spurious (a possibility that proponents dispute).

For a brief rundown of the former argument, see the Cato Institute's Michael Tanner's 1995 testimony before the U.S. Senate's Subcommittee on Youth Violence: Committee on the Judiciary (http://www.cato.org/publications/congressional-testimony/relationship-between-welfare-state-crime-0). For a synopsis of literature supporting the latter, see Cao et al., "Family, Welfare, and Delinquency," *Journal of Criminal Justice* 32 (2004): 565–576. These researchers determine that other forms of adult supervision and attachment to schools compensate for the association others see between welfare, female-headed households, and delinquency.

USING A THIRD VARIABLE TO TEST FOR AN EXPLANATORY LINK

Using a third variable to explain the reason *why* the two original variables are linked follows the same logic. If the individual subtables produce no percentage differences between or among independent variable categorical groups, then we can feel more comfortable in stating that we have found an explanation for the original relationship. If the outcomes remain the same, then we must look for other explanations.

Let's look at perceptions within the European Union (Table 10.6). In this real-world example, "X" stands for one's age (broken down into three categories), and "Y" one's acceptance of one's country's membership in the European Union. The data are from a 1995 study,[6] when, after formal organization had been established by the Maastricht Treaty, the European Union was expanding, economic rules were being standardized, and the movement toward a common currency was picking up support.

Older EU citizens were 10.2 percentage points less likely to accept EU membership than were the youngest group of citizens, 6.4 percentage points less likely than the "middle" age group. Obviously, we would not be able to

TABLE 10.6 Age and EU Acceptance

		Age			Total
		15–24	25–54	≥ 55	
EU Membership Is Good	Yes	1,797	4,510	2,452	8,759
		64.1%	60.3%	53.9%	59.1%
	No/ Neutral	1,008	2,966	2,094	6,068
		35.9%	39.7%	46.1%	40.9%
Total		2,805	7,476	4,546	14,827

Δ = –6.4 percentage points–10.2 percentage points, lambda = 0,[1] chi-square = 83.35.

[1] Remember that lambda is 0 under conditions of accord, and chi-square only under statistical independence. Each age group supported the EU, but at significantly different proportional levels.

consider this relationship spurious. Unless there is a transformation of a gene that occurs with age that also makes one less accepting of international agreements, we can't consider that age is an outcome of another, third, variable that causes both aging and international views. As part of our development of theory, we would be interested in asking instead *why* older citizens are less likely to accept EU membership. More than a decade ago, one of my talented undergraduates offered a reasonable explanation. Might it be the case that older citizens (as opposed to younger ones) are more likely to be employed in "traditional" occupations like agriculture or manufacturing, or retired and concerned about maintaining benefits under a common regional regime? For them, European integration, and the consequent removal of tariff and other boundaries, might present a threat to their jobs and way of life. On the other hand, younger citizens are more likely to be employed or, after education, seek employment in newer businesses like international finance, telecommunications and other high tech industries. For them, EU integration presented opportunity. The assumption seemed to be borne out by the data (recreated from my recollection of his work). For simplicity, Occupational Status has been combined into two categories—traditional and modern—reflecting the aforementioned logic (see Table 10.7).

Let's first test for the premise: were older citizens more involved in traditional occupations than younger ones? Yes, by differences of 49.5 and 17.1 percentage points, respectively.

If the differences in occupational classification explained all of the differences in EU acceptance, then the results would be similar to those presented in Table 10.2A–C.[7] If these differences were inconsequential, then the results would be similar to those in Table 10.5A–C. In actuality, the results (as is usually the case in real life) weren't perfect in either direction (see Table 10.8).

TABLE 10.7 Age and Occupational Status

		Age			Total
		15–24	25–54	≥ 55	
Status	Traditional	1,250	5,809	4,307	11,322
		45.3%	77.7%	94.8%	76.4%
	Modern	1,556	1,665	238	3,459
		54.7	22.3%	5.2%	23.6%
Total		2,762	7,474	4,545	14,825*

* It is often suggested that, when tables in use have different sample sizes, only those individual who answered all relevant questions be included. That practice is employed here (excluding those who had no opinion about EU membership and/or fit into one of the two occupational codes). Note that the sample size is so large that even small differences would be statistically significant (chi-square).

Δ = 17.1 percentage points/49.5 percentage points, lambda = .089, chi-square = 2,455.01.

TABLE 10.8 Age and EU Acceptance Controlled by Occupational Status

		Age			Total
		15–24	25–54	≥55	
EU Membership	Yes	1,797	4,510	2,452	8,759
Is Good		64.1%	60.3%	53.9%	59.1%
	No/Neutral	1,008	2,966	2,094	6,068
		35.9%	39.7%	46.1%	40.9%
Total		2,805	7,476	4,546	14,827*

Δ = –6.4/–10.2 percentage points, lambda = 0.

Occupation = Traditional		Age			Total
		15–24	25–54	≥ 55	
EU Membership	Yes	736	3,339	2,289	6,364
Is Good		58.9%	57.5%	53.1%	56.0%
	No/Neutral	514	2,470	2,018	5,002
		41.1%	42.5%	46.9%	44.0%
Total		1,250	5,809	4,307	11,366*

Δ = –4.4 percentage points/–5.8 percentage points, lambda = 0.

(Continued)

TABLE 10.8 (Continued)

Occupation=Modern		Age			Total
		15–24	25–54	≥55	
EU Membership Is Good	Yes	1,061	1,170	162	2,393
		68.2%	70.3%	68.1%	69.2%
	No/Neutral	495	495	76	1,066
		31.8%	29.7%	31.9%	30.8%
Total		1,556	1,665	238	3,459*

Δ = –2.2 percentage points/–0.1 percentage points, lambda = 0.
*Rounding error caused by fractional weights alters the sums marginally.

When that third variable (type of employment) was controlled for, the results looked more like the first scenario than the second, but some of the age/EU acceptance differences remained for those in traditional occupations. We still had some *residual* differences that needed to be explained by other factors (perhaps generational proximity to World War II). The notion of "residuals" will be explained in greater detail in our chapter on regression analysis (Chapter 11).

Let's look at another example. We know that, in 2008, older citizens were less likely to support candidate Barack Obama than younger ones, continuing a reversal of what was once viewed as doctrine ("older citizens are more likely to vote for Democratic candidates than younger ones").

Is there an explanation for this change? One can argue that Barack Obama represented the politics of change and that older citizens either because of age or social conditioning are more adverse to change than younger citizens; see the discussion of life cycle and generational theories in Chapter 1. The following table (10.9) breaks the original age (IV) and vote (DV) down by attitudes toward gay marriage, an obvious center piece of cultural change in the United States. The data come from the 2008 American National Election Studies (ANES) survey.

Note that for "All Respondents" the oldest group was 19.5 percentage points less likely to vote for Barack Obama than the youngest group, and 6.1 percentage points less likely than middle agers. Notice what happens when we control for that third variable, one's position about gay marriage. The distinctions based on age virtually disappear. Although not offering total proof, as we never can, this table should lead us to believe that there is something about cultural change, minimally defined by gay rights positions, that explains age differences and the partisan nature of the vote.

TABLE 10.9 Age by 2008 Presidential Vote

Gay Marriage Position		Age			Total
		Youngest	Middle	Oldest	
Pro–Gay Marriage	Obama	257	126	44	427
		78.4%	80.8%	75.9%	78.8%
	McCain	71	30	14	115
		21.6%	19.2%	24.1%	21.2%
	Total	328	156	58	542
		100.0%	100.0%	100.0%	100.0%
Anti–Gay Marriage	Obama	55	78	61	194
		40.7%	35.1%	37.9%	37.5%
	McCain	80	144	100	324
		59.3%	64.9%	62.1%	62.5%
	Total	135	222	161	518
		100.0%	100.0%	100.0%	100.0%
All Respondents	Obama	312	204	105	621
		67.4%	54.0%	47.9%	58.6%
	McCain	151	174	114	439
		32.6%	46.0%	52.1%	41.4%
	Total	463	378	219	1,060
		100.0%	100.0%	100.0%	100.0%

USING A THIRD VARIABLE TO TEST FOR SPECIFICATION/INTERACTION EFFECTS

In our first hypothetical example, we dealt with a potential internal validity problem (spuriousness), and, in the second, we introduced an explanatory thread. For our third let's consider an original relationship's generalizability (external validity). Is it, for example, more likely to occur in combination with changes in other variables or for certain subgroups? For quite some time, we have noted that older citizens, at least in the United States, are more likely to vote, in any given election, than younger ones. Figure 10.1 summarizes voter turnout among four standard U.S. Census age categories.

Note the greater shift among the youngest group between presidential and midterm elections. In particular, note the dramatic decline among young people between the presidential election of 2008 and the subsequent turnout in the subsequent midterm (2010), helping to return the U.S. House to Republican control.[8]

For our purposes, let's break our age groups into three standard generational specific categories: post–baby boomers, baby boomers, and pre–baby boomers or the generation that lived through the Great Depression and World War II (often called "the Greatest Generation").[9] As one test of the original hypothesis

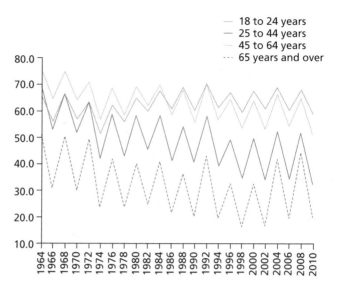

FIGURE 10.1 Voter Turnout by Age

("the Greatest Generation is more likely to vote than those that followed"), let us turn again to the 2012 U.S. Census Voter Supplement File.[10]

As expected, the Greatest Generation is the most likely to have (or stated that they had) voted, being 17.6 percentage points more likely to have done so than the post-boomer group, 2.4 percentage points more than the "baby boom" generation. Obviously, the greatest difference is between the greatest and post-boomer generation, with perhaps "baby boomers" carrying some of the civic obligation of their elders. Instead of using a third variable to explain why the oldest generation is most likely to vote (is it that they have a higher sense of civic obligation?), let us instead examine whether these differences are equally generalizable across genders. Presented in Table 10.10 are our original table and the tables for men and, separately, for women.

Notice that the generational difference in turnout increases for men (23.7 percentage points between the oldest and youngest generations), but decreases for women (12.4 percentage points). Evidently, a generational explanation for the differences in voter turnout is more relevant for men than for women. Interestingly, the lessened influence of generational experience on turnout for women comes from two generational features. The oldest cohort of women shows lower proportional voter turnout than men partially because it includes a subset of women who would have been socialized during a period where,

TABLE 10.10 Generation and Voting Turnout

| | | Generation | | | Total |
		Post	Boomers	Greatest	
Did R Vote in	All	53.9%	69.1%	71.5%	61.8%
2008 Election	Males	50.6%	67.6%	74.3%	59.7%
	Females	57.0%	70.6%	69.4%	63.7%

Raw frequencies are not listed as they are in the thousands. Even slight differences will be statistically significant. Lambda in all the associated tables is always 0 as a majority stated they voted in each generational category. The percentage for the "Greatest Generation" is somewhat lessened by the inclusion of the very oldest citizens who, even in this age of convenience voting, list physical impairment as the major reason for not voting.

although women had been granted the right to vote, societal mores expected greater participation among men. Among the youngest cohort, on the other hand, women are more likely to vote than their male counterparts, perhaps indicative of the growing sense of opportunity that women in this generation experienced.

We usually control as a way of statistically reducing our original differences when a third variable is introduced. It is possible, however, that we can under-generalize our results. What if we have two equally populated groups? For one (group A), turnout increases as one ages, and for the other (group B), turnout decreases at the same, but negative rate (see Figure 10.2). The two groups would cancel each other out and the data would appear as if the two variables (age and turnout) were not related at all. Age or generation, however, would have a significant impact on turnout for both groups, but in *opposite* directions.

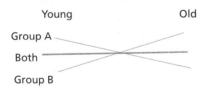

FIGURE 10.2 A Hidden Relationship

In the United States, white citizens tend to affiliate *less* with the Democratic Party as they move up the educational ladder (until one reaches post-bacca-laureate education). Black citizens, on the other hand, tend to lean *more* Democratic.[11] If the proportion of whites and blacks were the same, the educational effects would, when combining the two racial groups, cancel out. As the proportion of blacks in this country is only about 1/7 of the proportion

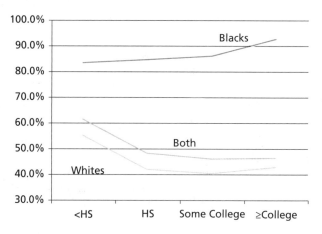

FIGURE 10.3 Race, Education, and Democratic Vote

of whites, however, the overall effects of education on party identification tends to be only partially moderated. The patterns are reflected in Figure 10.3. The Democratic percentage includes independent-leaning Democrats.

AN EXAMPLE WITH MEANS—SIMPSON'S PARADOX

As a special case of hidden effects, let's finish with a special example of how a relationship noticeable for the whole shows something different for subgroups within. Return to our hypothetical example of gender income inequality presented in Chapter 7. As you recall, we determined that, in this company, women made significantly less money than men. However, what if we were to separate individuals by their full-time or part-time status? Part-time employees work only half days, or 20 hours per week; full-time employees work full days, or 40 hours per week. Is it possible that even though our data indicate that males make more than females overall, within each status category, females can make more than males? Look at the following breakdown possible from our sample:[12]

Simpson's Paradox A unique type of specification effect where a "lurking" variable, when controlled for, *reverses* the direction of the original independent to dependent variable relationship.

	Males	Females
All	$\overline{X} = \$32,800$	$\overline{X} = \$32,000$
	$(N = 300)$	$(N = 200)$
Full-time	$\overline{X} = \$40,000$	$\overline{X} = \$52,000$
	$(N = 150)$	$(N = 40)$
Half-time	$\overline{X} = \$25,600$	$\overline{X} = \$27,000$
	$(N = 150)$	$(N = 160)$

Females make more, on mean average, than do males regardless of whether they work part-time or full-time. How then can it be possible that, in the entire sample, males make more on mean average than do females? The answer lies in the fact that females (in this example) are more likely to be part-time employees. Part-time employees make much less than do full-time employees. Since females make more than males in each category, can we then claim discrimination against men?

Sidebar 10.3: Simpson's Paradox

As we read in a previous chapter, demonstrating wage and other employment discrimination is far from an easy task. Data like this have often been used by both sides of the controversy. Perhaps full-time female employees had to work more years and therefore acquired more seniority and expertise than males in order to be rewarded full-time status. By the same logic, those females left in part-time jobs would on average have more seniority and expertise than their part-time male associates. Perhaps the firms in the profession would only elevate females to full-time status if they were exceptional, rewarding males with less talent or motivation. Perhaps the bias, if it exists, is societal rather than professional, with females more likely to accept and keep part-time employment in certain professions (real estate agent comes to mind) because of the greater likelihood that they will be primary care givers to their children and primary care takers of elderly relatives. Obviously, our statistical evidence only begins to explain the differences both between genders and between status categories. Again, more information is needed.

Whatever the determination, we have just presented an example of *Simpson's Paradox*, the possibility that the direction of an original relationship is reversed when another, lurking variable is taken into account.[1]

[1] E. H. Simpson, "The Interpretation of Interaction in Contingency Tables," *Journal of the Royal Statistical Society*, Ser. B, 13 (1951): 238–41.

Sidebar 10.4: A Warning about Inference When Using Tabular Controls

As we break our original cross table into separate tables controlled by a third variable, we may notice that the value of our inferential statistics have declined, and, subsequently, we are less likely to reject the null hypothesis of statistical independence between our original two variables. Keep in mind that this may occur for two reasons. The first is that the actual relationship that we observed has become weaker (as in our first analysis of education and income). The other, however, is that the size of the sample within each controlled table has decreased. It is possible for percentage differences to actually increase within our separated tables but for our inferential significance to decrease.

In Exercise 7, you will see a different type of specification effect, one that is called interactive. Look it over. We will then finish our discussion of the use of three or more variables in Chapter 12, multiple regression analysis.

KEY TERMS

classic experimental design (218)

control variable (217)

cross-contamination/spillover effect (220)

double blind (220)

explanatory relationship (224)

field experiments (221)

interaction effect (224)

random assignment (220)

Simpson's Paradox (238)

specification effect (224)

QUESTIONS AND EXERCISES

NOTE: Several more examples and exercises can be found in both the SPSS and Stata manuals that accompany this text. Crosstabular or contingency table analysis with more than two variables is covered in Section 4.5, and means tests in Section 4.3.

1. The presumed relationship between variables X and Y is said to be "spurious." This means that:
    a. The causal relationship between X and Y is reversed (Y is really the independent variable).
    b. Another variable influences changes in Y but NOT X. No causal link exists between the two.
    c. Both X and Y are both dependent on some third variable. They have no direct impact on each other.
2. A comparison is made between two countries with differing electoral systems. One operates under a winner-take-all/single member districting rule (as in most U.S. elections), and one under a form of proportional representation (as in most other countries). Turnout is higher in the second.
    a. Write a hypothesis for which this would be a potentially useful test.
    b. In that hypothesis, what is the independent and what is the dependent variable?
    c. Can you think of any alternate explanation for the outcome?
3. We find a positive mathematical relationship between two variables, but when we control for a third, the relationship is reversed

(negative) in all categories of the control variable. This is an example of

_____ .

4. A table lists the relationship between gender and the congressional vote in 2012. The table is then broken down according to one's views about social welfare spending. One's views about social welfare spending are most likely a third variable that we would:
   a. Use to test for a spurious relationship
   b. Use as an intervening, explanatory variable
   c. Use as a specification variable

5. For a design to be considered internally invalid, the cause of differences in the dependent variable cannot be differences in our originally hypothesized independent variable (T/F).

6. The following table represents data from the 435 districts of the U.S. House. The percentage of citizens who list themselves as black in the census is listed, as well as the percentage of the vote received by the Democratic candidates (Kerry and Obama) in 2004 and 2008, respectively. For simplicity, districts are divided on each variable by whether they are above or below the national value for each.

   Discuss what the tables tell you, especially what happens when we control for the relationship between %Black and %Obama by %Kerry. As part of your answer, and for each of the three tables (below median vote for Kerry/above/all districts), compute the relevant percentage differences, lambda, and chi-square (keeping note of the "special comment" specified in using inferential statistics for non-random samples in Chapter 7).

TABLE 10.11 2008 Vote for Obama

			%Black		
			< Median	> Median	Total
%Kerry < Median	%Obama	< Median	118	89	207
			92.9%	93.7%	93.2%
		> Median	9	6	15
			7.1%	6.3%	6.8%
	Total		127	95	222
			100.0%	100.0%	100.0%
%Kerry > Median	%Obama	< Median	13	5	18
			14.4%	4.1%	8.5%
		> Median	77	118	195
			85.6%	95.9%	91.5%
	Total		90	123	213
			100.0%	100.0%	100.0%

(Continued)

TABLE 10.11 (Continued)

			%Black		
			< Median	> Median	Total
All Districts	%Obama	< Median	131	94	225
			60.4%	43.1%	51.7%
		> Median	86	124	210
			39.6%	56.9%	48.3%
	Total		217	218	435
			100.0%	100.0%	100.0%

7. In 2008, Italian citizens were asked whether they intended to vote in the upcoming European elections. Look at the following table. Does whether or not citizens feel their voice counts in the EU help to determine whether or not they intend to vote? How would you describe how a third variable, whether or not citizens feel their vote counts in their own country, influences the original relationship? As part of your answer, and for each of the three tables (pro/anti/all), compute the relevant percentage differences, lambda, and chi-square.

TABLE 10.12 Voting Turnout in the European Union—Italy

			Vote Counts in EU		
			Yes	No	
VOICE	Do Not		11	20	31
COUNTS IN	Intend to Vote		9.6%	42.6%	19.3%
COUNTRY	Intend to Vote		103	27	130
			90.4%	57.4%	80.7%
	Total		114	47	161
			100.0%	100.0%	100.0%
VOICE	Do Not		10	188	198
DOES NOT	Intend to Vote		25.0%	33.1%	32.6%
COUNT IN	Intend to Vote		30	380	410
COUNTRY			75.0%	66.9%	67.4%
	Total		40	568	608
			100.0%	100.0%	100.0%
Total	Do Not		21	208	229
	Intend to Vote		13.6%	33.8%	29.8%
	Intend to Vote		133	407	540
			86.4%	66.2%	70.2%
	Total		154	615	769
			100.0%	100.0%	100.0%

8. There is general consensus that individuals will feel more inclined to vote if they feel their vote will make a difference in the outcome. They will be

more likely to feel that way if they sense that the vote will be close. They are also more likely to feel that way if they feel that a particular candidate is more likely to be advantageous to them, and therefore care about who wins. The following tables were produced from the 2012 ANES. The first helps to test the first hypothesis ("those who think the election will be close will be more likely to vote than those who feel it will not"), and the second tests the second hypothesis ("those who care who wins will be more likely to vote than those who don't care"). The third includes both "perception of closeness" and "caring about outcome" as variables that may cause voting turnout.

Answer the following:
■ Which independent variable seems to be a better predictor and explainer of voting turnout?
■ Is there an interactive effect between those two variables and voter turnout?

TABLE 10.13 Reasons for Voting 2012

		Not Close	Close	
Voted?	Yes	616	3206	3822
		70.0%	77.3%	76.0%
	No	264	944	1208
		30.0%	22.7%	24.0%
		880	4150	5030

		Don't Care	Care	
Voted?	Yes	414	3408	3822
		45.4%	82.7%	76.0%
	No	497	711	1208
		54.6%	17.3%	24.0%
		911	4119	5030

		Don't Care/ Not Close	Care/ Not Close	Don't Care/ Close	Care/Close	
Voted?	Yes	59	557	355	2851	3822
		36.0%	77.8%	47.5%	83.8%	76.0%
	No	105	159	392	552	1208
		64.0%	22.2%	52.5%	16.2%	24.0%
		164	716	747	3403	5030

9. The following set of tables presents data on a country's tax burden as a percentage of the GDP (gross domestic product), government expenditures

as a percentage of the GDP, and the unemployment rate in a given year. Data for each country are divided into two categories, below the mean for all countries or above. Does the tax burden percentage have a positive effect on unemployment? Does the government expenditures percentage have an effect on unemployment? Are there interactive effects when both are used to predict unemployment? Just use percentage differences and gamma to answer the questions. Of course, tax burdens and expenditures in one year may take some time (called a lag effect) before they can influence employment and other economic factors.

TABLE 10.14 Tax Burdens, Expenditures, and Unemployment

			GOVGDP		Total
			<mean	>mean	
UNEMPLOYMENT	>mean		26	23	49
			31.3%	30.3%	30.8%
	<mean		57	53	110
			68.7%	69.7%	69.2%
			83	76	159
Total			100.0%	100.0%	100.0%

			TAXGDP		Total
			<mean	>mean	
UNEMPLOYMENT	>mean		28	22	50
			31.5%	31.0%	31.3%
	<mean		61	49	110
			68.5%	69.0%	68.8%
			89	71	160
Total			100.0%	100.0%	100.0%

TAXGDP			GOVGDP		Total
			<mean	>mean	
>mean	UNEMPLOYMENT	>mean	8	14	22
			50.0%	25.5%	31.0%
		<mean	8	41	49
			50.0%	74.5%	69.0%
<mean	UNEMPLOYMENT	>mean	18	9	27
			26.9%	42.9%	30.7%
		<mean	49	12	61
			73.1%	57.1%	69.3%

Source: Heritage Foundation's Index of Economic Freedom database.

NOTES

1   Of course, even the best executed experiment's results might be limited to the population from which our experimental "subjects" were randomly drawn.

2   Of course, much of this may have been more than subconscious. See Sidebar 2.1 in Chapter 2.

3   For those who wish to investigate two powerful studies that not only offer alternate explanations but finds ways to test for them, allow me to suggest the following—one short, one long:

A review of Emily Oster's work on the disparity between male and female births in some developing countries discussed in Dubner and Levitt, "The Search for 100 Million Missing Women," Slate.com, 2005, http://www.slate.com/id/2119402/

Gary C. Jacobson and Samuel Kernell, *Strategy and Choice in Congressional Elections* (Yale University Press, 1981). The authors cast doubt on then standard assumptions about the causes of seat losses for the incumbent president's party during midterm elections, come up with a plausible alternate explanation, and then follow with the examination of logical derivatives from that explanation.

4   See, for example, Barasko et al., *Understanding Political Science Research Methods: The Challenge of Inference* (Routledge, 2013).

5   Of course, where parents go to college can make an additional difference in outcomes.

6   Karlheinz Reif and Eric Marlier, *Eurobarometer 43.1BIS: Regional Development and Consumer and Environmental Issues, May–June 1995*, Conducted by INRA (Europe), Brussels, 2nd SSD ed. (Swedish Social Science Data Service [producer], 1998; Swedish Social Science Data Service/Zentralarchiv fuer Empirische Sozialforschung/Inter-university Consortium for Political and Social Research [distributors], 1998).

7   Of course, we cannot conclusively prove this as there might be other differences associated with age that might be the true cause. Remember, alternate explanations always exist.

8   Source: U.S. Census Bureau, Current Population Survey, Registration and Voter Supplement File, 1964–2010.

9   "Baby boomers" include those born between 1945 and 1964. The generational theory, as it applied to voting, can be found in Chapter 1.

10 When possible, I suggest using census figures. The ANES is not as accurate as, for one reason, it contains many fewer cases than the U.S. Census Registration and Voter Supplement File. On the other hand, it does contain political and attitudinal items not possible in the census. Once we go beyond basic demographics and turnout, we can't garner any political attitudes or behaviors. However, note that the ANES overestimates turnout much more than does the census file. These figures are calculated as the number who stated they voted in each group by the number of citizens in each group. This lies between the voting age population and voting eligible population as those who were disfranchised due to felony convictions are not deducted from the base (see Sidebar 2.2, Chapter 2). Source: U.S. Census Bureau, Current Population Survey, November 2012.

11 Another former student found that this had more to do with the evangelical, church attending nature of lower status blacks. As opposed to their upper status

counterparts, they could be pulled away from their nominal Democratic attachments when cultural issues, such as gay rights, were in play.

12   The following calculations demonstrate how these subgroup means could produce the means for all of the individuals in each gender sample. Category 1 is full-time, and category 2 is part time:

$$\overline{X} = \frac{\overline{X}_1(N_1) + \overline{X}_2(N_2)}{N_1 + N_2}$$

This formula is an extension of the formula for the calculation of means when data have been categorized in a frequency distribution (Chapter 3). Although not everyone (N_1 or N_2) in each subgroup necessarily makes the same income, the mean is the income that each would receive if the total income for that subgroup was evenly distributed. Computing the subgroup means by adding each individual's income would produce the same result.

For males, this is calculated as follows:

$$\overline{X} = \frac{\$40,000(150) + \$25,600(150)}{150 + 150} = \$32,800$$

For females, this is calculated as follows:

$$\overline{X} = \frac{\$52,000(40) + \$27,000(160)}{40 + 160} = \$32,000$$

Different by How Much? Linear Regression

Learning Objectives:

■ To realize that you work with regression equations all of the time
■ To understand the concept and mathematics of regression
■ To understand the concept of a "best-fitting line"
■ To understand R^2 as a goodness of fit measure
■ To be able to judge regression equations inferentially
■ To realize the limitations of linear regression

Statistics like lambda help us measure the relationship between two variables measured at the nominal level. Ordinal statistics like gamma do so for variables measured at the ordinal level. In this chapter, we will start our discussion of a statistic that helps us test a hypothesis that links two variables measured at the interval level—**linear regression**.

As we develop our understanding of linear regression, we will come back to statistics and statistical concepts that were introduced in previous chapters. Means and variances will be used. Once again, we'll discover the importance of deviation scores. Standardization will come up as essential in statistical analysis. The concept of proportional reduction of error and variance (PRE/PRV) will be reintroduced, as will the interconnection among different types of statistics. As you learn a new statistic, use this and the next chapter (third variables) as a review of the key terms and concepts presented throughout the text.

linear regression A statistical technique that allows us to gauge the interaction of one variable on another if both variables are measured at the interval level.

■ YOU ALREADY KNOW THIS: READING A LINEAR REGRESSION EQUATION

Most students seem to have difficulty with interpreting or are just plain fearful when faced with a regression equation, even a simple linear one. They do not, however, realize that they use such equations in everyday life. Before we get into the mathematics of regression, let's demonstrate this point.

We all know how to convert feet into inches. For every 1 foot increase, we "expect" an increase of 12 inches. Of course, this "expectation" is exact, as the translation between the two has been created to be so. As a formula, the translation from feet to inches would be the following:

$$\text{\# inches} = 12(\text{\# feet}) \tag{11.1}$$

As another example, when we travel to a foreign country, we usually need to convert that country's currency into our own in order to know how much, in our terms, we are spending for a given purchase. At the time of this writing, 1 euro (the common currency of most of the European Union) was worth US\$1.36.

$$\text{US\$} = 1.36(\text{€}) \tag{11.2}$$

Notice that each formula allows us to convert any number of feet or euros to any number of inches or dollars: €15, for example, equals US\$20.40. In addition, for every increase of 1 euro, we "expect" an increase of US\$1.36. The difference between €20 and €25 would therefore be US\$6.80. In geometric terms, those conversion factors are the equivalent of the slope of a line, where the slope is equal to the change in dollars (1.36) for every 1-unit change in euros. We also know that any given line is defined not only by its slope or angle from the horizontal, but also its "intercept," where the intercept is the point at which a line crosses its vertical axis when the horizontal value is equal to 0. When the number of euros equals 0, the number of dollars (intercept) will also equal 0 (see Figure 11.1). The currency translator formula would therefore be equal to:

$$\text{US\$} = 0 + 1.36(\text{€}) \tag{11.3}$$

Not all conversions intersect at 0. What if we were to convert degrees Celsius into the less common (but used in the United States) degrees Fahrenheit? Water freezes at 0° Celsius, but 32° Fahrenheit. Every 1-degree increase on the Celsius scale corresponds to a 1.8-degree increase Fahrenheit. The formula for converting from Celsius to Fahrenheit is therefore:

$$\text{°F} = 32 + 1.8(\text{°C}) \tag{11.4}$$

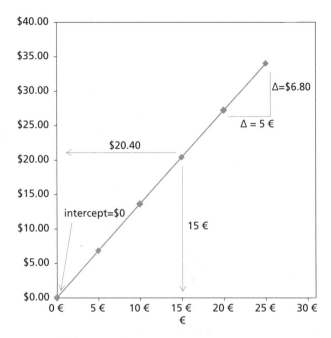

FIGURE 11.1 A Typical Linear Plot

or, more commonly presented as:

$$°F = 32 + \frac{9}{5}(°C) \qquad (11.5)$$

This is graphically represented in Figure 11.2.

In general, the equation for any line, where y represents the value on the vertical axis and x represents the value on the horizontal axis is as follows:

$$y = a + b(x) \qquad (11.6)$$

where a = the point at which the line crosses the y-axis when $x = 0$
(**intercept**)
b = the **slope** $\Delta y / \Delta x$

intercept The value of the dependent variable when the independent variable equals 0.

slope The expected increase in the dependent variable for every unit increase in the independent variable.

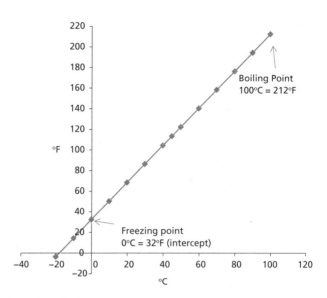

FIGURE 11.2 Fahrenheit versus Celsius

Thus far, we have worked with equations that perfectly "predict" the value of one variable based on the variable of the other. The data points are exactly on the predictor equation line. These "predictions" are perfect because humans created these conversions. In the real world, however, predictions are not so perfect, especially when we only have comparisons on two variables. Let's start by looking at two variables that should be highly correlated. The following graph, known as a **scatterplot**, shows the percentage of the vote won by candidate Barack Obama in 2008 compared to the vote won by the previous Democratic presidential candidate, John Kerry, in 2004 (Figure 11.3). For simplicity of representation, we only present those data for the 53 California congressional districts. Notice that the data points almost correspond to a straight line, but not exactly. Visually, a straight line would represent the scattered points extremely well, but there would be some degree of error in predicting how well Obama did compared to how well Kerry did four years before.

A less uniform example can be demonstrated by displaying the "scatterplot" representing the percentage of voting turnout in the 50 states, where our horizontal (x) axis represents the percentage of the voting age population with a college education or higher (2010 Census), and the vertical axis (y) represents the percentage of the voting age population that voted in the 2012 presidential election (Figure 11.4).

scatterplot A graphical representation of the relationship between two (or more) variables.

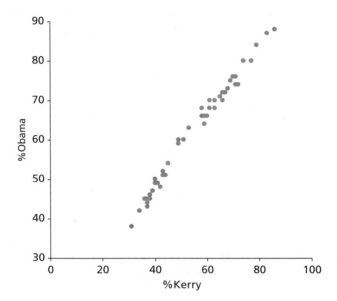

FIGURE 11.3 Democratic Presidential Vote 2004 versus 2008

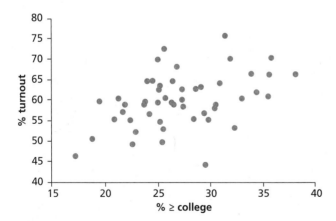

FIGURE 11.4 College Education and Turnout

Notice that although the plot seems visually to demonstrate a positive relationship between the percentage of college-educated citizens and voting turnout, the points are not nearly as "linearly" fitting as the previous graph. Because a "best-fitting" (to be defined later) straight line does not exactly allow us perfectly to predict our *y*-axis variable from our *x*, the linear regression equation becomes:

$$\hat{y} = a + b(x) \qquad (11.7)$$

where $\hat{y}$ = each value of *y* (turnout) predicted by the best-fitting line
$\hat{y} = a + b(x)$

Graphically, let's look at the point that represents Hawaii (see Figure 11.5). Notice that, for Hawaii, the difference between the actual turnout (44.2%) and the turnout predicted by the "best-fitting" line (calculated as 61.38%), is greater than for any other state.

WHICH LINE FITS BEST? MINIMIZING THE SUM OF THE SQUARED DEVIATION SCORES

We now need to discuss how that "best-fitting" line is determined. For each point (state) in the distribution, there exists a value equal to the difference between the value of *y* that we actually observe, and the value ($\hat{y}$) that we

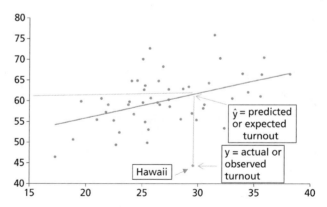

FIGURE 11.5 College Education, Turnout, and Hawaii as an Outlier

would predict or expect given our **best-fitting line**. This difference, also called the "residual" or "prediction error," is equal to:

$$y - \hat{y} \tag{11.8}$$

Remember that, as we are dealing with interval data, we are not just concerned about whether those two are different (nominal), or even just whether one is greater (ordinal), but *by how much* they are different (interval). In linear regression, the best-fitting line is calculated as the one that *minimizes* the sum of the squares of all of those differences or residuals (50 in this example). This notion of "sum of squares" should already be familiar to you, as it is part of the calculation of the variance (see Chapter 4),[1] where we first needed to calculate, for each case (state), the squared deviation score.

$$d_i^2 = \frac{\sum\limits_{i=1}^{N}\left(x_i - \overline{X}\right)^2}{N} \tag{11.9}$$

As with the variance, we need not worry about negative residuals canceling out positive residuals, as these residuals are squared.

How do we determine the slope and intercept of that line? As we are linking differences in both the independent (level of education) and dependent variables (turnout), we need to calculate the **covariance** between those two variables. For each case, we first calculate the deviation score on the X or independent variable. Next we calculate the deviation score on the Y or dependent variable. We do not square each individually as we are measuring the covariances between them. Instead we multiple them by each other:

$$\left(x_i - \overline{X}\right)\left(y_i - \overline{Y}\right) \tag{11.10}$$

As the degree of covariance between two variables is partially contingent on how much variance exists in our independent variable (the greater the variance on x, the greater the potential for variance on y), we need to *standardize* by that original deviation. The slope (b) is therefore calculated as follows:

$$b = \frac{\dfrac{\sum\limits_{i=1}^{n}\left(x_i - \overline{X}\right)\left(y_i - \overline{Y}\right)}{N}}{\dfrac{\sum\limits_{i=1}^{n}\left(x_i - \overline{X}\right)^2}{N}} \tag{11.11}$$

best-fitting line The line through a scatterplot of two variables that minimizes the sum of the squared deviation scores of the dependent variable.

covariance The degree to which two variables vary together.

This can then be simplified as:

$$b = \frac{\sum_{i=1}^{n}(x_i - \bar{X})(y_i - \bar{Y})}{\sum_{i=1}^{n}(x_i - \bar{X})^2} \qquad (11.12)$$

The intercept for our best-fitting line is then calculated as:[2]

$$a = \bar{Y} - b(\bar{X}) \qquad (11.13)$$

The slope of a simple linear regression line passes through the means of the two variables (see Figure 11.6). That is, a case that has as its value the mean of the independent (x) variable will also have as its value the mean of the dependent variable.[3] Let's return to our 50-state scatterplot.

Using our equation for the intercept and slope, our linear regression equation is the following:

$$\hat{y} = 43.72 + .59(x) \qquad (11.14)$$

Let's use these numbers to predict certain outcomes and differences.

If the percentage of adult citizens within a state with at least a college education equals 38%, what we predict voting turnout to be?

$$\hat{y} = 43.72 + .59(38) = 66.1\% \qquad (11.15)$$

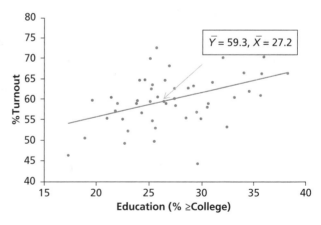

FIGURE 11.6 Best-Fitting Regression Line, and Means

For that value, our predicted or expected value is not that much off from our observed value. Our actual last data point has an $x = 38.2\%$ and a $y = 66.3\%$. On the other hand, our prediction or expectation if $x = 17\%$ would be a y of 53.8%. The closest observation is not so close ($x = 17.3$, $y = 46.3$). Our "best-fitting" line fits some data points better than others.

■ Two states differ on their percentage of adult citizens with a college degree or more by 15%. What would we expect the difference in turnout between those two to be?

Here we need only look at the slope. For every 1% point increase in education level, we would expect an increase of .59 percentage points in turnout (.5948% if carried out to four decimal places).[4] A 15% increase would therefore lead to an expected difference of .5948 × 15% = 8.922%.

Let's look at another set of data, this time comparing education levels within 32 European countries and turnout in their parliamentary elections.[5] The general slope this time is negative, not positive (Figure 11.7).

The best-fitting linear equation is calculated as follows:

$$\hat{y} = 84.731 - .2577(x) \tag{11.16}$$

The intercept tells us that, in the unlikely event that the percentage of citizens with higher education is 0, then the predicted percentage turnout will be 84.73%.[6] The slope this time is negative and tells us that for every 1-unit or percentage point increase in the proportion of adult citizens who have completed some level of higher education, we would expect a decrease of .25 percentage points in turnout in the most proximate parliamentary election.

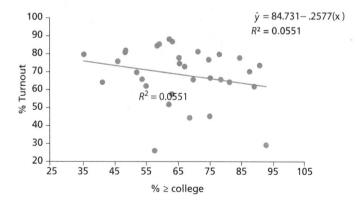

FIGURE 11.7 Education and Turnout, Europe

▮ REGRESSION AND PRE/PRV MEASURES (*R*-SQUARE)

The question that now needs to be answered is the following. As the "best-fitting" line fits the data with different degrees of "best," how do we measure how well the line fits the data? For that we return to a concept we used before, a PRE or PRV measure. Remember our discussion of lambda. We compared the *number* of errors we would observe if we guessed the mode within each independent variable group (i.e., the number of cases not in the respective modal categories) against the number of errors we would observe if we made our best, modal guess for the entire distribution.

$$\lambda = \frac{N(1) - N(2)}{N(1)} = \frac{E(1) - E(2)}{E(1)} \qquad (11.17)$$

where $E(2)$ is the number of errors we make by guessing within each independent variable category

$E(1)$ is the number of errors we would make by "blind guessing" (i.e., guessing the modal category without information about the independent variable, the mode for the entire distribution)

For ordinal data (gamma, Somers' D), we compared the number of times we would be wrong in predicting the *order* of an outcome against a 50% correct prediction. If we predicted concordance, then:

$$Gamma = \frac{[.5 \times (C + D)] - (D)}{[.5 \times (C + D)]} \qquad (11.18)$$

Linear regression takes into account not whether or not we are wrong in making a particular guess about the dependent variable (nominal), nor whether we are wrong in the order we guess (ordinal), but rather by *how much* we are off. In addition, as we discussed previously, that "how much" is squared, giving outliers even greater influence in our calculations. The PRE rule is much the same as lambda and gamma. First, we take the sum of the squared deviation scores $(y - \hat{y})$ from the "best-fitting" regression line (i.e., the formula calculated with information about the independent variable). That is our equivalent to $E(2)$. We then calculate the sum of the squared deviations we would take from our best guess without such information, this time the mean for the entire distribution, $y - \overline{Y}$. Our PRE measure thus becomes:

$$\frac{\sum\limits_{i=1}^{N}(y_i - \overline{Y})^2 - \sum\limits_{i=1}^{N}(y_i - \hat{y})^2}{\sum\limits_{i=1}^{N}(y_i - \overline{Y})^2} \qquad (11.19)$$

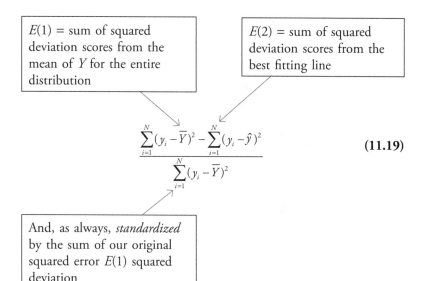

$$\frac{\sum_{i=1}^{N}(y_i - \overline{Y})^2 - \sum_{i=1}^{N}(y_i - \hat{y})^2}{\sum_{i=1}^{N}(y_i - \overline{Y})^2}$$

(11.19)

We can perhaps better understand this by a graphical representation of the two sets of residual or deviation scores. The following scatterplot represents, as our independent variable (X), the proportion of the vote won by then candidate Obama in 2008 in each of the 53 California districts. Our dependent variable (Y) is the proportion of times in 2009 that the winning congressional candidate supported the newly elected president on bills for which he had an expressed preference. The hypothesis we are trying to test would be the following:

> *The greater the proportion of the vote received by a president in a congressional district, the more likely the Congress member of that district will support the president.*

As we are not only concerned about order, but by how much, we also need to state:

> *There is a positive linear relationship between the proportion of the vote received in a congressional district and that district's Congress member's subsequent support for the president.*

The theoretical logic behind these hypotheses (we look at the obvious alternate explanation later) is that Congress members would be more inclined to support/not support a popular/unpopular president in their district for fear of alienating their voters before their next election. The assumption, of course,

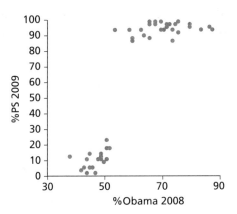

FIGURE 11.8 Presidential Vote and Presidential Support

is that the vote for the Congress member is actually contingent on the public's view of the incumbent president.[7] Figure 11.8 presents the scatterplot of these two variables.[8]

Let's look at the scatterplot in two ways. The first (Figure 11.9) shows the original deviation scores for each district from the mean (i.e., the observed support for the president's positions in 2009 subtracted from the mean level of support from all 53 members, $y_i - \overline{Y}$).

The second (Figure 11.10 on page 260) plots the deviation scores calculated with knowledge of the independent variable used in calculating the "best-fitting" line $(y - \widehat{Y})$.

Notice that the deviation scores in the second graph are generally smaller than the deviation scores using the mean. The discrepancy between the two, as you recall, increases as the respective deviation scores are squared before they are added.

The PRE calculation (equation 11.19),

$$\frac{\sum_{i=1}^{N}(y_i - \overline{Y})^2 - \sum_{i=1}^{N}(y_i - \widehat{y})^2}{\sum_{i=1}^{N}(y_i - \overline{Y})^2}$$

R-square A goodness of fit measure that calculates how much of the variance of the dependent variable is explained by the independent variable variance.

is known as the **R-square** value or coefficient of determination that, as with lambda, provides us with a measure of "goodness of fit." How much better off are we with knowledge of the 2008 presidential vote in each district (and

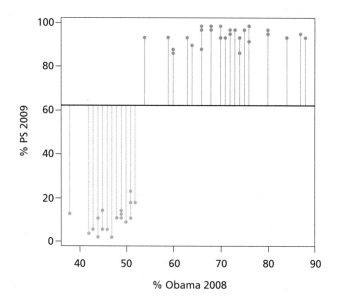

FIGURE 11.9 Deviations from the Mean

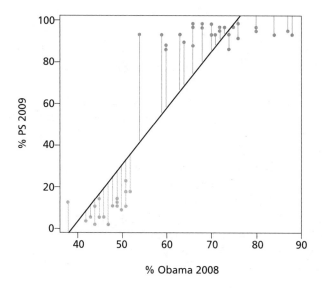

FIGURE 11.10 Deviations from the Regression Line

thus able to compute a slope and intercept) as opposed to "blind guessing" the mean of presidential support for each district representative?

Note that our PRE measure can also be listed as follows:

$$\frac{\dfrac{\sum\limits_{i=1}^{N}(y_i - \overline{Y})^2}{N} - \dfrac{\sum\limits_{i=1}^{N}(y_i - \hat{y})^2}{N}}{\dfrac{\sum\limits_{i=1}^{N}(y_i - \overline{Y})^2}{N}} \qquad (11.20)$$

which calculates the R-square as a difference between the two variances. Thus, we can discuss R-square as a PRV, or proportional reduction in variance measure. The first part of the equation, as well as the standardizing denominator, is the original variance (about the mean). The second part of the equation is what is called is the "regression" variance (i.e., the variance when using our best-fitting line as our y estimator). In our California group, the original variance (from the mean) is equal to 1690.4, and the residual (regression) variance is equal to 385.6.

R^2 is calculated as follows:

$$\frac{1{,}690.4 - 385.6}{1{,}690.4} = .772 \qquad (11.21)$$

Lambda told us by what proportion did we reduce our categorical error in guessing the dependent variable with information about the independent variable. R^2 indicates the proportion of the original variation (about the mean) that is explained by variation from the best-fitting line. For these 50 states, knowledge of (and utilization of) the percentage of the vote received in each district by president-elect Obama proportionately explains 77.2% of the original variance of presidential support. We are still left with 22.8% of the original variance unexplained or *residual* variance.

As with lambda, R^2 can vary from 0 (creating a best-fitting line gives us no proportional reduction from guessing the mean) to 1 (the regression line perfectly fits the data). That value of 1 would apply in guessing inches from feet or °F from °C. The regression variance will equal 0 (there is no deviation from the "best-fitting" line), thus leaving us with the original variance divided by itself. We come close to that in predicting the vote for Obama in 2008 with the vote for John Kerry in 2004, with an R^2 of .986.

Sidebar 11.1: Poverty Level and Crime

It is generally taken for granted that poor people are more likely to engage in criminal activity, especially property crimes like burglary and theft, than wealthier individuals both in the United States and across the globe.[1] The following scatterplot compares the proportion of individuals in a state (or the District of Columbia) who live below the poverty line and the number of crimes per 100,000 inhabitants.

Limiting ourselves to property crimes (burglary, larceny, and theft), we can see a reasonably strong relationship between the poverty rate and the crime rate. The relationship is not as strong for violent crimes (murder, aggravated assault, rape, and robbery). Assessing the effects of inequality and crime, Morgan Kelly explains the different motivations behind these two types of crime, attributing the latter less to poverty and inequality than to social disorganization.[2]

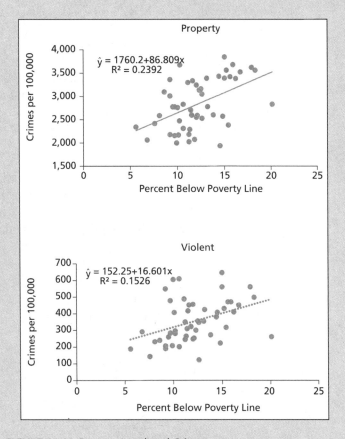

FIGURE 11.11 Poverty Level and Crime

Although the evidence seems to confirm our hypothesis, we should not, however, take any of this evidence to assume that all poor people are criminals or that all wealthier individuals are not. There are just different criminal probabilities within each group.

[1] For an international perspective, see "Poverty and Crime: Breaking the Vicious Cycle," 2013, http://www. poverties.org/poverty-and-crime.html.

[2] Morgan Kelly, "Inequality and Crime," *Review of Economics and Statistics* 82, no. 4 (2000): 530–539. Data sources: Crime: Federal Bureau of Investigation, *Uniform Crime Reports*, http://www.fbi.gov/about-us/cjis/ucr/ucr. Poverty Rate: Department of Commerce, U.S. Census Bureau.

GOING FULL CIRCLE: SLOPES, PEARSON'S *R*, AND BACK TO *R*-SQUARE

The slope tells us the predicted value of the dependent variable for each value of the real or possible value of the independent variable. It does not, however, give us any indication of the strength of the association between two variables. For that, we need to turn to another statistic, Pearson's *r*, more commonly referred to as the correlation coefficient. **Pearson's *r*** is the ratio of the products of the covariances between our independent and dependent variables, standardized (divided) by the product of their individual variances. Pearson's *r* can vary from −1 (a perfect linear negative relationship) to 0 (no relationship) to +1 (a perfect linear positive relationship).

There are several ways to calculate this statistic, but, in keeping with the theme in this chapter, we will use the simplest one based on deviation scores. In order to calculate Pearson's *r*, we need to first calculate the original deviations scores from the mean for our independent variable *x*, then the variation scores for our dependent variable *y*. We then enter them into the following formula:

$$r = \frac{\dfrac{\sum\limits_{i=1}^{n}(x_i - \bar{X})(y_i - \bar{Y})}{N}}{\sqrt{\dfrac{\sum\limits_{i=1}^{n}(x_i - \bar{X})^2}{N} \dfrac{\sum\limits_{i=1}^{n}(y_i - \bar{Y})^2}{N}}} \tag{11.22}$$

Pearson's *r* Also called the "product moment coefficient," it is a measure of the linear relationship between two interval variables. It is also the square root of *R*-square.

Or, alternately:

$$r = \frac{\sum\limits_{i=1}^{n}(x_i - \bar{X})(y_i - \bar{Y})}{\sqrt{\sum\limits_{i=1}^{n}(x_i - \bar{X})^2 \sum\limits_{i=1}^{n}(y_i - \bar{Y})^2}} \tag{11.23}$$

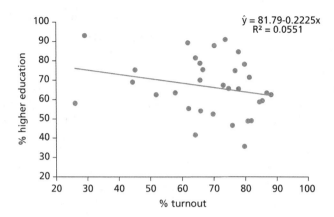

$\hat{y} = 81.79 - 0.2225x$
$R^2 = 0.0551$

FIGURE 11.12 Turnout and Higher Education

Notice any similarities with equations 11.11 and 11.12? Let's return to scatterplot 11.7. This time (Figure 11.12), however, let's use percent education as our dependent variable and percent turnout as our independent one (don't worry about the causal direction here; we're just going to make a point).

Notice that our R-square value stays the same. R-square assumes no direction (symmetrical) and therefore does not vary when the independent and dependent variables are switched. Now multiply the absolute values of the two slopes $(.2477 \times .2225)$. Remember that the slopes are based on direction—independent and dependent variables matter. Look familiar (.0551)? R-square, the symmetrical measure of fit, is the product of the individual slopes.

One last point. If we calculate the value of the Pearson's r for either table, it will equal $-.235$. Square that number, and you should get the R-square value. Remember, the bivariate tabular version of r is Φ, which is, in turn, connected to chi-square. Yes, statistics are related.

IS THE SLOPE REALLY DIFFERENT FROM THE MEAN? INFERENCE WITH REGRESSION

Normally, as mentioned previously, I'm hesitant to use significance tests with non-randomly sampled data (one entire Congress, a set of European countries, etc.). If we do have a sample, however, we still need to go from our descriptive analyses (r, R-square, and slopes) to an inferential one. Remember that, with linear regression, we are comparing estimates of the dependent variables using a best-fitting line against estimating the mean for all cases. If the slope is in the hypothesized direction, and the R-square is fairly high, then we have mostly satisfied our causal Step 4 (the observed results are as expected). We still need to test (Step 5) whether our results are significant enough to reject the possibility (our null hypothesis) that the independent variable has no effect on the dependent variable in the population from which the sample was drawn. With linear regression, the null hypothesis is that, in the population from which our sample was drawn, the true slope is 0, no different from the mean.

Linear regression assumes that, in that population, the values of the dependent value y are normally distributed for each value of our independent variable x.[9] When dealing with normal distributions previously, we used t-tests. A variation of that test, **t-test for slopes**, is used to compare our observed slope with a slope of "0." Let's bypass the math on this one (it's the slope divided by its standard error) and show the results from an analysis of feeling thermometer scores from the 2008 American National Election Studies survey. Our independent variable is one's rating of the Democratic Party, and our dependent variable is one's rating of candidate Barack Obama. The results are presented in Table 11.1.

The unstandardized coefficient (we'll get to the standardized beta in the next chapter) tells us that, using our calculated best-fitting line, an increase of 1 degree in feelings toward the Democratic Party predicts an increase of .761 degrees for candidate Obama. The R-square value of .467 indicates that, descriptively, the regression line fits the data reasonably well, with the variation on the independent variable explaining 46.7% of the variance on the dependent variable. The t-test is greater than the two-sided critical cutoff of 1.96, with a p of less than .0000. In all likelihood, assuming the requirements for linear regression are met, the true slope is between .726 and .797—both greater than 0. We can reject the null hypothesis with confidence.

TABLE 11.1 Regression, Feeling Thermometers: Democratic Party and President Obama

R	R-Square	Adjusted R-Square	Std. Error of the Estimate
.683[a]	.467	.467	20.950

[a]Predictors: (Constant), V18 B1h. Feeling Thermometer: Democratic Party.

	Unstandardized Coefficients	
	b	Std. Error
(Constant)	14.434	1.121
V18 B1h. Feeling Thermometer: Democratic Party	.761	.018

		95.0% Confidence Interval for B	
t	sig.	Lower Bound	Upper Bound
12.880	.000	12.236	16.631
42.339	.000	.726	.797

t-test for slopes A test of significance that determines whether the slope of our equation is significantly different from a slope of 0.

Sidebar 11.2: Remember the Law of Large Numbers

If we are testing a null hypothesis of a slope of 0, keep in mind that our ability to reject the null, as with all other statistics, is partially a function of sample size. Take, for example, the following list of ten cases on two variables.

x	y
10	30
20	35
20	42
10	35
30	47
45	50
80	35
20	65
65	80
10	80

Our slope is .152 with an R-square of .013—not a very good fit. Our t-value is only .617, not large enough to reject the null hypothesis. If we increase our sample to 300, however, by replicating our ten cases 30 times, our slope and R-square values remain exactly the same. Our t-value, however, increases to 2.012, significant at $p < .05$. Would we really consider this theoretically significant?

LINEAR IS NOT ALWAYS THE BEST FIT

Data can always be placed into a regression calculator, and a "best-fitting" line will always be calculated. With a large enough sample size (if we are randomly selecting a sample), even a regression analysis with a small R-square value can be statistically significant (slope in the population most likely not 0). A quick look at a scatterplot, however, will often move us away from a simple linear model. Take the following scatterplot, based on data taken from the World Bank's World Development Indicators collection. The independent variable is the amount spent per capita on health care (adjusted to U.S. dollars), and the dependent variable is the infant mortality rate per 1,000 live births.

A simple linear regression produces a decent R-square value, but it doesn't really pattern the data very well. It seems that most of the decline in the mortality rate occurs within the first $1,000 of additional health expenditures, then levels off. Above $1,000, increased expenditures seem to have a limited effect on infant mortality rates.

One can divide the data in two, separating countries with $1,000 in expenditures or less from those that spend more. The original linear slope is −0.0071 (an increase of $1,000 decreases the infant mortality rate by .71%, $R^2 = 0.217$). For countries spending below $1,000, the slope is −0.0581 ($R^2 = 0.368$). For countries that spend more, the slope is basically 0, with an R^2 of .0165.

We'll cover these types of specification effects in the next chapter. Let's end this vignette with a suggestion. There are different types of bivariate regression models, not all linear. A power model, for example (see the "best-fitting" curve displayed as dashes), produces a much more proximate fit to all of the data points (see Figure 11.13). That fit is measured as $R^2 = .776$.

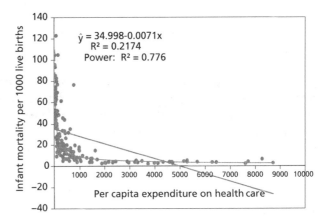

FIGURE 11.13 Health Care Expenditures and Infant Mortality

LINEAR REGRESSION CONSIDERATIONS

Usually, when we think about our hypothesis, it may be of the following form:

The higher the overall education level in a state, the higher we expect turnout to be.

However, note that this is an *ordinal* hypothesis. The interval equivalent would be as follows:

Education and income will be linearly related in a positive fashion.

We are asking not only if the variables differ in a particular order, but by how much. Order and the direction of a linear regression slope may not present the same results. Look at Figure 11.14, which presents a hypothetical distribution of two variables with six cases. If we compare the six cases and count the number of times an increase in x is associated with a *decrease* in y (discordant pairs), we will come up with ten possibilities (1 with 2, 3, 4, and 5; 2 with 3, 4, and 5; 3 with 4 and 5; and 4 with 5). The number of times an increase in x is associated with an increase (concordant pairs) in y occurs only with five comparisons (case 6 compared to the five others). Ordinally, the relationship is clearly negative. Yet, when we run these numbers through a simple linear regression, the slope is positive (.5714). That one outlier ($x = 12$, $y = 40$) pulls our slope upward, much as outliers pulled our mean from a distribution's median.

Is there a way to resolve this dilemma? One is to calculate a "best-fitting" equation that is not linear. Statistical packages such as SPSS and Stata provide us with a host of non-linear regression estimates. The other way is to eliminate the outlier as non-representative of the data, or to state the relationship as conditional: the two variables are linearly perfectly ($R^2 = 1$) and negatively associated until x exceeds a certain value. This does not mean that we eliminate all discussion of that outlier. Instead, we may use it, or any other of the outliers (Hawaii and others in Figure 11.5), as deviant cases worthy of study to determine why they do not fit the general pattern. **Deviant case analysis** is not only a fruitful way to come up with an undergraduate research topic (why is this state different?) but also adds to our understanding of the outcome we are trying to predict ("y should increase predictably with x unless . . ."). Such an analysis tells us how far we can generalize our results and adds to the broader theoretical knowledge of the discipline.

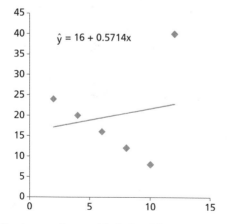

FIGURE 11.14 Ordinal versus Interval Relationship

deviant case analysis
Research that is used to extend our theoretical perspective of a relationship between two variables by intensively examining a case that does not fit the normal pattern.

KEY TERMS

best-fitting line (253)

covariance (253)

deviant case analysis (267)

intercept (249)

linear regression (247)

Pearson's *r* (262)

R-square (258)

scatterplot (250)

slope (249)

t-test for slopes (264)

QUESTIONS AND EXERCISES

NOTE: Several more examples and exercises can be found in both the SPSS and Stata manuals that accompany this text. Regression Analysis is covered in Section 4.6.

1. For lambda, we compared our guesses about outcomes using the mode. For linear regression, our comparison is based on which measure of central tendency?

2. Interpret each of the following:

   a. An *R*-square of 0. What would be the value of Pearson's *r*?
   b. An *R*-square of 1. What would be the value(s) of Pearson's *r*?
   c. An *r* (not *R*-square) of −1

3. Which of the following is most true?

   a. Correlation coefficients (*r*) and slopes do not differ if independent and dependent variables are reversed.
   b. Correlation coefficients (*r*) differ if independent and dependent variables are reversed, but not slopes.
   c. Correlation coefficients (*r*) and slopes both differ if independent and dependent variables are reversed.
   d. Correlation coefficients (*r*) do not differ if independent and dependent variables are reversed, but slopes do.

4. When doing a regression analysis, we run a *t*-test to determine if the observed slope is significantly different from _____ _____ .

5. It is possible for two variables to be related negatively if viewed as ordinal, but positively if viewed as interval. True or False?

6. Using the data presented in Sidebar 11.2 ("Remember the Law of Large Numbers"), hand calculate the slope, intercept, correlation coefficient, and *R*-square. Interpret each.

7. Using the data presented in Figure 11.13, hand calculate the slope (y dependent), intercept, correlation coefficient, and R-square. Interpret each.
8. For Sidebar 11.1 ("Poverty Level and Crime"), interpret the intercept, slope, and R-square values for the relationship between the percentage of households below the poverty line and property crimes.
9. For Sidebar 11.1 ("Poverty Level and Crime"), interpret the intercept, slope, and R-square values for the relationship between the percentage of households below the poverty line and violent crimes. Compare the results from Exercises 8 and 9.
10. The following corresponds to the scatterplot comparing the 2004 vote for Democratic candidate John Kerry with the 2008 vote for Barack Obama. Interpret the intercept, slope, and R-square values. In addition, assume for the sake of demonstration that this is a random sample of 435 districts, interpret the t-test values for the slope (both significance and confidence interval).

TABLE 11.2 Regression, Feeling Thermometers: John Kerry and Barack Obama

R	R-Square	Adjusted R-Square	Std. Error of the Estimate
.965[a]	.931	.931	3.903

[a]Predictors: (Constant), Kerry.

	Unstandardized Coefficients				95.0% Confidence Interval for b	
	b	Std. Error	t	Sig.	Lower Bound	Upper Bound
(Constant)	4.666	.668	6.985	.000	3.353	5.978
Kerry	.999	.013	76.558	.000	.973	1.025

11. The following represents the linear regression calculations of age and one's placement on a ten-point global warming scale that we will consider interval. A low score on the scale indicates a lack of concern about global warming, and a high value indicates serious concern. Interpret the intercept, slope, and R-square values. In addition, interpret the t-test values for the slope (both significance and confidence interval). Why can such a low R-square value be consistent with a significant t-test value?

TABLE 11.3 Regression, Age, and Global Warming

R	R-Square	Adjusted R-Square	Std. Error of the Estimate
.037[a]	.001	.001	2.109

[a]Predictors: (Constant), V28 D11 AGE.

	Unstandardized Coefficients				95.0% Confidence Interval for b	
	b	Std. Error	t	Sig.	Lower Bound	Upper Bound
(Constant)	8.033	.035	227.075	.000	7.964	8.103
V28 D11 AGE	−.004	.001	−5.991	.000	−.006	−.003

NOTES

1   If this information comes from a random sample, the denominator would be $N - 1$.

2   I'm using "a" to represent the intercept. Other texts will represent it as b_o.

3   As many courses would not include a hand calculation of slopes and intercepts, two examples are reserved as end-of-chapter exercises.

4   We can state "percentage point" here as both of our variables are measured in percent. If, on the other hand, our independent variable was "mean years of education," our statement would begin "for each year increase in a state's mean education …"

5   Derived from Eurotstat portal, European Union, http://epp.eurostat.ec.europa.eu/portal/page/portal/statistics/search_database, and *Voter Turnout Database*, "International Institute for Democracy and Electoral Assistance, Stockholm, Sweden, © International Institute for Democracy and Electoral Assistance," http://www.idea.int/vt/viewdata.cfm.

6   I have done analyses where the predicted turnout is over 100% or under 0%. The intercept might seem somewhat unusual. We can't have a turnout of 105%. On the other hand, we would also not have 0% of the population of a country without any higher education. "Best-fitting" lines will often have unusual intercepts, especially when a 0 value on the independent (X) variable is highly unlikely or impossible.

7   Edward Tufte and others advanced a similar notion that a president's popularity had a direct effect on how well the president's party did in midterm elections. Of course, this was only an explanation of between-election-cycle change, not the overall vote for the president's party, which is predominantly based on the partisan nature of a district. See Tufte, "Determinants of the Outcomes of Midterm Elections," *APSR* LXIX (1975): 812–826; and, for an updated view, see Jacobson and Kernell, *Strategy and Choice in Congressional Elections* (Yale University Press, 1981).

8　　Source for district vote for Obama: DavidNYC, "Presidential Results by Congressional District 2000–2008," http://www.swingstateproject.com/showDiary.do?diaryId=4161; source for presidential support scores (only non-unanimous votes used) courtesy of George C. Edwards III, "The Presidential Data Archive," http://presdata.tamu.edu/ArchiveData/support/text/House09_revised02052012.txt.

9　　There are ways to test for this, but I will leave that to an upper division course to pursue.

Retracing Our Methodological Steps

Hypotheses, Multiple Regression, and the Effects of Third Variables

Learning Objectives:

▮ To understand the use of three or more variables in multiple regression analysis
▮ To understand the use of a third variable in testing for a spurious relationship
▮ To examine the concept of a dummy variable
▮ To understand the use of a third variable in investigating explanatory effects
▮ To understand and be able to interpret the difference between standardized and unstandardized slopes
▮ To understand the use of a third variable in testing for additive effects
▮ To examine how we can inferentially test our multiple regression models
▮ To understand the use of a third variable in testing for a specification effect
▮ To bring all that we have learned together as we study multiple regression

As we demonstrated in Chapter 10, political and other life does not fit neatly into a two-variable model. In this chapter, we will conclude by applying the logic of third variable "controls" to test for spuriousness, suggest an explanatory scheme, and define interaction and specification effects. "Spuriousness" is one type of alternate explanation (Step 6), an explanatory scheme helps us to develop the theoretical connection between variables (Step 2), and interaction and specification effects allow us to determine how best to generalize our models (Step 7).

MULTIPLE REGRESSION AND SPURIOUS RELATIONSHIPS

You may have noticed that our district vote and support plot seemed to indicate that the major component of our line was reflective of the difference between two distinct sets of Congress members. In fact, the two clusters represent Republican members on the lower left, and Democratic members on the upper right. What we have is a type of spurious relationship, where a third variable is the true independent variable that causes both the district vote for Obama and the district member's subsequent support for him. Districts that vote Democratic for president will usually vote Democratic for Congress. These Democratic members will usually share many of the policy perspectives of a president of their party. Thus, it is the partisan nature of a district that influences both the presidential vote and, less directly, the support that district's representative affords the president (see Figure 12.1).

One way to examine this spurious effect, as we did when we looked at tabular data and means, is to control for the partisan direction of the district. With the assumption, certainly warranted in California's incumbent-friendly districts of 2008, that districts won by each party contain a majority of affiliates of that party, we can use the party winning each district as a surrogate for its partisan direction. The scatterplots for Democratic and, separately, Republican districts follow the plot for all California districts, along with their regression equations and R^2 measures. Plots have been adjusted to match axis differences (see Figure 12.4).

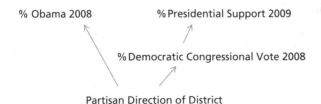

FIGURE 12.1 Presidential Vote and Presidential Support by District

Sidebar 12.1: Redistricting in the United States and the Power of Graphs

Each state sets up different rules governing how to geographically separate its allotted number of U.S. House districts. After a series of 1960s court cases, states were required to do so after each decennial census to equalize the population in each. Generally, when a state allows its legislature to make that decision subject to its governor's approval, and if the legislative and executive branches are controlled by the same party, a partisan gerrymander is likely to be the result.[1] A partisan gerrymander is one that attempts to maximize the number of seats for the majority party by making its safest districts somewhat less so in order to trade majority party voters into other seats to either make them safer or to capture them from the opposition.

Gary Jacobson created an excellent set of bar graphs to demonstrate this change.[2] The first shows the distribution of seats by party control based on party registration (data that can be easily obtained for electoral units as small as precincts and blocks) in the decade preceding the redistricting. White bars indicate seats that had changed party hands at least once. The second shows the distribution of seats in the election immediately after the redistricting (2002). Notice both the lack of "white" districts and the abrupt split between Republican and Democratic seats. The year 2002 was no exception. In the 265 house elections (53 seats, 5 election cycles) during this decade, a district changed party hands only once.

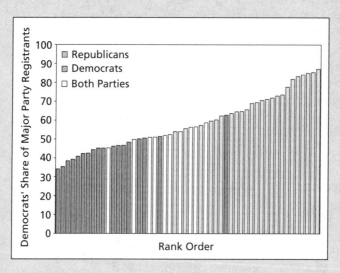

FIGURE 12.2 Registration and Party Control of California House Seats, 1992–2000

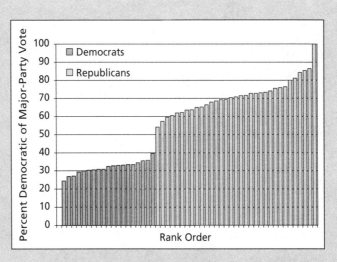

FIGURE 12.3 The Distribution of the House Vote, 2002

[1] In both *Davis v. Bandemar*, 478 U.S. 109 (1986) and *Vieth v. Jubilirer*, 541 U.S. 267 (2004), the U.S. Supreme Court determined that partisan gerrymanders could be declared an unconstitutional violation of the 14th Amendment's equal protection clause but set the bar so high that no partisan gerrymander has ever been successfully challenged.
[2] Gary C. Jacobson, "All Quiet on the Western Front: Redistricting and Party Competition in California House Elections," in P. Galderisi (ed.), *Redistricting in the New Millennium* (Lexington, 2005).

The most obvious difference in comparison to the original graph is the R^2 values. Once we separate out (control for) Democratic from Republican districts, our original high R^2 of .722 drops to a lowly .035 and .066, respectively. Knowledge of the vote received by Obama proportionately explains only 3.5% of the variance of presidential support for Democrats and 6.6% for Republicans. Additionally, the slopes are also dramatically reduced (although it is higher for Republicans, possibly indicative of the slight majority vote that Obama received in some of these otherwise Republican districts).

Although this separation of plots helps us to understand, as it did with the separation of cross tables, how much of the original relationship between vote and support is maintained and how much is lost, it doesn't give us a complete estimate of the importance of all the variables together. For this we turn to **multiple regression**, where two or more independent variables are used to explain our outcome or dependent variable.

multiple regression A regression model with two or more independent variables.

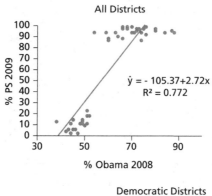

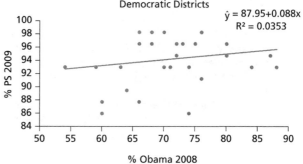

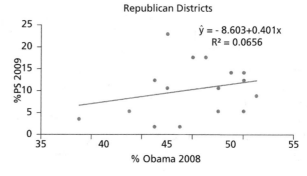

FIGURE 12.4 Regression Plot, District Presidential Vote, and Presidential Support

Dummy Variables

Of the three variables we already used, one, the party that holds the district, is nominal with just two categories—Democratic or Republican. However, as we saw in the Chapter 8 Appendix, dichotomous nominal data can be used in ordinal or interval statistics. In terms of regression analysis, we use the term **dummy variable**. In essence, we treat a dichotomy as having a code of 0 (the absence of a variable) or 1 (the presence). In this example, we will code the Democratic districts as 1 and the Republican districts (non-Democratic) as 0. Our new regression equation now takes on this generic form that applies to any three-variable regression, dummy variable or not:

$$\hat{y} = a + b_1(x_1) + b_2(x_2) \tag{12.1}$$

where x_1 and x_2 are the values for each case on two different independent variables

and b_1 and b_2 represent the slopes for the relationship between x_1 and $\hat{y}$ and x_2 and $\hat{y}$, respectively

For our example, x_2 refers to our original percent vote for Obama, and x_1 whether or not the district is Democratic. Two equations are now produced, one for Democratic districts (dummy = 1) and one for Republican districts (dummy = 0).

Democratic districts: $\hat{PS} = 1.915 + 80.102(1) + .172(\%Obama)$ **(12.2)**

$= 82.017 + .172(\%Obama)$

Republican districts: $\hat{PS} = 1.915 + 80.102(0) + .172(\%Obama)$ **(12.3)**

$= 1.915 + .172(\%Obama)$

The combined slope indicates that, regardless of which party holds the district, for every 1% point increase in the district vote for Obama, we would expect an increase in presidential support of .172 percentage points (much less than we would with the original plot). The base (%Obama = 0) of presidential support from Democrats starts at 82.017%, and from Republicans at 1.915%. Obviously, when using this model, we lose some of the distinctiveness that we enjoyed when looking at the regression models for Democrats and Republicans separately. The combined slope might also mask directional differences (one positive, one negative) for each party category. However, as mentioned in Chapter 2, when we summarize data we lose distinct information. Combining the party dummy with the vote for Obama, however, increases our R^2 to an almost perfect .989. Most of this comes from the party dummy variable, with, as would be expected, little explained by the vote for Obama.

dummy variable A nominal, dichotomous variable that can be used as an independent variable in a regression model.

Sidebar 12.2: Dummy Variables

A nominal variable with more than two categories can be used in a linear regression equation by separating the variable into a series of dichotomous dummies. For example, if we had a variable that split individuals into three categories of party (Democratic/Independent/Republican), two dummy variables could be created. The first would separate Democrats (1) from non-Democrats (0) (Independents and Republicans included), and the second would separate Independents (1) from both types of partisans (0). There would be no need to create a Republican/non-Republican variable as that is already subsumed by the first two. A 0 on both means you are a Republican. The operative number of dummy variables will always be equal to the number of nominal categories in a variable minus one.

MULTIPLE REGRESSION AND EXPLANATORY EFFECTS

Let's look at another version of multiple regression, this time with two fully interval variables. This time we will use all 435 congressional districts. The outcome we are trying to explain is the percentage of the 2008 presidential vote won by then candidate Obama. Let's start with the first explanatory variable, the percentage of the district population that is black. The linear regression formula calculates as follows:

$$\%OBAMA = 47.845 + .473\,(\%BLACK) \qquad (12.4)$$

with an $R^2 = .223$

The equation tells us that for every 1% point increase in the percentage of blacks in a district, we can expect a .473% point increase in the district vote for Obama. We might therefore conclude that black voters voted for candidate Obama because he was a person of color, generally identified as the first black major party presidential candidate. However, might there be an alternate explanation? Is it possible that one's race and one's vote are mediated by some third, explanatory variable? Is it possible that black voters normally vote Democratic, and that the main reason that the districts lined up the way they did was because Obama was a Democrat?

adjusted *R*-square A variation of the *R*-square statistic that takes into account the number of cases relative to the number of independent variables introduced into a regression model.

FIGURE 12.5 Explanatory Sequence: Race and Obama

Sidebar 12.3: The Aggregate or Ecological Fallacy

In analyzing the relationship between race and the 2008 vote, we are of course making an assumption that we can infer the behavior of individuals in our districts with the aggregated data for those districts.

When confirming our hypotheses about individual behavior based on this analysis of states, we need to be aware of a possible alternate explanation, the aggregate or ecological fallacy (i.e., erroneously deducing individual behavior from aggregations, like districts, states, or countries within which those individuals reside).[1]

After the 1968 U.S. presidential election, for example, some studies indicated that in certain areas of the South, the county vote for third-party candidate George C. Wallace, segregationist governor of Alabama, was positively correlated with the percentage of the county's citizens that were black. Did blacks vote for a segregationist? Most likely not. Rather, on further evaluation, white citizens became more concerned about the newly won civil rights of blacks as the proportion of blacks in a county increased. The percentage of blacks within a county helped explain why white voters were more or less likely to vote for Wallace. Causative? Most likely. But not indicative of black support for the candidate.

Although unlikely, it is at least possible that, as with Wallace in 1968, few black voters voted for Obama and that almost all of his votes came from the white population. Other than having no theoretical reason (STEP 2) to expect that, we should go one step further (STEP 8?) and investigate our hypothesis with other types of data, especially those based on individual responses. Were black citizens actually more likely to state that they voted for candidate Obama than were white ones? As a form of triangulization (Chapter 2), confirmation based on both aggregate- and individual-level data makes for a much stronger argument.

[1] The pioneering essay on the ecological fallacy is William S. Robinson's 1950 analysis of the positive relationship between immigration rates and literacy. See "Ecological Correlations and the Behavior of Individuals," *American Sociological Review* 15, no. 3 (1950): 351–357.

As a measure of the Democratic leaning direction of a district vote, let's take the vote that went to the previous Democratic presidential candidate, John Kerry. When added to the regression equation, we now have:

$$\widehat{\%\mathrm{OBAMA}} = 4.778 + .009\,(\%\mathrm{BLACK}) + .994\,(\%\mathrm{KERRY}) \qquad \textbf{(12.5)}$$

with an $R^2 = .931$

It appears that our alternate explanation is correct. Adding %KERRY to our equation explains almost all of the variance in the percent of the district votes that went for Obama. Increases in the black population have only marginal predictive effects on the presidential vote. In fact, if we just used %KERRY as our one independent variable, we would still have an R^2 of .931.

aggregate or ecological fallacy Erroneously inferring individual behavior from aggregated statistics.

Adding the percentage of the black population does nothing to help increase our explanation of the variance in the Obama vote at all. Assuming our aggregate district figures are indeed reflective of individual behavior, and that no ecological or aggregate fallacy has been made, then we have been able to explain the main reason why black voters chose Obama. It was because, as their normal voting pattern would dictate, Barack Obama was the Democratic candidate. His race did add to that vote, but only marginally. A contingency analysis of individual voters provides us with concurring evidence.[1]

Sidebar 12.4: Adjusted R-Square

Adding independent variables will always increase our R-square value, even marginally. Some analysts prefer, especially when sample sizes are small, to use a variation called the adjusted R-square. It adjusts the R-square value based on the number of cases of analysis against the number of independent variables entered into a linear regression model and only increases if newly entered variables increase our original R-square by more than would occur by the random luck of the draw. As such, it is not really relevant when populations or non-random samples are the focus of analysis.

As a statistic partially based on the laws of random selection, the adjusted and non-adjusted R-squares will converge as they sample size becomes large (the former can actually be negative with extremely small samples). Return to the data in Table 11.2. We will add a second set of independent variable values, x_2. As before, we'll replicate the ten cases several times to see the difference it makes in the adjusted and non-adjusted R-square values.

x_1	x_2	y
10	15	30
20	18	35
20	26	42
10	18	35
30	22	47
45	47	50
80	56	35
20	45	65
65	56	80
10	15	80

Two other ways exist to gauge the comparative effects of independent variables on an outcome. In the first, we standardize the slopes so they are more directly comparable. The second, if sampling conditions apply, is to test our slopes inferentially.

TABLE 12.1 Regression, %Black, %Kerry, and %Obama

	$R^2 = .931$	
	b	β
Intercept	4.778	
%BLACK	.009	.009
%KERRY	.994	.960

Standardized Slopes

Standardization is needed if the means and standard deviations (calculated with the mean) in the two independent variables are substantially different. Much as we did in our discussion of Z- and t-scores, our data need to be adjusted for these differences. In order to standardize our slopes, we carry out the following calculation for each variable:

$$\beta = b\left(\frac{s_x}{s_y}\right) \qquad (12.6)$$

where β = the standardized slope
    b = the unstandardized slope
    s_x = the standard deviation of the independent variable (x)
    s_y = the standard deviation of the dependent variable (y)

Table 12.1 now gives us the comparative information we need:
The standardized slopes would be interpreted as the following (notice that, as with Z- and t-values, the unit of measurement is dropped):

> For each standard deviation increase in %Black, we would predict a .009 standard deviation increase in %Obama.
> For each standard deviation increase in %Kerry, we would expect a .960 standard deviation increase in %Obama.

MULTIPLE REGRESSION AND ADDITIVE EFFECTS

Although standardization seems to make little difference in this example because the scales (percentages) for each are similar (although with different means and standard deviations), the differences would be much more pronounced if we were to, for example, try to predict Obama's vote percentage based on %Black and median household income. Not only are our units of measurement different (% and $), but the scales are also substantially different (per capita income can change by thousands).

Going back to our 435 district data, we produce the following figures (Table 12.2):

standardized slope A regression slope adjusted by the standard deviations of the independent and dependent variables.

TABLE 12.2 Regression, %Black, MHI, and %Obama

	$R^2 = .257$	
	b	β
Intercept	36.1	
%BLACK	.533	.531
Median Income	.000475	.194

The unstandardized slope for median household income (MHI) is so low because of its scale. For every $1 increase in a district's MHI, we would predict a .000475% point increase in the vote for Obama. Of course, district MHIs vary by more than $1. A $10,000 difference between two districts would equate to a 4.75% point increase in Obama's vote. The standardized slope still indicates that the black percentage of the district vote is more important than MHI, but the latter is not without statistical significance. The combination of both variables explains more of the variance in the vote for Obama than either alone.

A better example of interaction effects occurs when we attempt to explain the vote received by candidate Barack Obama with information on both the percentage of blacks within a district and the percentage of individuals 65 and older. The results are presented in Table 12.3.

TABLE 12.3 Regression, %Black, %PER65, and %Obama

	$R^2 = .241$	
	b	β
(Constant)	57.315	
%BLACK	.443	.442
%PER65	−.727	−.140

Both the unstandardized and standardized coefficients indicate a positive relationship between %Black and %Obama and a negative one between %PER65 and %Obama. Combined, they explain 24.1% of the variance of the vote, slightly above what they explain separately (22.3% and 5.4%, respectively). The standardized betas indicate the greater importance of the percentage of the black population than the percentage of older citizens.

INFERENCE WITH MULTIPLE REGRESSION

Another way to measure the relative importance of each independent variable is to test for its statistical significance.[2] Can we have come up with a positive

TABLE 12.4 Regression and Statistical Significance, %Black, %Kerry, and %Obama

	b	β	t	Significance (2-tailed)
Intercept	4.778		6.922	.000
%BLACK	.009	.009	.652	.515
%KERRY	.994	.960	66.739	.000

or negative slope in a sample even though the true population slope is 0?[2] Again, there is disagreement in the discipline as to whether or not significance tests are even relevant when no random sampling is performed (see Special Comment, Chapter 7). For illustrative purposes, however, we will use it with our district data (Table 12.4), even though these 435 districts are not a random sample of a defined population.

For this regression equation, indicated by the t-values and their associated significance, the black percentage of the district is not a significant predictor of the vote for Obama once we control for the vote John Kerry received in 2004; the percentage received four years earlier by John Kerry is. In Table 12.5 we see that both variables are statistically significant. Both the percentage of black residents within a district and the MHI help to explain the percentage of the vote received by Barack Obama.

TABLE 12.5 Regression and Statistical Significance, %Black, MHI, and %Obama

	Unstandardized Coefficients		Standardized Coefficients		
	b	Std. Error	β	t	Sig.
(Constant)	36.099901	2.755783		13.100	.000
%BLACK	.532593	.043673	.531	12.195	.000
MHI	.000214	4.801261E–5	.194	4.456	.000

MULTIPLE REGRESSION AND SPECIFICATION EFFECTS

As another example, representing a specification effect (generalizability), let's return to our European parliamentary turnout example from the previous chapter. The data represented in Figure 12.6 are divided as to whether the country is a former Soviet-bloc nation or not. The individual plots and regression data are presented for all countries and each of the two groups.

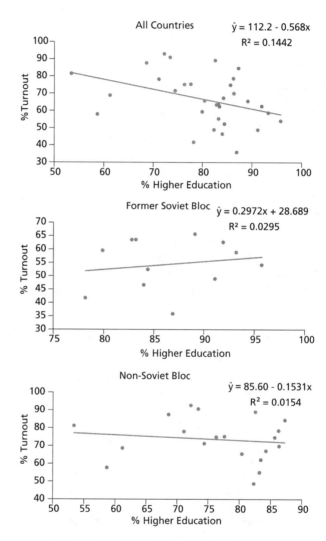

FIGURE 12.6 Education and Turnout: Former Soviet Bloc Status

TABLE 12.6 Regression with a Dummy Variable

$R^2 = .430$	b	β
Intercept	80.300	
% Higher Ed.	−.084	−.056
Dummy	−18.585	−.625

The same data are used, but this time with a dummy variable included indicating whether or not the country is a former Soviet-bloc nation (1 = yes, 0 = no).

The standardized slopes, both negative, indicate that the dummy variable, whether or not a country is a former Soviet-bloc member, is more mathematically important as an explainer of turnout than the percentage of those within a country with a higher education. Note, however, that the individual plots show a slight positive relationship between education and turnout for former Soviet-bloc nations and a slight negative one for other nations. Does the education and turnout relationship that we take for granted in the United States not exist when dealing with EU parliamentary elections? Or are these aggregations masking the true nature of voting in Europe, a sort of inverse aggregate or ecological fallacy?

What I call a specification effect is, in some ways, more commonly called in the regression literature an interaction effect. An interaction effect occurs when the influence of one independent variable on a dependent variable is different for each category of another independent variable. With regression we can directly test for this interaction by creating an additional variable that is the product of the two perceived interacting ones. In our education and turnout analysis, a new variable would be created by multiplying our dummy variable (Soviet bloc/non-Soviet bloc) by our education variable. This interaction variable would then be included as a third independent variable. This differs from a purely additive model in that it does not assume that the slopes for each country bloc would be the same (as evidenced by Figure 12.6). We will not go into any more depth on interaction effects, as we will leave this to a more advanced analysis course.

KEY TERMS

QUESTIONS AND EXERCISES

NOTE: You can replicate these results with the data sets available with the SPSS or Stata manuals that accompany this text. Regression analysis is covered in Section 4.6. These charts were produced using SPSS. The variable names used (V81R, COUNTRY, etc.) are those that appear in the codebooks for these data sets.

1. The following table (Table 12.7) was derived from the 2012 American National Election Studies (ANES2012A). The dependent variable is the post-election feeling thermometer rating (0 through 100) for Republican presidential candidate W. Mitt Romney (V17). The independent variables are one's feeling thermometer assessment of Mormons (V81M, Romney's religion) and for rich people (V81R, Romney among them). Both were issues during the campaign. Interpret the slopes (both standardized and unstandardized), R-square, and the t-test values (with such a large sample size, the adjusted R-square would be the same as the non-adjusted one). Was there a positive linear relationship between feelings toward Mormons and the rich and feelings toward Mitt Romney? How strong was it? Which of the independent variables explains feelings toward former Governor Romney better?

TABLE 12.7 Regression, Feeling Thermometers: Mormons, Rich People, and Romney

R	R-Square	Adjusted R-Square	Std. Error of the Estimate
.315	.099	.098	27.447

	Unstandardized Coefficients		Standardized Coefficients		
	b	Std. Error	β	t	Sig.
(Constant)	19.930	2.152		9.261	.000
Feeling Thermometer: MORMONS	.358	.034	.246	10.576	.000
Feeling Thermometer: RICH PEOPLE	.185	.032	.135	5.786	.000

2. The following table (Table 12.8) was derived from EURO69.SAV, a 2008 standard Eurobarometer survey.

The dependent variable is the ten-point ideological scale (V52), left to right. The independent variables are age and, as a dummy variable, whether or not one's country was formerly a Soviet-bloc nation (COUNTRY was reclassified with a RECODE to separate out the two sets of countries). Interpret the slopes (both standardized and unstandardized), R-square, and the t-test values (with such a large sample size, the adjusted R-square would be the same as the non-adjusted one). Was there a positive linear relationship between age and ideology (degree of conservatism), and how was that relationship influenced by country status? Which of the independent variables better explains differences in ideology?

TABLE 12.8 Regression, Age, Country, and Ideology

R	R-Square	Adjusted R-Square	Std. Error of the Estimate
.134	.018	.014	2.170

	Unstandardized Coefficients		Standardized Coefficients		
	b	Std. Error	β	t	Sig.
(Constant)	4.077	.060		67.467	.000
V28 AGE	.006	.001	.054	7.951	.000
COUNTRY	.646	.035	.125	18.412	.000

3. The following table (Table 12.9) was derived from the 2012 Cooperative Congressional Election Study (CCES2012A). The dependent variable is the 100-point survey question (V60) that asks:

   "If a state had a budget deficit, what percent should come from tax increases and spending cuts?"
   0 = All tax increases
   50 = Equal
   100 = All cuts

   The first independent variable is family income (V15). ("Income" is a qualified interval variable as it is broken down into 15 non-equally proportioned categories. Individuals with family incomes of $100,000 or more were reclassified together.) The second is gender (V1). Only one state (Indiana) is chosen for this analysis (data set = CCES2012I.SAV). Interpret the slopes (both standardized and unstandardized), R-square, and the t-test values. Was there a positive linear relationship between family income and deficit reduction preference toward cuts, and how was it mediated by gender? Which of the independent variables better explains differences in reduction preference?

TABLE 12.9 Regression, Income, Gender, and the Budget

R	R-Square	Adjusted R-Square	Std. Error of the Estimate
.107	.011	.009	25.885

	Unstandardized Coefficients		Standardized Coefficients		
	b	Std. Error	β	t	Sig.
(Constant)	65.333	3.790		17.240	.000
Family Income	.349	.356	.038	.982	.326
Gender	–5.146	1.991	–.099	–2.585	.010

4. The following table (Table 12.10) was derived from CONGRESS2008 (or the combined CONGRESS2008-2012 file). The dependent variable is a house member's party unity score (the proportion of times each voted with his/her party of bills where a majority of Republicans voted against a majority of Democrats [gamma=0]) in 2009 (PU09). The independent variables are the vote each member won by in 2008 (WV08), and their level of seniority going into the election (SENIORITY08). Newly elected members were given a seniority code of 0. One might argue that, as a Congress member becomes safer (i.e., wins by a large margin), he/she can afford to defect from party uniformity more often than others. If this is true, might the relationship be spurious—might both variables really be a function of seniority that tends to boost both electoral margins and one's sense of safety? Might it be additive?

Here's the analysis. You may wish not to consider *t*-tests relevant as this is not a random sample.

TABLE 12.10 Regression, Seniority, Winning Vote, and Party Unity

R	R-Square	Adjusted R-Square	Std. Error of the Estimate
.344	.118	.114	8.340

	Unstandardized Coefficients		Standardized Coefficients		
	b	Std. Error	β	t	Sig.
(Constant)	78.075	1.967		39.693	.000
SENIORITY08	.034	.047	.034	.738	.461
WV08	.211	.029	.334	7.183	.000

5. The following table (Table 12.11) was derived from the cross-national data file (CROSSNAT). The dependent variable is the percentage of males who live beyond 65 (WDI_65M), and the independent variables are the male employment rate (measured as percent of the male population 15 and over that is employed = WDI_EM) and a country's degree of urbanization (WDI_UP = percentage living in urban areas). Is there a positive or negative linear relationship between employment and male longevity, and how does urbanization change the outcome? Which of the independent variables better explains male longevity? Is there anything about the measure of employment that might influence the outcome?

Here's the analysis. You may wish not to consider *t*-tests relevant as this is not a random sample.

TABLE 12.11 Regression, Male Employment Rate, Urbanization, and %Males >65

R	R-Square	Adjusted R-Square	Std. Error of the Estimate
.643	.413	.406	11.476

	Unstandardized Coefficients		Standardized Coefficients			
	b	Std. Error	β	*t*	Sig.
(Constant)	41.375	6.892		6.003	.000
URBANPER	.417	.039	.649	10.702	.000
EMP15M	.039	.086	.028	.455	.650

NOTES

1   This should not imply the lack of a causal link between race and voting behavior, but only that it is mediated mainly through party, not candidate choice.
2   We will not go through all of the calculations here. Just remember that the *t* value is equal to the unstandardized coefficient divided by its associated standard error.

Concluding Remarks

This volume is intended to gently introduce students, especially those with a certain degree of math phobia, to the study of statistics and their use in political science. It should be a starting point, not an end point, for most of you. The influence of so-called big data and the ability to work with it will only grow in importance as time goes on. We are a far cry from when I was entering data on punch cards, and old-time supercomputers were necessary to even begin to tackle data sets as small (in relative terms) as 50,000 cases, not to mention U.S. Census data files. You can now run through those 50,000 cases in seconds on your laptop or tablet.

Remember, however, that data analysis is of little use without proper, methodologically sound development of hypotheses, awareness of the meaningfulness of our measurements and designs, and mindfulness of alternate explanations, including the peculiarities of different statistical techniques. This should not be viewed as a limitation but, rather, as an invitation and challenge to learn and analyze more. The skill sets that you will begin to learn from this text and the accompanying SPSS and Stata manuals will serve you well in the marketplace of the 21st century, but only if you maintain and enhance them.

We have discussed the nature of hypotheses and the multiple methods used to test them—both conceptually and mathematically. We have traced the steps necessary to use statistics within a proper methodological framework. You have been given an invitation and challenge to further your understanding of statistics and research methodology. It is now up to you, the student, to embark on your own research and do so. I wish you continued success.

Glossary

absolute frequency/tally/count The actual observed number of cases within each category of a frequency distribution.

accord A type of no association between two variables where percentages on the dependent variable can vary across independent variable categories as long as the modal categories remain invariant.

adjusted *R*-square A variation of the *R*-square statistic that takes into account the number of cases relative to the number of independent variables introduced into a regression model.

aggregate or ecological fallacy Erroneously inferring individual behavior from aggregated statistics.

alpha error The probability of erroneously rejecting the null hypothesis.

alternate explanations Reasons other than that which are hypothesized for why our properties/variables are related as hypothesized.

arithmetic mean The category that all cases would have if the total value of a variable for all cases were evenly distributed among them.

asymmetrical measure A measure of association that takes into account the direction of an association. Independent and dependent variables must be specified.

bar chart A graphical representation of data where each category is separated into bars. The height or length of each bar represents the number or proportion of cases within each category.

best-fitting line The line through a scatterplot of two variables that minimizes the sum of the squared deviation scores of the dependent variable.

bimodal symmetrical distribution A distribution in which both sides of the distribution are mirror images of each but two modes; one on each side of the distribution exist equally distant from the median.

bivariate statistics A class of statistics that allow us to measure and analyze the relationship between two variables.

Bradley effect The tendency for individuals to give responses that they feel are more politically or socially correct or reflect better on their own perceived moral values.

central limit theorem The distribution of sample means and dichotomous proportions will be normally distributed around the population mean, regardless of the shape of the original, individual data distribution.

central tendency A summary measure that describes the central or most prevalent category of a distribution.

Chicago effect The author's term for the intentional or unintentional misreporting of information by governmental or other agencies.

chi-square An inferential-only statistic that tests for the possibility that the proportions we observe in a sample could have been randomly drawn from a population with different expected proportions. The chi-square must be used when more than two categories of a variable exist.

chi-square (two variables) An inferential measure of association that compares the observed frequencies within a contingency table against a certain frequency expectation, usually one that matches statistical independence.

classic experimental design The standard against which all research designs are compared. This design assumes random assignment into two groups with the only difference between the groups being differences on the variable hypothesized to be the causal agent.

concordant pairs All pairs of two unique cases that differ in the same direction on two variables.

confidence interval A range of values that we use to safely predict a random choice.

contingency table A frequency table that represents the distribution of data simultaneously on two or more variables.

control variable A third variable that is used to eliminate the mediating effect that may cause us to misread the relationship between two variables specified in our hypothesis.

covariance The degree to which two variables vary together.

Cramer's *V* A nominal measure of association, similar to phi, where more than two categories exist for either or both variables.

critical value The value of a statistic, like chi-square, above which allows us to confidently reject a null hypothesis.

cross-contamination/spillover effect An experimental condition in which investigators cannot limit the influence of a test condition to only the test subjects.

crosstabulation *See* **contingency table**.

cumulative frequency A display within a frequency table that indicates the proportion or percentages that are contained within a certain category and categories ranked below it. Data must be measured at least at the ordinal level.

dependent property That property that we hypothesize was caused by another.

dependent samples test A test of significance for which the sampling of each case in the second group is contingent or dependent on the draw on the first.

descriptive statistics A class of statistics that allow us to measure and analyze what we actually observe.

deviant case analysis Research that is used to extend our theoretical perspective of a relationship between two variables by intensively examining a case that does not fit the normal pattern.

deviation score The difference between an individual case's value and the mean of all values within a distribution.

dichotomous variable/dichotomies A variable for which only two categories exist.

discordant pairs All pairs of two unique cases that differ in the opposite directions on two variables.

double blind An experimental condition in which neither the subjects nor the investigators are aware of the group in which each subject is placed.

dummy variable A nominal, dichotomous variable that can be used as an independent variable in a regression model.

expected frequency The number of cases in each category expected from a specified population from which a sample is randomly drawn.

explanatory relationship The reason (theoretical link) why our hypothesized variables should be linked as specified.

external validity of design Our hypothesized independent variable is actually the cause of our outcome or dependent variable for all targeted populations and circumstances.

external validity of measurement Our measurements are generalizable to our targeted populations and circumstances.

factual statement Test of a hypothesis that is proved true or false on limited investigation.

falsifiability The possibility that what we observe will not confirm what our hypotheses predict.

field experiments Experimental studies conducted in real-world settings.

frequency distribution A presentation of a distribution's cases summarized by their respective categories.

frequency polygon A graphical representation of data with bars representing each of a large number of categories. A line is then drawn connecting the tops of each bar.

gamma A measure of ordinal association that assesses the proportional difference between concordant and discordant pairs.

generational theory Explaining political behavior based on differences in what was occurring when an individual entered political awareness.

goodness of fit measure A statistical procedure that measures how well a measure of central tendency summarizes a distribution.

historical generalization Our hypothesized independent and dependent properties are only related accidentally and are not causally linked.

implicit perfect association A type of perfect association between two variables where adjustments are made if the number of independent and dependent categories is different.

independent property That property that we hypothesize has a causative effect on another.

independent samples test A test of significance for which the cases within each comparison group are drawn independently of each other.

index of diversity A variation or dispersion measure calculated as the total proportion of times that two unique cases that categorically differ on any variable can be drawn from any distribution.

index of qualitative variation A variation or dispersion measure that standardizes the index of diversity by dividing by the maximum qualitative variation possible.

inferential statistics A class of statistics that allow us to make inferences or estimates about populations based on our samples.

interaction effect The determination that a hypothesized relationship might be enhanced or weakened when a third variable changes.

intercept The value of the dependent variable when the independent variable equals 0.

internal validity of design Our hypothesized independent variable is actually the cause of our outcome or dependent variable.

internal validity of measurement We are actually measuring what we think we are measuring.

interquartile range The maximum categorical difference possible between any two cases in a distribution's middle 50%.

interval data Data for which we can discern differences among ranked categories and that allow us to answer the question, "different by how much?"

laboratory experiments In the social sciences, experimental studies that occur under controlled conditions that attempt to simulate real world settings.

lambda A nominal measure of association, based on the mode, that assesses how much better off we are with information about the independent variable.

law of large numbers As we increase our sample size, our estimates of population values draw closer to the true population value.

laws/hypotheses The actual and perceived relationships between or among properties/concepts.

life-cycle theory Explaining political behavior based on differences in circumstances that occur as one ages.

linear regression A statistical technique that allows us to gauge the interaction of one variable on another if both variables are measured at the interval level.

Literary Digest **poll of 1936** Poll infamous for making the wrong prediction about the outcome of the 1936 presidential election. The sample was biased toward individuals more likely to be Republicans than the voting population as a whole.

MAD (absolute or mean absolute deviation) The mean of the absolute values of deviation scores.

marginal sensitivity A condition that changes values of a statistic as the proportion of cases in each variable's categories change, even if the overall association remains the same.

marriage gap A recent U.S. electoral division where married couples, especially those with children, are more likely to vote Republican than non-married individuals, especially single females with children.

median The category that represents the midpoint of a distribution at or below which half of all cases lie. Data must be measured at least at the ordinal level.

mode The category within a distribution that has the most cases.

multiple regression A regression model with two or more independent variables.

multivariate statistics A class of statistics that allow us to measure and analyze the relationship among three or more variables.

negative skew *See* **skewness**.

nominal data Data that are assumed to be measured only by differences in categorization. All data are, by their very nature, nominal.

normal distribution A family of symmetrical distributions whose mathematical equation is determined by its mean and standard deviation.

number of cases The total units of analysis from which measurements are taken.

observed frequency The actual number of cases in each category observed in a sample.

one-tailed significance test A test to gauge the significance of the difference between our sample observation and expected population value when a direction is posited.

ordinal data Data for which we can discern differences among categories and for which a set rank ordering of categories makes conceptual sense.

Pearson's *r* Also called the "product moment coefficient," it is a measure of the linear relationship between two interval variables. It is also the square root of *R*-square.

phi A nominal measure of association between two dichotomous variables based on the interval statistic Pearson's *r* as well as chi-square.

pie chart A graphical representation of data where each category is separated into wedges. The area of each wedge represents the number or proportion of cases within each category.

positive skew *See* **skewness**.

PRE (proportional reduction of error) measure Any measure of association that assesses proportionately how much better off we are with information about the independent variable than without.

properties/concepts The generalizations we believe are important to measure from our cases.

random assignment An experimental condition in which cases have an equal chance of being placed in each test and control group.

random (equiprobable) sample A random sample assumes that any case within the target population we are analyzing has an *equal chance* of being drawn into the sample as any other case. Also referred to as an equiprobable sample.

range The maximum categorical difference possible between any two cases in a distribution.

relative frequency The proportion or percentage of observed cases within each category of a frequency distribution.

relevant percentage difference The difference in the percentages of cases between dependent variable categories for one or more independent variable categories.

reliability of measurement Measurements are consistent and meaningful.

R-square A goodness of fit measure that calculates how much of the variance of the dependent variable is explained by the independent variable variance.

sampling distribution of means The distribution of means drawn from an infinite or very large set of random samples from a population that results in a normal distribution around the true population mean.

scatterplot A graphical representation of the relationship between two (or more) variables.

Simpson's Paradox A unique type of specification effect where a "lurking" variable, when controlled for, *reverses* the direction of the original independent to dependent variable relationship.

skewness The degree to which a distribution (think frequency polygon) is pulled or stretched. A stretch to the right or highest values of the distribution indicates a **positive skew**, and to the left, a **negative skew**.

slope The expected increase in the dependent variable for every unit increase in the independent variable.

Somers' *D* A measure of ordinal association, based on gamma, with ties on one variable counting as half hypothesis confirming, half disconfirming.

specification effect The determination that a hypothesized relationship might change when applied to different subgroups within our cases.

spillover effect *See* **cross-contamination**.

spurious relationship Our hypothesized independent and dependent properties are actually both dependent on a third property.

standard deviation The square root of the variance.

standard error of the mean The standard deviation of sample means in sampling distribution of means based on dividing the standard deviation of the individual cases by the square root of the sample size.

standard error of the mean differences The standard deviation of the differences between two samples randomly drawn from a population.

standardization The application of a common numerical and/or conceptual base to different data so that different measurements can be compared.

standardized slope A regression slope adjusted by the standard deviations of the independent and dependent variables.

statistical independence A type of no association between two variables where percentages on the dependent variable are invariant across independent variable categories.

strict perfect association A type of perfect association between two variables where each category of one variable is uniquely matched with a category of another.

symmetrical distribution A distribution of a variable where the side to the left of the median is a mirror image of the side to the right.

symmetrical measure A measure of association that doesn't take into account the direction of an association. Independent and dependent variables are treated equally.

test implication An observable test of a hypothesis that is implied by that hypothesis.

theories/theory sketches A broad explanation of why we expect to observe what our hypotheses predict.

time series chart A graphical representation where data for one or more categories of a variable or variables are plotted for each year and where the yearly data points are connected. The area of each wedge represents the number or proportion of cases within each category.

triangulization Measuring our concepts and testing our hypotheses in as many different ways as possible.

t-test Also known as the Student's t is a series of symmetrical distributions based on sample size $(N - 1)$ that approaches the normal (Z) curve as the sample size increases.

t-test for slopes A test of significance that determines whether the slope of our equation is significantly different from a slope of 0.

unimodal symmetrical distribution A distribution in which both sides of the distribution are mirror images of each other and where the mode is the median category.

units of analysis, case, or fact Entities from which measurements are taken.

univariate statistics A class of statistics that allow us to measure and analyze only one variable at a time.

value (normative) judgment A moral or religious sense that a certain occurrence or action is "good" or "bad" that is based on religious or philosophical principles not subject to testing.

variable The actual, real-world measurement of properties/concepts.

variance The mean of the squared values of deviation scores.

variation ratio A goodness of fit measure that indicates the proportion of cases that vary from or are not within the modal category.

verifiability The ability of a factual statement or test implication to be proved true or false on limited investigation.

weak perfect association A type of perfect association between two variables where variation on the dependent variable occurs only within one category of the dependent variable.

weighted mean The arithmetic mean adjusted for the number or proportion of cases within each unit of analysis, used when a full listing of individual values is not obtainable.

Yule's Q A measure of nominal association for two dichotomous variables based on the cross products. It is derived from the ordinal measure gamma.

Z-score A measure of deviation from the mean standardized by the standard deviation of a distribution when the mean is 0 and the standard deviation is 1.

Sample Solutions Guide

Chapter 1

1. **Answer—c:** This is a generalizable characteristic that applies to and varies among a multitude of cases (people)

    "a" Represents a group of units of analysis (facts) that share the same characteristic on the property "religious denomination"

    "b" As phrased, this is the DEPENDENT variable. Of course, the causal direction would be reversed if we assumed that one's views on abortion rights determine which religion one joins. However, then it would be phrased as, "Individuals who support abortion rights are more/less likely to join . . ."

    "d" Is just one of several categories of "religious denomination." Remember, *variables must vary*.

3. **Answer—a:** This is generalizable and varies among people.

    "b" Represents one particular fact or unit of analysis

    "c" Represents a group of facts/units who share the same category of the variable "education level"

    "d" Is one *category* of "education level"

5. **Answer—d:** Although we still have to determine how to measure (variable) "difference," this is clear enough and has a clear direction.

    a. The economy is related to crime.

    Problem: "economy" and "crime" are not very specific or clear. Also "is related" has no direction.

    b. Educated individuals are tolerant.
        Problem: Even assuming we are fairly clear on what we mean by "educated" and "tolerant," we have no specific comparison.
    c. Younger Americans were more likely to vote for Obama than older people.
        Problem: This is a factual statement—it's either true or false with limited investigation. Take out the fact "Obama" and generalize. Also, what is the cutoff for "younger" and "older"?

7.   **Answer—a:** The others are all examples of alternate explanations.

9.   **Answer—False:** The confirmation of hypotheses (never entirely achieved) requires both direct (tests) and indirect (theory sketch) confirmation.

Chapter 2

1.   **Answer—b:** If a variable is measured unreliably, then we have no consistent measurement at all. One can't even consider whether that variable measures what it is supposed to measure.

3.   A "Chicago effect."

5.   Country of origin (a) is clearly nominal. We can't order these categories in any meaningful way and the numbers we would assign to each category would be purely arbitrary. Scales (c) are generally considered ordinal. Someone who is "Supportive" (3) is more supportive than one who is "Not supportive." The total percentage of Nigerian immigrants **(b)** and monetary contributions **(d)**, categorized as percentages and dollars, are easily seen as mathematically interval. Twelve percent is 7 percentage points higher than 5%; $560,000 is $200,000 more than $360,000. Note that, on occasion, scales are given interval properties by analysts for ease of comparison. Students are usually asked to evaluate their faculty using scales ranging from four to ten categories. At my university, students are given five options for each evaluative item (Strongly disagree . . . Strongly agree). Numbers, from 1 to 5, are assigned to each category. Whether that numerical assignment is conceptually justified is the subject of some debate. The same can be said for letter grades. Is an "A," normally given the numerical equivalent point score of 4, twice as good as a "C," normally given a "2"? Is an "F" (0) always the total absence of any demonstration of knowledge? A professor may give an "F" to someone who scored anywhere between 0 and 59 out of a total possible 100 points. When we use standard grade designations, we may lose a great deal of information about the differences between students with the same grade.

7.   All but "The party whose candidate won the district" are interval. Years, percentages, and proportions are all interval. If only Democrats and Republicans won, then we would have a dichotomous nominal variable that can be analyzed with ordinal statistics (a Republican district is more Republican than a Democrat one) and even interval statistics (see reasoning in Chapter 12).

9.   The total sample size (N) is 1,776. To compute the relative frequency, divide the absolute frequency of each category by 1,776 and multiply by 100. To

compute the cumulative frequencies, add the absolute frequency of each category and the frequencies of the categories that precede it, and then divide by 1,776 and multiply by 100. Notice that this may produce a figure somewhat different from adding the relative frequencies. This is because of the rounding error introduced in calculating each relative frequency. For example, 19.4% + 15.4% equals 34.8% (if we round off to one decimal place). (345 + 274)/1,776 × 100, however, rounds off to 34.9%. I suggest always going through the full calculation so that rounding error is not compounded.

Party ID (degree Republican)	Cat. Code	Absolute Frequency	Relative Frequency	Cumulative Frequency
Strong Democrat	0	345	19.4%	19.4%
Weak Democrat	1	274	15.4%	34.9%
Independent Leaning Democrat	2	275	15.5%	50.3%
Independent	3	221	12.4%	62.8%
Independent Leaning Republican	4	231	13.0%	75.8%
Weak Republican	5	209	11.8%	87.6%
Strong Republican	6	221	12.4%	100.0%
$N =$		1,776	1,776	1,776

Translation: 19.4% of the sample claimed to be (0) strong Democrats; 11.8% claimed to be weak Republicans (5). The largest single category, although not by much, is "Independent Leaning Democrats" with 275, or 15.5%, of the respondents claiming this position; 50.3%, slightly more than half, are Independent Leaning Democrats or even less Republican (more Democratic) in their partisan orientation.

Party ID (degree Republican)	Cat. Code*	Absolute Frequency	Relative Frequency	Cumulative Frequency
Democrat	1	619	34.9%	34.9%
Independent	2	727	.9%	75.8%
Republican	3	430	24.2%	100.0%
$N =$		1,776	1,776	1,776

*Category codes are arbitrary so long as they are in the proper order; "0, 1, 2" would also work.

Party ID (degree Republican)	Cat. Code*	Absolute Frequency	Relative Frequency	Cumulative Frequency
Democrat	1	894	50.3%	50.3%
Independent	2	221	12.4%	62.8%
Republican	3	661	37.2%	100.0%
$N =$		1,776	1,776	1,776

Combining categories differently in this survey presents us with a different assessment of the partisan preferences of the voting age population in 2000. The first combination (Table 2.2) indicates that a plurality of respondents (and, if the survey is an accurate assessment of the total eligible electorate, a plurality of voting age Americans), 727 or .9%, are Independents, and therefore up for grabs in any election. The second combination (Table 2.3) indicates a more partisanly polarized electorate, with minimal independence from party (12.4%), and with Democrats holding a slim majority (50.3%) of all respondents.

The difference is not insignificant. A major debate among election analysts over the past 50 years has centered on the question of whether partisanship within the electorate is dead. Over that time, the proportion of those claiming Independent status has increased. How large that increase has been depends on how we categorize the "Independent leaners," the group that has seen the largest growth since the 1960s. If we treat them as Independents, then there has been a substantial increase. The proportion of Independents (leaning or otherwise) in the 1960 ANES survey was only 23%. If we treat them, however, as partisans, the increase has not been so dramatic; 10% claimed pure independence in 1960. Many studies indicate that these "rhetorical Independents" are really closet partisans who claim independence as a politically correct answer (I vote the person, not the party) but who otherwise behave as partisans (that person almost always seems to be of the same party).

One question remains. If leaners are partisans, and Democrats outnumber Republicans, why have Republican presidential, Senate, and most recently, House candidates fared so well during these decades? Republicans are more likely to vote and are usually more loyal to their candidates than are Democrats. These tables and graphs represent a sample of all citizens eligible to vote. If we presented data only for voters, the graphs would look different.

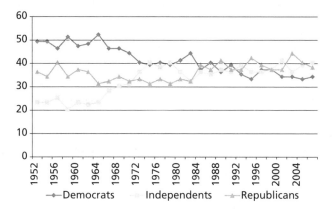

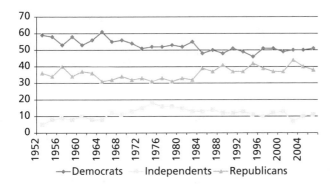

Grade	Absolute Frequency	Relative Frequency	Cumulative Frequency
A	8	14.5%	14.5%
B	24	43.6%	58.2%**
C	12	21.8%	80.0%
D	4	7.3%	87.3%
F	7	12.7%	100.0%
	$N = 55$	100.0%*	

* Rounding error-sum of individual percentages listed = 99.9%.
** Because of potential rounding error in each cell, it is best to divide the cumulative absolute (32) frequency by N (55).

Translation: 24/55 × 100, or **43.6%** of all 55 students, received a "B"; 80.0% of all students received a "C" or higher (better); and 87.3% of all students received passing grades.

Chapter 3

1. **Answer—b and c:** The median, an ordinal measure of association, can be used to summarize *any* data that carry ordinal traits. Interval data are also, by definition, ordinal ($50,000 is greater than $,000).
3. If symmetrical, the median and mean will be equal (there is no skew). The opposite is usually but not always true.
5. The state claims that it pays back .60 on every dollar gambled. As most who have purchased a lottery ticket know, many will walk away with nothing (.00), some will win a small amount, but a few will hit the jackpot, earning back many, many times what they spent. This distribution is **positively skewed**, in fact extremely so. As with any lottery

or gambling system, many must lose in order for very few to win big. Remember that 60% is not the chance of winning. That chance is extremely small. However, most will take the risk of gambling a small amount to chance winning a very large payoff. We'll cover more on gambling odds later in the text.

7. That distribution is most likely negatively skewed, with a few countries having inordinately low turnouts. Of course, if these are countries with limited populations, the actual turnout for the election from all EU countries would be higher.

9. Translations:

Mode: no single category is more prevalent than any other category.

Median: in both distributions, half received $60,000 or less in PAC contributions, and half $60,000 or more.

Mean: If we could redistribute the PAC contributions so that everyone received the same amount, everyone would receive $60,000 in the first distribution, but $2,000 in the second. The first distribution (mean = median) is symmetrical. The second distribution (mean > median) is positively skewed, with one extreme outlier's contributions having a much greater effect on the mean value. Perhaps that individual is a chair of an important appropriations committee, and several interest groups want to maintain their access to her.

11. In order to answer all of the questions, it is perhaps easier to first rank order each list of values separately. The listing of 1964 Democratic vote percentages would be:

35 45 48 56 57 62 65 67 71 72

The mode is that category of Democratic vote percentages that appears with the greatest frequency. **No mode** appears for the 1964 distribution since every category appears with the same frequency (once). To compute the **median**, divide the group of ten into lower and upper halves. Half (5) of the districts gave Democratic House candidates 57% of the vote or less, and half gave 62% or more. By convention, we choose the exact midpoint of these two values, **59.5%**. The voters of half (5) of all districts gave Democratic House candidates fewer than 59.5% of their votes in 1964, and half gave more. To compute the mean, add the sum total of all percentages for all ten districts (578%), and divide by the total number of districts (10). The **mean** Democratic House vote is **57.8%**. The distribution is (slightly) negatively skewed. If you could redistribute all of the *proportional* votes evenly, each district would have given the Democratic House candidate 57.8% of their votes. Note that this is not the same as saying that all ten districts gave 57.8% of their vote to the Democratic candidates unless the number of people voting in each district is the same.

The following table compares the statistics for the 1964 and 1966 percentages:

	1964	1966
MODE	None	62%
MEDIAN	59.5%	62%
MEAN	57.8%	58.1

Comparing these two sets of answers, we note that the ten districts gave Democratic House candidates higher proportional vote shares in 1966 than 1964, especially if we use the median as our measure of central tendency. The 1966 distribution is also more negatively skewed. This could be perhaps a function of equalizing populations. It may also have been caused by a Democratic partisan gerrymander. Most of the safest Democratic districts were made less so in order for the more marginal Democratic districts (especially D7) to become safer.

13. The median is equal to 53.55%, and the mean is equal to 55.64%. Half of the countries had turnouts equal to or greater than 53.55%, and half equal to or less. If every country had equal populations, and we redistributed the vote, each country would have a turnout percentage of 55.64. The distribution seems to have a positive skew, with the Seychelles' turnout anchoring the high end of the spectrum. Of course, given that nation's small population, and Egypt's large population, the real turnout for all 21 countries should be far less than 55.64%.

15. %Vote for Obama:

Median	51.10%
Mean	52.24%

a.

Median: half of the counties gave Obama more than 51.10% of the vote, and half less.

Mean: assuming the number of voters in each county were the same, if we redistributed the vote for Obama so each county's percentage were the same, that would be = 52.24%.

b.

With a slightly higher mean, we expect a slight positive skew in the distribution. Outlying counties were most likely more extreme on the high side of the vote percentage.

c–d.

	DEM	REP
Median	57.60%	42.60%
Mean	58.46%	44.24%

As expected, both the medians and means were higher for the Democratic counties and lower for the Republican counties than for all 16 counties combined. The combination tends to hide the differences between Democratic and Republican counties.

Note that the figures for Democratic counties more closely align with the figures for all 16 counties. This is partially due, however, to having more Democratic counties.

e. As with the 2012 U.S. and African nation data, not all counties have the same population. Los Angeles County's percentage counts no more than the percentages of much less populated counties. Counties also differ as to their percentage turnout, with counties with high minority populations generally having a lower turnout rate than others. In order to get the true total percentage vote for all counties, our figures would have to be weighted by the actual total number of individuals who voted in each election in those counties.

Chapter 4

1. The variation ratio (*VR*) tells us what proportion of cases is *not* in the modal category.

   A *VR* of .00 indicates that no cases are non-modal (i.e., every case is found in the modal category). There is no variation.

   A *VR* of 1.00 is impossible to achieve. If no cases are in the modal category, and the modal category is most prevalent, then no distribution exists. Values close to, but not equal to 1.00 are possible.

   A *VR* of .43 indicates that 43% of all cases are non-modal (i.e., vary from the mode). If you guessed the mode for any case, you would have a .43 probability of being wrong. Fifty-seven percent of all cases are found in the modal category.

3. The mean absolute deviation (MAD) measures deviation from the mean without regard to direction. It is the mean of those absolute deviations. On mean average, the number of terms served by each legislator varies from the mean (of all listed legislators) by 2 terms. Some legislators might be off by more than 2, some might be off by fewer than 2. They would all be off by exactly 2 only if 70 had 2 more terms than the mean (e.g., 7), 70 had 2 fewer (e.g., 3). The mean would be 5. That is a limited subset of all possibilities.

5. A standard deviation, like the MAD, can only equal 0 if everyone has the mean score (i.e., everyone has the same score). No one would deviate from the mean, or each other. Note that this is not the same as stating that everyone had a score of 0. That is one possibility among a myriad of possibilities. A standard deviation of 0 only tells us that everyone has the *same* score, not what that score is.

7. Distribution 1: $20,000, $40,000, $60,000, $80,000, $100,000
   Distribution 2: $20,000, $40,000, $60,000, $80,000, $1,000,000

   The range is the maximum difference between the values of any two cases in a distribution. The range for distribution 1 is $100,000 – $20,000 = **$80,000**. The values for that distribution differ by no more than $80,000. In the second distribution, the range is much greater, heavily influenced by the distribution's positive skew. Those values differ by as much as **$980,000**.

   Before we can compute the MAD and standard deviations, we must first compute the means for each distribution, which are $60,000 and $2,000, respectively. We then can compute a deviation score $(x_i - \overline{X})$ for each individual in each distribution. The MAD is the mean of the absolute deviations. The standard deviation is the square root of the mean of the squared deviations.

Case	Value	Deviation Score	Absolute Deviation	Squared Deviation	Case	Value	Deviation Score	Absolute Deviation	Squared Deviation
1	$20,000	−$40,000	$40,000	$$1,600 E6	1	$20,000	−$220,000	$220,000	$$48,400 E6
2	40,000	−20,000	20,000	400 E6	2	40,000	−200,000	200,000	40,000 E6
3	60,000	0	0	0	3	60,000	−180,000	180,000	32,400 E6
4	80,000	+20,000	20,000	400 E6	4	80,000	−160,000	160,000	25,600 E6
5	100,000	+40,000	40,000	1,600 E6	5	1,000,000	+760,000	+760,000	577,600 E6
		Σ =	$120,000	$$4,000 E6			Σ =	$1,520,000	$$724,000 E6
		Mean =	$24,000	$$800 E6			Mean =	$304,000	$$144,800 E6
			SD =	$28,284.27				SD =	$380,525.95

Both the MAD ($24,000/$1,520,000) and the standard deviations ($304,000/$380,525.95) are much greater in the second distribution than the first because of the extreme nature of the last case in the second distribution. The standard deviations are greater than the MAD for each distribution because extreme values carry even greater weight in the computation of the standard deviation. In the first distribution, the MAD is roughly 85% of the standard deviation. In the second, it is only roughly 80% because of the greater influence of that highly extreme value.

9. The following table represents the original and deviation scores for each set. Note that the deviation scores change when we analyze within each party because the mean is different for each. Republican figures are italicized.

Original PS Score	Deviation Score		
	(All) $(x - 54.4\%)$	(D) $(x - 72.9\%)$	(R) $(x - 38.0\%)$
78%	23.6%	5.1%	
85	30.6	12.1	
65	10.6	−7.9	
81	26.6	8.1	
39	−15.4		1%
34	−20.4		−4
72	17.6	−0.9	
42	−12.4		4
41	−13.4		3
66	11.6	−6.9	
43	−11.4		5
37	−17.4		−1
34	−20.4		−4
33	−21.4		−5
75	20.6	2.1	
39	−15.4	1	1
61	6.6	−11.9	

Mean $(\bar{X})$	Median	Range	MAD
All = 925%/17 = 54.4%	43%	85 − 33 = 52%	295.4%/17 = 17.38%
Dem = 583%/8 = 72.9%	73.5%	85 − 61 = 24%	55%/8 = 6.88%
Rep = 342%/9 = 38.0%	39%	43 − 33 = 10%	28%/9 = 3.11%

To compute the median and range, list each PSS in order from lowest to highest:

All 17:   33% 34 34 37 39 39 41 42 43 61 65 66 72 75 78 81 85%

With 17 cases, the median would be the value of the 9th ordered case (43%). Half of these 17 members of Congress supported the president 43% of the time or less, and half 43% of the time or more. The range, the difference between the highest and lowest support score is 52%. The maximum difference in support between any two of these 17 would be 52%.

Democrats: 61% 65 66 72 75 78 81 85%

With 8 cases, the median would lie between the 4th (72%) and 5th (78%) ordered case. Half of the Democrats supported the president less than 73.5% of the time, and half more. The range (maximum difference between any two Democrats) is 24%.

Republicans: 33% 34 34 37 39 39 41 42 43%

With 9 cases, the median would be the value of the 5th ordered case (39%), which also happens to be the value of the 6th. Half of the Republicans supported the president 39% of the time or less, and half 39% or more. The range for Republicans is 10%.

To calculate the mean, add all the values in each respective list, and divide by the number of cases in that list. Interpret the mean as that level of support that each member would have if each gave the same support. The MAD is the mean average of the absolute deviation scores within each listing (how much, not in which direction).

A few observations:

- For all 17, the mean is greater than the median, indicating a positive skew. Within each party, the distributions are fairly symmetrical.
- All Republicans seem to be more unified in their opposition than the Democrats are in their support. Both the range and MAD confirm this. Party does seem to matter, especially for Republicans. No two Republicans differed by more than 10%. Democrats differed by as much as 24%. If you guessed the mean for all Republicans, you would be off by a (mean) average of 3.11%. A similar guess for Democrats would produce a (mean) average error of 6.88%.
- Another indication that party matters is that the range and MAD for all 17 members far exceeds the range and MAD for either party. Note also that no Republican is more supportive than any Democrat.

11. Further supporting the assumption of a Democratic gerrymander (see Chapter 3, Question 11), the range (27% vs. 37%), MAD (7.28% vs. 9.60%), and standard deviations (8.57% vs. 11.46%) show less variation in 1966 than in 1964. Democratic voters were more evenly distributed once the Illinois legislature was forced to redistrict in order to satisfy the equal population demands of the Supreme Court.

13. The variation/dispersion is, as expected, greater for all 16 counties than for either the Democratic or Republican ones.

    We do note that both measures of variation (range and MAD) is higher for Democratic counties than Republican ones, indicating greater consistency in voting patterns for counties with more Republican than Democratic registrants. Here are the results of the Presidential Vote percentages.

	All	Dem	Rep
RANGE	29.3%	17.4%	9.3%
MAD	7.94%	5.86%	2.78%

14. Using the data in Question 13, compute the range and MAD for *both* the county vote for Obama and the county vote for Feinstein for ALL 16 counties. Describe and interpret **fully** what each figure tells you *in words*.

Chapter 5

1. If a distribution is symmetrical, the mean will be equal to the median. The mean is therefore at the **50th** percentile. A Z-score is a standardized deviation score. The mean value does not deviate from the mean, standardized or not. The relevant Z-score is therefore **0**.

3. Remember that the normal curve slopes out with a smaller proportion of cases from Z-point to Z-point. An income with a corresponding Z of, for example, 2.5 does not have an associated percentile twice as high as an income with a corresponding Z of 1. Check the values in the table for this.

5. Look at the table of areas under the normal curve: 34.13% of that area or proportion of cases in a normal distribution lie between a Z-score of -1 and the mean ($Z = 0$), and. 45.82% lie between the mean and a Z-score of 1.73 (50 − 4.28). Adding these two figures gives us a total proportion of **79.95%**.

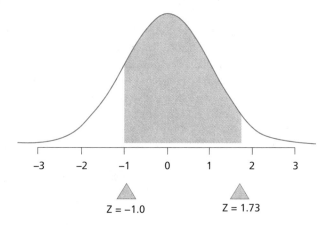

7. Let's look at this logically. The calculations follow the standard Z-score formula.

$$Z = (x_i - \overline{X})/s_x$$

We have the mean ($42,000) and the standard deviation ($17,000) for every family. We need to calculate the family income (x_i) that would correspond to the 15th percentile (bottom 15%).

Step 1: find the Z-score that corresponds to the 15th percentile (.3500 on the chart); 1.04 is close. As this is on the bottom end of the distribution, the appropriate Z-score is −1.04.

Step 2: Solve for x_i.

$1.04 = (x_i − \$42{,}000)/\$17{,}000$

$−1.04\ (\$17{,}000) = x_i − \$42{,}000$

$−1.04\ (\$17{,}000) + \$42{,}000 = x_i$

$−\$17{,}680 + \$42{,}000 = x_i$

$x_i = \mathbf{\$24{,}320}$

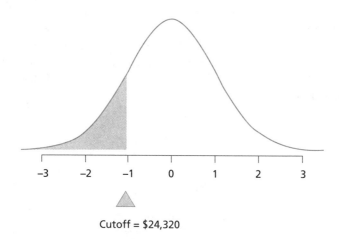

Cutoff = $24,320

The 15th percentile corresponds to a family income of $24,320. That ($17,680 less than the mean) is the maximum that you could earn before becoming ineligible for the voucher program.

9. Yes, but only 5% of the time or a probability of .05.

Chapter 6

1. **Answer—c:** With a large enough sample size, the sampling distribution of means will be normal or approximately normal regardless of the shape of the original distribution (central limit theorem).

3. Remember that since the sampling distribution of means is normally distributed around the true population mean (μ_x), the mean of those sample means must also be 47.

5. **Answer—False.** It also applies to dichotomous proportions. See the next chapter for a fuller explanation.

7. You could proceed as you did in Exercise 6 to produce a range of estimates of the true means of the population from which the sample of 600 was drawn. Is 30,000 euros within that range? If so, then we can't confidently reject 30,000 euros as the true mean of the entire town's households, and the town would not be disqualified. Because we are given an exact population value against which to compare, however, we can take a more straightforward approach. The question becomes rephrased as: could we have randomly drawn a sample of 600 households from a population and, just by the random luck of the draw, derive a sample with a mean that deviated 500 euros (30,500 − 30,000) from the true population mean (i.e., the mean we would expect if the sample exactly matched the population)? Is 500 euros within the margin of error that we have to allow just by the random luck of the draw? Stated differently—if we randomly drew samples of 600 from a population with a true mean of 30,000 euros, would 30,500 be within the 95% confidence interval of that sampling distribution?

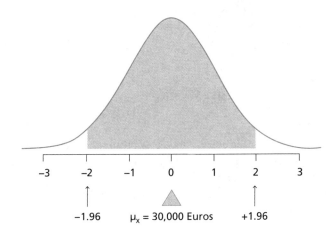

Using the Z-score formula for means, and substituting the standard deviation of the sample for the standard deviation of the population from which that sample was randomly drawn, compute the Z-score for our problem:

$$Z_{\overline{X}} = \frac{\overline{X} - \mu_x}{\frac{s_x}{\sqrt{N}}} = \frac{30,500€ - 30,000€}{\frac{7,000€}{\sqrt{600}}} = \frac{500€}{285.77€} = 1.75$$

We need to allow a margin of error of 560.1 euros (equivalent to a Z of ± 1.96). Because 1.75 is less than 1.96, we cannot confidently reject the possibility that this sample (with a mean 500 euros higher than the cutoff) could have been randomly drawn from a population with a true mean household income of 30,000 euros. Five hundred euros is within our calculated margin of error; 30,500 is not significantly different enough from 30,000 to reject 30,000 euros as a possibility.

However, what if we used a one-tailed test? The Z-score cutoff would then be 1.645, and we would be able to confidently 30,000 euros as a possibility. Ninety-five percent of a large number of random samples will produce a mean value associated with a Z-score of 1.645 *or less*. Because we are specifying an upper limit, we have what is called a directional test of significance. The town would thus qualify.

9. First, we need to calculate the standard error of the mean, substituting the sample standard deviation for the population standard deviation:

$$\sigma_{\overline{X}} = \frac{\sigma_x}{\sqrt{N}} \approx \frac{s_x}{\sqrt{N}} = \frac{21.902}{\sqrt{5385}} = 298.46$$

Plugging this into our formulas:

+1.96 = (50.48° − μ_L)/298.46°   − 1.96 = (50.48° − μ_H)/298.46°
+.298° = 50.48° − μ_L   − .298° = 50.48° − μ_H
−μ_L = .298° − 50.48°   − μ_H = −.298° − 50.48°
−μ_L = −50.182°   − μ_H = −50.778°
  μ_L = 50.182°   μ_H = 50.778°

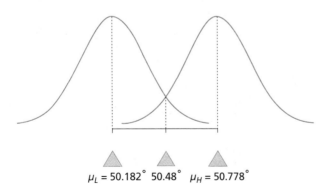

$\mu_L = 50.182°$ 50.48° $\mu_H = 50.778°$

Note: One problem with feeling thermometers is that, if one is not fully knowledgeable about the person or group in question, they may give a response of 50° or neutral. There is no way to adequately separate out those who wouldn't they didn't know and those who were genuinely neutral about Mormons. The percentage who gave this rating was a very large .2%. For other groups and, especially, presidential candidates, the "neutrals" tend to constitute a smaller percentage.

11. No, we can only give a range of estimates as shown previously.

Chapter 7

1. $\mu_1 - \mu_2$. Just as with individual means, the mean of the sample differences will always be equal to the difference of the means of the individual values.

3. **Answer—False.** Just as with flipping 100 coins and getting 100 heads, 0 is still a possibility, but it is highly improbable. "Confidently" does not mean "absolutely."

5. This breaks down to a difference of means calculations, with the null hypothesis (the expectation against which we compare our sample differences) = 0, so the second half of the formula is 0. If the calculated Z-score of the differences is greater than 1.96 (or 1.645 if we are calculating with a one-tailed test), then we can confidently reject the possibility that the true differences between men and women in the population from which this ample was drawn is 0. Some difference > 0 probably exists. If the calculated Z-score is less than either of those scores, then we can't reject that possibility. Again, remember that *not rejecting* is not the same as *accepting*. A difference of 0 is just one of many possibilities that we cannot reject.

First calculate the combined standard error of the mean differences. We substitute the standard deviations of the sample as an estimate for the true population standard deviations (which, obviously, we don't know).

George W. Bush thermometer ratings:

$$\sigma_{(\overline{X}_1 - \overline{X}_2)} \approx \sqrt{\frac{s_1^2}{N_1} + \frac{s_2^2}{N_2}}$$

$$\sigma_{(\overline{X}_1 - \overline{X}_2)} \approx \sqrt{\frac{24.55^2}{781} + \frac{25.12^2}{980}} =$$

$$\sqrt{\frac{602.70}{781} + \frac{631.01}{980}} = \sqrt{1.42} = 1.19$$

Next, calculate the Z-score for the mean differences:

$$Z_{\overline{X}_M - \overline{X}_F} = \frac{(56.65 - 55.74) - (0)}{1.19} = \frac{.91}{1.19} = 0.76$$

The value of .76 is well below either the one-tailed or two-tailed cutoffs. Therefore, based on mean differences in the sample, we can't confidently reject the null hypothesis H_0 of no difference in the population from which these two samples were drawn. Based on this measure, we really can't confidently claim that a gender gap existed in 2000 as far as it relates to feelings about George Bush. However, what about feelings toward Al Gore?

7. Both descriptively and inferentially, we have more evidence of a gender gap with the feeling thermometers for Al Gore than for George W. Bush.

9. As we went through similar calculations in Exercise 5, we will just present the answer here.

$N = 200$ $Z = 1.61$

As we are not specifying direction (which country is greater), we would need the Z-score to be less than -1.96 or more than $+1.96$ if we are using a 95% confidence interval. In actuality, with a sample of only 200, we would be using a lower/higher t-score cutoff (the combined degrees of freedom is about 396, a calculation we didn't go through in this chapter but one that programs such as SPSS and Stata will provide).

The differences that we observe in these two countries (€25) is not large enough to confidently reject the null hypothesis that the true population means are the same (€0).

Chapter 8

1. If the sample were truly random, we could not confidently reject the possibility that this sample came from a population with a true level of support within 4.4% of the sample value. Thus, we would not be able to reject any true population proportion between 67.6% and 76.4%.

   Although we can confidently reject the possibility that this sample came from a population with a true level of support of 66%, we cannot do so with certainty, just as we couldn't absolutely reject the possibility that a coin can be flipped 100 times and produce 90 or more heads. It is, however, unlikely.

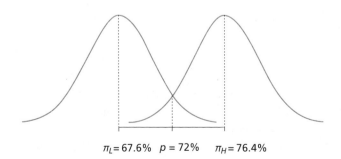

$\pi_L = 67.6\%$ $p = 72\%$ $\pi_H = 76.4\%$

3. We first need to compute the standard error of the proportions. Using our sample statistics as substitutes for the true population values, that is calculated as follows:

$$\sigma_p = \sqrt{\frac{p \times (1-p)}{N}} = \sqrt{\frac{.72 \times (.28)}{500}} = .021$$

Next, place that value in the general equation:

$$Z_p = \frac{p - \pi}{\sigma_p} = \frac{.72 - \pi}{.021}$$

and solve for both the lowest and highest populations proportions. That is, populations whose distribution of sample populations would include 72% within its 95% confidence interval:

$+1.96 = (.72 - \pi_L)/.021$ $-1.96 = (.72 - \pi_H)/.021$

$+.0412 = .72 - \pi_L$ $-.0412 = .72 - \pi_H$

$-\pi_L = .0412 - .72$ $-\pi_H = -.0412 - .72$

$-\pi_L = -.6788$ $-\pi_H = -.7612$

$\pi_L = .6788$ $\pi_H = .7612$

$$.6788 < \pi < .7612$$

5. $df = K - 1$. Thus we have **7** degrees of freedom. The critical cutoff (for a 95% confidence interval) equals **14.0671**. If we took a population with eight categories, took a large number of independent samples from that population, compared the observed sample frequencies with the expected population frequencies, and, using that comparison, computed the chi-square value for that eight-category table, then 95% of the time, the chi-square value would lie between 0 (the sample is proportionately identical to the population) and 14.0671. We could produce a sample with a chi-square greater than that, but it is highly unlikely ($< .05$).

7. The expected frequency for each ideological category would be $240/3 = 80$.

Category	f_o	f_e	$f_o - f_e$	$(f_o - f_e)^2$	$(f_o - f_e)^2/f_e$
Left	90	80	10	100	.125
Center	80	80	0	0	0
Right	70	80	−10	100	.125
					$\Sigma = .250 = \chi^2$

Most anything is possible. However, with such a low chi-square value (.250), we cannot confidently reject the possibility that this sample came from a population where individuals are evenly distributed among the three categories. With three categories and 2 degrees of freedom, we could not confidently reject that possibility with any sample distribution that produced a chi-square value below 5.9914. Of course, as with means, not being able to confidently reject an even population distribution does not mean that an equal distribution does exist—just that it is one possibility that cannot be confidently rejected.

9. The expected frequencies would be 144 (60%), 48 (20%), and 48.

Category	f_o	f_e	$f_o - f_e$	$(f_o - f_e)^2$	$(f_o - f_e)^2/f_e$
Left	90	144	−54	2,916	2.056
Center	80	48	32	1,024	21.333
Right	70	48	22	484	10.083

$$\sum = 33.472 = \chi^2$$

The calculated chi-square value is much greater than our 95% cutoff of 5.9914. We can therefore confidently reject the possibility that this sample could have been randomly drawn from a population with a 60%/20%/20% distribution. Impossible? No, but highly unlikely.

Chapter 9

1. Fill in the following to represent an example of statistical independence: For statistical independence to obtain, the proportional breakdown within each independent variable (region) category must be EXACTLY the same.

	Southern	Non-Southern
Agree with Tea Party Positions	35%	35%
Disagree with Tea Party Positions	65%	65%

3. For accord to obtain, any values that maintain the same modal category (disagree) will work. Statistical independence (Exercise 1) is a subset of accord. Other examples include:

	Southern	Non-Southern
Agree with Tea Party Positions	35%	40%
Disagree with Tea Party Positions	65%	60%

. . . or

	Southern	Non-Southern
Agree with Tea Party Positions	35%	*0%*
Disagree with Tea Party Positions	65%	*100%*

. . . or, as either category can be considered modal for non-Southerners

	Southern	Non-Southern
Agree with Tea Party Positions	35%	*50%*
Disagree with Tea Party Positions	65%	*50%*

5. Knowing whether one is an American or European helps us to reduce our error in guessing one's views about Afghanistan proportionately by 29.7%, but we can't tell from that value which group is more supportive.

7. $df = (2 − 1)(5 − 1) = 4$

9. We are positing a negative relationship (the more Republican, the less supportive).

Relevant percentage differences:

% Republicans who support = 0/178 = .0 or 0%
% Democrats who support = 219/253 = .866 or 86.6%

Republicans were 86.6% less likely to support the measure than were Democrats.

Hypothesis is confirmed.

Lambda
[215 − (34 + 0)]/215 = .721
Knowing party reduces our error in guessing the vote proportionately by 72.1%.

The observation is in the hypothesized direction (lambda would be the same if we switched the values for Democrats and Republicans).

Hypothesis is confirmed.

Yule's Q (gamma)
$[(34 \times 0) - (178 \times 219)]/[(34 \times 0) + (178 \times 219)] = -38{,}948/+38{,}948$
$= -1$
We hypothesized a negative relationship (more Republican, less support).

Hypothesis is confirmed.

Somers' *D* (vote dependent):
$[(34 \times 0) - (178 \times 219)]/[(34 \times 0) + (178 \times 219) + (219 \times 0)$
$+ (34 \times 178)] = -38{,}948/+45{,}000 = -.866$

Hypothesis is confirmed.

Lambda tends to be lower as it can reach 0 under the condition of accord and is sensitive to marginal variations (more Democrats than Republicans).

Yule's *Q* will reach it maximum absolute value even under the condition of weak perfect association.

Somers' *D* counts ties against us by adding them to the denominator.

11. a. 324 of the 507 males considered immigration to be beneficial (61.5%)
334 of the 526 females did (63.4%)

Women were 1.9 percentage points more likely to consider immigration to be beneficial than were men.

124 of the 527 males considered immigration not to be beneficial (23.5%)

116 of the 526 females did (22.1%)

Men were 1.4 percentage points more likely to consider immigration to be not beneficial than were women. Note that these two numbers would be reciprocals if only two categories of choice existed. The "Don't Know" category causes the difference. It is possible, with a large enough number of "Don't Knows" among females that males could be more likely to answer both "beneficial" and "not."

Category (Age/Support)	f_o (Observed)	f_e (Expected)	$f_o - f_e$	$(f_o - f_e)^2$	$(f_o - f_e)^2/f_e$
Male/Beneficial	324	322.9	1.1	1.21	0.00(4)
Male/Don't Know	59	66.3	−7.3	53.29	0.80
Male/Not Beneficial	124	117.8	6.2	38.44	0.33
Female/Beneficial	334	335.1	−1.1	1.21	0.00(4)
Female/Don't Know	76	68.7	7.3	53.29	0.78
Female/Not Beneficial	116	122.2	−6.2	38.44	0.31
				$\Sigma = 2.22 = \chi^2$	

b. Lambda = (135 + 2) − [(59 + 124) + (76 + 116)]/(135 + 2) = (375 − 375)/375 = 0

Knowing one's gender does not reduce our error in guessing one's views of immigration at all.

c. Chi-square (f_e rounded to one decimal place)—full calculation = 2.21

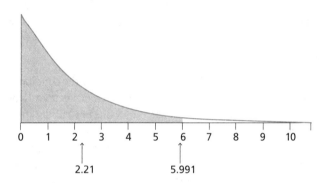

With 2 degrees of freedom (2 − 1)(3 − 1), 95% of the time we would randomly sample a group on two variables and come up with observations that would produce a chi-square between 0 and 5.991. Our calculated value of 2.22 tells us that the differences between what we observed in the sample and what we would have expected if this sample came from a population where statistical independence obtained would not be different enough to reject the null hypothesis that no differences existed in that population. We therefore cannot confidently reject that null hypothesis. Differences might exist in the population, but we can't confidently reject statistical independence as a possibility.

d. You should find that the relevant percentage differences and lambda will not change. The chi-square value will, however, be significant (22.1). Numbers do matter when we deal with inference.

13. In order to answer this question, we must first calculate the number of concordant pairs (different in the same direction), discordant pairs (different in opposite directions), and pairs that are only tied on the outcome, support for improved U.S. relations.

In order to calculate concordant pairs (older, more supportive), multiply the frequencies of each cell by the sum of the frequencies of each cell above and to the right. These will constitute pairs where the second case is both older and more supportive. Add these.

IMPROVED U.S. RELATIONS	Age			Total
	1 Younger	2 Middle	3 Older	
Support	120	110	360	590
	.0%	55.0%	72.0%	59.0%
Do Not Support	180	90	1	410
	60.0%	45.0%	28.0%	41.0%
Total	300	200	500	$N = 1,000$
	30.0%	20.0%	50.0%	100.0%

$C = 180 (110 + 360) + 90 (360) = 117,000$

In order to calculate discordant pairs (older, less supportive), multiply the frequency of each cell by the sum of the frequencies of each cell below and to the right. These will constitute pairs where the second case is both older and less supportive. Add these.

$D = 120 (90 + 1) + 110 (1) = 43,000$
Gamma $= (C - D)/(C + D) = (117,000 - 43,000)/(117,000 + 43,000)$
$= 74,000/160,000 = .4625$

When comparing an older to a younger individual we will be comparing a more supportive to a less supportive individual 46.25% more often than comparing an older individual to one who is more supportive. Or, as we increase age, we observe an increase in support 46.25% more often than a decrease. Or, knowing the order of two individual's age reduces our error in guessing the order of their level of support proportionately by 46.25% (over blind guessing 50/50). Hypothesis is confirmed, if not perfectly.

In order to calculate ties on the dependent variable (support) only multiply the frequencies of each cell by the sum of the frequencies to the right (as we have our table set up, these will constitute pairs that are different in age but similar in support). Add these.

$T_y = 120 (110 + 360) + 110 (360) + 180 (90 + 1) + 90 (1) = 150,000$
Somers' $D_y = (C - D)/(C + D + T_y) = 117,000/310,000 = .239$

The interpretation would be as previously given, but with ties on the dependent variable counting half as concordant, half as discordant.

Chapter 10

1. **Answer—c**
3. Simpson's Paradox
5. **Answer—True:** Changes in some third variable causes changes in our dependent variable. If spurious, it causes changes in both of our originally hypothesized variable.
7. For the entire sample, those who felt that their voice counted in the EU were 20.2 percentage points more likely to indicate an intention to vote in the upcoming EU parliamentary elections than those who felt their voice didn't count. This sense of political efficacy seems to play a partial role in explaining turnout. The next question is to determine whether political efficacy is specific to the EU or to electoral politics generally. One could easily assume that one's sense of the impact of their own voice and opinions generally would alter their intention to vote in any election, including one for the European Parliament. If that is the case, then we would expect controlling for one's sense of efficacy within their country would explain the differences in EU vote intentions. The results are not quite what this scenario would predict:

For all Italian citizens in this survey, those who felt that their vote counted in the EU were 20.2 percentage points more likely to express an intention to vote in the EU parliamentary election than those who did not. Among those who felt that their vote did not count in their own country's politics, the difference drops to 8.1. However, among those who felt that their vote did count, the difference increases to 33 percentage points. These results indicate a type of interactive or additive effect, with a sense of efficacy within country and within the EU having cumulative (if somewhat uneven) effects. To place this in perspective, look at the percentage of individuals who intend to vote in the EU Parliamentary elections within each two-variable category:

VOICE COUNTS

In neither	In country only	In EU only	In both
66.9%	57.4%	75.0%	90.4%

The lambdas and chi-squares are as follows:

	Lambda	Chi-Square
All	.00	23.04, $p < .001$
Voice Counts in Country	.00	21.07, $p < .001$
Voice Does Not	.00	.78, Not Significant

Why do you think that the lowest intention to vote in the EU election comes from those with a country-specific sense of political efficacy rather than a lack of efficacy generally?

Why is the chi-square twice significant, yet lambda = 0?

9. For each variable separately, the percentage differences are minimal (and against our hypotheses' direction). Gamma is also slightly negative (−.025, −.011). There does, however, seem to be an interaction effect. Where the tax burden is high, countries with relatively high government expenditures are 24.5 percentage points less likely to have relatively high unemployment. Where the tax burden is low, the comparable figure is +16 percentage points. We seem to have a classic case of countervailing influences. The gamma figures are, respectively, −.491 and .342. The partial order gamma, a statistic that we did not cover but is a controlled version of gamma is just .008.

Chapter 11

1. The arithmetic mean
3. **Answer—d:** Slopes are asymmetrical measures, Pearson's r is symmetrical.
5. **Answer—True.** As seen in Figure 11.12, one extreme outlier can change the direction of the "best-fitting" line. Remember that the deviation scores from that line are squared.
7. We first need to make two sets of calculations. For each case, we need to calculate the deviation scores from the mean of both variable x and variable y. We also need to calculate the covariances (reduced to the product of) those deviation scores.

x_i	$x_i - \bar{X}$	$(x_i - \bar{X})^2$	y_i	$y_i - \bar{Y}$	$(y_i - \bar{Y})^2$	$(x_i - \bar{X})(y_i - \bar{Y})$
2	−5	25	24	4	16	−20
4	−3	9	20	0	0	0
6	−1	1	16	−4	16	4
8	1	1	12	−8	64	−8
10	3	9	8	−12	144	−36
12	5	25	40	20	400	100

$$slope = b = \frac{\sum_{i=1}^{n}(x_i - \bar{X})(y_i - \bar{Y})}{\sum_{i=1}^{n}(x_i - \bar{X})^2} = \frac{40}{70} = 0.571$$

For every one unit increase in X, we predict a .571 increase in y.

$$a = \bar{Y} - b(\bar{X}) = 20 - 0.571(7) = 16$$

When $X = 0$, we predict a Y of 16.

$$r = \frac{\sum\limits_{i=1}^{n}(x_i - \bar{X})(y_i - \bar{Y})}{\sqrt{\sum\limits_{i=1}^{n}(x_i - \bar{X})^2 \sum\limits_{i=1}^{n}(y_i - \bar{Y})^2}} = \frac{40}{\sqrt{70 * 640}} = 0.189$$

The interval relationship between X and Y is .189. The relationship is positive, but not very strong.

$$r^2 = 0.036$$

The variance of X explains only 3.6% of the variance of Y.

9. Intercept = 152.25. If no one (0%) lives below the poverty line in a state, we would still expect 152.25 violent crimes per 100,000 inhabitants.

    Slope = 16.601. For every 1% increase in the poverty rate, we would expect an increase of 16.601 violent crimes per 100,000 inhabitants.

    R-square = .1526. The variance of the poverty rate explains 15.26% of the variance of crime.

    Comparison: Every percent increase in the poverty rate predicts a greater increase in violent crimes than violent crimes. However, the linear fit is not as good.

    We will touch on standardized slopes in the next chapter. They provide a relative, standardized way of comparing two scatterplots that reaffirms the greater effects of poverty on property crimes. The standardized slopes are .489 for property crimes and .391 for violent crimes.

11. Although we wouldn't see anyone zero years old in our sample, the equation predicts that such a person would have a score of 8.033 on the ten-point global warming scale. For every one-year increase in age, we would expect a very slight *decrease* in one's position on global warming of .004 on a ten-point scale. With this sample, we would estimate the true population slope to be somewhere between –.006 and –.003.

    There doesn't seem to be much of a relationship, confirmed by the low R^2 value of .001—the data hardly fit the "best-fitting" line at all. However, given the large sample size (more than 25,000), it is still enough to confidently reject the null hypothesis that the true population slope is 0. Obviously, inferential significance in this situation does not equate to conceptual significance.

Chapter 12

1. Slope:

For every one degree increase in feelings toward MORMONS, we would predict a .358 degree increase in feelings toward Mitt Romney (holding feelings toward RICH PEOPLE constant).

For every one degree increase in feelings toward RICH PEOPLE, we would predict a .185 degree increase in feelings toward Mitt Romney (holding feelings toward MORMONS constant).

Standardized slope:

For every one standard deviation increase in feelings toward MORMONS, we would predict a .246 degree standard deviation increase in feelings toward Mitt Romney (holding feelings toward RICH PEOPLE constant).

For every one standard deviation increase in feelings toward RICH PEOPLE, we would predict a .135 standard deviation increase in feelings toward Mitt Romney (holding feelings toward MORMONS constant).

t-test:

Both are statistically significant ($p < .000$); that is, we can confidently reject the possibility that, in the population from which this sample was drawn, the slope for either independent variable is 0 degrees.

R-square:

Both independent variables combined explain 9.9% of the variance of feelings toward former Governor Romney.

The standardized betas indicate that one's feelings toward Mormons were more important in estimating feelings toward Romney than were feelings toward rich people. A variation of the standard linear regression model stepwise regression (the use of which has come into question), also indicates the greater weight of Mormons (with a R^2 of .083) with RICH PEOPLE independently adding .016 to that value.

3. The results here are rather interesting and will be developed both by looking a multiple regression, and individual regressions by gender.

Slope:

Holding gender constant, for every category increase in family income, one would predict a .349% increase toward cuts. As men are coded as "1," and women are coded as "2," the regression model for each would be as follows:

$$\text{Men: } \widehat{Cuts} = 65.333 - 5.146(1) + .349(faminc)$$

$$= 60.187 + .349(faminc)$$

$$= 55.041 + .349(faminc)$$

The intercepts if the codes were 0 and 1 would be 60.187.

Standardized slope and *t*-test:

Gender has about three times the influence on variance of preferred deficit reduction allocations, and it is the only variable whose contribution is significant ($p < .10$). The negative beta (slopes) indicate a negative relationship between gender (male to female) and a preference for solving the budget deficit by cuts.

R-square:

Both independent variables combined explain only 1.1% of the variance of preferred deficit reduction allocations.

If we calculate a different linear regression model for men and women separately, our results are rather intriguing. I leave it to the student to interpret the results.

R

Gender = 1 Male	R-Square	Adjusted R-Square	Std. Error of the Estimate
.166	.028	.024	27.442

	Unstandardized Coefficients		Standardized Coefficients		
	b	Std. Error	β	*t*	Sig.
(Constant)	52.880	3.437		15.385	.000
Family Income	1.669	.556	.166	3.004	.003

R

Gender = 2 Female	R-Square	Adjusted R-Square	Std. Error of the Estimate
.091	.008	.006	23.992

	Unstandardized Coefficients		Standardized Coefficients		
	b	Std. Error	β	*t*	Sig.
(Constant)	61.077	2.718		22.472	.000
Family Income	−.777	.449	−.091	−1.732	.084

5. The percentage of male employment, according to our data, when controlling for urbanization, is hardly associated with male longevity. Urbanization, however, is positively associated and carries much greater weight in the outcome. Together, differences on those two variables explain 41.3% of the variance of longevity (almost all coming from URBANPER). While a high employment rate may seem to be a measure of a country's wealth and therefore one would assume that longevity would be greater, the fact that in some countries a greater proportion of employment comes from young men (15–21) may confound that assumption.

Compare this with the statistics for females:

R	R-Square	Adjusted R-Square	Std. Error of the Estimate
.653	.426	.419	11.797

	Unstandardized Coefficients		Standardized Coefficients		
	b	Std. Error	β	t	Sig.
(Constant)	60.888	4.068		14.969	.000
URBANPER	.397	.040	.596	9.942	.000
EMP15F	−.145	.056	−.156	−2.599	.010

Does either set of results prove that people living in cities live longer?

Index

Note: For a listing of tables, figures, and sidebars, see pages xiii–xvii